This Day
IN
ILLINOIS HISTORY

Jeff Ruetsche

emmis
books

Dedicated to

Stacy—thanks for supporting (and tolerating) me during this whole process—and to Sam, Marcus, and Zoe—thanks for being such great kids.

This Day

IN
ILLINOIS HISTORY

For further information, contact the publisher at:

Emmis Books
1700 Madison Road
Cincinnati, OH 45206
www.emmisbooks.com

Library of Congress Cataloging-in-Publication Data

Ruetsche, Jeff
  This day in Illinois history / by Jeff Ruetsche
      p. cm.—(This day in history series)
  Includes index.
  ISBN-13: 978-1-57860-243-8
  ISBN-10: 1-57860-243-2
  1. Illinois—History—Chronology. 2. Illinois—History—Miscellanea. I. Title. II. This day in Illinois history.
  F541.R84 2005
  977.302'02—dc22

                                2005024256

Produced by Menasha Ridge Press
Cover design by Susan Young
Interior design by Andrea Kupper

Front-cover photos courtesy of (clockwise from top left) Library of Congress, Ted Villaire, Library of Congress, National Aeronautics and Space Administration, Library of Congress, Wikipedia.

Back-cover photo courtesy of Wikipedia.

All photos courtesy of Library of Congress are from Prints and Photographs Division unless noted.

- TABLE OF CONTENTS -

- INTRODUCTION -

Illinois is a remarkable state.

When a young James Monroe toured the then-western frontier in 1786, he wrote Thomas Jefferson to say that Illinois was "miserably poor" and dismissed its unsettled prairies as unable to support enough inhabitants to ever earn "membership in the confederacy." Thirty-two years later—on December 3, 1818—Monroe found himself in the White House signing into law the act that granted Illinois its statehood. And so was born the 21st state of the Union.

The first state capital, Kaskaskia, was nearly wiped off the map in 1881 by a flood that left it the only Illinois town on the Missouri side of the Mississippi River. Due to a channel cut by the river, Kaskaskia can no longer be reached by land from the Land of Lincoln. Galena, the nation's first western boomtown (mined for lead, not gold), sits farther north than Boston, Massachusetts. Our southernmost town, Cairo, is farther south of the Mason-Dixon Line than Richmond, Virginia. (This straddling of North and South would play out hugely in the Civil War era.) And Illinois' highest natural point, the 1,235-foot Charles Mound, just south of the Wisconsin border, is not, in fact, Illinois's highest point—two city blocks at 233 South Wacker hold claim to that distinction.

Ah, Chicago . . . the only world-class city to be described as "the pulse of America," as "inhabited by savages," or as "a city where they are always rubbing a lamp and fetching a genii, and contriving and dreaming new possibilities" by such 19th-century luminaries as Sarah Bernhardt, Rudyard Kipling, and Mark Twain, respectively. Perhaps Illinois's own native son, Carl Sandburg, understood the city best: "Here is the difference between Dante, Milton, and me. They wrote about Hell and never saw the place. I wrote about Chicago after looking over the place for years and years." And what he looked over for years and years has been home to industrialists and anarchists; to artists, entrepreneurs, and scientists; to faceless laborers and world-famous athletes; to social revolutionaries and machine politicians who—all of them—helped define America's greatest city; and to the architects who dreamed to build it. A day-by-day history of Chicago itself could be written again and again.

But Illinois has far more to offer than Sandburg's "City of the Big Shoulders" alone. Southern Illinois—nicknamed "Little Egypt" for its fertile river deltas—is a world unto itself. Here is Cahokia, site of the largest pre-Columbian civilization on the map north of central Mexico; here are the earliest European outposts of what was for 150 years the original Wild West; and here, during the tumultuous era of Prohibition, raged a mob war whose key players rivaled all the flamboyance and brutality of their big-city counterparts up North. General George Rogers Clark doubled the size of the budding United States of America by capturing southern Illinois (and thus the entire Old Northwest) from the British in 1778. Twenty-five years later, his youngest brother, William, would return to southern Illinois to plan for, prepare, and launch the momentous Lewis & Clark Expedition (after the Louisiana Purchase again doubled the size of the nation). And southern Illinois also, notably, claims the one and only Metropolis, hometown of Superman.

Illinois's own real-life superman, Abraham Lincoln, occupied the central part of the state from the early 1830s until the day—on February 11, 1861—he left for the White House. He was largely responsible for moving the capital to Springfield, where Illinois legislators became the first in the Union to ratify the 13th Amendment, banning slavery; the first in the Union to enact child labor, work safety, and workman compensation laws; and the first in the Union to grant its women their long sought right to vote. Lincoln never returned to Springfield (alive), but fellow Illinoisans who succeeded him in the White House include Ulysses S. Grant and Ronald Reagan, and Adlai Stevenson and Charles Dawes (Vice Presidents).

The 16th president of the United States may be the most celebrated son of Illinois, but he is by no means the only one. Those who were born or who made their mark in the Prairie State (just to name a few) include Jane Addams, Louis Armstrong, Jack Benny, Chuck Berry, Black Hawk, Gwendolyn Brooks, Daniel Burnham, Al Capone, Charlie Chaplin, Miles Davis, Eugene Debs, John Deere, John Dillinger, Wyatt Earp, Red Grange, Benny Goodman, George Halas, Ernest Hemingway, "Wild Bill" Hickok, Bobby Hull, "Shoeless Joe" Jackson, Vachel Lindsay, Frank Lloyd Wright, Virginia Marmaduke, Harriet Monroe, Eliot Ness, Jesse Owens, Walter Payton, Popeye, Marjorie Merriweather Post, Sally Rand, Ron Santo, William Shirer, Phyllis Schlafly, Louis Sullivan, Gloria Swanson, Dick Tracy, Bob Woodward, and Orson Welles—all of whom joined Carl Sandburg for a time in "looking over this place."

And just who did originally look over Illinois? The state's name derives from *Illiniwek,* meaning "superior men," a self-description used by tribes of the Illini Confederacy, who were the dominant force when French missionaries and explorers first arrived in the 1670s. The Illiniwek Indians were driven off by the Sauk, the Fox, and the fierce Iroquois—each in turn replaced by successive waves of French, British, and American settlers who came to claim the very territory shunned by James Monroe. For about half a decade, in fact, from the end of the Revolutionary War to the establishment of the Northwest Territory, Illinois was the westernmost county of Virginia. Perhaps even more alarming, were it not for the skillful negotiations of Nathaniel Pope, Illinois's territorial representative to Congress in 1818, the state's northernmost 14 counties—including the city of Chicago—would today be part of Wisconsin. And the Chicago City Council actually voted to secede from the state in 1924—one boast the Windy City never made good on.

There's much to learn in the wondrous story of Illinois. This day-by-day history offers just a small portion of it, and in bite-size form. No cover-to-cover continuity can be found within, but there are numerous related entries to sample. For the story of Illinois's rise to statehood, begin with November 20 and then turn, in order, to January 23, April 1, August 12, and December 3. The incredible tale of a Mormon utopia (May 9, June 27, and February 4), or the heartbreaking drama of the Black Hawk War (November 3, June 8, April 7, May 13, May 20, June 24, August 2, and August 20), or vignettes of Lincoln's days in his old Illinois stomping grounds (March 7, September 9, April 24, June 26, June 16, July 29, September 15, October 15, February 11, and May 3) can likewise be explored by flipping back and forth through the pages of this book. In between lie a variety of stand-alone people and events that together add to the story of Illinois history. They are, for example, a great train robbery in Lake County, a jazz genius from East St. Louis, a Joliet-born queen of film noir, or an underemployed astronomer who in the midst of the Great Depression built the nation's most advanced radio telescope in his Wheaton backyard. Baseball fans will not be disappointed with entries from mid-October. And there are plenty of sports entries throughout, including the greatest high school basketball story in the annals of March Madness—on March 22, 1952.

One constant source of frustration in compiling this day-by-day history of Illinois was the dilemmas faced when two or more significant events landed on the same calendar date. Take our nation's birthday as an example: July Fourth in Illinois history saw General Clark's capture of Kaskaskia from the British in 1778; the groundbreaking for the Illinois & Michigan Canal in 1836; the laying of the cornerstone for the Old State Capitol in Springfield in 1837; and the submission of Daniel Burnham's revolutionary Chicago Plan in 1909. Such dilemmas were sensibly resolved by a series of coin flips, followed by a frantic search for secondary dates relating to whatever came up tails.

Not much these days is cut from whole cloth, and this book is certainly no exception. I would first like to thank Bill Nunes, southern Illinois historian extraordinaire, whose *Incredible Illinois* renewed my enthusiasm for our state's history. His *Southern Illinois* and *Illinois Crime* also helped inspire this book. My interest in Illinois's past was first piqued more than ten years ago, when I found an old reprint of the WPA Guide to Illinois (Federal Writers Project, 1939) at a neighborhood garage sale—the best buck I've ever spent. That old paperback was once again thumbed through furiously while compiling the present volume. Other titles that I had the joy and benefit of reading while researching for this book include *Chicago Days: 150 Defining Moments in the Life of a Great City* (*Chicago Tribune* staff, 1996), *Illinois: A History of the Prairie State* (Robert P. Howard, 1986), *American Pharaoh: Mayor Richard J. Daley—His Battle for Chicago and the Nation* (Adam Cohen and Elizabeth Taylor, 2001), *Frontier Illinois* (James E. Davis, 1998), The Illinois River (James Ayars, 1968), and the wonderful series of local pictorial histories, *Images of America,* created by Arcadia Publishing (a catalog of Illinois titles can be found at www.arcadiapublishing.com). Of the innumerable Web sites from which dates and information were gleaned, the most useful by far were the Illinois Historic Preservation Agency (www.state.il.us/hpa), the Encyclopedia of Chicago (www.encyclopedia.chicagohistory.org), Court TV's Crime Library (www.crimelibrary.com), and the free Web-based encyclopedias Wikipedia (www.en.wikipedia.org) and Information Please (www.infoplease.com). Plus, WUIS-91.9 in Springfield has a terrific series, John A. Lupton's *Illinois Political Journal,* posted at its Web site (www.wuis.org). Also found online were Robert A. Braun's "Black Hawk War: A Chronology" and "A Chronology of Illinois History," complied by the Secretary of State's office—both extremely helpful. Finally, my thanks go to the editorial staff at Menasha Ridge Press, especially Russell Helms, whose patience, sense of humor, and fine taste in Irish whiskey were greatly appreciated, and to whom I'm grateful for reminding me that June has only 30 days.

If you enjoy this book, I suggest going out and seeing Illinois for yourself. Take a road trip; Route 66 and the Lincoln Highway are waiting. Paddle the Illinois or Fox or Rock rivers. Take a riverboat down the Mississippi. Visit Grant's home, Lincoln's tomb, or Reagan's birthplace. Chicago has some the world's most magnificent museums and some unrivaled architectural gems. The Abraham Lincoln Presidential Library and Museum in Springfield opened to much hype (deserved) while this book was being compiled; it is but a few blocks from the grandest statehouse in the entire nation. Go see them both. Check out your local historical society. And the Superman Museum in downstate Metropolis is en route to Fort Massac State Park, where Lewis and Clark first made camp with their Corps of Discovery.

Explore Illinois. . . .

—Jeff Ruetsche, June 2005

- ILLINOIS AND ITS COUNTIES -

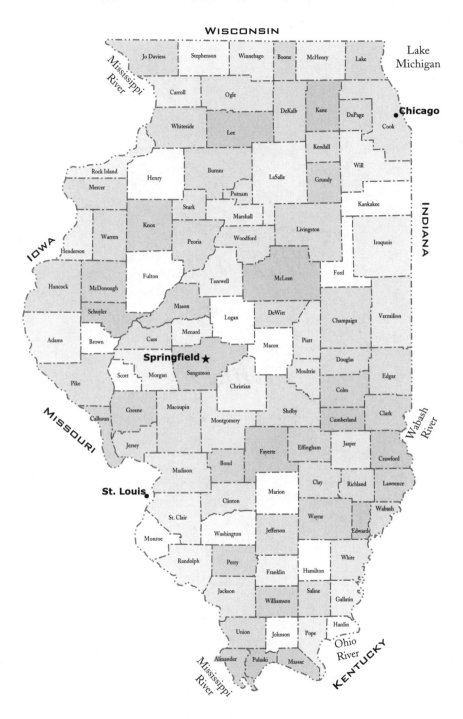

This day in January

- JANUARY 1 -
1680
LA SALLE AND TONTI EXPLORE THE ILLINOIS RIVER

French explorer René de La Salle and his Italian lieutenant, Henri de Tonti, approached the great village of the Illiniwek, near present-day Starved Rock in La Salle County, on this day in Illinois history.

France claimed the yet-undiscovered wilderness of Illinois on June 14, 1671, and the earliest explorers soon set forth to expand French influence in the New World. Their mission was twofold: plant the seeds of Christianity and exploit the lucrative fur trade with the native Indians. La Salle had secured exclusive trading rights in the western frontier of New France from King Louis XIV in 1678. The following year, with dreams of personal glory, he left Montreal to establish a network of outposts in Illinois Country.

The 33-man expedition traveled in eight canoes down the Illinois River, spurred by reports of an "Indian metropolis" visited by Jesuit missionary Father Jacques Marquette and his colleague Louis Jolliet half a decade earlier. According to La Salle, his party found it on New Year's Day. The great village consisted of more than 400 arch-shaped lodges constructed of wooden posts and interwoven mats of rush, or cattails, and large enough to host several families each. But the fires in these lodges were smokeless. The entire village was empty. The Illiniwek—an Indian confederation of several area tribes, including the Cahokia, Kaskaskia, and Peoria—had abandoned the site for their traditional winter hunting grounds.

La Salle's men, desperately low on food after a long December journey, searched the town and found the Illiniweks' sacred cache of corn. They took just enough to sustain themselves for a month.

Three days later, at a lake formed by the widening of the river near what is now Peoria, the Frenchmen came upon a small hunting camp. Within musket shot range of the wigwams, or temporary huts, the Frenchmen called out to the unsuspecting native Indians. Startled warriors gathered up their weapons and headed for cover, while the women and children fled to the nearby woods. Stepping ashore, La Salle raised a calumet, or Indian peace pipe, and ordered his soldiers to lower their guns. Moments later an Illiniwek chief appeared holding up his own peace pipe, avoiding potential bloodshed. According to the Frenchman's own account, the native Indians' joy "was as great as their apprehension had been," and a celebratory feast was held among new friends.

The Frenchmen offered gifts of tobacco and metal tools as payment for the stolen corn, which—according to La Salle's journal—they had planned to replace all along.

- JANUARY 2 -
1900
FLOW OF CHICAGO RIVER IS REVERSED

On this day in Illinois history, after eight years of construction by more than 8,000 workers, the Sanitary and Ship Canal opened, forcing the unprecedented permanent reversal of the Chicago River.

Begun in 1893, the 28-mile canal was an engineering feat born from the need to relieve the city of the ravages of cholera, typhoid fever, and other sewage-borne diseases that had been wreaking havoc on its citizens for decades. Chicago's drainage system, despite incremental improvements, was still relatively primitive by big-city standards. Remains from the slaughterhouses, factory discharge, and tons upon tons of various refuse created annually by denizens of the booming metropolis had been fouling Chicago's water supply for years. Disease thrived, and thousands were dying annually. The Sanitary and Ship Canal was designed to wash away Chicago's waste down the Des Plaines, Illinois, and Mississippi rivers. While the plan was undoubtedly promising for the city's sanitary conditions, downstaters were far less enthusiastic about the project.

The canal, a 24-foot-deep by 202-foot-wide trench dug through earth and limestone, ran from a high point on the Chicago River to the suburb of Lockport, about

Photo courtesy of Wikipedia

30 miles southwest, where it met up with the waterway flowing toward the Mississippi. At the time, the dig was the most ambitious earth-moving construction project ever undertaken in North America. When the massive machines broke the final barrier between canal and river, there was no ceremony, no media invite, and practically no one on hand to witness the historic spectacle. The scene was rather secretive. Trustees of the Sanitary District of Chicago, who had devised the plan back in 1887, stood nervously by, almost anticipating a last-minute injunction to stop at the behest of St. Louis, and watched quietly as the final earthen wall gave way. The water rushed through, and soon people thronged alongside the canal's edge to see the formerly static and stagnant river moving—amazingly—in the opposite direction of its natural current.

Deaths from waterborne diseases fell to record lows, and despite rumors and threats to the contrary, St. Louis and southern Illinois cities neither suffered ill effects nor took legal action against Chicago.

- JANUARY 3 -

1985

PAUL SIMON BEGINS FIRST OF TWO U.S. SENATE TERMS

Paul Martin Simon, the amiable Democrat from Jackson County with the trademark bowtie and wide-rimmed glasses, entered the U.S. Senate on this day in Illinois history.

The son of a Lutheran minister from Eugene, Oregon, Simon came to Troy, Illinois, after college in 1948. At 19, he became the nation's youngest newspaper publisher-editor and soon had a chain of 14 weeklies. He soon earned the reputation of a "crusading liberal" for exposing and taking down a local gambling syndicate. After serving his country during the Korean War from 1951 to 1953, Simon returned to Illinois to launch his political career. He was elected to the Illinois General Assembly in 1954, serving as a representative (1955–1963) and state senator (1963–1968) for two decades, with distinction. The popular Democrat then served as lieutenant governor of Illinois from 1969 to 1973 before setting his sights on Washington, D.C.

Photo courtesy of U.S. Senate Historical Office

Simon was elected to the U.S. House of Representatives in 1974 and served five successive terms (1975–1985) representing the state of Illinois. He was then elected to the U.S. Senate. For 12 years Senator Simon advocated smarter government spending. "Government is not the enemy," he told his colleagues. "Government is simply a tool that can be used wisely or unwisely. We can do better, my friends." In the Senate, he coauthored the Balanced Budget Amendment with Republican Orrin Hatch of Utah (it has yet to be ratified). Simon was instrumental in revamping the federal student-loan program, allowing students to borrow directly from the government, cutting waste. He was also alarmed by the proliferate waste in pop culture and campaigned vigorously against television violence.

Simon authored more than a dozen books. *Winners and Losers* was a reflection on his unsuccessful 1988 run for the Democratic presidential nomination. *Our Culture of Pandering*—a biting condemnation of failed American leadership and the selling out to moneyed interests across the political spectrum—was his last title, published only weeks before his death. Simon, well in advance of his companions on Capitol Hill, had offered public disclosures of his political finances since the 1950s and railed against corruption through his final days.

The senator died on December 9, 2003, at the age of 75 after open-heart surgery, and is buried at his family plot near Makanda, Illinois.

- JANUARY 4 -
1896
SENATOR EVERETT DIRKSEN BORN IN PEKIN

Everett McKinley Dirksen—longtime U.S. Representative (1933–1949) and U.S. Senator (1951–1969)—was born in Tazewell County on this day in Illinois history.

Dirksen, who once flippantly stated, "A billion here, a billion there, pretty soon it adds up to real money," honed his fiscal conservatism while serving as commissioner of finance for his hometown of Pekin, Illinois, from 1927 to 1931. In 1932 he was elected to the first of eight consecutive terms as a Republican in the U.S. House of Representatives. In 1950, he campaigned for a seat in the U.S. Senate and defeated the incumbent, Democratic Senate Majority Leader Scott Lucas. Dirksen would serve until his death.

Selected Senate Minority Leader in 1959, Dirksen earned national renown for the contentious legislation he often championed. In 1963, working closely with President John F. Kennedy from across the aisle, he helped secure passage of the Nuclear Test Ban Treaty. And in 1967, he introduced a Constitutional amendment allowing prayer in public schools.

His greatest moment, however, came with the Civil Rights Act of 1964. Facing the longest filibuster in Senate history, led by Southern Democrats like West Virginia's Robert C. Byrd, the bill was going nowhere. President Lyndon Johnson, a Democrat who strongly backed the bill, turned to Dirksen to rally Republican support. Dirksen invoked cloture—whereby a two-thirds vote would break the filibuster—and, in the presence of all 100 senators, delivered a stirring speech. " 'Stronger than all the armies is an idea whose time has come,' " he said, quoting Victor Hugo. "The time has come for equality of opportunity in sharing of government, in education, and in employment. It must not be stayed or denied. It is here!" The filibuster was broken, and the act passed on the Senate floor, 73–26—a tally divided more by regionalism than by party lines.

Dirksen died in Washington, D.C., on September 7, 1969, and is buried at Glendale Memorial Gardens in Pekin.

- JANUARY 5 -
2004

CHICAGO BOARD OF TRADE TRANSFERS ALL ACTIVITY TO STATE-OF-THE-ART ELECTRONIC TRADING PLATFORM

The world's most advanced electronic-trading platform, the Chicago Board of Trade's Common Clearing Link, became fully operational and accessible worldwide on this day in Illinois history.

The Chicago Board of Trade (CBOT) was organized on June 10, 1848, just as Chicago was emerging as an industrial and economic powerhouse, to help Illinois farmers distribute their produce to the world. Buyers and sellers throughout the Midwest now had a central meeting place to exchange agricultural goods, and both groups benefited: Higher financial returns for growers were complemented by lower-priced products for merchants. For the first time, farm prices began to stabilize, and in 1855 the French government purchased wheat from the CBOT rather than through New York City; it was the first time a major European buyer had looked to the Midwest. By the 1870s—despite losing its original building and all the records therein to the Great Fire of 1871—the Chicago Board of Trade was selling grain by the millions of bushels to markets throughout the world. In 1929 a new trading facility was built at LaSalle Street and Jackson Boulevard to accommodate the ever-expanding board. The 44-story Art Deco tower, topped with a gilded statue of Ceres, the Roman goddess of agriculture, overlooks the Chicago financial district today.

Photo courtesy of Library of Congress, LC-US262-120484DLC

By the 1990s, the CBOT was breaking its own world records in trading contracts (154 million in 1990, 219.5 million in 1994, and 281 million in 1998) and showing no signs of slowing down. Mayor Richard J. Daley and CBOT executives broke ground on January 17, 1995, for the new $175 million trading facility, which added 60,000 square feet of floor space to handle this massive volume of trade. The floor—referred to as "The Pit"—is a madhouse of frantic traders and transactions totaling 400 million bushels of grain per year, as well as oats, rye, barley, soybeans, corn, wheat, and silver. It conducts half of all commodities trading in the United States, mostly in the futures markets, while continuing to perform as the nation's leading agricultural exchange.

The CBOT's new Electronic Trading Platform, unparalleled in speed and functionality, helps manage this ever-increasing volume of trade and ensure Chicago's place at the center of the international market.

- JANUARY 6 -
1878
CARL SANDBURG BORN IN GALESBURG, ILLINOIS

Pulitzer Prize–winning poet and historian Carl Sandburg was born in a three-room cottage in Knox County on this day in Illinois history.

The son of an immigrant railroad worker, Sandburg had a working-class midwestern upbringing that developed in him a reverence for the common man. He left school after the eighth grade to sweep barbershop floors, deliver milk, harvest wheat, and shine shoes. After roaming America as a hobo for several months, Sandburg enlisted in the 6th Illinois Infantry in 1898 to fight in the Spanish-American War. He was based in Puerto Rico, where the oppressive heat and mosquitoes posed a far greater threat than Spanish guns. Sandburg returned to Galesburg and enrolled at Lombard College, where he embraced both poetry and socialism, and paid for his classes through employment as an on-call fireman. He also assumed duties in 1899 ringing the bell to call students to class.

Sandburg was a prolific writer. His first book of poetry, *In Reckless Ecstasy,* was printed by a college mentor in 1904. He later moved to Chicago, where he was hired to cover labor issues for Victor Lawson's *Chicago Daily News.* A work of biography, *Abraham Lincoln: The War Years,* and his collected works of poetry, *Complete Poems,* each earned him the Pulitzer Prize, in 1940 and 1951, respectively. Sandburg was also a folksinger, a political lecturer, and an author of children's books. He once remarked on his own versatility: "I had studied monotony. I decided whatever I died of, it would not be monotony." Sandburg's best known lines, however, come from "Chicago," a celebration of his adoptive city published in *Poetry* magazine in 1914: "Hog Butcher for the World, / Tool Maker, Stacker of Wheat, / Player with Railroads and the Nation's Freight Handler, / Stormy, husky, brawling, / City of the Big Shoulders: / They tell me you are wicked and I believe them. . . ."

Carl Sandburg died on July 22, 1967, and his ashes were buried, per his request, beneath Remembrance Rock, behind his Galesburg birthplace.

- JANUARY 7 -
1901

CAVE IN ROCK, ILLINOIS, INCORPORATED
NEAR ITS LEGENDARY NAMESAKE

On this day in Illinois history, the village of Cave In Rock was incorporated on the banks of the Ohio River, near the notorious Hardin County criminal hideout from which its name derives.

The quiet hamlet (population 350) sits peaceably upon the bluffs in stark contrast to the bloody past of its nearby namesake. Cave-in-the-Rock, a yawning cavern 20 feet wide by 55 feet high at the mouth and 200 feet deep, invited nothing but mischief in the early frontier days of Illinois. It served for decades as refuge to all manner of thieves, cutthroats, and scoundrels. In 1797, for example, a Continental Army officer–turned–river bandit named Samuel Mason used Cave-in-the-Rock in an elaborate ruse to engage in piracy. Hanging a great sign above the cave mouth, reading "Liquor Vault and House of Entertainment," Mason and his band preyed upon unsuspecting pioneers traveling west down the Ohio River, who thought they had come across a rather curious, but welcome, riverside inn. Once ensnared, the crew was attacked and killed, the boat robbed, and the bodies of the victims weighed down with rocks and sunk to the riverbed. Mason was just one in a long line of outlaws who sought refuge in Cave-in-the-Rock while on the lam and seeking plunder. (Illinois was, after all, the original Wild West.)

Photo courtesy of Wikipedia

Most notorious of all were the brutal Harpe Brothers. "Big" Harpe and "Little" Harpe were actually cousins who held three wives between them, and maimed and murdered with such reckless glee as is found only in those possessed of pure evil. On the run from a Kentucky posse, wanted for multiple murders, they crossed the river and holed up in Cave-in-the-Rock for about a month in 1799. There, they managed to trap several more victims, adding another five grisly murders to their tally. In one attack they pushed a couple of young lovers off the 50-foot bluffs, and watched as they miraculously fell to the sands below unharmed. Both Harpes were eventually captured by vigilante groups; Big Harpe's head delivered to authorities on a platter.

The cave is now the centerpiece of a 60-acre state park just outside Shawnee National Forest, and visitors today will find far more hospitable accommodations in Cave In Rock, Illinois, than those offered by Samuel Mason more than 200 years ago.

- JANUARY 8 -

1917

FRANK O. LOWDEN INAUGURATED ILLINOIS'S 27TH GOVERNOR

Frank Orren Lowden, who before campaigning vowed to limit himself to a single term in which to enact sweeping change, was inaugurated as the state's 27th Governor on this day in Illinois.

Lowden was born in Minnesota on January 26, 1861, graduated from Iowa State University in 1885 and Union College of Law (now Northwestern University) in Evanston, Illinois, in 1887. He was admitted to the bar in Chicago and started a law practice there within a few months. Lowden married into great wealth in 1896 after

courting Florence Pullman, the daughter of millionaire industrialist George Pullman (inventor of the Pullman Sleeping Car), and then served as a lieutenant in the Illinois National Guard from 1898 to 1903. With a military background and large war chest on which to campaign, Lowden was ready to run for public office. He moved to Oregon, Illinois, and was elected to the U.S. House of Representatives, serving from 1906 to 1911. The Ogle County Republican chose not to run for reelection in 1910 and instead set his sights on the state capitol.

Governor Lowden earned national praise within the first two months of his administration for forcing through the state legislature long-overdue reorganizations of Illinois government. Springfield was bogged down by more than 100 lumbering, inefficient agencies. Governor Lowden scrapped these entirely, reassigning their various and often blurred responsibilities among nine new state departments: Agriculture, Education, Finance, Labor, Mines and Minerals, Public Health, Public Welfare, Public Works, and Trade and Commerce. He also revolutionized the state's banking system. Based on his newfound national popularity, Lowden gave Illinois its first contender for the White House since Ulysses S. Grant. In 1920, he was a favorite candidate for the Republican nomination but ultimately lost out to Warren G. Harding after ten ballots. He then retired from public office, refusing the vice presidential ticket in 1924.

Lowden died March 20, 1943, and was buried at Graceland Cemetery in Chicago.

- JANUARY 9 -
1895
EUGENE DEBS ENTERS WOODSTOCK JAIL

Eugene V. Debs—labor activist and five-time Socialist candidate for U.S. president—began his six-month prison term in McHenry County, convicted for his role in the Pullman Strike the previous year, on this day in Illinois history.

The strike originated at the Pullman Car Co. south of Chicago, but soon spread across the nation as the Union of Railroad Workers (URW), under Debs's leadership, united in support of its Illinois brethren. Federal troops and local Pinkerton agents were called in to break the strike. Debs and other URW leaders were arrested for conspiracy to interfere with the U.S. mail, which depended on the railways for delivery, and for violating a government injunction against continuing the standoff.

The judge sentenced Debs to the remote Woodstock Jail to avoid mass protests and keep the charismatic leader out of the public eye. This information was leaked, unsurprisingly, and half the small town's male population showed up to greet Debs and six other cohorts at the Woodstock train depot. Debs issued a manifesto to the public immediately upon entering his jail cell: ". . . for participation in the late strike we have no apologies to make nor regrets to express . . . six months—or six years—in jail will fail to purge me of contempt."

Debs's prison term was in fact quite cozy. He dined on roast chicken, slept on a comfortable bed with clean sheets, and received a number of distinguished guests. One of his visitors was Victor Berger, a prominent Milwaukee Socialist who brought him a copy of Karl Marx's *Das Kapital;* soon after, Debs decided to commit his life to the socialist cause.

When he was released in June, a "huge throng of townspeople carried Debs to the train station on their shoulders," and he returned to Woodstock in 1908 in his "Red Special" campaign train while running for U.S. president on the Socialist Party ticket; Debs never made it to the White House.

- JANUARY 10 -

1905

SECOND OF THREE DEADLY EXPLOSIONS AT ZEIGLER COAL MINE

A 26-man cleanup crew died in an explosion at the Zeigler Coal Mine in Franklin County on this day in Illinois history.

Southern Illinois was one of the top coal-producing regions in the country during the first quarter of the 20th century. Spurred by the railroads, which both consumed the coal and transported it to Chicago steel plants, the state's 810 mines were producing more than 86 million tons of the valuable resource annually by 1917. Tragedy and labor strife were all too common.

The Zeigler Coal Company was owned by Joseph Leiter and his father Levi Leiter, who had acquired the mine in 1901 and built a company town nearby. The mine soon led the state's thriving coal industry in productivity, and the town stood as a model work community for the rest of the nation. It boasted weatherized homes, a modern schoolhouse and hospital, and a central park. But in 1904 the Leiters lowered workers' wages from 50 cents to 38 cents per ton and declared the mine "open"—that is, noncompulsory union. Since the Zeigler mine featured the latest machinery, the owners felt justified in ignoring union wage scales, which were based on tonnage mined by hand. Union miners disagreed. They went on strike that year, nonunion workers and strikebreakers were brought in, and violence ensued.

In 1905, the first Zeigler explosion killed 54 nonunion workers trapped inside the mine. The Leiter brothers blamed strike sympathizers for the disaster—an accusation first supported by a coroner's jury, which suggested that gunpowder may have been used to detonate the mine. This claim was later rejected by investigators who concluded that poor ventilation and marsh gases had caused the explosion. Whatever the cause, the shaft was ordered closed. Joseph Leiter refused to recognize the order and in 1909 sent the cleanup crew down to prepare the mine for reopening. All 26 men in that crew perished in a second explosion. A third explosion killed an additional three men inspecting the shaft a few weeks later, and thereafter the mine was finally, permanently closed.

Coal remains one of Illinois's most abundant natural resources.

- JANUARY 11 -
1847
DOROTHEA DIX SUBMITS PROPOSAL FOR ILLINOIS'S FIRST MENTAL HOSPITAL

The State Hospital for the Insane, built in Jacksonville, was proposed to the General Assembly by the whirlwind social reformer Dorothea Lynde Dix on this day in Illinois history.

Dix arrived in Illinois a 45-year-old gadfly with some radical ideas of how to change the way America treated its mentally ill. She'd been touring the states encouraging institutional change. Rather than advocate locking away the insane as incurables, she urged the construction of new mental hospitals with healthier conditions than the callous sanitariums of the day, and to treat the afflicted as patients rather than inmates. Many former "raging maniacs" under the proper stewardship, she argued, could eventually reenter society as happy citizens. The city of Jacksonville, in the center of the state, was the perfect location for such a hospital. It had two precedents in the State Asylum for the Deaf and Dumb (established in 1846) and the Institution for the Education for the Blind (to be opened in 1848). Dix convinced the Illinois legislature that the state needed a "well established, skillfully conducted hospital" to best confront the scourge of mental illness that afflicted its larger cities. On March 1, 1847, an act was passed for the appropriation and establishment, "within four miles of the town of Jacksonville, county of Morgan, an institution to be known as the Illinois State Hospital for the Insane."

Construction began in 1848 and the first of many patients arrived on November 3, 1851. Patients were to be cared for at the state's expense, and the original building, which was designed to hold 250, was soon turning them away at the door for lack of vacancies. In 1869 to prevent overcrowding, the Illinois General Assembly ordered two more state mental hospitals built, one in Elgin to the north and one in downstate Anna. The Jacksonville site was thereafter named Illinois Central Hospital for the Insane. Its original five-and-a-half-story central building with two single-story wings has since been expanded by a number of halls, buildings, and separate cottages.

From the 1940s through the 1970s, the hospital was a national center for training psychiatric nurses, and is known today as Jacksonville Developmental Center.

- JANUARY 12 -
1926
GOLDEN AGE OF RADIO BORN ON
WGN'S *SAM 'N' HENRY* SHOW

On this day in Illinois history, WGN Radio aired the first-ever situation comedy, *Sam 'n' Henry*, which two years later became the then-uncontroversial *Amos 'n' Andy* show.

Radio was a mere half decade old, and Chicago's WGN ("World's Greatest Newspaper," after the station's owner, the *Chicago Tribune*) was a pioneer in the midwestern market. Its powerful signal reached throughout Illinois and the better part of all surrounding states. Two popular radio personalities—Freeman Gosden and Charles Correll—conceived of a new show, the premise of which would likely get them banned from the airwaves today. *Sam 'n' Henry* featured the comical exploits of two recently arrived migrants to Chicago from the South. Performing live and joined by an in-studio supporting cast, the two actors assumed exaggerated "black" accents and were listened to by thousands every day.

The show lasted only two years (with more than 500 episodes) in its original form, but it was an integral part of the Golden Age of Chicago radio. In 1927, WGN's rival, WMAQ, bought out the rights to Gosden and Correll. The name of the show was changed to *Amos 'n' Andy*, and it was syndicated nationally on the NBC radio network and later on CBS. It lasted until 1960 before losing popularity amid increasing controversy, and the dominance of television forced it off the air (the spinoff TV series, *The Amos 'n' Andy Show*, which ran on CBS from 1951 to 1953, was even more controversial, engendering widespread criticism in the African American community). In Chicago, Gosden and Correll's show was just one of several old-time radio classics that earned a nationwide audience. *Fibber McGee and Molly*, the country's most popular Hollywood-based radio show in 1941, had likewise been created in Chicago as *Smackout* ten years earlier. *Little Orphan Annie, National Barn Dance*, and *The Breakfast Club* were other titles born in Chicago that reached large national audiences.

By the time TV overtook radio as the primary medium for sitcoms and variety shows in the 1960s, Chicago no longer reigned as the radio capital of American entertainment.

- JANUARY 13 -

1999

MICHAEL JORDAN RETIRES—AGAIN

Chicago Bulls superstar Michael Jeffrey Jordan retired from the National Basketball Association for the second time in five years on this day in Illinois history.

Few will argue that Jordan was basketball's most dominant player ever. During his career in Chicago, he won a league-record ten scoring titles. He was Rookie of the Year in 1984, five-time league MVP, and six-time league finals MVP (having led the Bulls to two "three-peats" in the 1990s). Jordan made the NBA All-Star team 14 times. "God disguised as Michael Jordan," was how NBA legend Larry Bird described the Bull's number 23 after he dropped 63 points against the Boston Celtics in a 1985 playoff game.

Photo courtesy of Jeff Ruetsche

Jordan shocked Chicago fans by announcing his retirement from basketball the day before training camp in 1994. The Bulls had just won three straight championship titles, and Jordan was still in his prime. His father, James Jordan, had been murdered by a robber during the off-season, and championship titles no longer drove the devastated superstar. Later that year Jordan pursued a dream of his father's—to play professional baseball—and spent the summer with the Birmingham (Alabama) Barons, a minor-league affiliate of the Chicago White Sox. Jordan never made the major leagues, but he did begin again to hunger for the competition of the basketball court.

In the middle of the 1995 season he made a celebrated return to the Bulls and, beginning the following year, guided his team to yet another three successive NBA championships. The 1996 team—Jordan's first full season back—won an unprecedented 72 regular season games with just ten defeats; in the closing seconds of the victorious final championship game, which happened to be on Father's Day, Jordan clutched the ball and fell to the center of the United Center stadium floor, overwhelmed with emotion. He announced his second of ultimately three NBA retirements after the sixth championship run, his final season as a Chicago Bull.

Before his rookie season, after being drafted by the Bulls, Jordan told a *Sports Illustrated* interviewer, "I'd like to play in at least one All-Star game."

- JANUARY 14 -

1896

JOHN DOS PASSOS BORN IN CHICAGO

John Roderigo Dos Passos, a giant literary figure of the first half of the 20th century, was born in Chicago on this day in Illinois history.

Dos Passos was an Illinois export. Like Ernest Hemingway, Wyatt Earp, and Walt Disney, he was born in the Prairie State and spent part of his childhood here, but left early in life to make his mark on the outside world. The son of a wealthy Chicago attorney, Dos Passos was sent off for a classically grounded education at a Connecticut boarding school in 1907, took a six-month tour of Europe with a private tutor, and later enrolled at Harvard College to further study the masterpieces of western civilization. After graduating in 1916, Dos Passos left for Europe as a volunteer ambulance driver in the Great War to defend that civilization. He stayed in Paris, France, one among a number of American expatriates—the so-called "Lost Generation"—to write, socialize, and study after the brutal conflict. His first novel, *One Man's Initiation: 1917,* was published in 1920, followed by the bitterly antiwar *Three Soldiers,* which won him critical acclaim in 1921. Dos Passos' early works were infused with impressions from his war service, and—enamored as he was then with Marxist ideology—condemned American materialism and the very capitalist system from which he had so richly benefited as a young man. His early masterpiece written in the vein was the *U.S.A.* trilogy: *The 42nd Parallel* (1930), *1919* (1932), and *The Big Money* (1936).

With the coming of World War II, however, Dos Passos had become disillusioned with Communism. He began to abandon—and in fact criticize—the political rhetoric of his youth, and because of this his popularity suffered internationally in his old circles. John Dos Passos spent 1942 through 1945 in Europe as a war journalist and was elected to the American Academy of Arts and Letters (cofounded by Mark Twain in 1898) in 1947. He continued to write until his death in September of 1970, having produced more than 40 novels, essays, and plays, often returning to the defining experience of his life, World War I.

Dos Passos was also a prolific painter, and in 2001 an exhibition of his work, *The Art of John Dos Passos,* toured several cities of the United States.

- JANUARY 15 -
1680
LA SALLE BUILDS FIRST FRENCH FORT IN ILLINOIS COUNTRY

Construction of Fort Crevecoeur on the banks of the Illinois River near present-day Peoria, by Frenchmen under the command of René de La Salle, began on this day in Illinois history.

Fearing that their hosts, the Illiniwek, might become hostile, La Salle removed himself and his men from the Indian village to build a fort about one mile downriver. It was the first European fortification built in Illinois. Crevecoeur—meaning "broken heart"—was so named, according to one contemporary, "because the desertion of our men, with the difficulties we labored under, had almost broken our hearts." Other versions have La Salle naming the fort while lamenting the loss of the *Griffin,* the magnificent sailing ship he had commissioned for the purpose exploring the lower Mississippi River, and which had failed to arrive at a scheduled rendezvous, disappearing upon the Great Lakes forever. La Salle ordered that a new boat be built at Fort Crevecoeur, but he still needed rigging and tackle for the journey. In March, with no other option, La Salle and six men left for their base at Fort Frontenac, 1,000 miles distant on Lake Ontario, to secure the necessary supplies. His lieutenant, Henri de Tonti, was left in command of Fort Crevecoeur with 2 friars and 13 other Frenchmen.

René de La Salle

The weary voyagers had not been paid for two years and were on the verge of mutiny. When Tonti set off with four men to survey a better site for a more permanent fort upriver at present-day Starved Rock, the remaining Frenchmen acted on their discontent and stole what food and provisions they could carry, abandoning the outpost. Tonti would soon be swept up in a war between his Illiniwek friends and an invading army of Iroquois—a war that had begun before the arrival of any Europeans to the area. La Salle returned to the site in December of that year, after an arduous nine-month journey, arriving with the additional men, provisions, and sailing equipment needed to continue the journey. Fort Crevecoeur was completely deserted.

Beside the fort sat the unfinished sailing ship with the words *Nous sommes touts sauvages*—"We are all savages"—carved into its hull.

- JANUARY 16 -

1836

GALENA & CHICAGO UNION RAILROAD,
SEED OF THE GREAT NORTH WESTERN, CHARTERED

The first railroad to run out of Chicago, and the first to be built in the West, the G&CU Railroad was chartered on this day in Illinois history.

The line was intended to connect the Lake Michigan port community with the Mississippi River boomtown of Galena. Chicago was incorporated as a town of 300 on August 12, 1833, and had already mushroomed to more than 4,000 residents. Galena at the time was likewise flourishing as the first mining boomtown of the West—driven by lead, not gold—and had a growing population of approximately 5,000. Construction on the G&CU did not begin until March of 1848, and the first locomotive to operate in Illinois, the "Pioneer," arrived that October. Despite the name, the G&CU never reached Galena and instead connected Chicago to Freeport. It was completed in 1853 and consolidated with the larger Chicago & North Western Railroad 12 years later. (Thus the G&CU, which began operating at an earlier date, is considered the origin of the C&NW, also called the "Great North Western" line.) The North Western, with Chicago as its hub, operated from 1865 to 1995, and over the decades merged with rival railroads. It acquired thousands of miles of track extending out from the City of the Big Shoulders as far as Omaha, Nebraska, to the west; St. Paul, Minnesota, to the north; and St. Louis, Missouri, to the south.

One curious aspect of the C&NW is its running "left-hand main" on major double-track lines—routing traffic to the left track rather than the right, as was the standard practice. This is because the original G&CU line had arbitrarily placed its inbound stations (toward Chicago) on the left-hand side of the track. When the North Western expanded service and a second track was added specifically for outbound traffic, it was placed on the distant side of the station platforms so as to accommodate Chicago-bound passengers. To reconfigure this system—changing all those signals and switches—was a cost the railroad chose to avoid.

In April of 1995, the Chicago & Northwestern Railroad merged into the Union Pacific Railroad.

- JANUARY 17 -

1920

VOLSTEAD ACT LEADS TO RISE OF CHICAGO UNDERWORLD

The National Prohibition Act of 1919, better known as the Volstead Act, went into effect on this day in Illinois history, spawning the bloody Chicago gang wars of Al Capone, Bugs Moran, and company.

The bill, named for its promoter U.S. Representative Andrew Volstead (Minn.), was passed by the U.S. Congress in October of 1919—over the veto of President Woodrow Wilson—to enforce national Prohibition. The banning of "beer, wine, or other intoxicating malt or vinous liquors" provided a golden opportunity to would-be bootleggers who populated the nefarious underworld. The demand for alcohol would remain high, spurring crime—proved that very day when a group of Chicago men robbed a railroad car full of whiskey marked for "medicinal purposes only." It was the first recorded violation of Prohibition.

Johnny Torrio, with his rising protégé and partner in vice, Al Capone, took quick advantage of the situation. Selling illicit liquor would be a huge moneymaker, especially with Chicago's large Irish and German communities, and others culturally unsuited for a "dry" world. A vast bootlegging enterprise was born. Organized crime thrived as legitimate competition was nonexistent and the enforcers of Prohibition were easily bought off. Speakeasies proliferated across the city, with countless saloons, restaurants, and cabarets hosting smoke-filled backrooms where thirsty customers could consume banned alcohol. All were supplied by the Torrio-Capone monopoly. Or, almost all . . .

Bugs Moran was one local bootlegger who refused to merge with Torrio or submit to his powerful crime czar. He referred to Capone as the "behemoth" and delighted in challenging him to move in on his North Side Irish turf. But in 1924, Moran's mentor, Dion O'Bannion, was gunned down by a pair of Capone's thugs in a grab to consolidate the city's 10,000 speakeasies and their $100 million annual revenue. Moran responded by attempting to assassinate Torrio in January of 1925; he botched the assassination but succeeded in scaring the crime boss into retirement. Capone was now in charge, and he and Moran spent much of the remaining decade attempting to get one another to "push up the daisies."

The ensuing "beer war," which dominated the city headlines of the late 1920s and early 1930s, cooled down after Capone was imprisoned in 1931, but never really ended until Prohibition was repealed on December 5, 1933.

- JANUARY 18 -

1939

ROCK 'N' ROLL PIONEER PHIL EVERLY BORN IN CHICAGO

Phil Everly, cofounder of the seminal rock 'n' roll duo The Everly Brothers, was born in Cook County on this day in Illinois history.

Phil, along with his brother Don, who was born two years earlier in Kentucky, were the sons of country-music performers Ike and Margaret Everly. The country duo brought their Appalachian-inspired pop songs to the tops of the charts in the 1950s and 1960s. From the ages of 6 and 8, the boys were being taught to sing and play guitar by their parents. They began performing in Chicago as teenagers and had composed a song titled "That's the Mood I'm In," which, left unprotected by copyright, was reportedly "borrowed" by Glenn Miller to become the Big Band hit "In the Mood." The brothers began playing live radio shows and touring in the late 1940s, settling for a short while in Edwardsville, Indiana, and then Knoxville, Tennessee. There they met guitarist Chet Atkins, who got Phil and Don their first big break—a six-month contract with Columbia Records.

Thus began a recording career that produced 26 Top 40 hit singles and helped define the very sound and image of early rock 'n' roll. The Everly Brothers, now recording for Archie Bleyer's Cadence label, had their first chart-topper with "Bye Bye Love" in 1957—a song that was offered to but rejected by Elvis Presley—which also became their first million-copy seller. Following the lead of Presley, Chuck Berry, and Little Richard, The Everly Brothers added to their harmonizing vocals and soft acoustic sounds the pluck and twang of the electric guitar, driving rhythms of a backup band, and teenybopper lyrics so popular in the emerging rock 'n' roll music of the day. Other hits like "Wake Up Little Susie," "All I Have to Do Is Dream," and "Cathy's Clown" soon followed. In turn, their singing style had a profound influence on virtually all top rock bands of the 1960s.

In 1986, The Everly Brothers were among the first inductees to the Rock and Roll Hall of Fame, and Phil and Don continued performing as a duo into the 21st century.

- JANUARY 19 -

1841

CHICAGO-BASED *PRAIRIE FARMER* HITS ILLINOIS NEWSSTANDS

On this day in Illinois history, the first issue of John S. Wright's influential *Prairie Farmer* newspaper was distributed throughout the state.

Wright was not a farmer, but as a successful Chicago entrepreneur he was a determined advocate of Illinois business, which in the mid-1800s was based predominantly on agriculture. He arrived to the city as a 15-year-old in the same year Chicago received its city charter (1833) and, working first with his father, Wright became a real estate tycoon by the age of 23. A tireless promoter of Illinois, he toured the state to meet with and hear the concerns of its farmers. He published his magazine as a forum where Illinois farmers could share ideas and read up on the latest methods in crop rotation, fertilization, or fighting off pests and insects. "Farmers, write for your paper," he encouraged in that inaugural January issue, and soon the pages of *Prairie Farmer* featured articles by experts in everything from the latest farm equipment to new ideas in conservation. Subscriptions skyrocketed as the information in Wright's publication helped boost the productivity and livelihood of Illinois agriculture.

Burridge D. Butler bought the paper in 1909 and extended its circulation through surrounding states in the Midwest. *Prairie Farmer* then became a major sponsor of the popular corn-husking competitions, and Butler was prone to engage in such stunts as landing the newspaper's plane in cow pastures during county fairs. On September 15, 1928, he bought WLS Radio in Chicago, which operated under the auspices of the *Prairie Farmer* for the next few decades—a tremendous promotional tool. (For years, before its transition to rock 'n' roll, the station's most popular program was the Sunday evening Farm Dance Show.) WLS's 50,000 watts reached the entire subscription base, which peaked at 370,000 subscribers in 1950. Together, the newspaper and the radio station became the collective voice of the common farmer, championing such causes as FDR's profarming New Deal and campaigning against corruption and deceptive marketing schemes.

Subscriptions to *Prairie Farmer*—still published today—were down to below 60,000 by the onset of the 21st century, a sign of the changing times.

- JANUARY 20 -
1970
U.S. SUPREME COURT DECIDES *ILLINOIS VS. MISSOURI*, KASKASKIA'S FATE

Kaskaskia "Island" in the Mississippi River, the territorial capital (1809–1818) and first state capital (1818–19), was declared by the U.S. Supreme Court to be a part of Illinois, not Missouri, on this day in Illinois history.

Kaskaskia—where Illinois began—played a key role in the state's early history. The town was located on the Kaskaskia River, five miles from its confluence with the

Mississippi. Named for the Kaskaskia Indians, for whom Father Marquette built the Church of the Immaculate Conception in 1675, the town became a vital frontier outpost to successive waves of French, British, and American pioneers. It was here that George Rogers Clark began his campaign to evict the British from Illinois during the Revolutionary War. A 650-pound cast-iron bell, a gift from King Louis XV of France, was rung in celebration and has been called "The Liberty Bell of the West" ever since. In 1814, Illinois's first English-language newspaper, the *Illinois Herald*, was founded in Kaskaskia. The town's mixed population of French, British, American, and the few remaining native Illiniwek residents peaked at more than 6,000 at the time.

Kaskaskia's Liberty Bell of the West

But its precarious location in the Mississippi River flood basin guaranteed Kaskaskia's demise. Intermittent flooding had forced the move of the state capital to Vandalia and continued to force residents to flee throughout the mid-19th century. On April 18, 1881, a deluge finally destroyed Kaskaskia, cutting a new channel through the land and severing a small island from the eastern bank. (Though it abuts the Missouri shore, locals refer to it as an island.) The old administrative capital was totally submerged. Those who remained settled on the high ground, where the original liberty bell and a rebuilt Church of the Immaculate Conception survive to this day. The state of Missouri claimed Kaskaskia within its territorial and sovereign rights, and a boundary dispute between it and Illinois continued for decades. The U.S. Supreme Court finally decreed that the boundary line of Illinois embraced Kaskaskia Island, irrespective of the river's course.

Today Kaskaskia and its nine inhabitants (according to the most recent census) can be reached only through St. Mary, Missouri, after crossing the river at Chester, Illinois.

- JANUARY 21 -

1972

METROPOLIS DECLARES ITSELF "HOME OF SUPERMAN"

The city of Metropolis in downstate Massac County, the only town in the United States so named, was granted permission by DC Comics on this day in Illinois history to promote its official slogan: "Home of Superman."

Photo courtesy of Jeff Ruetsche

The scenic town of 6,000 on the Ohio River may not be exactly what Jerry Siegel and Joe Shuster had in mind when they created the Man of Steel in the early 1930s. There are no hulking skyscrapers, no criminal masterminds, and no bustling masses to provide anonymity to the superhero's mild-mannered alter ego, Clark Kent. But today there is the world's largest collection of Superman memorabilia, housed in the multimillion-dollar Super Museum, and an annual Superman Celebration that draws thousands of devoted fans, collectors, and celebrities on a pilgrimage from across the globe.

In the early 1970s a local businessman, Robert Westerfield, campaigned for the town to embrace the comic book hero as its own. Recently arrived from Kentucky, he was astonished that city leaders had not yet capitalized on the name recognition—the obvious marketing potential was huge. The movement gained momentum—faster than a speeding bullet—and once permission was granted by DC Comics, the Illinois General Assembly passed house resolution No. 572 recognizing Metropolis as the "Home of Superman."

The city's newspaper changed its name to the *Metropolis Planet,* after Clark Kent's fictional employer, and helped organize the first Superman Celebration in 1979—the same year the first Superman movie starring Christopher Reeve was released. The event has grown larger and larger ever since, attracting such movie stars as Kirk Alyn (the original film *Superman*), Noel Neill (Lois Lane in the 1950s *Adventures of Superman* TV series), and Jimmy Olsen actors Tommy Bond and Jack Larson, among others.

A 1993 fund-raising venture netted $100,000 to erect a 15-foot bronze statue of the Man of Steel on a solid brick foundation—inscribed with, "Truth, Justice, and the American Way"—in front of the city courthouse.

- January 22 -

1925

"Big Jim" O'Leary Dies

On this day in Illinois history, "Big Jim" O'Leary, Chicago gambling lord and son of the defamed Catherine O'Leary—whose cow *did not* cause the 1871 Chicago Fire—died in the Windy City.

Born in 1860, Jim O'Leary grew up at 137 DeKovan Street, Chicago. This, or rather the O'Leary's backyard barn, was the starting point of the Great Chicago Fire of 1871 that thoroughly destroyed the commercial core of the city. The home itself was spared. But neighbors, and soon the entire city, attributed the deadly conflagration to Mrs. O'Leary's Cow. The myth holds that the cow kicked over a lantern, and within minutes the flames had spread across the drought-stricken city. Never proved, the story too spread, and though exonerated by a city investigation the O'Learys were vilified in public opinion. His mother, father, and sister lived out their lives in relative seclusion, avoiding the press and the nosy public; James turned to the Chicago underworld.

"Big Jim" grew up to become a true villain, the kind that inspires romanticized crime fiction rather than scorn. O'Leary started working for local bookies at the age of 15. He began operating off-track betting parlors in the 1880s, and in 1904 "Big Jim" O'Leary opened the first-ever gambling boat on Lake Michigan, *The City of Traverse*. He got involved with Mike McDonald, boss of the city's first true crime syndicate, and by 1907 had inherited control of the gambling and vice district around Chicago's busy Union Stockyards. Soon all of the Southwest Side was Big Jim's territory. In later years he worked with Johnny Torrio—Al Capone's mentor—in providing illicit booze to speakeasies during the early years of Prohibition.

Big Jim O'Leary had become a multimillionaire by the time of his death, but he was never able to clear the name of his mother, or the family bovine, over the great fire that defined his childhood.

- JANUARY 23 -

1818

NATHANIEL POPE PUSHES ILLINOIS'S BORDER 40 MILES NORTH

Territorial delegate to the U.S. Congress, Nathaniel Pope persuaded legislators in Washington, D.C., to move the state's northern boundary up an extra 40 miles on this day in Illinois history.

Pope was in the Nation's Capital lobbying for Illinois's entry to the Union. At the time, he was Illinois Territory's lone representative to the U.S. government. As pre-scribed in the Northwest Ordinance of 1787, the northern boundary was to run west through the southern tip of Lake Michigan (contiguous from the northern edge of neighboring Indiana). Pending in the U.S. House of Representatives was the Illinois Enabling Act, which set the course for statehood with borders according to the old ordinance, but to this Pope submitted an amendment extending the proposed state line 40 miles northward. His motivation was to give Illinois a strong foothold on Lake Michigan, and thus balance the Mississippi River trade to the south with Great Lakes commercial shipping to markets in the north and east. In addition, he argued, this would "afford additional security to the perpetuity of the Union, inasmuch as the State would thereby be connected with the [northeastern states] through the Lakes." The bill passed easily on April 18, 1818, and Nathaniel Pope's prescience paid big divi-dends nearly half a century later when Illinois, because of these northern bounds, remained within the Union rather than joining the upstart Confederacy.

Another current consequence is that more than 60 percent of the state's current population is located in its 14 northern counties, which otherwise would have become part of Wisconsin. The added territory includes not only Chicago but the valuable lead mines at Galena and the cities of Rockford, Waukegan, and many others as well—more than 8,000 square miles in all. Nathaniel Pope returned home and served as a federal district court judge for Illinois until his death on January 22, 1850, almost 48 years to the day of his bold and historic proposal in Congress. He ran unsuccess-fully for Illinois's U.S. Senate seat in 1824.

Without Pope's maneuvering in Congress, Illinois would have a much different face today, and so too might the nation.

- JANUARY 24 -
1925
SOUTHERN ILLINOIS KLAN LEADER S. GLENN YOUNG KILLED

S. Glenn Young, audacious Ku Klux Klan front man for the southern part of the state during Prohibition, was gunned down in "Bloody" Williamson County on this day in Illinois history.

Young, a former Prohibition agent brought in and reinstated to clean up bastions of organized crime in towns like Benton, Marion, and Madison, Illinois, was also a prominent member of the Ku Klux Klan. Klansmen, he reasoned, would make perfect federal agents in the war against local bootleggers, as those who engaged most in the illicit sale and consumption of alcohol were largely Catholics and foreigners. On December 22, 1923, nearly 500 Klansmen were sworn in as federal Prohibition enforcement agents in Carbondale. Young was, essentially, their director, and he immediately set about skirting the local (and often corrupted) authorities in enforcing the law. As he did so, he made quite a few enemies, not the least of which were southern Illinois mob bosses Charlie Birger and the Shelton Brothers, whose bottom line Young's raids were cutting into. Birger and the Sheltons formed a short-lived alliance to take out their common nemesis, and the war between "wets" and "drys" was on.

On this January evening, Young, whose influence in the area had already suffered a series of defeats against the allied bootleggers and local authorities, met his fate at the European Hotel in Herrin. In a formal challenge–turned–ambush, three of Charlie Birger's gunmen met Young with his lackeys for an Old West–style showdown in the hotel lobby. Young, a former Texas Ranger with a legendary draw, took out two of his attackers but was struck fatally in the chest, causing the remaining Klansmen to run in fear. One year earlier, he had been leading raids with impunity, arresting hundreds, and intimidating the civil authorities of Franklin and Williamson counties through a strong showing of public support; but now S. Glenn Young, along with the KKK in southern Illinois, was finished.

Young's funeral attracted 20,000 people and he was buried in the purple robes of a Klan Kleagle (recruiter), eulogized as a martyr to the 18th Amendment, and put to rest with more than 70 indictments to his name.

- JANUARY 25 -
1924
FLORENCE FIFER BOHRER ANNOUNCES CANDIDACY FOR ILLINOIS STATE SENATE

On this day in Illinois history, after much cajoling from friends, Bloomington's Florence Fifer Bohler announced the candidacy that would result in her becoming the first woman elected to the state senate.

She was born in 1877, daughter of Illinois Governor "Private Joe" Fifer, who held office from 1889 to 1893, and became very active in reform movements as a young woman. After marrying Jacob Bohrer, whom she met while studying music at the University of Chicago in the late 1890s, and the births of their son Joseph, and daughter, Gertrude, Florence Fifer Bohrer became deeply concerned about creating a safe environment in which to rear her children. She adopted the philosophy that a good mother must be socially active and "push out the walls of her home to include the community." She formed the Mothers' Club of McLean County to form stronger bonds between the home and the school, which eventually led to the national Parent Teacher Association. In 1910, Fifer Bohrer led a campaign to build a tuberculosis sanitarium in Bloomington, Illinois, which formally opened to wide praise in 1919 with her sitting as the secretary of the board. She was also active in the women's suffrage movement and served as the local director of the American Red Cross during World War I.

The 1924 elections were the first in which women nationwide had full voting rights. In some states, it was the first time they could run for office, and Florence was encouraged by many to take her civic activism to Springfield. She ran as a Republican and was elected the first woman to sit on the Illinois State Senate. She was reelected in 1928, and during her eight years in the General Assembly was a champion of the rights of women, children, the sick, and the poor. One important act she sponsored allowed women to sit on juries. She was also instrumental in the enactment of several new child welfare laws. State Senator Fifer Bohrer also introduced the bill, passed into law, establishing the official state song, "Illinois."

She died at the age of 83 in July of 1960, having lived her life in accordance with her personal motto: "I saw a thing to do, and I did it."

- JANUARY 26 -
1986
CHICAGO BEARS WIN SUPER BOWL XX

The 1985 Chicago Bears put the grand finale to one of the greatest seasons in National Football League history, a 46–10 Super Bowl XX rout over the New England Patriots, on this day in Illinois history.

Photo courtesy of Red Label Records

Not only did the team, led by charismatic coach Mike Ditka, dominate the NFL that season, but its members became virtual rock stars: It was the year of Jim McMahon, William "The Refrigerator" Perry, and the hit single "Super Bowl Shuffle." The Bears had the entire city whipped into a Super Bowl frenzy. The famous lions at the entry steps to the Art Institute of Chicago sported giant Bears football helmets, and the Chicago Symphony Orchestra performed a resounding version of "Bear Down, Chicago Bears" to cheer on the team.

The team's pop-culture appeal was surpassed only by its gridiron dominance. The defense, with five Pro Bowl selections, including future Hall of Fame linebacker Mike Singletary, ranked first in the league. Walter Payton led the offensive charge, punishing opposing defenses with more than 2,000 yards from scrimmage and 11 touchdowns. The Bears finished the season 15-1 and completely shut down both NFC playoff opponents en route to Super Bowl XX.

Their 36-point margin of victory against the Patriots set an NFL record. New England's game plan was to stop number 34, evidently at all costs; with Payton serving as a decoy, the field seemed wide open to the rest of the Chicago offense. Matt Suhey rushed for an 11-yard touchdown to put the Bears up 7–3, and they never looked back. The defense sacked Patriot quarterbacks seven times and held New England running backs to a mere seven yards rushing. Ditka's team was unstoppable.

The Bears have not returned to the Super Bowl since.

- JANUARY 27 -
1982
CHICAGO CUBS PICK UP ROOKIE INFIELDER RYNE SANDBERG

On this day in Illinois history, the Chicago Cubs, in a trade with the Philadelphia Phillies, acquired an unknown minor-leaguer who would go on to become one of the greatest second basemen to ever grace the major leagues.

Ryne Sandberg started slow with just one hit in his first 32 at-bats, but soon broke the slump to launch a baseball career that would earn him the nickname "Baby Ruth," landing in Cooperstown 23 years later. In that Hall of Fame career, "Ryno" played all 16 seasons with the Cubs (1982–1994, 1996–97), setting club records for a second baseman across the board and winning the adoration of millions at Wrigley Field. As a Cub he appeared in ten consecutive All-Star games (1984–1993), won nine straight Gold Glove Awards (1983–1991), and led the Cubs to the oh-so-unfamiliar National League Championship Series in both 1984 and 1989. The team floundered both years despite Sandberg batting a combined .385 in those games. He set a major-league record of 123 errorless games in a row at second base, and in 1984 won the league MVP while belting out 40 home runs—most ever for any player in that position after Roger Hornsby's 42 in 1922.

Ryno's signal performance came on what has since been dubbed simply "The Sandberg Game," on June 23, 1984. He went 5 for 6 at the plate, hitting dramatic game-tying home runs off All-Star relief pitcher Bruce Sutter in the 9th and 10th innings. His seven RBIs and stellar fielding helped the Cubs to a 12–11 win over the Cardinals. "One day I think he's one of the best players in the National League," said St. Louis manager Whitey Herzog after the game. "The next day, I think he's one of the best players I've ever seen." Ryne Sandberg signed a then-record $28.4 million, four-year contract extension with the Cubs in 1992, making him the highest paid player in baseball history at that time.

He was inducted to the National Baseball Hall of Fame in Cooperstown on July 31, 2005, joining such Cubs greats as Billy Williams, Ernie Banks, and Ferguson Jenkins.

- JANUARY 28 -
1922

ILLINOIS FARMER FRED HATCH
CREDITED WITH INVENTING THE SILO

Dairyman Magazine published an article crediting McHenry County farmer Fred Hatch with inventing the vertical silo—nearly 50 years after the fact—on this day in Illinois history.

Agricultural landmarks are often not heralded with the trumpets and drums that accompany other historical events; and so it was when Fred Hatch and his father,

Old, overgrown McHenry County silo

Lewis, quietly built the nation's first vertical silo, in August of 1873, on their Spring Grove, Illinois, farm. Fred had just returned from studying agriculture at the University of Illinois in Urbana, a member of the school's second graduating class, when he approached his dad with plans for the silo. "I never had seen a silo when I [built] mine and even my own father considered it a very 'crazy idea.'" But the revolutionary idea took root, and a silo 10 feet wide by 24 feet tall (16 above ground) was soon filled with fine-cut corn silage (cow feed).

"We first dug a pit eight feet deep and laid stone walls around it. The part above ground was built of flooring, with a layer of tar paper and another thickness of flooring board," recalled Hatch in the *Dairyman* article. "This made it almost airtight." Soon their fattened cows were giving more milk than ever before. Lewis, who had gone along with his son's college-inspired scheme only reluctantly, quickly built two more silos for the farm. The Hatches' original silo—precursor to the now ubiquitous grain towers dotting the landscapes of rural America—was used every year and filled a total of 46 times through 1919, when the farm was sold and the new owner tore it down.

A historical marker set by the McHenry County Historical Society beside the dilapidated foundation of the original silo quietly marks its location.

- JANUARY 29 -
2005
FIGHTING ILLINI ALL-CENTURY BASKETBALL TEAM HONORED

Twenty great players from the first 100 years of U of I basketball were recognized during a halftime ceremony at Assembly Hall in Champaign, on this day in Illinois history.

Banners went up declaring University of Illinois the All-Century Team as the No. 1–ranked Fighting Illini were in the midst of an 89–66 rout of the Big Ten rivals, the Minnesota Gophers. The 20-man team was elected by thousands of Illini fans and announced on October 15, 2004. An Illinois Basketball Centennial Weekend—commemorating the 100th anniversary of the program—was held January 28–31, 2005.

The earliest players selected for the team were Ray Woods (1915–17) and Chuck Carney (1920–22). Woods led the Illini to a perfect 16–0 record and a National Championship in 1915. He was also National Player of the Year in 1917. Carney was a first-team All-American all three seasons at Illinois, and was National Player of the Year in 1922.

Plenty of Illini greats—young and old—were on hand for the ceremonies. Former stars in attendance included Johnny "Red" Kerr (1952–54), Eddie Johnson (1978–1981), and Bruce Douglas (1983–86). Kerr, who scored 1,299 points for the Illini before going to the NBA, later became the analyst on Chicago Bulls broadcasts. Douglas, whose 765 assists are still an Illinois record, stated with perfect player comportment, "I'm just thankful to have had the opportunity to play here."

Frank Williams (2000–02) and Brian Cook (2000–03) were the most recent players to make the illustrious top 20 all-time list. Williams, who earned Big Ten Player of the Year honors in 2001, holds the Illini record of 24 free throw attempts in a single game. Cook, the 2003 Big Ten Player of the Year, set the Illini single-season record in 2002 by sinking 96 of 110 free throw attempts. Both have gone on to the NBA. Three veterans of the 1989 "Flying Illini" that made the Final Four—Kenny Battle, Nick Anderson, and Kendall Gill—were also honored.

All present that day witnessed a 2005 Fighting Illini team that would finish the season ranked No. 1 in the nation but fall gracefully in the final seconds by a 3-point margin to South Carolina in the NCAA Championship Game.

- JANUARY 30 -
1885
RICHARD J. OGLESBY BECOMES ILLINOIS'S FIRST THREE-TERM GOVERNOR

Governor Oglesby was inaugurated for the third time to the state's highest office on this day in Illinois history. He was Illinois's first three-term governor—though his second term had lasted only ten days.

Oglesby came to Illinois as an 8-year-old Kentucky orphan in 1833 and was raised by his uncle in Decatur. After working first as a farmer, carpenter, and rope-maker, he studied law in Springfield and was admitted to the bar, opening up a practice in Sullivan,

Illinois, in 1845. Oglesby left for the California Gold Rush in 1849, returning to Illinois with a small fortune of $5,000 in gold two years later. He then turned to politics.

Oglesby was elected to the Illinois State Senate in 1860, sitting for one session before resigning to join the Union Army when the Civil War broke out. He led troops first as a colonel, then as brigadier and major general of the Eighth Regiment, Illinois Volunteer Infantry. Serving under the command of fellow Illinoisan, General Ulysses S. Grant, Oglesby led his brigade in the successful assault on Fort Donelson, Tennessee. He was later wounded while leading a charge at the Battle of Corinth, after which he returned home.

The war hero ran for and won the governorship of Illinois, serving his first term from 1865 to 1869. He was elected Illinois governor again in 1872, but left office a mere ten days after inauguration to join the U.S. Senate. After one six-year term representing Illinois as a Republican in the U.S. Senate, Oglesby declined to run for reelection, and returned once again to his adoptive state. His third and final term as Illinois governor (1885–89) was marked by labor strife, most notably the drama surrounding Chicago's Haymarket Square Riot of 1886. Oglesby, on the eve of the executions, commuted two of the controversial seven death sentences to life imprisonment. The governor was close friends with Abe Lincoln, whom he encouraged to campaign for office in the 1850s with the newly-born Illinois Republican Party, and beside whose deathbed Oglesby would sit a decade later.

Richard J. Oglesby died at Oglehurst, his Elkhart, Illinois, estate, in April of 1899. He is buried at Elkhart Cemetery.

- JANUARY 31 -

1937

OHIO RIVER FLOOD DESTROYS SHAWNEETOWN

The downstate city of Shawneetown—early financial center and transportation hub—suffered a devastating flood on this day in Illinois history.

The Ohio River merges with the Wabash at the southeastern border of Illinois and flows along the banks of Gallatin, Hardin, Pope, Massic, Pulaski, and Alexander counties before emptying into the Mississippi at the southernmost tip of the state. It drains more than 525,000 square kilometers of water annually. Heavy rains in of January 1937 and a month of melting snow combined to threaten disaster for the low-level towns like Shawneetown, in Gallatin County, and Cairo, in Alexander County.

Postflood destruction at Shawneetown

The river began to rise on January 5, causing little worry as this was typical (if early), and by January 20 experts predicted the water level would top off at 52 feet—several feet below the 60-foot levees built along the shorelines in both towns. Flooding was not new, and both Cairo and Shawneetown thought they were prepared. On January 22, however, a downpour of rain, sleet, and hail began and lasted several days, increasing the water level 2 feet per day. Even the experts started to worry.

At the end of the month, the ever-swelling Ohio River raged over its banks and the entire region was hemmed in by a great flood. Shawneetown was nearly fully submerged. Nearby Golconda, Rosiclare, and Elizabethtown became virtual islands in the middle of the deluge. State Highway 13, some 25 miles distant from the riverbed, sat under eight feet of water. Cairo, which anticipated the worst flooding, attracted a national media frenzy for the coming catastrophe and had already been largely evacuated. It, alone among Illinois cities along the Ohio, withstood the flood. The river's waters rose to within inches of the levee's crest before receding.

The situation in Shawneetown was desperate. Terrified residents huddled on rooftops and street corners. With telephone service down, the town sent out pleas for help over an amateur's short-wave radio, and motorboats from throughout the region arrived to evacuate the marooned townspeople. By the time the waters subsided in mid-February, authorities decided to relocate the entire town several miles inland; there exist today an "Old Shawneetown" and a "New Shawneetown" in Gallatin County.

Overall, the Great Flood of 1937 caused more than $75 million in damages, destroyed hundreds of bridges, and left thousands of Illinoisans homeless.

This day in
February

- FEBRUARY 1 -
1865
ILLINOIS BECOMES FIRST STATE TO
RATIFY THE 13TH AMENDMENT

On this day in Illinois history, legislators of the 21st state in the Union became the first to ratify the 13th Amendment to the Constitution, formally banning slavery.

The U.S. Congress sent the amendment to the states for ratification on the last day in January of 1865. It had been drafted in Alton, Illinois, by Senator Lyman Trumbull, an old friend and political ally to Abraham Lincoln. A two-thirds approval—at that time 27 of the 36 states in the Union—was needed to adopt the amendment. The following morning, Illinois was the first state to ratify, but the amendment did not receive final approval until Georgia ratified on December 6, 1865.

Photo courtesy of Library of Congress, Geography and Map Division

Illinois itself had a long and contentious history of slavery. The earliest European explorers encountered a deeply rooted slave culture among the Illiniwek Indians. In 1715, King Louis XIII issued an edict recognizing slavery in France's American colonies; the British extended these rights while loosely administering Illinois from 1763 to 1778, as did the state of Virginia, which had claimed conquest of Illinois during the Revolutionary War, through 1783.

After that, Illinois became part of the Northwest Territory. Its laws forbade slavery, but the official deed of secession from Virginia established the practice's continued tolerance in specific French and Canadian settlements. Territorial Illinois, established in 1803, finally and formally banned slavery. But with historical roots in French-Indian culture and deep bonds to slave states like Kentucky and Tennessee, which heavily settled Illinois in the early 1800s, many Illinoisans petitioned Congress to end the ban. Nevertheless, the Illinois Constitution, written in 1818, declared that "neither slavery nor involuntary servitude shall hereafter be introduced to this state." (That ambiguous language, however—"hereafter be introduced"—allowed certain Illinois residents who already owned slaves some latitude.) Many transplanted New Englanders and Southerners with strong abolitionist sentiments tipped the balance of state opinion on the divisive issue, and in 1824 a popular vote officially ended the debate.

It is fitting that Illinois, whose most famous son had issued the Emancipation Proclamation three years earlier, was the first state to give his words the power of federal law.

- FEBRUARY 2 -
1882
CHICAGO GETS CHARTER FRANCHISE FOR THE NATIONAL LEAGUE

On this day in Illinois history, Chicago became one of eight cities (along with Boston, Cincinnati, Hartford, Louisville, New York, Philadelphia, and St. Louis) to form a new professional baseball league.

Referred to simply as the National League today, the National League of Professional Baseball Clubs was very much the brainchild of Chicago businessman William Ambrose Hulbert. He was also cofounder of the Chicago White Stockings (now the Cubs, who won the inaugural National League pennant and went on to dominate professional baseball through the 1880s). Hulbert was a silver-tongued businessman who venerated the city of Chicago. "Better a lamppost in Chicago," he once said, "than a millionaire anywhere else." He was born in 1832, just a few miles west of the future site of the National Baseball Hall of Fame in Cooperstown, New York, and became part owner of Chicago's first professional baseball team in 1870 and assumed its presidency in 1875.

Hulbert was instrumental in cleaning up the game of professional baseball at a time when gambling, drunkenness, and unruly behavior ran rampant, on and off the field. Baseball games often broke out in fistfights, and "almost every team," according to one report, "had its 'lushers.'" Hulbert was determined to change this. And he was unwavering in his belief that Chicago be the center of reform. He conspired in 1875 with Albert Spalding, a Rockford, Illinois, native then starring as a pitcher for the Boston Red Stockings, to pilfer the top players from the National Association and form a new league that demanded integrity and upright behavior from its players. They began to reform baseball—these moral crusaders—by stealing star players from the East. By this coup Hulbert and Spalding assembled one of the most dominant ball clubs in the history of the national pastime, the 1876 Chicago White Stockings. They then persuaded other teams, four from the East and three more from the West, to also defect from the N.A. and join the upstart National League. Hulbert, Spalding, and company ran the National Association out of business virtually overnight.

Hulbert is buried at Chicago's Graceland Cemetery beneath the unmistakable gravestone of a large concrete baseball, and his team, the Cubs, continue to play just a few blocks down the street, at Wrigley Field.

- FEBRUARY 3 -
1809
ILLINOIS TERRITORY CREATED BY FEDERAL GOVERNMENT

On this day in Illinois history, land bounded in part by three great rivers was separated from Indiana Territory to create Illinois Territory, and Kaskaskia was made its capital by an Act of Congress.

The initial boundaries of Illinois Territory were somewhat amorphous. The western edge was clearly delineated by the Mississippi River. Its southern and southeastern borders were likewise marked by the Ohio and Wabash rivers. A line extending due north from the Wabash, about halfway up the eastern border, ended at the southern tip of Lake Michigan. Those boundaries are all familiar to Illinoisans today, but at the time, Illinois Territory to the north included all of present-day Wisconsin, the Upper Peninsula of Michigan, and large sections of northeast Minnesota. The political, economic, and cultural center of this vast territory was the region referred to as the America Bottom, a southwestern corner of the present state first settled by the French. The territorial capital was set up at the old French administrative center of Kaskaskia. Here, Ninian Edwards was appointed territorial governor, a position he'd hold until statehood in 1818, and Nathaniel Pope soon became the territory's lone representative to the U.S. Congress.

Illinois Territory in 1809 was sparsely populated outside of the capital, and was fertile land for fur trappers and Indian traders. By the early 1800s, with ermine, lynx, and beaver fur in demand by East Coast and European elites, a single pelt was worth a pound of shot, musket powder, and 20 flints, as well as a week's worth of supplies, to the average trapper or trader. Virtually all the area's permanent settlements clustered around the America Bottom and the banks of the Ohio and Illinois rivers, and Chicago was nothing more than a tiny port and trading outpost. The first land office opened in Kaskaskia in 1804, the second in Shawneetown in 1812. The American population of Illinois at the time was roughly 12,000, still outnumbered by the many Indian tribes who also called Illinois home. Meanwhile, the rest of the territory served those seeking great wealth in this lucrative fur trade. Illinois Indians—the Sauk, Fox, and Potawatomi up north, and the Shawnee and other nations in the south—were more than happy to oblige, seeking whiskey and rifles in return.

Illinois back then was the gateway to the West, from whence Lewis and Clark had launched their historic journey through the newly acquired Louisiana Territory half a decade earlier.

- FEBRUARY 4 -
1846
BRIGHAM YOUNG LEADS MORMON EXODUS FROM ILLINOIS

Brigham Young, who assumed leadership of the Mormon Church after the martyrdom of Joseph Smith in June of 1844, led the initial wave of his followers westward from their capital city of Nauvoo, Illinois, on this day in Illinois history.

In the wake of the Joseph and Hyrum Smith murders, carried out by a mob while the brothers were incarcerated at Carthage Jail and awaiting trial for the destruction of a rival printing press, a two-year period of violence called the Mormon War exploded in western Illinois. Before surrendering to authorities, Joseph Smith had mobilized the Mormon militia (the state's largest) and enacted martial law in Nauvoo. Bracing for repercussions from the vigilante killings, the residents of nearby towns expected the Mormons to seek revenge. Fabricated stories of Governor Thomas Ford being held hostage at Nauvoo and other Mormon depredations were circulated throughout the state to gather support. Militias organized in Carthage, Quincy, and Warsaw to seize the Mormon stronghold, though an all-out siege never came.

Meanwhile, Young prepared the mass exodus of his flock, vowing in September 1845 to lead them to a new utopia "as soon as the grass turns green." That next February, 5,000 faithful left on a westward trek that would end in Salt Lake City, Utah. One of the few Latter-day Saints to remain behind was Emma Hale Smith, Joseph's first wife and widow, who later married a non-Mormon, abandoning the church and its (former) practice of polygamy.

In 1848, the Icarians, a secular utopian sect inspired by French philosopher Étienne Cabet, arrived from Texas to establish a commune where Joseph Smith's Christian city had failed. They rebuilt the Mormon Temple, which had been burned after the exodus, to serve as their administrative center, but it was again destroyed by a tornado. The Icarian experiment, too, was a failure, and the community eventually dissolved and dispersed. The city remained a shell of its former self for more than a century.

In 1962, major restorations of the historic city were launched, and today the site is one of Illinois's top tourist attractions along the Mississippi River.

- FEBRUARY 5 -
1954
CHICAGO'S LYRIC OPERA OPENS

The internationally acclaimed Lyric Opera of Chicago opened with a celebrated first performance at the Civic Opera House on this day in Illinois history.

The Chicago Opera Company had closed after its 1948 season, and the city was in an eight-year opera draught when the Lyric Opera debuted with a presentation of Mozart's *Don Giovanni*. It was a huge financial risk at a time when recent events did not bode well for the theater's success. Seven opera companies had folded in the city over the previous four decades, and critics predicted the latest endeavor would likewise end in debt. But the Lyric Theater of Chicago, as it was called for season one, pulled out all the stops for the opening show, and a sold-out house was left standing in enthusiastic applause as one notable Chicago theater critic declared the inaugural performance equal to that of "an established troupe of long standing." The Lyric was founded by an insurance broker, an Italian composer, and a student-singer, 28-year-old Carol Fox. Fox served as general manager through 1980, one year before her death. For $30,000, much of it donated by friends, they hired an all-star cast for two performances of *Don Giovanni*. Opera legend Rosa Raisa attended Opening Night as guest of honor.

The Civic Opera House, home to the Lyric Opera now for 50 years, has been selling out its 3,600 seats ever since. It is the second-largest opera auditorium in North America. The company's most ambitious event was a 1996 performance of Wagner's *Ring* cycle, the first time the epic was presented in its entirety. Put on at a cost of $6.5 million, the sold-out *Ring* cycle had an estimated $34.7 million economic impact on the city. The opera was a tremendous success, and it returned for the 2004–05 season, to mark the Lyric's 50th anniversary. But the world-renowned theater does not confine itself to the classics. Recent performances include contemporary works such as *The Great Gatsby* and even original musicals based on popular films, such as Robert Altman's *Wedding*, which premiered and was directed by Altman himself in 2004.

Thanks to the Lyric Opera's five decades of intrepid world-class performances, Chicago ranks internationally among the top cities for opera.

- FEBRUARY 6 -

1911

RONALD REAGAN BORN IN TAMPICO, ILLINOIS

Ronald Wilson Reagan, 40th president of the United States, was born in Whiteside County on this day in Illinois history.

Reagan—"The Great Communicator"—was raised in Illinois. His family moved from rural town to rural town before settling in Dixon, Illinois, along the Fox River, when Ronald was a ten-year-old boy. There, he became a lifeguard in the summer of 1926 and is credited with saving more than 70 lives through the summer of 1932. He was elected student body president of Dixon High School and again at Eureka College, in central Illinois, before graduating with the class of 1932.

After college, the ambitious Reagan went west and set off on a wide-ranging career. He broadcasted Chicago Cubs baseball games (re-creating the play-by-play as it was

Photo courtesy of Library of Congress, LC-USZ62-13040

wired to the studio) for WOC/WHO Radio in Davenport, Iowa. He enlisted in the Army Reserves in Los Angeles, California, where he soon launched an acting career highlighted by the film *Knute Rockne: All American* (1940). He made training and recruitment films for the U.S. Army during World War II, became president of the Screen Actors Guild, and appeared in 53 Hollywood movies through 1964.

Reagan also engaged in California politics. He gradually changed party affiliation, campaigning as a Democrat for Truman in 1948 and Eisenhower in 1952 and 1956, but supporting Richard Nixon, a Republican, in 1960; he officially changed his party registration in 1962. In 1966, he was elected governor of California and served two terms.

In 1980, Ronald Reagan defeated Democratic incumbent Jimmy Carter to become the 40th president of the United States. He defeated Carter's vice president, Walter Mondale, in a 49-out-of-50-state landslide to win reelection in 1984. Reagan's two-term administration was marked by supply-side economics (with mixed success, lowering inflation and unemployment while doubling the national debt) and a bold foreign policy. Derided by opponents at the time, Reagan is widely credited today for facilitating victory in the Cold War and ushering in the demise of Soviet communism.

Reagan died after a long bout with Alzheimer's disease on June 5, 2004, and a candlelight vigil was held at his boyhood home in Dixon.

- FEBRUARY 7 -
1990
ILLINOIS RIVERBOAT GAMBLING ACT ENACTED

The Prairie State, on this day in Illinois history, became the second state in the nation to allow riverboat gambling.

The Riverboat Gambling Act, like all controversial pieces of legislation, had its staunch supporters and its passionate opponents. The bill's chief proponent was a Democratic state representative from Rockford named E. J. "Zeke" Giorgi, dubbed "Father of the Illinois Lottery" by Governor Dan Walker in 1975. Zeke and his Springfield allies argued that the revenue collected through taxation would be used to fund public schools, help support worthwhile charities, and create jobs and a general economic boon for many of the state's struggling river cities. Detractors called that "poppycock." They saw in the prospect of riverboat casinos a social panacea, a predatory scheme that would systemically victimize the state's poor who, as proved by their disproportionate participation in the state lottery, would throw away what few dollars they owned in hopes of striking the jackpot. But Giorgi, after two years of debate, won the day, and the Alton Belle Casino on the Mississippi River became the state's first fully operating water-bound casino on September 11, 1991.

The Gambling Board established by the Riverboat Gambling Act was allowed to grant ten riverboat casino licenses. Each casino could host up to 1,200 gambling sites (consisting of blackjack tables, slot machines, etc.) between no more than two vessels. The Board consists of five members, appointed by the governor and confirmed by the state senate, who oversee and regulate the operation of Illinois riverboats. More than 100 agency employees audit and investigate each casino to ensure integrity and to collect on the dual system of taxation—they've reaped more than $3 billion since 1991—imposed on the amount wagered and the number of admissions. Critics call it a draw, though— win some, lose some—as this economic windfall has come at the unquantifiable price of emptied wallets, broken lives, and displaced tourism from other parts of the state.

By 1993, the Alton operation had been joined by riverboats in Aurora, Galena, East St. Louis, Joliet, Metropolis, Peoria, and Rock Island, with Elgin soon to follow.

- FEBRUARY 8 -
1910
BOY SCOUTS OF AMERICA FOUNDED
BY OTTAWA, ILLINOIS, MILLIONAIRE

On this day in Illinois history, William D. Boyce, a Chicago publishing tycoon and resident of LaSalle County, incorporated the Boy Scouts of America.

He was motivated to bring scouting to America by a chance encounter while visiting London, England, in August of 1909. Boyce was wandering astray in the famous "pea-soup fog" of that city when he stumbled upon an anonymous British Boy Scout, perhaps 11 or 12 years old, who then used his lantern to guide the American millionaire to his destination. Offering to pay the young lad for his service, Boyce was told, "No, sir, I am a Scout. Scouts do not accept tips for Good Turns." Boyce was impressed. He asked the boy to take him to his leader, obtained a truckload of scouting literature from the organization's founder, Lord Robert Baden-Powell, and returned to his Ottawa, Illinois, mansion determined to promote the Boy Scouts in the United States. The following February, Boyce traveled to Washington, D.C., and filed incorporation papers for the Boy Scouts of America.

He helped the fledgling organization stay on its feet with a $4,000 gift that first year, and joined with scouting leaders from places like the YMCA in recruiting new members across the nation. His business acumen and organizational skills (he had gotten rich, in part, by employing up to 30,000 boys as sales agents—the first newspaper boys—for his Chicago Ledger in the 1890s and early 1900s) were a boon to early scouting. Hundreds of troops popped up in cities all over America. Their purpose, as established by Boyce, was ". . . to promote, through organization, and cooperation with other agencies, the ability of boys to do things for themselves and others, to train them in Scoutcraft, and to teach them patriotism, courage, self-reliance, and kindred virtues, using the methods which are in common use by Boy Scouts."

Every June, in Ottawa, Illinois, the nation's Boy Scouts and Scout leaders make a pilgrimage to the W. D. Boyce Grave Site and Memorial, placing a ceremonial wreath at the final resting place of their founding father.

- FEBRUARY 9 -
1862
FIRST CONFEDERATE PRISONERS ARRIVE AT ALTON PRISON

Confederate soldiers captured in battle during the Civil War first arrived at Alton Federal Military Prison on this day in Illinois history.

Alton Prison opened in 1833 as the first state penitentiary in Illinois, but was closed down in 1860. Prison reformers like Dorothea Dix had forced its abandonment due to overcrowding and poor sanitation, and a new facility was built in Joliet. But with two prisons in nearby St. Louis filling up with prisoners of war, the U.S. Congress passed legislation in December of 1861 to reopen the Alton site. Nearly—or merely, critics will say—$2,500 was spent to improve conditions at the prison before the first prisoners arrived. But as with most war prisons—North and South—those conditions were miserable. The 144th Illinois Infantry, composed mostly of Alton area recruits, was assigned to guard the prison.

Between 1862 and 1865, Alton Federal Military Prison saw more than 11,760 Confederate soldiers pass through its gates. Along with these prisoners of war, hundreds of local traitors—those guilty of expressing anti-Union sentiment, aiding escaped Southerners, or engaging in guerrilla attacks against Union interests in Illinois—found themselves locked behind the inhospitable jail bars. Disease ran rampant at Alton. Before long, the prison lived up to its former reputation and, owing to lack of sanitation, insufficient nourishment, and overcrowding, the mortality rate of its inmates soared. A smallpox epidemic broke out in the winter of 1862–63, and an estimated six to ten inmates perished per day. Alton citizens demanded that all infected prisoners be transported to an empty island on the Mississippi River, where an uninhabited dwelling was transformed into a temporary hospital; none of the several hundred victims of smallpox sent there ever returned.

After the Civil War ended, Alton Federal Military Prison was evacuated and razed to the ground, and a monument listing more than 1,500 known Confederate prisoners to have perished there was raised at a nearby cemetery.

- FEBRUARY 10 -
1851
ILLINOIS CENTRAL RAILROAD CHARTERED

On this day in Illinois history, five years before construction was completed, the Illinois Central Railroad was chartered by the General Assembly.

It was the nation's first rail line to receive a federal land grant, owing to President Millard Fillmore's signing of the landmark Federal Land Grant Act in 1850. The plan was to build a line running northwest from Cairo, Illinois, up to Galena, with a "Chicago Branch" running northeast up from Centralia. Rails were shipped from England, twisted into U-shape form to fit into ships for their ocean passage, and

Depot of the Illinois Central Railroad

heated and bent straight again upon arrival. It was worth the effort. The impact on Illinois's economy, by revolutionizing industry, trade, and transport—along with the subsequent population boom—was immeasurable. Once completed, the Illinois Central's tracks constituted the longest contiguous railroad in the world.

The Illinois Central took over, reorganized and consolidated neighboring short lines, acquired public land, and expanded at an amazing rate over the next four decades. By 1890, the main line and its subsidiaries consisted of more than 10,000 miles of track crisscrossing the state of Illinois. Towns such as Champaign, Carbondale, and Mattoon mushroomed overnight at railroad junctions, and Chicago became the transportation hub of the nation. The line was extended south to the Gulf of Mexico in 1881, when 550 miles of 5-foot track (from Cairo to New Orleans) were transformed to standard gauge (4.85 inches) in a single day. A luxury train, the Panama Limited, offered an 18-hour trip between Chicago and New Orleans. Later that decade the IC branched out farther, to Sioux Falls, South Dakota, and Omaha, Nebraska.

In 1855 an accomplished lawyer from Springfield, Abe Lincoln, defended Illinois Central Railroad against McLean County's challenge to the railroad's tax-exempt status in the Illinois Supreme Court. Lincoln and Illinois Central won, but the rising politician had to return to court twice in 1857 to collect from the powerful railroad his $5,000 fee for services rendered.

One hundred and fifty years after its completion, the Illinois Central is the only line from the great age of railroads still operating under its original name.

- FEBRUARY 11 -
1861
PRESIDENT-ELECT ABRAHAM LINCOLN
BIDS FAREWELL TO SPRINGFIELD NEIGHBORS

On this day in Illinois history, at Springfield's Great Western Railroad Station, Abraham Lincoln said good-bye to the city he called home.

He was heading toward the all-but-certain maelstrom of civil war, leaving behind the Midwestern comforts and warm-hearted people who for a quarter century had nurtured him to great success as a homesteader, lawyer, and politician. Before departing to Washington, D.C., to be inaugurated the 16th president of the United States, Lincoln issued a brief but unforgettable tribute to his Springfield friends and neighbors. "My friends, no one, not in my situation, can appreciate my feeling of sadness at this parting. To this place, and the kindness of these people, I owe everything," said an emotional Lincoln. "I now leave, not knowing when, or whether ever, I may return, with a task before me greater than that which rested upon Washington. I bid you an affectionate farewell." And then he boarded the train.

Lincoln's old law office in Springfield

The sign board at the Lincoln-Herndon law office, where the future president had had a practice with partner William H. Herndon since 1844, was left hanging per Lincoln's instructions. He promised Herndon that when he returned from the White House, they would go on to practice law "as if nothing had ever happened."

Twelve days after issuing a "Farewell Address," Lincoln arrived secretly in Washington, D.C. He was warned, along the way, by legendary Chicago detective Alan Pinkerton, of an assassination plot. Secessionist sympathizers—a conspiracy of "plug uglies"—were planning an ambush in Baltimore. Pinkerton guards escorted Abraham Lincoln anonymously through the southern city. Traveling in an unmarked train, Lincoln was disguised as a Scottish sleuth (or dressed as a woman, depending on which newspaper account one chooses to believe), before arriving safely in the capital to address the nation. Four years later, following Lincoln's assassination, Pinkerton would express in grief, "If only I had been there to protect him as I had done before."

Lincoln would not return to Illinois until 1865, when his funeral train rolled into Chicago in early May.

- FEBRUARY 12 -
1869
ILLINOIS WOMEN'S SUFFRAGE MOVEMENT BORN IN CHICAGO

Chicago's Liberty Hall was packed by delegates promoting a woman's right to vote, among other reform issues, for the first meeting of its kind in the "West" on this day in Illinois history.

The two-day convention (February 11–12) was organized by Mary Livermore, a Boston-born schoolteacher who in 1857 moved to Chicago, where, with her husband Daniel, a pastor, she began publishing the reform newspaper *New Covenant*. The purpose of the convention was to organize a women's suffrage movement in Illinois and demand that the upcoming state constitutional convention remove all legal barriers to a woman's right to vote. On day two, Mary was duly elected president of the Illinois Women's Suffrage Association and, within weeks, was publishing a new city newspaper, *The Agitator*, to counterbalance the less sympathetic Chicago papers of the day. (The *Chicago Tribune* had opined during the convention: "The public will now be annoyed for six months by the characteristic ill humor of a lot of old hens trying to hatch out their addled productions.")

The two days of sessions featured a Who's Who of early suffragists. Chicagoan Myra Bradwell—one of the nation's first female attorneys and publisher of the prominent law journal, *Chicago Legal News*—was in attendance. Susan B. Anthony and Elizabeth Cady Stanton—the two leading advocates of reform from New York—came to support their fellow Illinois suffragists. Anna Dickinson—who had achieved national renown as an antislavery orator during the Civil War—engaged in a spirited debate with an opponent of women's suffrage, Reverend Robert L. Collier, who insisted that women best influenced society from behind the scenes at home. The crowd nearly broke into a riot during the exchange and Livermore had to restore order several times. Livermore and company were unable to force reform on the Illinois General Assembly that year. But the convention did succeed in spawning local suffragist associations throughout the state, which, in incremental steps, achieved over the next five decades everything that those who packed Liberty Hall had hoped to accomplish.

On June 19, 1891, state legislators passed a bill that entitled Illinois women the right to vote for local school officials, the first of many steps toward universal suffrage.

- FEBRUARY 13 -
1920
ANDREW "RUBE" FOSTER ORGANIZES NEGRO NATIONAL LEAGUE

On this day in Illinois history, Rube Foster, star pitcher and manager for the Chicago American Giants and visionary of black baseball, founded the Negro National League.

Foster, who made his 1901 debut with the Chicago Union Giants by pitching a shutout, became a player, manager, and baseball executive of unsurpassed skill in any league. After winning the 1903 Black World Series with the Cuban X-Giants and repeating in 1904 with a team from Philadelphia, the burly 6-foot-4-inch Foster returned to the City of the Big Shoulders in 1907. There, as a player-manager, he guided the Leland Giants to a league-best 110-10 record. On the mound he was wily yet disciplined, and always in control: "Do not worry. . . . appear jolly and unconcerned. I have smiled often with the bases full with two strikes and three balls on the batter. This seems to unnerve." Foster brought that psychological mastery of the game to the dugout as well. In 1909, his Leland Giants narrowly lost a best-of-three series (two games to one) to the World Series champion Chicago Cubs; the following season, when Foster's team had gone 123 and 6, no major-league club stepped forward to accept the challenge. In 1911, he formed the Chicago American Giants, who dominated top black and semipro teams across the nation throughout the decade.

But despite all the excitement in the ballpark, black baseball was plagued by instability at the gates—until Rube Foster founded the Negro National League in 1920. It was the first viable major league for top black players who were barred from competing with their white counterparts. As league president and owner, Foster recruited several high-caliber clubs (including the touring Cuban X-Giants), set the league's schedule, and realized unprecedented profits through 1926, when he was forced to retire due to illness. His Chicago American Giants won the first three championships (1920–22), and Foster would help other clubs meet payroll out of his own pockets to keep the league together. Sadly, Rube Foster—"Father of Black Baseball"—spent his final years in a hospital sick ward and died on December 9, 1930, in Kankakee, Illinois. The Negro National League folded within the next 12 months.

Foster was elected posthumously to the National Baseball Hall of Fame in Cooperstown, New York, on March 11, 1981.

- FEBRUARY 14 -
1894
JACK BENNY BORN IN WAUKEGAN

One of the most prominent stars of American radio and television in the 20th century, Jack Benny, was born in Lake County on this day in Illinois history.

His birth name was Benjamin Kubelsky. He started studying the violin (his trademark instrument) at the age of six, learning on a half-size fiddle at twice-weekly lessons for which his parents, who earned a modest income, paid 50 cents per session. By his freshman year at Central High School in Waukegan, Benny was playing professionally at a local vaudeville theater. Flunking all his classes, the young musician dropped out of school in 1911 to pursue a career in show business. From the orchestra pit he caught the attention of an emerging comedy act—the Marx Brothers—who played the theater while touring the Midwest. The comedians' manager (their mother) invited Benny to grab his violin and accompany her sons' onstage antics on the road; Benny's own parents, however, refused to send their 17-year-old son off on what they thought to be a "boondoggle."

Jack Benny was nevertheless undeterred. After a stint in the Navy (during which he entertained the troops with his music and stand-up comedy) Benny started touring the vaudeville circuit with the Marx Brothers. In 1927, while attending a Passover seder at the invite of Zeppo Marx, he met his future wife and longtime comedy partner, Mary Livingstone. Benny first achieved national fame with the *Jack Benny Program*, which hit the airwaves in 1932 and remained one of the most listened-to radio shows through the mid-1950s. A colorful cast of sidekicks (including Livingstone as Benny's wisecracking girlfriend) became staples in the weekly exploits of an accomplished but petty comedian, played by Benny as a caricature of himself. The show was such an immediate success that Jack was deemed "Most Popular Comedian on the Air" by the nation's radio editors. He attracted a string of big-name sponsors, including Canada Dry Ginger Ale, General Motors, and General Foods. Benny's radio sketches were the predecessors to the television sitcoms of later decades. The show moved to television from 1950 to 1965, and Benny also appeared on the big screen in 1963's *It's a Mad, Mad, Mad, Mad World*.

Jack Benny became a Hollywood fixture, but he often returned to visit his hometown of Waukegan before dying of cancer in 1974.

- FEBRUARY 15 -

1933

CHICAGO MAYOR ANTON CERMAK SHOT WHILE VISITING FDR

Anton J. Cermak, Chicago's first foreign-born mayor, was struck by an assassin's bullet while touring with President-elect Franklin Delano Roosevelt in Miami, Florida, on this day in Illinois history.

Cermak was born near Prague in the Czech Republic (Bohemia at the time) in 1873, and emigrated to downstate Illinois with his family as a child. Following his father's lead he worked as a teenager in the Braidwood, Illinois, coal mines. He moved to Chicago in 1890, got involved in local politics, and by 1902 was serving in the Illinois General Assembly. Seven years later he was back in Chicago, serving as alderman of the city's 12th Ward—the Bridgeport neighborhood—where he became a rising star consolidating power in the Democratic Party machine.

In 1931, Anton Cermak defeated incumbent "Big Bill" Thompson in the city's mayoral election. Thompson had taunted Cermak during the campaign, directing a condescending rhyme at his opponent's ethnicity: "Tony, Tony, where's your pushcart at? Can you imagine a World's Fair mayor, with a name like that?" (The World's Fair would be coming to Chicago in a couple years.) Cermak responded skillfully, turning the taunt back on Thompson while scoring points for himself among Chicago's many ethnic populations: "He don't like my name . . . It's true I didn't come over on the Mayflower, but I came over as soon as I could."

As mayor, Cermak campaigned to bring Illinois into the Roosevelt camp during the 1932 Democratic National Convention, and again during the general election against President Herbert Hoover. He was in Florida visiting his political ally when a bullet intended for the president-elect missed, striking instead the big-city mayor at FDR's side. On his way to the hospital, Cermak allegedly whispered to Roosevelt, "I'm glad it was me and not you, Mr. President." The assassin—an antiauthoritarian zealot named Joseph Zangara—was caught, convicted, and sent to the electric chair within two months.

Mayor Cermak's funeral procession

Photo courtesy of Library of Congress, Prints and Photographs Division

Cermak succumbed to his wounds on March 6, 1933, and is buried today at Chicago's Bohemian National Cemetery.

- FEBRUARY 16 -
1903
VENTRILOQUIST EDGAR BERGEN BORN IN CHICAGO

Actor, radio personality, and world-renowned ventriloquist Edgar John Bergen was born in Cook County on this day in Illinois history,

He discovered the voice-throwing trick from studying a how-to manual as an 11-year-old boy. After mastering the technique, the young Bergen asked a neighbor-

Photo courtesy of Radio Hall of Fame

hood carpenter to build him a dummy, which was soon delivered, and the persona for Bergen's wisecracking companion, Charlie McCarthy—who was modeled on a local newspaper boy—was born. As a student at Northwestern University in Evanston, Illinois, Bergen took Charlie on stage with him in amateur talent shows. The wooden sidekick with trademark cape, top hat, and monocle soon stole the show. Students and faculty alike adored the duo. In 1938, Charlie received a "Master of Innuendo and Snappy Comebacks" degree from the university, the only such honor awarded to a wooden dummy in American history.

After leaving the campus, Edgar and Charlie headed for Hollywood, where they made it big in the national spotlight. Though he first broke into professional show business by falling in with vaudeville acts and performing in movie shorts, Bergen made his big break on radio where, ironically, audiences could not see the gist of his ventriloquist act. *The Edgar Bergen/Charlie McCarthy Show* (which later included sidekick puppets Mortimer Snerd and Effie Klinker) was among radio's top-rated programs from 1937 through the mid-1950s. Charlie was never short on comedic quips—"Ambition is a poor excuse for not having sense enough to be lazy" or "Hard work never killed anybody, but why take a chance." And on October 30, 1938, Bergen and his character-creations were credited with "saving the world" because the majority of America's radio audience tuned into them rather than Orson Welles's panic-inducing broadcast of *War of the Worlds*.

Edgar Bergen died of kidney disease at the age of 75 in 1978, had *The Muppet Movie* dedicated to him the following year, and was inducted into the Radio Hall of Fame in 1990.

- February 17 -

1967

Lottie Holman O'Neill Dies in Downers Grove, Illinois

Lottie O'Neill, a native of DuPage County and the first woman elected to the state's General Assembly, died at her Downers Grove home on this day in Illinois history.

Lottie Holman was born in November of 1978 in Barry, Illinois, and moved to Chicago after college to pursue a business career. There she met and married William Joseph O'Neill, an Australian immigrant, and the couple moved to suburban Downers Grove in 1904. They remained there for more than 60 years as Lottie launched a pioneering political life with the full support of her husband, who shared her conviction that the fundamental principle of democracy is that all people be represented.

When her two sons were teenagers, O'Neill, inspired by a visiting congresswoman from Montana, campaigned for the Illinois House of Representatives. She spoke throughout the 41st District (DuPage and Will counties) contradicting the conventional wisdom of the day that women were indecisive and ill-equipped, mentally, to either vote or hold office. She energized large crowds of women voters: "All that DuPage County women have to do in the Forty-first District and elsewhere is to hang together and show the masculine citizen that they do know what they want, and, furthermore, that they intend to have it."

She won the election, serving several successive terms as a state representative (1923–1931 and 1933–1951); later, as a state senator (1951–1964), she was a leading advocate for women's issues, education, and civil rights. O'Neill ran as an independent Republican for the U.S. Senate in 1931 and represented the Illinois GOP at the 1944 Republican National Convention. A staunch conservative who earned the respect of Democrats, Senator O'Neill was strongly opposed to the utopianism of the United Nations, the federal income tax, and the intrusions of the government into private business.

O'Neill is buried at Oak Crest Cemetery in Downers Grove, Illinois, and a statue commemorating her 38 years in the Illinois General Assembly was erected in the capitol rotunda in Springfield in 1976.

Photo courtesy of Jeff Ruetsche

- FEBRUARY 18 -
1934
STATE ARSENAL BURNS IN SPRINGFIELD

On this day in Illinois history, a ten-year-old boy started a fire that would cause the State Arsenal Building to be razed.

The State Arsenal was a massive, castlelike structure about one block north of the State Capitol, and one of Springfield's most distinguished buildings. It was dedicated in a grand 1903 ceremony officiated by President Theodore Roosevelt and Governor Richard Yates. In the three decades thereafter, notable speakers at the Arsenal included presidents Calvin Coolidge, William H. Taft, Herbert Hoover, and Franklin D. Roosevelt, and leading Illinoisan William Jennings Bryan, among others. Perhaps the most grandiose event ever to be hosted by the Arsenal was a centennial banquet in 1912, commemorating President Abraham Lincoln's birthday. The Arsenal was Springfield's cultural center. Legendary bandleader John Philip Sousa performed there, as did the Chicago Grand Opera. It was from that auditorium, at the ground floor of the hulking three-story building, that a young pyromaniac started a fire that would leave the place thoroughly gutted. Everything—from the lower-level firing range, to the third-floor officer's quarters, to the vast ammunition stores that occupied the west wing—was utterly destroyed. The young boy tossed a burning paper sack onto the wooden stage, which soon caught fire, spread to the nearby curtains, and engulfed the whole armory.

Every member of Springfield's 88-man fire department battled the flames throughout the evening. More than 1 million rounds of ammunition went off, but the bullets, fortunately, were confined within the Arsenal's walls. Hoses kept a constant flow of water to douse the hundreds of pounds of dynamite stored in the basement. The once medieval-looking fortress was left in smoking, toppled ruins. In all, more than 3,000 rifles and $900,000 worth of supplies were destroyed. Thousands of war records were gone. Miraculously, nobody was seriously injured. Beyond repair, the building's remains had to be bulldozed.

The new State Armory was built on the site in 1937, and Illinois State Archives beside it in 1938, at a combined cost of nearly $2 million.

- FEBRUARY 19 -
1943
BIG INCH OIL PIPELINE DEDICATED AT NORRIS CITY, ILLINOIS

On this day in Illinois history, the town of Norris City in downstate White County became the axis of hope for the Allies during World War II, as the Big and Little Big Inch oil pipelines were formally dedicated.

American shipments of crude oil were being havocked by German U-boat operations off the Atlantic Coast, threatening to cripple the war efforts of the United States and Britain. Dubbed "Operation Drumbeat," five German submarines were dis-patched in December of 1941 with orders to ravage American shipping. By the end of February they had sunk 46 oil tankers, damaged 16 others, and cut the flow of crude oil from the Gulf of Mexico to the Eastern Seaboard by well over 50 percent. Without that oil—critical to the laying of runways, the manufacture of rubber tires, and, of course, for fueling innumerable ships, tanks, and airplanes—World War II would be lost.

Photo courtesy of Library of Congress, FSA-OWI Collection, LC-USW4-029615

The solution, in part, was to build an oil pipeline across America's heartland.

Norris City, Illinois, was chosen as the halfway terminus for the 1,800 miles of pipe that would stretch from eastern Texas to New York City. It had two legs. Big Inch, at 24 inches in diameter, carried 300,000 barrels of crude per day to Norris City, where half of it would be refined and another half sent on to Pennsylvania or New York refineries via Little Big Inch, a 20-inch pipeline. The construction of this, the largest and longest oil pipeline in the world, began in August 1942 and was fully completed (though operational in part months before) by April 1943. Big and Little Big Inch were the results of an unprecedented collaboration between the U.S. government and private industry. Washington covered the bill—$35 million—while a consortium of 11 companies including Texaco, Standard, and Shell Oil, provided the staff and supervised the construction of the pipelines.

By war's end, 6 billion of the 7 billion barrels of oil consumed by the Allies came from the United States, much of it passing through southern Illinois.

- February 20 -
1969
Five Members of the "Chicago 7" Convicted

On this day in Illinois history, five members of the so-called Chicago Seven were found guilty of intent to incite a riot (at the 1968 Chicago Democratic National Convention), sentenced to five-year prison terms, and fined $5,000 each.

The 1968 Democratic National Convention in Chicago turned into a maelstrom of protests, counterprotests, and ensuing violence in a city—and national party—bitterly divided by the Vietnam War. Thousands of activists descended on Chicago that August, and not all—most notably some of the ringleaders—could rightly be called peaceful. The Chicago Police in turn made matters worse after Mayor Richard J. Daley, in draconian fashion, allegedly ordered they "shoot to kill" arsonists and "shoot to maim" looters.

The atmosphere going in was intense. There were rumored (yet unconfirmed) threats to assassinate Daley and the prowar Democratic candidate, Vice President Hubert Humphrey; absurd threats to dump LSD in the Chicago River; ludicrous intimations from activists to seduce delegates' wives and daughters. Much of this reflected the unserious mindset of the Yippies, a movement fronted by Abbie Hoffman that had long planned the week's activities. Daley took the threats seriously (or used them as justification), and he reinforced the Chicago Police—already on 12-hour shifts—with several thousand federal soldiers and National Guardsmen.

When the antiwar platform was voted down inside the convention walls, all chaos broke out in the streets. The American flag was torn down in Grant Park and a communist flag rose in its place. While most protesters had been peaceful, agitators threw rocks and bottles at the police and Guardsmen, who in turn used tear gas and nightsticks indiscriminately. In the end, there were 650 arrests and scores of protesters injured.

Eight ringleaders were arrested and went on trial for conspiracy on September 24, 1968. One, Black Panther Bobby Seale, was found in contempt of court after numerous courtroom tantrums and sent to jail. The other seven—Jerry Rubin, Abbie Hoffman, Rennie Davis, Tom Hayden, David Dellinger, and professors John Froines and Lee Weiner—were defended by attorney William Kunstler. Their many antics during the trial, while basing the defense on "free speech," included challenging Mayor Daley to a fistfight, wrapping themselves up in the North Vietnamese flag, and promising hallucinogens to the prosecutor's children.

All had the charges of conspiracy dropped; but all but the two academics were found guilty of inciting a riot.

- FEBRUARY 21 -

1938

CHICAGO ASTRONOMER GEORGE E. HALE DIES

George Ellery Hale, who for years headed the largest, most advanced astrophysical laboratory in the world at the University of Chicago, died on this day in Illinois history.

Hale, born in Chicago on June 29, 1868, developed his lifelong fascination with the stars as a young boy. His father, a successful elevator designer and salesman in the post-fire city of Chicago (emerging as the birthplace of the skyscraper) had to keep bringing home newer, better, and larger microscopes, telescopes, and other scientific equipment as young George was never satisfied for long with the instruments at hand. His father even built him his own backyard observatory, he said, "when I was 13 or 14 years old." Hale later recalled his days as an amateur astronomer: "I built a telescope . . . and I mounted it on the roof of the house. The astonishing views it afforded of Saturn, the Moon, Jupiter, and other objects excited an intense desire to carry on actual research."

He would carry on that research to astonishing inventiveness and discovery.

After graduating from the Massachusetts Institute of Technology in 1890, and volunteering at the nearby Harvard College Observatory, Hale returned to Chicago. There, he incorporated the Kenwood Physical Observatory—again in his father's backyard—and gained worldwide recognition for groundbreaking experiments with his invention, the spectroheliograph, which advanced the ability for isolating, photographing, and measuring waves of spectral light. It had a 12-inch refracting telescope. William Rainey Harper, president of the University of Chicago, took notice and offered Hale a faculty position. Hale accepted the position under the condition that the university construct for him a new observatory, one large enough to support the world's largest telescope. The Yerkes Observatory (named for its financial sponsor and actually located in Williams Bay, Wisconsin), with its 40-inch lens, was dedicated by the University of Chicago in 1897.

Photo courtesy of Yerkes Observatory

George E. Hale, professor of astrophysics at the University of Chicago from 1892 to 1905, had by his death founded several leading observatories across the county and won the prestigious Bruce Medal for astronomical excellence in 1916.

Robert Pershing Wadlow, the "Alton Giant" who at 8 feet, 11.1 inches was the tallest man to ever live, was born on this day in Illinois history.

The Philistine warrior, Goliath—who according to biblical tradition stood at 9 feet, 6 inches—is the only man in all of recorded history to be taller. Robert Wadlow was an average 8-pound, 6-ounce newborn baby, but by six months had reached 30 pounds; he had grown to an astonishing 5 feet, 6.5 inches by kindergarten. At 13, young Robert was the world's tallest Boy Scout, at 7 feet, 4 inches. By 18, he was an 8-foot-4, 390-pound giant who wore size 37 shoes that costs $100 per pair. His parents and his four siblings—two brothers and two sisters—were all of average height. Wadlow's abnormal height was the result of a tumor in his pituitary gland, which caused it to produce irregular amounts of the human growth hormone.

At age 20 the International Shoe Company provided Wadlow shoes for free; in exchange, Robert and his father drove cross-country to promote the company—with the front passenger seat torn out so Robert could sit in back seat, stretch his legs, and enjoy the ride. He had joined the Ringling Brothers and Barnum & Bailey Circus the previous year, but he preferred the company of his family and Alton neighbors.

Wadlow died in July 1940 from a blood infection caused by a blister on his foot, the type from which he had suffered throughout his young adult life. His 1,000-pound casket required more than a dozen men to carry it, and he was buried with an unremarkable gravestone that reads simply "At Rest." The entire town closed down for the funeral and more than 40,000 mourners signed the guest register.

Robert earned the nickname of "The Gentle Giant," and in 1985 a life-size statue was erected in his memory in downtown Alton.

CHAMPAIGN'S BONNIE BLAIR WINS FIFTH OLYMPIC GOLD METAL

On this day in Illinois history, Bonnie Kathleen Blair—raised on the ice rinks of Champaign County—won her world-record fifth Olympic gold metal in speed skating.

Blair was born in 1964 in New York and came to Illinois, where she was raised, at the age of 2. She started skating then, following the lead of her five older siblings. She began competing at age 7 and, after graduating from high school in Champaign, with the support of funds raised by the Champaign Policemen's Benevolent Association, she left to train with the United States Olympic Speed Skating Team. Bonnie Blair made her Olympic debut at the 1988 Winter Games in Calgary, Canada, taking the gold in the 500 meter by setting a new world record of 39.1 seconds. Blair, with a ferocious will for victory, was just getting warmed up on the ice.

Over the next six years, Blair established herself not only as the most decorated woman in the history of speed skating, but one of the most successful of all athletes in any sport. Her second gold medal came as an exhilarating win over the pack in the 500 meter during the 1992 Olympic Games in Albertville, France. This made her the first woman ever to win back-to-back golds in that event. She added a third gold by defeating the top Chinese speed skater by a mere two hundredths of a second in the 1,000 meter that same year. Two years later, at the 1994 Winter Olympics in Lillehammer, Norway, Bonnie—with the full 60-plus-member "Blair Bunch" in tow to root her on—won again both the 500 meter and the 1,000 meter, for her fourth and fifth career gold metals—an unrivaled feat among U.S. Olympic athletes. For the shorter sprint, she became the first woman to shatter the 39-second barrier, clocking in at 38.99 seconds.

Blair, who has since become a tireless fund-raiser for the American Brain Tumor Association, among other charitable causes, was elected to the United States Olympic Hall of Fame in 2004.

- FEBRUARY 24 -
1837
STATE LEGISLATURE VOTES TO MOVE CAPITAL TO SPRINGFIELD

The General Assembly, bowing to the persistent campaigning of a group of Sangamon County representatives dubbed the "Long Nine," passed into law a bill designating Springfield the new state capital on this day in Illinois history.

Illinois's second capital city, Vandalia (the first was Kaskaskia), had proven inadequate for a number of reasons, and in 1834 state legislators motioned for its replacement. Vandalia was located in southern Illinois. But Chicago was growing and settlements (in the wake of the Blackhawk War of 1832) were likewise increasing in other northern parts of the state. A number of more centrally located cities, including Alton, Peoria, and Jacksonville, were in the running to be named site of the new capitol building, but it was Springfield that finally prevailed on the fourth ballot in an 1837 referendum. The Long Nine, led by state representative Abraham Lincoln, with eight others who also bested 6 feet in height (hence the nickname), had pledged Springfield's town square and a contribution of $50,000 for the construction of a new statehouse unlike any that existed in the nation at that time. The persuasive group won the agreement of the state legislature, and Springfield was thus awarded the honor of becoming Illinois's third capital city.

Old State Capitol

The Illinois Statehouse—now called the Old State Capitol—was a grand Greek Revival building designed by John F. Rogue, resident architect of Springfield. The cornerstone was laid on July 4, 1837, and its foundation and walls were built entirely of limestone quarried in Illinois. Four massive Doric columns support a portico at the main entrance and a majestic classical dome tops the center of the building. The Illinois House of Representatives convened here on December 7, 1840, and it served as administrative center for the General Assembly through 1876. It was here that Abraham Lincoln, as attorney, pled more than 400 cases in the 1840s and 1850s; as senatorial candidate, delivered his famous "House Divided" speech in 1858; and as slain president of the United States, lay in state May 3–4, 1865.

After the new (but as yet incomplete) Statehouse opened in 1876, the old Capitol was transformed into the Sangamon County Courthouse, and later designated an Illinois State Historic Site.

- FEBRUARY 25 -
1779
GENERAL GEORGE ROGERS CLARK CAPTURES VINCENNES

General George Rogers Clark—younger brother to the better-known explorer of Lewis and Clark fame—forced the British surrender of Fort Sackville at Vincennes, just east of the present Indiana state line, on this day in Illinois history.

The conquest came at the end of a punishing, 20-day slog through 180 miles of frigid, overflowing streams and Illinois wilderness. The general and his men waded waist-deep at times through icy waters, Clark's youthful cajoling—and orders to shoot any stragglers—keeping moral high. Having captured several important British posts in western Illinois the previous summer, Clark now led this rugged band of frontiersmen to drive the King's soldiers from a regional stronghold at Vincennes. Roughly half his troops were volunteers from the largely French citizenry whose allegiance Clark had won, without firing a shot, at the Mississippi River towns of Kaskaskia, Cahokia, and Prairie du Rocher. The day before the 170-man force departed, a Mississippi flatboat, the *Willing,* had cast off with six cannons and 40 additional men for the coming battle. They were to rendezvous at the mouth of the Wabash River, near Fort Sackville, for a coordinated assault.

After reaching the Wabash River and camping two full days within two miles of the fort, waiting in the freezing rain for the *Willing* to arrive, Clark received word from local hunters that much of the British garrison had returned to Fort Detroit for the winter. Those who remained were unsuspecting of any assault, and the French residents of the town were eagerly awaiting their American liberators. With still no sight of the flatboat and its additional men and firepower, and his own men becoming more weather-beaten and frail by the day, Clark ordered the immediate attack of the fort.

Lieutenant Governor Hamilton had personally marched down from Detroit, along with a contingent of 500 British troops and allied Indian warriors, to capture Fort Sackville from the Americans two months earlier. He was planning to retake Illinois in the spring. After reinforcements arrived, Vincennes was to serve as the campaign's headquarters. Now Hamilton was trapped with fewer than 50 soldiers and, after a short-lived and feckless defense, he surrendered unconditionally to Clark's superior forces. Capturing Fort Sackville was the crowning jewel in George Roger Clark's remarkable Illinois campaign, earning him the designation "George Washington of the West."

The *Willing* sailed into view the following day.

- FEBRUARY 26 -
1995
FINAL DEPARTURE FROM GLENVIEW NAVAL AIR BASE

The final U.S. aircraft to take off from Glenview, a northern Chicago suburb's 66-year-old Naval Air Base, did so on this day in Illinois history, ending an era of military training that lasted three generations.

What would eventually become Glenview Naval Air Base was built on 450 acres of farmland about 25 miles northwest of Chicago's congested city center. The Curtiss-Wright Corporation, a newly formed aviation conglomerate, purchased the base with the ambitious plan to make this new site the region's chief private and commercial air field, and the showpiece of a network of passenger-friendly airports stretching from New York to California. Its Hangar One was at the time the largest in the world. It was designed in a country club mindset with a restaurant, lounge, and upper-level promenade that allowed guests an unobstructed view of the runways. After $3 million in construction costs, with financing directed by Chicago banker Earle H. Reynolds, Curtiss-Reynolds Airport was dedicated on October 20, 1929. The daylong celebrations attracted more than 35,000 people to a "Pageant of Aerial Progress" that included more than 100 flying machines. Nine days later Black Friday hit and threw the nation into the Great Depression.

Curtiss Airfield was able to hang on during the Depression. It had some successes, most notably hosting the International Air Races in 1933, which featured both Charles Lindbergh and Amelia Earhart, but fell far short of fulfilling its original vision. Its financiers hoped contracts awarded to the base for instructional courses given to Army and Navy pilots would help keep Curtiss afloat. By 1940, with World War II approaching and the older runways at Great Lakes Naval Air Base in nearby Lake County proving insufficient, all major military flight training in the region was transferred to Curtiss. The Navy bought the base for about half a million dollars from Curtiss-Wright, and over the next six decades the renamed Glenview Naval Air Base graduated thousands of our nation's finest pilots, including a 19-year-old future U.S. president, George Herbert Walker Bush.

Immediately after the final aircraft took off—three P-3 Orions—a great yellow X was painted on each runway, signaling closure, and Hanger One has since been converted to a memorial park honoring those who had served.

- FEBRUARY 27 -

1979

JANE BYRNE WINS CHICAGO'S MAYORAL PRIMARY

On this day in Illinois history, Jane Byrne scored a stunning upset in Chicago's Democratic primary against Mayor Michael Bilandic, all but securing her as the city's 41st mayor.

Mayor Bilandic succeeded longtime machine boss Richard J. Daley after Daley's death in 1976. He was a big favorite going into the campaign season for the 1979 primaries. Byrne was first appointed head of consumer affairs by Mayor Daley in 1968 but released from that post by Bilandic nine years later, after criticizing the mayor over a taxicab fare hike. She was a lesser-known but politically talented underdog who would avenge her firing by capitalizing on a timely blizzard. In January of 1979, just weeks before the primary, more than 90 inches of snow dumped on Chicago, grinding city services to a halt. Bilandic ignored the snowstorm. Byrne made it her central campaign issue, hammering away at an ill-prepared Mayor Bilandic, who embraced Chicago's moniker of "The City That Works," at a time when city streets were closed, public transportation stalled, and garbage sat uncollected. She defeated her former boss by 15,000 votes out of 800,000, to capture the Democratic nomination for city mayor.

No Republican had been elected mayor of Chicago since "Big Bill" Thompson in 1937. The Democratic primary, in effect, was the city's mayoral election. Byrne beat the Republican nominee handily, with 82 percent of the vote on April 3, and took office as the city's first woman mayor on April 16, 1979.

Mayor Byrne was supported by an unlikely coalition—lakefront liberals, northside conservatives, and inner-city African Americans—but was never able to endear herself to the "old guard" machine Democrats. She did pull some memorable stunts, such as moving into the notorious Cabrini-Green housing projects and hiring her husband for $1 per year as an advisor. Unable to galvanize a base, however, in the 1983 Democratic primary Byrne was defeated by Harold Washington, who went on to become Chicago's first African American mayor. Byrne became a machine outsider and sharp critic of the younger Mayor Richard J. Daley. She published her political memoir, *My Chicago*, in 1992.

Robert Green Ingersoll—"The Infidel Orator"—was appointed Attorney General by Governor Oglesby on this day in Illinois history.

Photo courtesy of Library of Congress, LC-DIG-cwpbh-04126

Ingersoll was admitted to the bar, along with his brother, Ebon C., on the same day—December 20, 1954. They had studied law together in Marion, Illinois, for just one month. The Ingersoll boys came to Illinois with their father as teenagers and immersed themselves in a vigorous study of the classics and philosophy. Though Ebon C. Ingersoll became a successful Shawneetown lawyer and three-time U.S. Representative from Illinois (1864–1871), it was Robert who achieved greater fame. After teaching, practicing law, and serving 21 months as colonel in the Union Army, Ingersoll became 19th-century America's most commanding and controversial public orator. (He had resigned his military commission, having seen "enough of death and horror," in June 1863.) After serving as Illinois Attorney General from 1867 to 1869, Robert Ingersoll toured the nation giving tireless two- and three-hour lectures, excoriating religious orthodoxy while charging $400 to $7,000 per venue.

Ingersoll, son of a poor Congregationalist minister, delivered such antireligious sermons as "Hell," "Progress," and "Orthodoxy"—unrelenting and at times satirical assaults on religion. In "The Gods," he declared, "Give me the storm and tempest of thought and action, rather than the dead calm of ignorance and faith." He championed "progress" in thought and abhorred "superstition," earning the reputation as the "Great Agnostic." In 1868, Ingersoll was campaigning for the governorship of Illinois but lost the support of many delegates when he refused to tone down his unorthodox views.

Ingersoll amassed tremendous wealth. In 1876, he moved into Cockle Mansion, which was completed after two years and $50,000 worth of construction. It was the most extravagant residence in all of Peoria. By 1880 he was earning an estimated $200,000 annually as an attorney for the railroads; and he kept busy in politics, often stumping for fellow Republicans, and always opposing organized religion.

The antithesis of his father—a man of profound faith and material poverty—Ingersoll died on July 21, 1899 of a heart attack, and his ashes were spread over Arlington National Cemetery.

This day in

March

- MARCH 1 -
1874
EVANSTON'S GROSSE POINT LIGHTHOUSE
ILLUMINATES LAKE MICHIGAN

The lantern atop the newly built, 113-foot Grosse Point Lighthouse, among the largest of its kind on the Great Lakes, first sent its welcoming beam across the waters of Lake Michigan on this day in Illinois history.

The federal government ordered construction of Grosse Point in 1873, after Evanston residents had petitioned Congress for years to fund a local lighthouse. By the 1850s, Chicago had become the hub of a great inland waterway, and with increased maritime traffic came more and more shipwrecks. On September 8, 1860, a passenger ship, *Lady Elgin,* collided with a schooner carrying lumber off the Evanston shores and within site of the town's citizens. Along the lakefront they gathered and watched, unable to help as the *Lady Elgin* broke apart and sank and its hundreds of passengers struggled to reach land. Nearly 300 died. From this tragedy was born the campaign to build a great lighthouse that could safely guide the many ships approaching Chicago's busy harbor.

Built on a promontory named Grosse Point, or "Great Point," by 17th-century French explorers, the Evanston, Illinois, landmark served from 1873 to 1941 as the principal lighthouse on Lake Michigan's southern shores. Its Second Order Fresnell Lens, one of only five employed in all the Great Lakes, sent a beacon of light that could be seen for 21 miles, warning navigators of shallow water and guiding them in poor weather to Chicago's shores. Two fog signals were added in 1880, and a staff of three keepers and a daytime laborer were needed to operate Grosse Point Lighthouse before it was fully electrified in 1923, when the staff was reduced to two keepers. In 1934, with the installation of the first-ever photoelectric device used in a lighthouse, the service house was decommissioned and Grosse Point stripped of its full-time staff. The light was shut off in 1941, as part of the government's Air Raid Protection program, and has been used only intermittently since 1945 to aid Lake Michigan luxury cruisers, the railroads having long replaced the lake as the main route for commercial traffic.

In 1999, Grosse Point became the first lighthouse on the Great Lakes to be designated a National Historic Landmark.

- MARCH 2 -

1868

UNIVERSITY OF ILLINOIS AT URBANA-CHAMPAIGN OPENS

The state's first government-funded facility for higher learning, then called the Illinois Industrial College, first opened its classroom doors on this day in Illinois history.

In the early years the school was limited in scope to the Agricultural College and vocational studies, and, under the auspices of the Morrill Act (establishing Congressional land grants to the states for such schools) funding for further departments was withheld. The prospect of the school becoming a vehicle for the academic meritocracy was roundly mocked. One contemporary cartoon derisively showed farm boys trudging in from a muddy plowing lesson, sitting down awkwardly to read Plato. But all that began to change during the governorship of John Altgeld (1893–97) when the state of Illinois expanded aid to the school, which was declared the University of Illinois in 1885. Its motto: "Learning and Labor."

Photo courtesy of Jeff Ruetsche

Lorado Taft's Alma Mater at the University of Illinois

The university has since contributed greatly to the development of the state and the nation. With its roots in agriculture, the U of I dispatched "farm advisors" to every county in Illinois to encourage local farm leadership and keep local farmers abreast of the latest in agricultural experimentation, a practice from which was born the American Farm Bureau Federation. The school's College of Agriculture was soon recognized among the best in the nation. The U of I's colleges of Engineering, Physics, and (later) Computer Science have likewise achieved world renown. No fewer than ten alumni have won the Nobel Prize, and the College of Arts & Sciences has produced 16 Pulitzer Prize recipients. The list of accomplished graduates over the decades also includes Roger Ebert (Pulitzer Prize–winning movie critic), Hugh Hefner (founder of *Playboy*), and Ron Popeil (creator of the infomercial). The campus newspaper, *The Daily Illini,* is the longest-running college newspaper in the nation. The school's symbol, Chief Illiniwek—often misunderstood to be a mascot—appears only for a ceremonial dance during halftime of major sporting events, in authentic Native American dress and headset donated by Chief Frank Fool's Crow of the Oglala Sioux.

The University of Illinois today boasts 18 colleges at its Urbana-Champaign campus, with sister universities in Chicago (UIC) and Springfield (UIS).

- MARCH 3 -
1873
LYMAN TRUMBULL ENDS THIRD
SUCCESSIVE TERM AS U.S. SENATOR

Senator Lyman Trumbull, who changed party affiliations several times during his career, ended his distinguished tenure in the United States Congress on this day in Illinois history.

A former Connecticut schoolteacher, Trumbull heeded Horace Greeley's advice to "Go West Young Man, Go West" and moved to Belleville, Illinois, in 1837. He practiced law and then pursued Illinois politics along with his new friend, Abe Lincoln, and rose from the state legislature (1840–41) to serve as Illinois Secretary of State (1841–43) and justice of the Illinois Supreme Court (1848–1853). As an attorney, he'd often argue escaped slaves' cases pro bono. He argued and won the landmark case *Jarrot v. Jarrot* in 1845, without pay which put an end to constitutional loopholes allowing involuntary servitude in Illinois. In 1854, Trumbull was elected to the U.S. House of Representatives, but before Congress convened he was appointed to the Senate. He served in the U.S. Senate from 1855 to 1873.

As a Senator, Trumbull was at the heart of the most contentious issues of the Civil War and Reconstruction era, often skirting party loyalty to vote on principle. Elected as a Democrat, he became a Republican in 1856 after his opposition to slavery had made his former party inhospitable. In 1872, Trumbull split with the Republicans over the impeachment of President Andrew Johnson, being one of only seven Republicans who voted to acquit Johnson. This, combined with his disapproval of the Grant administration's lenient stand on Reconstruction, led Trumbull to back Horace Greeley on the Liberal Republican ticket for the 1872 presidential election.

Returning to Chicago to practice law after his third Senate term had ended, Trumbull finally returned to the Democrat Party. He served as counsel to Samuel J. Tilden during the heavily contested 1876 presidential election. (Tilden eventually lost when the bipartisan Congressional Electoral Commission awarded the disputed election results of several states to Republican candidate Rutherford B. Hayes.) Senator Trumbull's greatest achievement in Congress was drafting and proposing the 13th Amendment to the U.S. Constitution, which abolished slavery, in 1864.

He died in Chicago in June 1880 and is buried at the city's Oakwood Cemetery.

- MARCH 4 -
1978
DAILY NEWS SAYS, "SO LONG, CHICAGO"

The *Chicago Daily News,* which ran from 1876 through 1978, revolutionizing the newspaper industry, published its final issue on this day in Illinois history.

The paper was founded by Melville E. Stone to compete with the more elite *Chicago Tribune,* and thrived under the guidance of Victor Fremont Lawson, the *Daily's* visionary publisher and business manager. It was the first Midwest paper to sell for 1 cent, at a time when Chicagoans had to pay three to five pennies for one of its competitors. The *Chicago Daily News* was the first big-city paper in the nation to dispatch teams of foreign news correspondents, to print photographs, and to devote a column to the budding phenomenon of radio; it also broke ground by employing notable writers, such as Eugene Field and Carl Sandburg, as literary columnists. By 1888, the *Daily News* had a circulation exceeding 200,000, ranking it among the top two or three newspapers in the nation.

Victor Lawson, who became sole owner in 1888 until his death in 1925, donated much of his wealth to those less fortunate than he. Among his top beneficiaries were the Congregational Church and the Young Men's Christian Association. And he was widely credited for making large donations, anonymously, to numerous local charities. His grave at Chicago's Graceland Cemetery, a larger-than-life Crusader sculpted by Lorado Taft, bears no name, no dates, and no epitaph. It is inscribed simply with the following words: "Above All Things Truth Beareth Away the Victory."

In 1929 the paper moved into its new home, a 26-floor Art Deco landmark skyscraper designed by Chicago architects Holabird & Root, and was widely syndicated through the 1950s. The *Chicago Daily News* won the Pulitzer Prize 13 times for everything from commentary to editorial cartooning to international reporting. But at the age of 102, the once-revolutionary daily had succumbed to a lack of ingenuity, rising expenses, and an American public enamored by TV sitcoms and no longer interested in an afternoon newspaper.

For years, the *Chicago Daily News* kept its price at one penny to be attainable by the city's working classes after a long day at the rail yard, factory, or slaughterhouse.

- MARCH 5 -
1980

ALTON ACTIVIST PHYLLIS SCHLAFLY TESTIFIES
IN CONGRESS AGAINST THE ERA

On this day in Illinois history, Madison County's Phyllis Schlafly appeared before the U.S. Armed Services Committee in the Nation's Capital to oppose passage of the Equal Rights Amendment.

The Equal Rights Amendment was first introduced in 1923, four years after women had won the right to vote, and brought to session year after year, but did not make it past the floor of Congress until 1972. That year both the House and Senate passed it quickly, and the ERA finally went to the states for ratification, needing the support of 38 states to become law. By the time it reached its seven-year time limit (eventually extended to ten by Congress) it had been ratified by 35 of the necessary 38 states. Illinois—the first state to grant its women the right to vote and the first to

Photo courtesy of Library of Congress, *U.S. News & World Report Magazine Collection*, LC-U9-33889A-31/31A

ratify the 19th Amendment in 1920, extending this right to all women across the nation—was one of the key holdouts. Opposition was spearheaded by an Alton woman named Phyllis Schlafly, whose grassroots organization, Eagle Forum, stood steadfast against the National Organization of Women and other advocates for the amendment. Her organization was founded the same year the ERA went to the states.

The two camps of female activists had vastly different interpretations of the wording of the proposed ERA, which was all of three sentences long. Supporters argued that this amendment would further guarantee against gender discrimination in all walks of life. Opponents argued that the U.S. Constitution and Bill of Rights already offered such protections, and that the ERA would open the door to judicial activism and lead to such things as women being compelled to register with the selective service and serve combat roles in the military. It was this fear—not the auspices of the Christian Right, as some of her critics accused—that motivated Schlafly. Citing the potential drafting of women and the threats posed to female prisoners of war, among other concerns, she made a reasoned case against the ERA. This argument played well with the Illinois General Assembly, which refused to ratify the controversial amendment seven years in a row.

Defeat of the ERA was the "greatest victory for women's rights since the women's suffrage amendment of 1920," declared Schlafly, who announced the death of the ERA by throwing a celebratory bash in 1981.

- MARCH 6 -
1848
ILLINOIS'S SECOND STATE CONSTITUTION RATIFIED

On this day in Illinois history, after weeks of debates, drafts, and revisions, more than 75 percent of the state's voters ratified a new constitution.

By the 1840s, the frontier-era Illinois Constitution of 1818 had become outdated, and calls for its replacement were heard from many quarters. Democratic demands included ending life terms for Illinois Supreme Court justices, rolling back the influence of state banks, and arming the governor with veto power. Whigs were mainly concerned with blocking non-Illinoisans from voting, which in their eyes was a privilege of citizenship being violated under the current laws that granted suffrage to any white male inhabitant over age 21. Ending government spending on extravagant public works was another general concern. A proposal for a new constitution was at first narrowly defeated in 1842 but passed with 72 percent of the vote in 1846. Under Governor Augustus C. French, a Democrat and the first native New Englander elected to that office in Illinois, a second constitution would take root.

From early June through the end of August the following summer, 162 delegates assembled at the old State Capitol in Springfield to mold the new document. The changes were sweeping. To prevent Supreme Court packing (under the 1818 constitution, judges were appointed for life), the number of justices was reduced to three, each elected by geographic districts to nine-year terms. The governor could now wield a limited veto, which could be overturned by a majority in the General Assembly. To address growing debt, official salaries were scaled down to $1,500 per year for the governor, $1,200 for a Supreme Court justice, and a very modest $800 for both the secretary of state and the state treasurer. The right to vote was reserved for Illinois citizens alone; a proposal to extend suffrage to freed slaves was voted down 137–7. Amendments could be added by popular vote rather than by having to call for further conventions.

French ended his first term early so gubernatorial elections could coincide with the implementation of the new constitution; still, he won a full four-year term in 1848.

- MARCH 7 -

1833

LINCOLN APPOINTED POSTMASTER OF NEW SALEM

On this day in Illinois history, President Andrew Jackson appointed Abraham Lincoln postmaster of New Salem.

The post was only part time, earning young Abe a meager salary of about $30 per year. It was one of many occupations he held in New Salem before leaving for the more promising locale of the up-and-coming Springfield in 1837. Lincoln arrived at New Salem in 1831 and immediately built a strong reputation for himself in the small prairie settlement of roughly 100. Besting the local braggart, Jack Armstrong, in a much-publicized wrestling match, Lincoln soon found tales of his unrivaled physical strength spreading throughout the region. This reputation surely had much to do with his appointment as postmaster, as delivering mail in such a rugged frontier setting demanded great stamina. It was in New Salem, too, that Lincoln fell in love with a woman named Ann Rutledge, a romance that ended in heartbreak and a prolonged period of melancholy when she died suddenly in the summer of 1835. (In later years, rumors surrounding this brief courtship would haunt Lincoln's already tormented widow, Mary Todd Lincoln.) By the 1840s,

Lincoln statue at New Salem

with the nearby Sangamon River proven to be non-navigable, virtually all of New Salem's residents had followed Abe's lead and packed up for more promising towns like Springfield, Peoria, or the newly appointed seat of Menard County, Petersburg.

New Salem was revived as a state park in the early 20th century. Newspaper mogul William Randolph Hearst purchased the site in the name of the Old Salem Lincoln League, which subsequently deeded the land to the State of Illinois. The original cooper's shop, where barrels, coffins, and other wooden goods were handmade, was the only building still standing when restorations began. An ambitious effort headed by the league—spanning decades, and based on original plats and records found at the Sangamon County archives, archeological digs, and interviews with descendants of the town's settlers—has since reconstructed the old settlement. Dozens of buildings have been restored, including the Rutledge Tavern, Denton Offut's Store (where Lincoln was hired as a clerk), and the log schoolhouse.

Illinoisans and others seeking to "discover Lincoln" are free today to roam the 16th president's former stomping grounds, still administered by the Lincoln League.

- MARCH 8 -

1892

PULITZER PRIZE–WINNING JOURNALIST
EDGAR A. MOWRER BORN IN BLOOMINGTON

Edgar Ansel Mowrer, Berlin correspondent for the *Chicago Daily News* who won a Pulitzer Prize in 1933, was born in McLean County on this day in Illinois history.

Mowrer came from a family of journalists. He and his brother, Paul, were both assigned to the foreign office of the *Chicago Daily News* during World Wars I and II. Both had distinguished careers. Paul published ten books of poetry in addition to his reporting, and in 1933 married Hadley Richardson Hemingway, former wife of another Illinois author whose work was inspired by the European conflicts. That same year, Edgar A. Mowrer published his most celebrated work, *Germany Puts the Clock Back*. It analyzed the decline of democracy in Germany in the post–World War I years as Mowrer had witnessed it firsthand, and warned presciently against the rise of Hitler's fascism. Chapter XVIII, "Perish the Jew: Hitlerism Exposed!" anticipated the Holocaust a full decade before its true horror was revealed to the world.

Arguably, no other American journalist of the 20th century was witness to so much seminal history of the era. He won his Pulitzer for the Best Foreign Correspondent of the Year and returned home to speak before audiences at the Chicago Council on Foreign Relations. Topical lectures such as "The Sickness of a Great People," further elaborating on the plight of a German nation spiraling toward catastrophe, reached an estimated 200,000 Midwesterners via radio broadcast. By 1937, Mowrer was broadcasting from Paris, France, as the German war machine he had foreseen was preparing to roll across Europe. He later reported on the fall of France in 1940–41 from Lisbon, Portugal, where he had escaped to safety. His observations throughout led Mowrer to believe dreams of peaceful coexistence to be "the opium of the West," and he campaigned for harsh terms of surrender as the war came to an end. Other important titles published by Mowrer include *Triumph and Turmoil: A Personal History of Our Time, An End to Make-Believe*, and *A Good Time to Be Alive*.

Edgar Ansel Mowrer, who is largely forgotten today, died in March 1977.

- MARCH 9 -
1832
ABRAHAM LINCOLN ANNOUNCES FIRST BID FOR PUBLIC OFFICE

A 23-year-old Abraham Lincoln announced his candidacy as a Whig for the state legislature on this day in Illinois history.

Lincoln had recently arrived in Illinois and settled in New Salem, where he would take on numerous occupations but set his sights early on a political career. The young candidate ran on a platform centered on improved navigation of the Sangamon River, which he hoped would attract steamboats and provide a boon to commerce, population, and prosperity in the region. (Later efforts would prove it to be non-navigable, leading Lincoln and most others to leave the village virtually abandoned.) He also called for more stringent usury laws, as money-lending schemes had preyed victim on many new settlers in frontier Illinois, and for universal education for all state residents. With the guidance of some local mentors, Lincoln had this platform published in the *Sangamon Journal* within a week of announcing his candidacy.

Much of his campaign, however, was spent on the road, serving in the Black Hawk War throughout the summer. He had joined the state militia in Beardstown, Illinois, in April, and was elected captain of a mounted rifle company by his peers. He served about two months in northwestern Illinois—without seeing battle—before his return to New Salem. (It was Lincoln's company that arrived on the scene of Stillman's Run—the first engagement of the war—to bury the remains of 11 militiamen killed during the rout by Black Hawk's warriors in present-day Ogle County.) When the August 6 election results were made public, Abe had finished eighth in a field of 13 candidates but received 277 of 300 votes from his own precinct. Ironically, during his presidential bids of 1860 and 1864, Lincoln lost Sangamon County by tallies of 42 and 380 votes, respectively, while winning the White House.

Two years later Lincoln returned to the campaign trail as a Whig, this time winning a seat in the Illinois General Assembly on August 4, 1834.

BILL VEECK ACQUIRES MAJORITY SHARE
OF THE CHICAGO WHITE SOX

Bill Veeck, the ingenious and eccentric promoter of the national pastime, purchased 54 percent of the Chicago White Sox on this day in Illinois history.

A native of Hinsdale, Illinois, Veeck was the son of sportswriter–turned–president of the Chicago Cubs William Veeck Sr., and first broke into the baseball business as a soda vendor at Wrigley Field. He was chief groundskeeper by 1936, and directed the planting of that stadium's ivy during the off season. Veeck joined the U.S. Marines, was wounded in the leg in the South Pacific, and returned home an amputee in 1945. The dynamic young entrepreneur then set his sights on the major leagues. Veeck's first ownership of the White Sox was brief (1959–1961) but memorable. After similarly brief stints with the Cleveland Indians (1946–49) and the hapless St. Louis Browns (1951–53), followed by a few years as a special advisor to Phil Wrigley, owner of the Cubs, he began to inquire about Chicago's South Side team. Charles Comiskey— grandson of the Sox original owner, "Old Roman" Comiskey—was reluctant to see the team go to Veeck, a perceived maverick. But his sister, White Sox president Dorothy Comiskey Rigney, owned a majority of the franchise and agreed to sell it to a conglomerate fronted by Veeck for $2.7 million in 1959.

That season, the White Sox won the American League pennant and doubled their attendance numbers. Led by second baseman Nellie Fox and a brilliant pitching staff, the team went 96-40 but fell to the Los Angeles Dodgers, four games to two, in the World Series. Veeck's innovations included an "exploding" scoreboard, putting the players' names on the backs of uniforms, and promotional events such as Fireworks Night and amusing ballpark giveaways. The charismatic owner was a mainstay at the "Bard's Room," the Comiskey Park restaurant and bar, buying drinks and trading stories with the Chicago media well past midnight. "There are only two seasons," he once intoned, "winter and baseball." Bill Veeck sold the Sox in 1961 but would return to own the team again from 1974 to 1980. His most unforgettable promotion during that stretch was Disco Demolition Night in July 1979, when fans stormed the playing field; burned, exploded, and otherwise destroyed disco records and forced through mayhem the cancellation of game two of a doubleheader.

Veeck died in 1986 and was inducted posthumously to the Baseball Hall of Fame, as "A Champion of the Little Guy," in 1991.

- MARCH 11 -
1868
GROUNDBREAKING FOR NEW STATEHOUSE IN SPRINGFIELD

Ground was broken for a new (and the present) State Capitol Building in Springfield on this day in Illinois history. Construction was not fully completed until 1888.

In 1865, a bill was introduced in the General Assembly to move the state capital to Peoria. Though that bill did not pass the legislature, nervous Springfield residents set about raising $200,000 for the construction of a new building. (Three short decades earlier, citizens of Vandalia, Illinois, had taken similar action—but failed—before the state capital was relocated from their city to Springfield.) The official groundbreaking occurred unceremoniously at the State-house Grounds. "Yesterday afternoon about three o'clock, quite a concourse of people assembled at the State House site, to witness operation of breaking ground," reported the *Illinois State Journal.* "No speeches were made on the occasion and the whole operation was performed in a sensible and businesslike manner." (Springfield's leading citizens had originally wanted this site to be the final resting place of President Lincoln, but they were overruled by a grieving Mary Todd Lincoln, who had plans for the tomb moved to nearby Oak Ridge Cemetery.)

Photo courtesy of Jeff Ruetsche

Original cornerstone to the Illinois Statehouse

The laying of the official cornerstone several months later, on October 5, 1868, by contrast, was witnessed by the largest crowd ever assembled in Springfield to that date. Illinoisans from far and near traveled by foot, wagon, and railroad to view the ceremony. Two bands played patriotic songs for the occasion. The 8- by 3- by 4-foot concrete block to be set in the building's foundation contained a time capsule. The metal box held official documents from the founding of Illinois as a territory, photographic portraits of prominent men, and sample products of the day, such as whiskey bottled in Riverton and a watch built in Elgin. The original cornerstone, however, proved to be a problem. Cracks developed and it quickly deteriorated, threatening the entire foundation. The stone was removed, discarded, and replaced by a solid block of Joliet limestone. The original cornerstone, with its historic treasures, was buried in the 1880s beneath the Statehouse's north entrance. It was completely forgotten about for several decades until unearthed during renovations in 1944.

The first cornerstone now sits as a historical marker just a few feet from its original location, along with a second Illinois time capsule dedicated by Secretary of State Jim Edgar in 1988 to commemorate the 100th anniversary of the Statehouse's completion.

- MARCH 12 -
1902
GOVERNOR ALTGELD DIES IN JOLIET

On this day in Illinois history, John Peter Altgeld, the state's 22nd and most vilified governor, died while delivering a speech in Will County.

Altgeld emigrated to Ohio from Germany as a young child, joined the Union Army at 16—lying about his age—and finally settled in Chicago a few years after the Civil War. There, he became a prosperous lawyer and real estate agent. A Democrat, Altgeld ran for the U.S. House of Representatives in 1884, and though he lost to incumbent George Adams, his strong showing in Illinois's heavily Republican Fourth Congressional District bade well for a future in Illinois politics. He was then elected to the Illinois Supreme Court, serving as a judge from 1886 to 1991.

Photo courtesy of Abraham Lincoln Presidential Library

Altgeld narrowly defeated Joseph W. Fifer for the Illinois governorship in 1892, and his single term (1893–97) was among the most contentious in state history. Governor Altgeld was admired by progressives but scorned by industrialists and the press. He was incorruptible, principled, and often took the highly unpopular stand of defending the working class. In an 1893 act of political suicide, Governor Altgeld pardoned the three remaining Haymarket anarchists—Samuel Fielden, Oscar Neebe, and Michael Schwab—for lack of evidence regarding their involvement at the 1886 riot that killed seven police officers. (The others convicted had already been hanged or had committed suicide while in prison.) For this, Altgeld was attacked mercilessly in Chicago newspapers. The *Chicago Tribune*, for example, called him a "friend of murderers," and he was burned in effigy across the nation.

Governor Altgeld received less recognition for enacting the state's most rigorous child-labor laws and increasing funding for Illinois schools. But his casting off into political oblivion was cemented in 1894 when he publicly protested President Grover Cleveland's ordering federal troops in to break up the Pullman Strike and then sent in the state militia, which killed several strikers. Altgeld's political enemies of course blamed him for the bloodshed, and he was soundly defeated for reelection in 1896.

He died at only 54 years of age and was interred at Chicago's Graceland Cemetery. A monument to Governor Altgeld (sculpted by Gutzon Borglum, creator of Mount Rushmore) sits in Chicago's Lincoln Park.

- MARCH 13 -
1980
JOHN WAYNE GACY JR. CONVICTED OF MASS MURDER

On this day in Illinois history, John Wayne Gacy Jr.—the Killer Clown—was convicted on 33 counts of first-degree murder.

Gacy, outwardly an ordinary family man, inwardly harbored personal demons that drove him to commit monstrous acts. Born in Chicago on St. Patrick's Day 1942, he was raised a devout Catholic and left home at age 20 for a few months to work at a Las Vegas mortuary. Returning to Illinois, Gacy settled in Springfield and excelled as a shoe salesman, marrying a coworker in 1964. They had two children. The family moved to Iowa, where Gacy managed his father-in-law's restaurant, winning numerous awards and commendations from the local business community. There, having nothing more than a few traffic violations on his record, Gacy was arrested for sexually abusing a young boy (an employee) and, later, when he was out on bond, of attempted burglary while serving on Merchant Patrol, a community-watch group that looked after one another's businesses. He was convicted and sentenced to ten years in prison but was released on good behavior after 18 months. With his marriage in ruins, Gacy returned again to Illinois to wreak terrible havoc on dozens of unsuspecting families.

He moved into a home in suburban Des Plaines and enjoyed a good measure of popularity around town, as the crimes of his recent past remained secret. He bowled, played cards, and attended Chicago Blackhawks hockey games on complimentary tickets given him by players who frequented the downtown diner where Gacy worked as a cook. He also began performing as Pogo the Clown at neighborhood birthday parties and the children's wards of local hospitals. In 1972 he remarried and held his wedding reception at his Des Plaines home. When guests complained of a strange odor, Gacy claimed it was from dampness in the crawl space and covered the stench with lime salt.

Soon, teenage boys began disappearing from the surrounding area, which the police at first chalked up as runaways, though several of them had worked part time for Gacy's new construction company. Finally, in March of 1979, one of Gacy's intended victims survived an attack, began his own investigation of his abductor, and eventually led the authorities to the heinous discovery of 29 bodies buried in the dank crawl space of the suburban home. Four more were dredged up from the Des Plaines River.

Gacy—despite pleading not guilty by reason of insanity—was sentenced to death and sat in prison for 15 years before he was executed by lethal injection at midnight, May 10, 1994.

- MARCH 14 -
1914
CHICAGO'S WRIGLEY FIELD COMPLETED

On this day in Illinois history, after construction costs of $250,000, a new ballpark was completed at Clark and Addison streets on the city's North Side.

It was then called Wheegham Park and home not to the National League Cubs, who played at the city's West Side Grounds, but to the Chicago Whales of the upstart Federal League. The stadium's seating capacity was 14,000, and it featured four acres of Kentucky bluegrass covering an outfield that stretched 310 feet to left, 440 feet

Photo courtesy of National Historic Landmarks

to center, and 356 feet down the right-field line. There were as yet no bricks and no ivy. The first professional baseball game to ever take place in this Mecca for the national pastime was an April 23, 1914, Whales victory over the Kansas City Federals. When that struggling Federal League folded after the 1915 season, the Chicago Cubs moved in, and the name was changed to Cubs Park.

Renovations began in the 1920s and continued intermittently through final years of the 20th century. Wooden bleachers were installed during the 1922–23 off-season, increasing capacity to 20,000. In 1926, the name was changed to honor team owner William Wrigley Jr. And in 1937, team president William Veeck introduced many of the features so identified with the ballpark to this day, including the outfield bleachers (dwelling to some of the major leagues' most boisterous fans), the 27- by 85-foot hand-operated scoreboard (still in use—a rarity in the major leagues today), and, of course, the park's characteristic ivy (Japanese bittersweet and Boston ivy being the flora of choice). A 15-foot clock was added to the scoreboard in 1941 and home-run baskets set atop the outfield walls in 1970. In 1988, Wrigley Field, owned by the Tribune Company since 1981, finally added lights despite neighborhood protestations; ironically, the first-ever scheduled night game was rained out that August. Various seating additions over the years, including second-story grandstands, have brought game-day capacity to more than 38,000. Fans gracing those seats have seen plenty of baseball history, including Babe Ruth's mythical called shot during the 1932 World Series.

Wrigley Field has hosted six World Series (1918, 1929, 1932, 1935, 1938, and 1945)—the Cubs have lost them all.

MARJORIE MERRIWEATHER POST BORN IN SPRINGFIELD

Marjorie Merriweather Post, founder of General Foods and notable collector of art, was born in Sangamon County on this day in Illinois history.

Post was the heiress to a fortune at age 27. Her father, Charles W. Post, a pioneering figure in the processed food industry, left to her the increasingly successful Postum Cereal Company when he died in 1914. C. W. had personally mentored his daughter in every aspect of running a successful company. She joined him in everything from overseeing factory production to sitting in on board meetings. Along with the responsibility of owning her father's company came a considerable financial empire built on products like Postum (a coffee substitute), Grape-Nuts, and Post Toasties. Marjorie, along with her second of four husbands, Wall Street financier E. F. Hutton, expanded the company's operations throughout the 1920s. With a keen business sense and her father's entrepreneurial spirit, Marjorie Merriweather Post earned the reputation of America's leading businesswoman. Based in Battle Creek, Michigan, her Postum Cereal Company gobbled up the competition, acquiring Jell-O in 1925, Baker's Chocolate in 1927, and Maxwell House Coffee in 1928 before becoming General Foods Corporation in 1929.

Post was also a very public figure, a socialite who turned her many lavish homes and mansions into personal art museums. (Her father had also instilled in her a love for collecting expensive and exotic artwork.) She began seriously collecting in the early 1920s and even enrolled at New York's Metropolitan Museum of Art while hiring celebrated art dealer Sir Joseph Duveen as her personal tutor. She purchased an enormous estate in Washington, D.C., in 1955, to house her vast collection of mostly French and Russian pieces. Called Hillwood, this mansion was bequeathed to the public after her death on September 12, 1963.

With mansions in Illinois, New York, Florida, and D.C.—along with *Sea Cloud*, the world's largest privately owned yacht—Marjorie Merriweather Post had plenty left over for charitable causes such as the American Red Cross, the Salvation Army, and the National Symphony Orchestra.

- MARCH 16 -

1880

AVIATOR-INVENTOR WILLIAM BUSHNELL STOUT BORN IN QUINCY

On this day in Illinois history, the great engineer, inventor, and pioneer of aviation W. B. Stout was born in Adams County.

"Never resort to mathematics," he was fond of saying, "until you have exhausted all the possibilities of a couple of toothpicks and a piece of string." When Stout had an

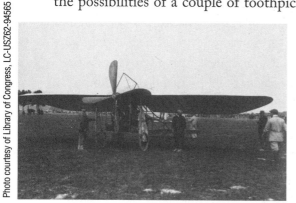

idea, he ran with it. As a 14-year-old, Stout discovered an article in *Youth Companion* magazine showing how to design and build a flying machine from cardboard and rubber bands. He immediately ran out and acquired the necessary supplies, followed the directions carefully, and executed a successful test run with the model airplane on his first try. An ambitious aviator was thus born. Stout enrolled at the University of Minnesota in St. Paul to pursue a degree in mechanical engineering; before he could finish, however, he was diagnosed with an acute eye condition that prevented him from reading, and therefore forced his dropping out of classes. It was 1903, and doctors urged him to rest his eyes for two full years. Undeterred, the nearly blind but industrious Stout spent his time hammering out aviation articles on his typewriter; they were featured in a number of publications.

Stout resumed his tinkering once his eyesight recovered. In 1907, after touring Europe on a motorbike, he designed an all-new type of motorcycle, which led to his hiring as an engineer to several budding American automobile companies in following years. In 1912, having built a fair reputation for himself, he was hired by the *Chicago Tribune* as its technical editor. Stout's most notable invention was a monoplane dubbed "Stout's Cootie"—the first successful airplane design devoid of exterior struts, wires, and other wind obstructions. It debuted in 1919 and forever changed the course of aviation history. Another revolutionary design was the Stout All-Metal Air Sedan, which took flight in 1923 and became the forerunner to today's commercial airplanes.

Stout founded the Airplane Model League of America, offering kits from 65 cents to $3, and he died in 1956 having inspired thousands of youngsters across the country to tinker with cardboard and rubber bands.

- MARCH 17 -

1965

A. A. STAGG DIES AT AGE 102

Amos Alonzo Stagg, legendary football coach and director of the University of Chicago's department of physical culture, died in his California home on this day in Illinois history.

Stagg's tenure as football coach at U of C lasted from 1892 to 1932; three years after his departure, the program folded. He held the first football practice on October 1, 1892, the same day the university first opened its classroom doors. That season he was player coach for the football Maroons. The squad soon dominated the newly formed Big Ten Conference, winning seven conference championships under Stagg's guidance between 1899 and 1924. A collegiate football powerhouse in the early 20th century, the U of C Maroons were the first local football team to be called the "Monsters of the Midway." They compiled a 242-112-28 record under Stagg—and five unbeaten seasons.

Innovations credited to Stagg include the forward pass, the onside kick, and the T formation. He was also the first coach to assign numbers to jerseys and pass out varsity letters to his players. Stagg, who once planned on becoming a minister, considered coaching "one of the noblest and perhaps the most far-reaching [profession] in building up the manhood of our country . . . a fine chance to do Christian work." For him, football shaped virtue, and thus through his national influence it came to dominate collegiate athletics in America. A firm disciplinarian, Stagg donated $1,000 to the University of Chicago for the purchase of chimes that would ring on campus to announce bedtime for his athletes. Stagg continued coaching until he was 98 years old and—characteristically—turned down a Hollywood offer to base a movie on his life.

Amos Alonzo Stagg High School in Palos Hills, Illinois, was dedicated in his honor in 1964.

- MARCH 18 -

1925

ILLINOIS'S TORNADO ALLEY RAVAGED BY GREAT TWISTER

Southern Illinois was devastated by a tornado that killed nearly 700 people throughout the Midwest on this day in Illinois history.

The Great Tri-State Tornado (Missouri, Illinois, and Indiana) left 15,000 homes destroyed—and more than one ghost town—in its 129-mile wake. The greatest toll was exacted on southern Illinois, where it plowed northeastward, killing more than 500 people in 40 minutes as it cut across the state. Property damage exceeded $10 million. Worst hit were the Illinois towns of Murphysboro, West Frankfort, and DeSoto. Murphysboro lost 234 residents, with hundreds more injured as nearly half the town was leveled. One third of West Frankfort lay in ruins as well, and the town suffered approximately 150 deaths and 400 injuries. Desoto lost 69 people—half of them children—when the massive twister touched down directly on a school. Also hard hit were Carbondale, Gorham, Parrish, and Vergennes. Scores were killed on southern Illinois farms along the tornado's path.

The tornado traveled at an estimated 73 miles per hour as it tore through Illinois, its funnel said to be flexing between one-quarter mile and one mile in width. The *St. Louis Post-Dispatch* described the scene: "The air was filled with 10,000 things. Boards, poles, cans, garments, stoves, whole sides of the little frame houses, in some cases the houses themselves, were picked up and smashed to earth. And living beings, too . . . A cow, picked up by the wind, was hurled into the village restaurant." The *East St. Louis Journal* reported on a traveling salesman who was "sucked through the roof" in Carbondale only to land across the street, injured but still alive.

Relief arrived from across the state; so too did curious onlookers who flooded the highways days later.

- MARCH 19 -
1848
WYATT EARP BORN IN MONMOUTH, ILLINOIS

A legendary lawman of the Wild West, Wyatt Earp was born in Warren County on this day in Illinois history.

The man lionized in Western lore and immortalized in the movies and on TV left Illinois with his family as an infant, but returned to Monmouth six years later. There, young Wyatt and his not-as-famous brothers, Virgil and Morgan, learned about law enforcement from their father, Nicholas P. Earp, who served as a city constable. Nicholas earned additional income by peddling beer and liquors, which, with a budding temperance movement in western Illinois, led to his acquiring enemies among local prohibitionists. In November 1859, Nicholas Earp was tried and convicted for bootlegging and tax evasion, publicly humiliated, and subsequently run out of town by advocates of the temperance movement based at Monmouth College. The family headed west, where 11-year-old Wyatt would soon become famous.

A teenage Wyatt worked as a stagecoach driver, rejected whiskey but embraced gambling and boxing, and settled in as constable of Lamar, Missouri, by 1870. There, he earned the reputation of a skilled lawman, keeping order with a minimum of casualties; however, with a proclivity for side jobs that skirted the law, Wyatt (like his father) was forced to flee town the following year under accusations of embezzlement and horse theft. (Neither charge was ever proved.) He then joined the Wichita, Kansas, police force—where reportedly he met fellow Illinoisan–turned–hero of the Wild West, "Wild Bill" Hickok—and was later appointed assistant city marshal of Dodge City.

In 1880, Wyatt and Morgan Earp were appointed "special deputy policemen" of Tombstone, Arizona, by the city marshal, their older brother, Virgil. There, in a vacant lot, on October 26, 1881, occurred an event of legendary proportions: the Gunfight at the O.K. Corral. Wyatt, Morgan, and Virgil Earp, joined by gunslinger "Doc" Holliday, faced notorious ruffians and cattle thieves Billy Claiborne, Frank McLaury, Tom McLaury, Billy Clanton, and Ike Clanton. Thirty shots were fired in as many seconds, and the lawmen were victorious; both McLaury brothers, along with Billy Clanton, lay dead.

Wyatt never returned to his boyhood home in Monmouth, but 1872 records prove that he had been arrested for "keeping and being found at a house of ill-repute" in Peoria, Illinois.

- MARCH 20 -

1920

GEORGE S. HALAS HIRED TO COACH
DECATUR STALEY'S FOOTBALL CLUB

George Halas, a University of Illinois football star–turned–engineer for the Chicago, Burlington & Quincy Railroad, received a phone call on this day in Illinois history, after which he "ceased to be a railroad man."

On the line was a representative of the A. E. Staley Corporation, located in downstate Decatur, offering Halas the chance of a lifetime. He was hired to coach the Decatur Staleys football team (company teams being popular at the time), which had

Photo courtesy of Roy Taylor

been organized the previous year and done well locally. He was expected to take the team to the next level, compete with top semipro squads across the nation, and thus promote the company name. After spending the summer of 1920 recruiting top collegiate talent, Staley organized the upstart American Professional Football League (later renamed the National Football League) that began play in October. Competing against teams from Rock Island, Illinois, to Rochester, New York, the Decatur Staleys finished the season with an impressive 10-2-2 record.

He moved the team to Chicago the following year for better economic opportunity but was contractually bound to keep the Staleys name for one more season. The Chicago Staleys played at Cubs Park (later renamed Wrigley Field) and went 9-1-1 to be named the 1921 league champions—and a tradition unrivaled in professional football was thus born. In 1922, they became the Chicago Bears. And in 1925 the Bears won their first of eight NFL championships (nine including the 1921 Staleys). Halas coached the Bears for the better part of five decades.

During his September 7, 1963, induction into the Football Hall of Fame in Canton, Ohio, "Papa Bear" Halas addressed the crowd: "To all of you who have contributed so much to the realization of this Hall of Fame . . . let me say for all the Chicago Bears right from the original Staleys in 1920 down to the 1963 [NFL Champions], just two heartfelt words: thank you!"

Halas died in 1983 and is entombed at Chicago's St. Adalbert Catholic Cemetery.

- MARCH 21 -
1866
GALESBURG'S "MOTHER" BICKERDYKE RESIGNS AS ARMY NURSE

Mary Ann "Mother" Bickerdyke—famous "angel of the battlefield"—retired after four years of nursing wounded soldiers on the front line of the Civil War, on this day in Illinois history.

Bickerdyke came to Galesburg, Illinois, from Ohio in 1856, and was soon widowed and left without an income. To support herself and her two sons, she used her knowledge of healing herbs to sell "botanic medicines" to the sick. In 1861, Bickerdyke was elected by her church congregation to deliver a contribution of money and supplies to the Army hospital in Cairo, Illinois. She was appalled at the poor conditions of the hospital and immediately set out to stay and care for the wounded, teaching the soldiers how keep the place clean and sanitary. It was there that Bickerdyke earned the nickname "Mother." The patients adored her, welcoming the nurse's visits far more than the doctors who ran the hospital, who felt Bickerdyke's efforts were an intrusion.

In 1862, Mother Bickerdyke went on a fund-raising tour for the Sanitary Commission, a group organized by Chicago women to do relief work during the war. Stories of her Cairo experience moved the audience, who in city after city made generous contributions. General Ulysses S. Grant appointed Bickerdyke to head the Gayoso Block Hospital in Memphis, Tennessee, which soon came to be called Mother Bickerdyke's Hospital. After that she was sent to General William Tecumseh Sherman at Vicksburg, where she endured cold weather and low supplies side-by-side with the soldiers with whom she traveled. The legend of Mother Bickerdyke nursing soldiers on the frontlines back to health earned her fame that at the time rivaled that of generals Grant or Sherman.

Her final stop before resigning was Camp Butler in Springfield, Illinois, to help prepare soldiers there for their return home after the war.

- MARCH 22 -
1952
HEBRON GREEN GIANTS WIN STATE
HIGH SCHOOL BASKETBALL CHAMPIONSHIP

On this day in Illinois history, the Hebron High School Green Giants basketball team completed a miracle season by defeating Quincy Senior High School 64–59 in overtime to capture the state tournament title.

Photo courtesy of Don Peasley

Champaign's Huff Gymnasium was filled to the rafters with fans hoping to witness Hebron's rendezvous with destiny. It was a classic David-versus-Goliath scenario. Tiny Hebron, with only 98 students, was the smallest high school in state history to ever make it through the Sweet Sixteen. Quincy, by contrast, had more than 1,000 students and a pool of 480 boys from which three teams were formed—their 45 players exceeded the total number of boys who attended Hebron High School by three.

The Green Giants, most of them McHenry County farm boys, had developed their skills as children, shooting baskets in haylofts with makeshift hoops set up at either end. Star center Bill Schulz didn't see a real basketball court until eighth grade. Coach Russ Ahearn had never been in a varsity overtime contest before the night of the championship, which his Green Giants won in thrilling fashion, pulling out of reach on free throws in the final minute before being swarmed by the crowd.

The team captured the hearts and imaginations of the entire state. The *Champaign News-Gazette* trumpeted the victory with a headline that took front-page prominence above a blurb about the U of I's Fighting Illini basketball team making the NCAA Final Four. *Chicago Sun-Times* sportswriter Jerome Holtzman declared, "Hebron's Green Giants . . . can't be blamed if they pinch themselves in disbelief. The dream has come true." The return trip became a celebratory parade escorted by police along the final 60 miles of Route 47. The original caravan of 30 cars swelled to more than 100 as it passed through Carpentersville, Algonquin, and Crystal Lake, picking up fans along the way. Once home, the team enjoyed a victory dinner at Ernie Heinmann's Hebron Café.

- MARCH 23 -

1901

INAUGURAL AUTO SHOW AT CHICAGO COLISEUM

On this day in Illinois history, a long-standing annual event was begun when the Chicago Coliseum hosted its first Chicago Auto Show.

What is today one of the largest auto shows in the world had comparatively humble beginnings. The 1901 Chicago Auto Show was staged March 23–30, and attracted 6,000 curious patrons on opening night. More than 50 pioneering automakers displayed their latest models. "If I owned the whole bunch of them," one attendee declared, "I would turn them out to pasture . . . for all time to come." Others were more enthused by this unprecedented showcase for what was then the cutting edge in modern transportation. Most vehicles back then were driven by tiller (rather than steering wheel), had four tires that resembled those found on a bicycle, and topped out at less than 20 miles per hour. An indoor track encircled the exhibit floor, upon which demonstrations continued throughout the week, forcing spectators to literally dodge the "traffic" en route to the display floor. While the show was an overall success, no one then could anticipate what was yet to come.

For more than 100 years, Illinoisans (and others) have flocked to the Chicago Auto Show to see the latest models and spectacular dream cars of the future. The Studebaker "Gold Car," finished in a coating of pure gold and valued at more than $25,000, was the hit of the 1917 show. The event became more grandiose as the years progressed. Displays became more decorative, using elaborate lighting, banners, and music to attract prospective buyers. And, of course, attractive women—a "procession of beauty queens" as one press release phrased it—became annual staples along with the cars they adorned. It was here every winter that features such as hidden headlights, "suicide doors," and the electric doorman (garage-door opener) were debuted. By the mid-1930s, the Chicago Auto Show had become a full-blown extravaganza, and, attracting ever-increasing numbers of exhibitors and spectators, was moved to the vast Chicago International Amphitheater. It would move yet again to the McCormick Place three decades later.

For the Chicago Auto Show's 100th Anniversary in February of 2001, a black-tie gala was held—starting at $150 per plate—raising more than $1.7 million for local charities.

- MARCH 24 -

1924

ARCHBISHOP GEORGE WILLIAM MUNDELEIN BECOMES CARDINAL

On this day in Illinois history, George William Mundelein, archbishop of the Roman Catholic Diocese of Chicago—the "American Pope"—was elevated to the College of Cardinals.

Mundelein was born to German immigrants in 1872 in New York City, ordained a priest at 22 for the Diocese of Brooklyn, and arrived in Illinois when appointed as the eighth bishop of Chicago on December 9, 1915. He was the youngest archbishop in America. George Cardinal Mundelein, as he came to be known, was tremendously popular, and he left an indelible mark on his adopted city. With his characteristic style,

Photo courtesy of Wikipedia

conviction, and poise, Mundelein focused on Chicago's massive immigrant population, which had been previously overlooked. One of his major efforts was to unify the city's Catholics—Poles, Germans, Italians, and others—into territorial rather than ethnic parishes. Cardinal Mundelein also greatly expanded Catholic charities during the Great Depression. His most notable accomplishment, however, was the Eucharistic Congress celebrated in the summer of 1926, when Catholicism was boldly on display in the City of the Big Shoulders. That June, during the annual gathering of the faithful, an estimated 1 million pilgrims from around the world descended upon Chicago. It was a five-day spiritual pep rally: 6,000 masses were said throughout the diocese on the first day alone, 150,000 pilgrims packed Soldier Field to receive the Cardinal's blessing, and 4.5 million communion wafers were prepared by the city's nuns.

Mundelein founded the large seminary St. Mary of the Lake in the Lake County town named for him, about 40 miles north of Chicago. "Since we have a great diocese and must provide for the future, we must erect a great institution," he declared in 1919. "It will take years to complete it. . . . but if we do it, we must do it well." It opened two years later. Today the seminary is home to a prestigious theological university and center for priests' continuing education, and its Feehan Memorial Library houses more than 180,000 volumes on Catholic theology and church history.

Cardinal Mundelein died on October 2, 1939, and his ceremonial hat hangs above the sanctuary of Holy Name Cathedral in Chicago, where he said mass for a quarter century.

- MARCH 25 -
1864
OWEN LOVEJOY, ILLINOIS ABOLITIONIST LEADER, DIES

Owen Lovejoy, younger brother of the martyred Elijah Lovejoy and one of the state's leading organizers of the Underground Railroad, died on this day in Illinois history.

Owen was born in Maine in 1811 and moved with Elijah to the Midwest, where he assisted the staunch abolitionist in publishing the *St. Louis Observer* and the *Alton Observer* in the early 1830s. After his brother's murder by a proslavery mob in Alton, Illinois, in 1837, Owen devoted his life fully to the antislavery movement. The following year he coedited (with his second brother, Joseph) Elijah's memoirs for the American Anti-Slavery Society; then he settled in upstate Bureau County where, as a Congregationalist minister, he became an abolitionist politician and one of Illinois's chief conductors in the Underground Railroad, a religiously motivated and racially mixed movement for social reform that guided untold thousands of runaway slaves through Illinois to freedom in the decades preceding the Civil War. Lovejoy's home in Princeton played such a central role that the route through Bureau County came to be called the "Lovejoy Line." During the 1840s and 1850s, he often boasted of his harboring of fugitive slaves, hoping to spur more abolitionists into action, as he believed only public action could end slavery.

Lovejoy, one of the founding members of the Illinois Republican Party, had a profound influence on Abe Lincoln. In 1856 Lovejoy was elected to the U.S. House of Representatives. He gained a reputation in Congress for delivering fiery antislavery speeches—"Human Beings, Not Property" (1858), "The Fanaticism of the Democratic Party" (1859)—which excoriated slavery as being adverse to the U.S. Constitution, the American conscience, and the law of God. Lincoln would mimic this very theme in his own speeches while campaigning for public office. Lovejoy predicted that Lincoln would become the "emancipator," and when Lovejoy died, the 16th president wrote of him, "He was my most generous friend."

Owen Lovejoy's home in Princeton, Illinois, is now a National Historic Landmark.

- MARCH 26 -
1943
BOB WOODWARD BORN IN GENEVA

One of the nation's most celebrated journalists, two-time Pulitzer Prize winner Bob Woodward, was born in Kane County on this day in Illinois history.

The son of an Illinois judge, Woodward grew up in Wheaton, Illinois, where he graduated from high school in 1961. While working as a janitor in his father's law office as a teenager, Woodward developed a nose for investigation. By perusing his father's files (after hours) he learned that many of the people in town led quite different lives than their public personas suggested. Woodward went on to major in journalism at Yale University. He served as a communications officer for five years in the U.S. Navy before being hired in 1970 by the prestigious *Washington Post* on a two-week trial basis. Fourteen days later, he was gone. But Woodward persisted, got a job as a reporter of the *Montgomery Sentinel* (in the Washington, D.C., suburbs), and informed his father back in Illinois that he was going pursue a career as a reporter rather than enrolling in law school. "You're crazy," Judge Woodward intoned. One year later—with 12 months of journalistic polish—he was taken on full time by the *Washington Post*. Woodward was only 28 years old but would soon become one of the most significant names in American media history.

"I think that the decision to nominate the story for a Pulitzer is of minimal consequence," Woodward reflected after one of the most successful careers any journalist could hope for. "I also think that it won is of little consequence. It is a brilliant story—fake and fraud that it is." Nevertheless, he had won two Pulitzers. The first and most famous came in 1973 for his *Post* stories breaking the Watergate scandal, along with fellow investigative journalist Carl Bernstein. With the shadowy informant dubbed "Deep Throat" (who finally revealed his identity in June 2005), their investigation and exposure of "dirty tricks" led to the eventual impeachment and resignation of President Richard M. Nixon. Woodward's second Pulitzer came 30 years later for his stellar coverage of the atrocities of September 11, 2001.

Bob Woodward has also written 12 best-selling books, including one about the 1982 drug overdose and death of comedian and movie star (and fellow Wheaton High School graduate) John Belushi.

- MARCH 27 -
1914
LEGENDARY JOLIET HIGH SCHOOL BAND
HOLDS ITS FIRST PRACTICE

On this day in Illinois history, the Joliet High School Band—arguably the most dominant band ever in the nation—held its inaugural practice on an otherwise customary after-school afternoon.

The band was affiliated with the accomplished Joliet Grade School Band, composed of grade-schoolers through high school seniors, and they set off on a 50-year championship run unrivaled in the history of state and national competition. With uniforms and instruments purchased by the Rotary Club of Joliet, and directed by the high school's shop teacher, A. R. McAllister, Joliet High School Band rose from humble beginnings to national fame. They won regional championships every year from 1924 to 1964, with the exception of finishing a close second in 1930, before Joliet High School was split up into three separate schools. They won the National Championship Trophy in 1926, 1927, and 1928, and then were banned from the 1929 competition (as stipulated by the rules to give others a chance) and invited to the same tournament that year in Denver, Colorado, as honored guests.

Joliet's proud band members, with trusty trumpets, tubas, and oboes by their side, have played before a litany of 20th-century American dignitaries. They performed for local soldiers departing for both World Wars and Korea. The Joliet High School Band played for all sitting presidents from Woodrow Wilson to John Kennedy (with the exception of President Harry Truman), and in 1953 led the Illinois delegation at Dwight D. Eisenhower's inaugural parade. They won the highest marking of any musical group participating in the procession that day. The championship tradition looked to be secure in 1955 when, at the Midwest National Band Clinic in Chicago, the grade-school band broke a long-standing tradition that frowned upon applause during a performance and the audience exploded in a ten-minute standing ovation during a break in Tchaikovsky's Symphony no. 6.

By the time those young musicians had graduated from high school, however, the Joliet High School Band would be no more.

- MARCH 28 -
1990

ILLINOIS CIVIC LEADER JESSE OWENS AWARDED CONGRESSIONAL MEDAL OF HONOR

On this day in Illinois history, Jesse Owens, who settled in Chicago after winning four gold medals at the 1936 Olympics, was posthumously awarded the Congressional Medal of Honor by President George H. W. Bush.

Owens, who was born in 1913 in Alabama and raised in Ohio, first came to Chicago in 1928 for a national interscholastic track meet. There, he won the 100-meter dash, setting a new world (high school) record of 9.4 seconds as well as winning

the 200-meter dash. After dominating Big Ten track from Ohio State University, Jesse Owens famously went on to claim four gold medals at the 1936 Olympics in Berlin—the so-called "Hitler Olympics." He won in the broad jump, 100-meter dash, 200-meter dash, and as the lead-off man in the 4- by 100-meter relay. In a myth that persists to this day, it was not the despicable Hitler who snubbed the victorious Owens (who in his own biography claims the Nazi leader even waved to him), but U.S. President Franklin Roosevelt, who refused to invite the Olympic champion to the White House for fear of the political implications in the American South. In any case, Owens returned home a hero and soon relocated to Chicago, where he would excel in public service.

Owens wore many hats as a Chicagoan. He continued to promote himself as a world-class athlete, appearing in exhibition races against local sprinters, professional baseball players (always giving them a ten-meter head start), and even racehorses. He also landed a gig spinning jazz records as a Windy City disc jockey. He had an outgoing personality and knack for self-promotion, and these characteristics led to great success in the public arena. He became deeply involved in working with the city's disadvantaged youth. He sat for years as a board member, and eventual director, of the Chicago Boys Club, and spent another half decade as sports specialist with the State of Illinois Youth Commission. Jesse Owens was appointed President Dwight Eisenhower's personal representative to the 1956 Olympic Games in Australia, and he was later honored by presidents Gerald Ford and Jimmy Carter.

Jesse Owens—who smoked a pack of cigarettes a day—died of lung cancer on March 31, 1980, and was interred at Chicago's Oak Woods Cemetery.

- MARCH 29 -
1864
CIVIL WAR RIOT IN CHARLESTON, ILLINOIS

On this day in Illinois history, a melee between Union soldiers on leave and local Copperheads at the Coles County Courthouse square resulted in 9 dead, 12 wounded, and more than 50 arrests.

Opposition to the war intensified in southern Illinois with the enactment of the national draft in 1863. Cities like Charleston, divided into pro-Northern and pro-Southern camps, saw increased violence as the latter group felt violated by the prospect of being drafted into a war they did not support, for a cause—emancipation—they feared. These Peace Democrats, referred to as "Copperheads" (after the snake) by their patriotic neighbors, felt that conscription was unconstitutional. Some of them joined up with the secretive Knights of the Golden Cross, who conducted a low-level guerilla war in the name of the Confederacy against Illinois and other Northern states.

Throughout February and March of 1864, confrontations between known Copperheads and Union soldiers home on leave increased both in frequency and in intensity. The county had supplied 2,700 volunteers in response to President Abraham Lincoln's call to arms, and many were then in town on furlough, drinking a great deal and acting quite boisterous. In some instances the soldiers would single out Southern sympathizers for humiliation, forcing a public oath of allegiance to the Union. The bitterness between these two groups culminated in the infamous Charleston Riot, which the *Charleston Plain-Dealer* called the most "dreadful affair . . . that has ever occurred in our part of the state."

Early that morning gangs of Copperheads, armed with rifles and Bowie knifes, descended on Charleston determined to confront the soldiers. They kept arriving throughout the day. The entire town was apprehensive of the coming clash when, at four o'clock in the afternoon, a Union soldier approached a known Southern sympathizer and asked, tauntingly, if any Copperheads were in town. The man's response—"Yes, God Damn you, I am one!"—was accompanied by a drawn revolver. The ensuing skirmish lasted all afternoon before Copperheads finally fled to the surrounding country when about 100 reinforcements from nearby Mattoon were rushed in by locomotive. Of those captured, 15 Copperheads were imprisoned but released before the end of the year.

The Charleston Riot became the best-known episode of bloodshed to occur in Illinois during the Civil War.

- MARCH 30 -
1981
CENTRALIA'S JAMES BRADY WOUNDED
DURING ASSASSINATION ATTEMPT

White House Press Secretary James Brady, a native of Marion County, suffered a near-fatal gunshot wound to the head during an assassination attempt on President Ronald Reagan, on this day in Illinois history.

Brady, born on August 29, 1940, was a local Eagle Scout, graduate of the University of Illinois, and staffer at the office of Senator Everett Dirksen by the early 1960s. He then worked in the private sector until 1973, when he moved from Chicago to Washington, D.C., to become special assistant to the Secretary of Urban Housing and Development in the cabinet of President Richard Nixon and, later, President Gerald Ford. He then served as press secretary to presidential candidate John Connally in 1980 and was appointed to that same position for newly elected President Ronald Reagan— a fellow Illinoisan—the following year. This had been a lifelong goal of Brady's.

His service was interrupted when a lone and demented gunman, John Hinckley Jr., attempted to kill President Reagan—wounding "The Gipper," a police officer, a Secret Service agent, and, most severely, Secretary Brady. (Hinckley, who was inspired by the 1976 film *Taxi Driver* to impress its star, child actress Jodie Foster—over whom he obsessed—by assassinating a major political figure, had actually stalked President Jimmy Carter for years. That assassination opportunity never presented itself, but for Hinckley, whose hero was John F. Kennedy assassin Lee Harvey Oswald, any sitting U.S. president would do.) The scene took place after the president had spoken at an AFL-CIO conference in Washington, D.C., and was exiting the Hilton Hotel. Television cameras captured the chaos live. Brady, though permanently disabled and unable to return to his former role with the administration, retained the title of press secretary through Reagan's second term in the White House, ending in January 1989.

Ever since, Brady, with his wife, Sarah, has been a leading advocate of gun control, sponsoring the Brady Bill to prevent gun violence, which was signed into law by President Bill Clinton in 1993.

- MARCH 31 -
1908
JAZZ GREAT RED NORVO BORN IN BEARDSTOWN

On this day in Illinois history, Kenneth "Red" Norville, one of the most influential jazz musicians of the early 20th century, was born in Cass County.

Legend states that, as a child, Norville sold his pet pony to buy his first instrument—a marimba. As a teenager he followed the road traveled by so many aspiring jazz artists of the day and landed where the scene was hot—Chicago—to make a name for himself. There, he joined a band called "The Collegians" in 1925, and also played his marimba with an all-percussion vaudeville troupe in the late 1920s. He also played the xylophone, but Norville soon emerged as the jazz scene's leading vibraphonist. When being introduced on stage one night, he heard the announcer mispronounce his last name—Norvo. "It stuck . . . so I kept it," he said, and a legendary stage name was born.

Norvo was in demand by the biggest names in the music world, and remained so for decades. He performed with the great orchestras of Bix Beiderbecke, Benny Goodman, and Woody Herman. In 1930, he met, married, and eventually formed a band with the popular singer Mildred Bailey. They were known as "Mr. and Mrs. Swing." Noted for his improvisational skills—Norvo's solos were often described as "effervescent" and "bouncing," with an "underlying darkness"—he also established himself as a gifted bandleader and led some of the most creative arrangements of the era. He recorded with everyone from Billie Holiday to Charlie Parker to Frank Sinatra. The experimental Red Norvo Trio, put together in 1950, merging the various styles of Charles Mingus on bass, Tal Farlow on guitar, and Norvo himself on vibraphone, is considered one of the finest three-player combos in the history of jazz.

Norvo continued performing across the country through the mid-1980s, when he suffered a debilitating stroke, and he died at the age of 91 on April 6, 1999.

This day in April

- APRIL 1 -

1818

ILLINOIS CENSUS TAKERS APPOINTED

Ninian Edwards, who had been territorial governor since 1909, appointed local census commissioners in hopes of procuring the required tally for statehood, on this day in Illinois history.

The Illinois Enabling Act would not be signed into law until April 18, but anticipating that no stone could be left unturned (and, in fact, a few stones would likely need inventing), Edwards began the head-counting early. U.S. Representative Nathaniel Pope, a wily negotiator, was able to secure a few highly favorable revisions to the bill. First, he lowered the population requirement by one-third from 60,000 to 40,000. Second, he won an extended deadline—by six months—for completion of the census, which was now due December 1 instead of June 1. Third, and most importantly, he was able to strike down the provision demanding that federal agents be assigned to oversee the entire project. This allowed Edwards to appoint census commissioners of his own choosing—fellow Illinoisans with a vested interest in reaching, by any means available, that magic number of 40,000 residents. Even Pope and Edwards expressed private doubts that this number could be reached.

The counting began immediately, and it was an early display of Illinois's long-established tradition for creative polling. Residents were bribed to inflate the numbers of their households. Travelers were tallied as if they resided in Illinois, some a second time as they passed through on the return trip to their true homes. There were even 600 residents of one town in the present state of Wisconsin, well outside the proposed boundary of the new state, who for the matter of this survey were considered as future Illinoisans. By the end of it all, the census takers had counted 40,258 residents. Illinois had met the population requirement, and that December it became the 21st state of the Union.

A later report—after statehood was an irrevocable fact—showed that Illinois had only 34,620 residents at the time of the census, making it the least populous state ever to be admitted to the Union.

APRIL 2
1908
ACTOR-SINGER-DANCER BUDDY EBSEN BORN IN BELLEVILLE

On this day in Illinois history, Buddy Ebsen—a showbiz renaissance man—was born in St. Clair County.

Buddy, born Christian Rudolph Ebsen, began putting on dance shows for family and neighbors, along with his sister, Vilma, as children at their Illinois home. Their father owned a dance studio. The duo left for New York in the late-1920s where they headlined a vaudeville act on Broadway. After a brief stint in medical school, Ebsen left with his sister for Hollywood in 1935. There, he achieved great success, starring on stage and screen for MGM Studios along with leading women like Eleanor Powell, Shirley Temple, and Judy Garland. (His sister retired from acting soon after coming to California.) Ebsen was originally cast to play the Tin Man in Victor Fleming's sensational 1939 hit, *The Wizard of Oz,* but fell gravely ill from inhaling aluminum dust (from the makeup) and had to be replaced. Ebsen, however, after serving as a lieutenant for the U.S. Coast Guard from 1941 through 1946, would have further opportunities for fame.

His most memorable roles were born in two classic television series. Ebsen played the unsophisticated but sensible Jed Clampett in *The Beverly Hillbillies* (1962–1971) and later a retired private eye in *Barnaby Jones* (1973–1980). Buddy had long since resigned from MGM, citing a matter of conscience over "selling his soul" to a seven-year, $2,000-per-week contract. He appeared in several B westerns and Walt Disney's *Davy Crockett* television movies (as Fess Parker's sidekick) before landing in the nation's living rooms on a weekly basis for nearly 20 years. In 1993, he made a tongue-in-cheek cameo appearance as Barnaby Jones in the *Beverly Hillbillies* movie.

Ebsen, who wrote five screenplays, choreographed the dance steps for Disney's Mickey Mouse, and even published one novel while appearing in dozens of films, died at the age of 95 on July 7, 2003.

- APRIL 3 -
1839
CORNERSTONE LAID FOR JUBILEE COLLEGE IN BRIMFIELD, ILLINOIS

The cornerstone for Jubilee College, one of the state's earliest institutions for higher learning, was set on this day in Illinois history in Peoria County.

Jubilee College was the dream of Philander Chase, the first Episcopal bishop of Illinois and founder of Kenyon College in Ohio. Its primary role was to train missionary priests, but Chase had more elaborate plans. He envisioned a financially and socially independent educational community amidst an isolated, 2,500-acre wooded setting. Jubilee College opened in 1840 with a theological department, a men's college, and boys' and girls' grammar schools. The two-story Gothic building at the center of campus featured classrooms, a library, and student dormitories. Its centerpiece was the decorative, medieval-looking chapel. By 1850, Bishop Chase had added 1,500 acres, along with faculty homes, a general store, and a print shop. His dream was taking form.

Bishop Chase came close to realizing his vision of a self-sufficient community for Jubilee College. The school had its own farms, managed by Chase's sons, which produced food for campus residents and surplus to vend in nearby Peoria. The school owned a flock of 2,000 sheep, from which the wool was sold and shipped to eastern markets. But despite Chase's pious sermons from the chapel's pulpit, Jubilee never succeeded in its primary task as a seminary. The number enrolled in the preparatory schools (boys and girls) and the college (young men) outnumbered theology students at times by a ratio of ten or twelve to one.

Philander Chase

Jubilee College went into decline after Chase's death in 1852 and never recovered from a devastating fire five years later. The truth was that as successful as the farming and fleecing experiments had been, it was Chase's ebullient personality and considerable fund-raising skills that translated into such early success for Jubilee College. (He once secured a $10,000 endowment from five South Carolinians for the tiny school's South Carolina Professorship.) In 1862, Jubilee finally closed its doors.

The restored college building, with its Gothic spire and buttresses, sits today in the center of a 90-acre historic site maintained by the Illinois Historic Preservation Agency.

- APRIL 4 -
1968
ILLINOIS HOOLIGAN JAMES EARL RAY ASSASSINATES MARTIN LUTHER KING JR.

On this day in Illinois history, Alton native James Earl Ray murdered civil rights leader Martin Luther King Jr. at a Memphis, Tennessee, hotel.

Ray was born in Alton in March 1928 and led a life of crime that kept him busy with Illinois authorities for years. He dropped out of high school at the age of 15 and moved in with his uncle in Quincy, Illinois, and accompanied him as a collector for the mob. Ray soon began burglarizing homes and selling the stolen items, and was arrested by the Alton police at age 17. He then joined the Army and was stationed in Germany in the late 1940s. There, he reportedly expressed admiration for Adolf Hitler, saying America needed someone like him to rid the country of Jews and others minorities. After spending 90 days in the stockade for being drunk and disorderly, and then going AWOL, the misfit was discharged and returned to Illinois a bitter recluse. He later did two years in prison for the armed robbery of a Chicago taxi driver, and his sociopathological behavior continued to spiral into self-destruction, leading to further crimes, convictions, and the fateful assassination.

Ray escaped prison in April 1967 by hiding in a bread truck, and one year later found himself in Memphis, Tennessee, at the same time Martin Luther King Jr. was there to attend a labor rally. He had been stalking King across the country for two weeks and checked into a small hotel room across from where he was staying. A single bullet from Ray's rifle took the life of the civil rights leader. Three days of widespread looting and rioting, in angered response to the murder, took the lives of nine more people on Chicago's South and West sides.

Meanwhile, Ray slipped out from a Memphis police dragnet, led the FBI on a two-month goose chase, and was finally apprehended with false passports and a loaded .38 revolver at London's Heathrow Airport. At first wanting to plead guilty, believing that no Southern jury would convict a white man for killing a black man, Ray eventually pleaded not guilty and claimed to be the victim of an elaborate government setup. He was convicted to 99 years in prison and died in jail in 1998.

To this day, conspiracy theorists—including members of King's family—believe that Ray was the innocent pawn of an elaborate CIA conspiracy, but have little in the way of real evidence to back up their claims.

- APRIL 5 -
1955
MAYOR RICHARD J. DALEY ELECTED IN CHICAGO

Richard J. Daley—"last of the big-city bosses"—was elected to his first of several terms as Mayor of Chicago on this day in Illinois history.

Daley, former state senator (1943–46) and clerk of Cook County since 1950, had attained great influence in the Illinois Democratic Party as boss of the so-called Chicago "machine." He won the Democratic primaries in February against a machine outsider, sitting Mayor Martin H. Kennelly, who had declared his reelection bid as a battle "of the people against the bosses." The people lost. Daley would reign supreme in city politics until his death in 1976.

Photo courtesy of Abraham Lincoln Presidential Library

Daley campaigned by fine-tuning the old-machine politics of the past. He met with all 50 ward committeemen and with as many of the 3,000-plus precinct captains as possible. He engaged in small talk with city workers at every turn, knowing that this would ultimately deliver more votes than going out to meet the general voting public or articulating campaign proposals to the press. Presenting himself as a kid from the stockyards—at one point rallying on horseback before 500 workers to recall his days as a stockyard cowboy—Daley connected with the city's rank and file.

A young, charismatic Democratic alderman–turned–Republican, Robert Merriam, posed a serious challenge to Daley in the general election. Chicago's three major newspapers—the *Tribune,* the *Sun-Times,* and the *Daily News*—all supported Merriam, who actually spoke to the issues. But the Chicago machine, as it is said, has a knack for turning out the voters (living or otherwise), and Daley won by a comfortable margin of 126,000 votes.

Power was placed in Daley's hands in return for loyalty at the polls. Patronage jobs and a disciplined city hierarchy that allowed Chicago to function—to respond effectively to individual, family, or neighborhood problems—right down to the city block, were trademarks of Daley's Chicago. He came under criticism for the continued segregation of the city's housing and public schools, and for harsh measures taken against protestors at the 1968 Democratic National Convention, but was never seriously challenged for the office of mayor.

His son, Richard M. Daley, was elected mayor of Chicago in 1989 and has been serving in that office ever since.

- APRIL 6 -
1866
GRAND ARMY OF THE REPUBLIC (GAR) FOUNDED IN DECATUR

On this day in Illinois history, the Grand Army of the Republic—preeminent organization for Union veterans of the Civil War—was chartered in Macon County.

The first post, which met in Decatur, consisted of 12 members. The idea to organize Union war veterans came from Benjamin Franklin Stephenson of Springfield, Illinois, who had served two years as a surgeon with the 14th Illinois Infantry. Their

slogan—"Fraternity, Charity, Loyalty"—gained fast popularity and by the following summer 39 posts, large and small, had formed in Illinois. GAR was spreading to the other states as well, and by 1890 membership peaked at more than 400,000 veterans distributed throughout 7,000 posts—Illinois had the most, with nearly 800. A member of GAR could be identified easily as a "bronze-button hero," as they came to be called, for the small bronze star each wore on his lapel. They wore double-breasted blue overcoats with black wide-brimmed hats, and greeted one another as "comrade."

The GAR was very active both politically and socially throughout its existence. It supported legislation creating pensions for military personnel, launched the tradition of Memorial Day (originally Dedication Day), and spawned a number of auxiliary groups that, like the GAR, engaged in charitable activities, such as the Women's Relief Corps, the Ladies of the Grand Army of the Republic, and the Sons Of Union Veterans of the Civil War. It is said that no Republican candidate ran for the office of U.S. president without a GAR endorsement from 1868 to 1908. And any local politician—in virtually any district across the United States—who opposed GAR-sponsored legislation would run the risk of inviting the wrath of the national organization.

In July 1956, the last surviving member of the Grand Arm of the Republic died at the age of 109.

- APRIL 7 -

1832

BLACK HAWK'S "INVASION" OF ILLINOIS

On this day in Illinois history, the old Sauk warrior Black Hawk, two days after recrossing the Mississippi River, set up camp in present-day Whiteside County.

Black Hawk had been evicted from Illinois the spring of 1831 by the state militia and promised never to return. He now led 1,500 Sauk and Fox Indians, along with a few allied Kickapoo, defiantly back into northwestern Illinois from Iowa. The lands he sought, which in his eyes were stolen by the Americans via devious treaties, had in fact been stolen from the Illiniwek by his own people via war just a few generations earlier. His party—called the "British Band" for their friendliness with America's recent adversary—consisted of about 500 warriors and 1,000 women and children, with full lodges for temporary settlement. It clearly was not a war party, though it could easily birth one. Many young men, bitter over the selling off of their land by tribal elders, had joined Black Hawk—against the wishes of Chief Keokuk and the tribal council—armed and ready for conflict. It was not long before they found it.

Black Hawk's band settled with White Cloud, a sympathetic Winnebago prophet, at a village along the Rock River at present-day Prophetstown, Illinois. Both claimed that Black Hawk had returned to farm the fertile lands. General Henry Atkinson, who commanded U.S. Army troops from nearby Fort Armstrong at Rock Island, was seeking a number of Black Hawk's warriors for the murder of 24 friendly Menominee Indians the previous summer. The old warrior would not turn them in. Negotiators then warned Black Hawk that he must leave or be overrun "like fire over the prairies" by American forces. Black Hawk again refused. The 15 weeks of conflict that ensued have come to be known as the Black Hawk War. It was the final Indian-American conflict of the Old Northwest. The Sauk and Fox were driven apart and chased by overwhelming numbers throughout northwestern Illinois and southwestern Wisconsin. Black Hawk was himself ultimately captured, and nearly half his people decimated. The several thousands of U.S. troops and state militiamen suffered more from cholera than battlefield casualties, though entire white settlements in the region were massacred by marauding native Indians—some loyal to Black Hawk, others simply taking advantage of the frontier chaos.

The sad, brief war was owed in large part to Black Hawk's rashness and inability (willful perhaps) to comprehend American land treaties and white settlers' loathing of the native Indian.

- APRIL 8 -

1674

FATHER JACQUES MARQUETTE ARRIVES TO FOUND THE FIRST MISSION IN ILLINOIS

Father Jacques Marquette, a Jesuit priest who, along with Louis Jolliet, had established the first recorded European contact with the Illiniwek Indians, returned on this day in Illinois history, to establish the Mission of the Immaculate Conception.

Marquette, just 35 years old and animated by his zeal to evangelize the natives, had received generous tokens of friendship from the Illiniwek on his first trip to the "Unknown Countries." He had departed in 1673, according to his narrative, to a great feast of corn porridge, fish, dog (which he and Jolliet declined), and buffalo meat. Six hundred Kaskaskia and Peoria Indians saw him off with words encouraging them to return with their Great Spirit. Marquette was also given two gifts—a calumet (peace pipe) and a ten-year-old slave boy—from one Illiniwek chief. Sick and bogged down by poor weather, Marquette, on his return, spent the winter in a small hut at what would become Chicago before traveling to revisit his new friends down the Illinois River. Weakened by illness but inspired to complete the mission, he resumed the journey in early spring.

When he arrived at present-day Ottawa (near Starved Rock), Marquette was welcomed back with open arms. It was Good Friday. Before a great assembly with 500 chiefs and elders, surrounded by thousands of men, women, and children from the various Illiniwek nations, Marquette declared possession of the village of the Kaskaskia in the name of Christ and named it the Mission of the Immaculate Conception. It was Illinois's first mission. The fact that Jolliet and Marquette had told the Illiniwek that the French, under the guidance of the Christian God, had vanquished their fierce eastern enemies, the Iroquois (which was not entirely true), may have had something to do with the natives' embrace of the missionary's message. Marquette's fluency in six Algonquin dialects, which the local tribes spoke, was another key benefit. A second return trip to the Jesuit's western base at St. Ignace on Mackinac Island, Michigan, proved too much for the frail Marquette to endure, and he died on March 18, 1675, in the wilderness.

The Mission of the Immaculate Conception was then taken over by Father Claude-Jean Allouez, who has been credited with baptizing 10,000 native Indians over his 24-year career.

- APRIL 9 -
1973
FORMER GOVERNOR OTTO KERNER JR. DIES

Otto Kerner Jr., who served two terms as the state's governor from 1961 to 1969, before he was convicted of taking bribes in a horse-track scandal, died on this day in Illinois history.

Kerner was born in Chicago on August 15, 1908, son of a federal judge and Illinois Attorney General. He followed his father's footsteps to achieve great success in the Democratic Party. Kerner received a JD from Northwestern School of Law in 1934. He served eight years (1947–1954) as U.S. Attorney for the Northern District of Illinois after a distinguished military career where he was decorated with the Bronze Star during World War II. When Kerner was elected governor in 1960, Illinois was about to enter one of the most tumultuous decades of the 20th century, and he distinguished himself in those trying times by promoting economic opportunity, education, and job access in the state's more underdeveloped regions, both rural and urban. After his eight years in Springfield, Otto Kerner was appointed to the U.S. Court of Appeals, 7th Circuit, in 1968. There, he most notably chaired the famous National Advisory Commission on Civil Disorders (the Kerner Commission) to help right the wrongs of racial disharmony in America. "Our nation is moving toward two societies, one black, one white," he warned in the commission's key findings, "separate and unequal."

But these achievements were soon eclipsed by charges of corruption. In 1973 Kerner resigned his post amid allegations that he had been a key player in a bribery scandal involving Illinois horse-racing venues. In a quid pro quo backroom deal with prominent racetrack owner Marjorie Everett, Kerner had passed legislation favorable to the industry (and Everett's track) in exchange for $300,000 in racetrack stocks and campaign contributions. He was indicted on federal charges of mail fraud, bribery, perjury, and income-tax evasion, and convicted to serve three years in prison. He was released after seven months, after being diagnosed with terminal cancer.

Otto Kerner died on May 9, 1976, and, owing to his exemplary war record, he was buried at Arlington National Cemetery in Virginia.

- APRIL 10 -
1848
ILLINOIS AND MICHIGAN CANAL OPENS

On this day in Illinois history the I&M Canal opened, connecting the Great Lakes to the Mississippi River and ushering in a new era of unrivaled growth and prosperity for Chicago and the region.

The dream of building the canal had spanned many generations. Louis Jolliet had suggested linking Lake Michigan to the Des Plaines River via the Chicago portage—"but half a league of prairie"—back in 1673 when he first explored Illinois Country. In 1822, four years after Illinois was admitted to the Union, Congress made an initial land grant to the young state for constructing the canal. By the early 1830s, canal commissioners and private land speculators had begun plotting communities along the proposed route, including Chicago's Bridgeport neighborhood, Lockport, Joliet, Ottawa,

Illinois and Michigan Canal and Drainage Channel, looking North, Joliet, Ill.

Photo courtesy of Lewis University and the Canal and Regional History Special Collection

and LaSalle. Many of these towns would throw grand celebrations, complete with bands and full fanfare, to welcome their first cargo shipment through the canal.

Construction began in 1836 but was delayed for several years due to an economic depression. Irish immigrants composed the bulk of the workforce, digging a 96-mile ditch that ran from Bridgeport to Peru, Illinois. The 60-foot-wide by 6-foot-deep canal was completed in 1848 at a cost of nearly $6.2 million.

Mule-drawn towlines pulled commodities—wheat, sugar, limestone—along the canal, from lock to lock along paths than ran the entirety on either side, until steam-propelled boats took over by the early 1870s. By then, however, the I&M's usefulness was being eclipsed by a parallel railroad route, and by 1890 commercial traffic had greatly diminished. Finally, in 1933, the canal ceased operating entirely. The Civilian Conservation Corps later restored several of the original 15 locks in an attempt to preserve the historic waterway, and similar restoration efforts continued for years.

In 1984, President Ronald Reagan signed into law the creation of the Illinois & Michigan Canal National Heritage Corridor, the first of its kind in the United States.

On this day in Illinois history, the state's oldest living veteran of the Civil War, "Uncle Bob" Wilson, died at the age of 112 in his room at the veterans' home at Elgin State Hospital.

Wilson, a former slave who had served in the Confederate Army, led a remarkable life. The lines between fact and fiction recalling that life often blur. Slave records indicate that he was born on January 13, 1836, in Richmond, Virginia. He took the name of the plantation's owner and was reportedly present in Jamestown, Virginia, to witness the hanging of volatile abolitionist John Brown in 1859. In October of 1862 Wilson joined Company H of the 16th regiment of the Virginia Infantry, and was discharged the following May, making his way for Illinois. Owning his new freedom under the Emancipation Proclamation—issued one month before he enlisted, curiously, in the Confederate Army—Wilson headed for the Land of Lincoln to establish a new life as a freedman.

It is in Illinois that the legends and lore of Uncle Bob's remarkable life begin to take form. Sometime before Wilson's war service he had reportedly escaped slavery but been captured in a sort of reverse Underground Railroad that had been operating for years in southern Illinois. Escaped slaves, or those perceived to be escaped slaves, were kidnapped and forced back into bondage—illegally—in Illinois, or sold back to their Southern plantation owners. According to Wilson, he was captured and forced into service at the infamous Hickory Hill mansion in Saline County, which (according to some researchers) harbored hundreds of slaves in the 1840s. Most worked the nearby salt mines in the ironically named town of Equality. Wilson, his story goes, was locked up in the third-floor slave quarters and served as a stud, fathering some 200 children, a plan devised by the mansion's owner, John Hart Crenshaw, to create an endless supply of slaves to bring to Southern markets. Wilson was later sold back to his Virginia owner. This tale cannot be proved, but it's a story Wilson was fond of recalling to his dying days. Uncle Bob returned more certainly to Illinois in 1863, where he spent many years as farmer and preacher.

He celebrated his 112th birthday at the Elgin hospital with much fanfare, including a visit by honored guest, Illinois Governor Dwight Green.

- APRIL 12 -
1938

CHICAGO BLACKHAWKS BECOME
UNLIKELY WINNERS OF STANLEY CUP

On this day in Illinois history, the Chicago Blackhawks stunned the world (or at least hockey fans) by claiming their second Stanley Cup, defeating Toronto 4–1 in game four of the best-of-five finals.

The 1937–38 Blackhawks were unlikely candidates to win the Stanley Cup, much less appear in the final round of the playoffs. Under first-year coach Bill Stewart—the first American-born coach to lead an NHL team to claim the league championship—they had squeaked into postseason play with a less-than-spectacular 14-25-9 third-place finish. They turned into a completely different team once the Stanley Cup playoffs began. Led by future Hall of Fame defenseman Earl Siebert and top scorer Paul Thompson (22 goals, 22 assists in the regular season), they took the quarterfinal from the Montreal Canadiens two games to one; the semifinals from the New York Americans two games to one; and the finals three games to one over what was supposed to be a far-superior Toronto Maple Leafs squad.

Blackhawks Monument outside Chicago's
United Center

Also remarkable was the fact that these Stanley Cup–winning Blackhawks remain to this day the only team in NHL history to claim the Cup with a roster that was 50 percent American. Eight of their 16 players were born in the United States. One of them was goaltender Mark Karakas, from St. Paul, Minnesota, who started every game of the regular season. But he broke his toe in the semifinals against New York and sat out while his team split the first two contests with Toronto. Karakas returned for games four and five—wearing a steel-capped boot—allowing a total of just two goals, helping his team to victory.

The Blackhawks—the worst regular-season team to ever contend in the Stanley Cup finals—returned to form in the 1938–39 campaign with a 12-28-8 last-place finish.

- APRIL 13 -
1928
CHARLIE BIRGER SENTENCED TO HANG IN BENTON, ILLINOIS

Shachnai Itzik "Charlie" Birger—the highly feared, charismatic, and swashbuckling bootlegger from Williamson County—became the last man in the state sentenced to die at the gallows on this day in Illinois history.

The son of Russian immigrants, Birger grew up in the coal-mining towns around East St. Louis, to which he returned after Army service, met up with some unsavory characters, and got wrapped up in the vice-laden underworld. In the 1920s, with an opportunity provided by the Volsted Act, whish prohibited the sale of alcohol, Charlie moved to Harrisburg, in southern Illinois, to peddle illicit beer and whiskey to the local coal miners. He soon became the Al Capone of Saline County. Based from the notorious Shady Rest establishment in neighboring Williamson County, Birger controlled a network of speakeasies, brothels, and gambling halls in and around Harrisburg. The Birger Boys—Charlie's gang—enforced these "halfway houses," which generated tremendous profits for the self-described "Protector of Harrisburg." Birger had a charm and swagger about him that rivaled any of the big-city crime bosses; he walked the streets tossing coins to children, looked after the welfare of his neighbors, and helped many in need out of a tough set of circumstances. He never allowed his neighbors to waste their money at his gambling tables.

A life of crime soon took its toll on Birger. Bloody warfare erupted between the Birger Boys and fellow bootleggers (and former allies) the Shelton Gang. Battles roared throughout Saline, Williamson, and Franklin counties—violence that ultimately destroyed Birger's entire enterprise. His Shady Rest hangout lay in smoldering ruins, victim of a midnight bombing that left four of Birger's men dead by mid-January of 1927. Later that year Birger, southern Illinois's most feared gangster, was convicted for the cold-blooded murder of West City Mayor Joe Adams (an ally of the Shelton Gang) and sentenced to hang. After a failed attempt to save his own life by feigning insanity, the 48-year-old Birger was marched to the gallows on April 19. (That same month, the Illinois state legislature banned death by hanging.)

Stepping up to the scaffold, the cocksure Birger tipped his hat to the crowd, shook the hand of the executioner, and left this life with the words "It's a beautiful world."

- APRIL 14 -

1924

LOUIS SULLIVAN, LEADER OF CHICAGO
SCHOOL OF ARCHITECTURE, DIES

On this day in Illinois history, the father of modern functionalism in American architecture, Louis Sullivan, died in Chicago.

Sullivan had been studying at École des Beaux-Arts in Paris, France, but became restive. He moved to Chicago, the place to be for aspiring architects in the wake of the Chicago Fire of 1871, and joined the firm of Dankmar Adler in 1879. His 14-year partnership with Adler produced more than 100 buildings, including the Chicago Auditorium—a mammoth combination hotel, office building, and grand-opera house with a 17-story tower. Built in 1889, it still stands as a city landmark and home to Roosevelt University today. Other Adler & Sullivan gems, such as the Grand Opera House and original Chicago Stock Exchange Building, have been lost to the wrecking ball.

Sullivan's motto was "Form follows function." Of the skyscraper—a revolutionary structural design—Sullivan wrote pithily, "It must be tall." But his practical buildings were far from boring. His designs are notable for the elaborate ornamentation and geometric, almost mystic facades that adorned them. This style became known as the Chicago School of Architecture, and Sullivan was its great champion.

Adler and Sullivan's Chicago Auditorium

In 1893, Sullivan's career went into sudden decline. The planners of Chicago's World's Columbian Exposition—in favor of Daniel Burnham's more classical eclecticism, which borrowed heavily from the past—had rejected the innovations of the Chicago School. Sullivan had lost out, in effect, to the very antithesis of his own architectural theory. He was crushed. "The damage wrought by the World's Fair will last for half a century if not longer," he bitterly exclaimed. His last major commission was for the Carson Pirie Scott Building, completed in 1904, in Chicago's Loop. With zero commissions in the last five years of his life, Sullivan died bitter, poor, and nearly forgotten in 1924. But one important individual did remember him—a former apprentice for six years back in the Adler & Sullivan heyday—Frank Lloyd Wright.

Five years after Sullivan's death, Wright and other admirers commissioned an elaborate headstone to their idol, who is buried at Chicago's Graceland Cemetery.

- APRIL 15 -

1955

FIRST-EVER McDONALD'S FRANCHISE OPENS IN DES PLAINES

Ray Kroc, founder of McDonald's Corporation, opened the doors to the nation's first franchised McDonald's restaurant on this day in Illinois history. Ever since, as they say, it's been "over 100 billion served."

Kroc, who was born in Oak Park, Illinois, in 1902, sold milkshake mixers in California in 1954. His favorite customers, Dick and Maurice "Mac" McDonald, ran a little hamburger joint in San Bernadino that used eight of Kroc's machines. Kroc saw the opportunity for an endless milkshake-mixer cash cow were the McDonald brothers to open up more restaurants across the country. So optimistic was Kroc that he even volunteered to run the chains.

In Des Plaines, Illinois, the following year, he opened the first McDonald's franchise. It was a big hit. The original site is now a museum, a landmark to the entrepreneurship and brand consistency that characterize the king of America's fast-food palaces. The original restaurant logo was a mascot named Speedie, but Kroc replaced him with the trademark yellow arches and, eventually, a red-and-yellow clown named Ronald. (The original Ronald McDonald was played in TV spots by future weatherman Willard Scott.) Burgers were 15 cents, fries 10 cents, and the Happy Meal still a twinkle in Ray Kroc's eye. In 1959, the 100th franchise opened in Chicago.

Ray Kroc understood that Americans did not sit and dine; rather, they ate and ran. "I believe in God, family, and McDonald's—and in the office, that order is reversed," Kroc once opined. His business card simply showed his name, the golden arches, and the word *Founder*.

In 1961, Kroc bought rights to the business from the McDonald brothers for $2.7 million. Their California restaurant—renamed "The Big M"—survived until the Golden Arches were raised a few doors down the street.

The first McDonald's franchise

Photo courtesy of McDonald's

- APRIL 16 -

1961

CHICAGO BLACKHAWKS WIN STANLEY CUP

On this day in Illinois history, the Chicago Blackhawks claimed the Stanley Cup with a 5–1 Game Six victory over the Detroit Red Wings in the NHL Championship.

The team had a mediocre 1960–61 season, going 29-24-17 to finish third in the six-team league. Goaltender Glenn Hall, who played all 70 games and recorded six shutouts, was the team's anchor. The offense was led by Bobby Hull and Stan Mikita, both of whom would dominate the league throughout the decade, winning a pair of MVP awards each over four successive seasons (1965–68). The Blackhawks' top defender was Pierre Pilots, who likewise had a great decade, winning Outstanding Defenseman honors in 1962, 1963, and 1964. All four of these players enjoyed stellar careers in Chicago and ultimately landed in the Hockey Hall of Fame.

In 1961, however, they were all still relatively young and starred for a team that was the underdog going into the semifinals against the five-time Stanley Cup champion Montreal Canadiens. Under head coach Rudy Pilous, the Hawks defeated the "Habs" four games to two. Propelled by Glenn Hall, who earned two more shutouts during the series, the Chicago Blackhawks were on their way to challenge their arch rivals, the Detroit Red Wings, for Lord Stanley's coveted trophy.

The Blackhawks led three games to two, with both teams undefeated at home, when the series returned to Detroit. The Hawks walloped the Red Wings 5–1, before 14,328 fans, to secure the Cup. The Blackhawks were behind 1–0, with one man in the penalty box when they turned the Detroit power play on its head, tying the game and winning momentum for the rest of the contest. "The tying goal, coming while they were short-handed, fired up the Blackhawks and they were unbeatable thereafter," the *Chicago Tribune* reported. "Conversely, the Red Wings seemed to collapse as the second period progressed and appeared to be a defeated club when they came out for the final period."

It was the Blackhawks' first Stanley Cup in 23 years, and they haven't returned since.

On this day in Illinois history, with the onset of the Civil War, many in the southern-most part of the state were declaring their loyalty to the Confederacy.

A mere five days after the Confederates fired on Fort Sumter, the *Golconda Herald,* in Pope County, issued the following warning: "Should you of the North attempt to pass over the border of our state, to subjugate a southern state, you will be met. . . . you will not shed the blood of our brothers until you have passed over the dead bodies of the gallant son of Egypt."

Little Egypt, as the southern tip of the state was called, had one foot in each camp—North and South—and amid this divided loyalty were some who argued for outright secession from Illinois. The *Cairo Gazette,* in Alexander County, had declared, "The sympathies of our people are mainly with the South." A crowd of citizens from Marion, in Williamson County, had publicly resolved to join the Confederacy, but reversed themselves at the first whiff of Union troops. And the St. Louis, Missouri, papers featured rampant headlines about thousands of southern Illinoisans taking to the streets to oppose "Lincoln's war."

A pro-Southern militia called the Knights of the Golden Circle rose up and spread panic throughout much of southern and central Illinois. They plotted to blow up bridges, attacked small bands of Union loyalists, and caused riots as far north as Peoria. This secret society was associated with the Peace Democrats, who opposed Lincoln and the war and expressed general sympathy for the South.

But southern Illinois had its Union defenders as well. The *Jacksonville Journal,* for example, published in a known abolitionist town in Morgan County, openly mocked its anti-Union neighbors. "Resolved: That coloreds is contagious, and, if permitted to come here, having a strong predisposition, we might catch 'em," it satirically published the Golden Circle's resolutions. "Resolved: That coloreds have no business being coloreds nohow." In fact, enlistment in the Union Army in the lower half of the state rivaled that of many northern counties.

All-out revolution never came to southern Illinois, owing in part, no doubt, to Cairo serving as General Ulysses S. Grant's headquarters and base of the western armada.

Photo courtesy of Library of Congress, LC-USZ62-64127

- APRIL 18 -

1865

GENERAL ULYSSES S. GRANT RECEIVES A HERO'S WELCOME IN GALENA

Ulysses S. Grant, having led the Union Army to victory over Confederate forces, returned home to a hero's welcome in Jo Daviess County on this day in Illinois history.

The Grants had first come to Galena nearly penniless in 1860. After resigning from the U.S. Army due to a drinking problem in 1854 and falling on hard times in St. Louis, Missouri, Ulysses moved with his wife and four children to join family in town. He worked at his father's leather-goods store for a salary of $800 per year. He rented a small

Photo courtesy of Wikipedia

home on Cemetery Hill for $125 per year. Grant could be identified in the city of 14,000 as he still wore his old blue Army coat—the only man in town so attired. When the Civil War broke out, a local resident, John A. Rawlins, gave a patriotic speech at the city court-house. "It is simply union or disunion, country or no country . . . ," the lawyer spoke. "Only one course is left for us! We will stand by the flag of our country and appeal to the God of Battles!" Moved, Ulysses S. Grant left for Springfield, where he was appointed colonel of the 21st Illinois Regiment. Grant worked his way up the ranks and eventually led the Union to victory as a three-star general.

On April 9, 1865, General Robert E. Lee surrendered to Grant at Appomattox Court House, Virginia, effectively ending the Civil War. (Ely Parker, a Seneca Indian from Galena, Illinois, who was Grant's secretary, had written up the terms of surrender.) Grant returned home to a grand celebration nine days later. A jubilant parade with a brass band and fireworks was followed by the official presentation of a gorgeous brick home on Bouthillier Street. Grant's wife, Julia, remembered "a tremendous and enthusiastic outpouring of people . . . a glorious triumphal ride around the hills and valleys, so brilliant with smiles and flowers, we were conducted to a lovely villa exquisitely furnished with everything good taste could desire."

Grant would leave his Galena home again, just a few years after his triumphant return, to become the 18th president of the United States.

- APRIL 19 -
1946

ARGONNE NATIONAL LABORATORY
ESTABLISHED IN COOK COUNTY WOODS

On this day in Illinois history, the University of Chicago accepted a contract to run Argonne National Laboratory at a site chosen in a Cook County forest preserve.

The location was not random: The site had been a part of the Manhattan Project in 1941; the first atomic experiments were conducted there. In 1943, Chicago Pile 2—a water-cooled nuclear reactor disassembled at the university and reassembled at the Palos Hills Forest Preserve—had achieved criticality (a controlled nuclear reaction) there. In July 1943, Walter Zinn was appointed the lab's first official director, and the name was changed from Manhattan Engineering District's Metallurgical Laboratory (METLab) to Argonne National Laboratory. One month later, President Harry S. Truman signed the Atomic Energy Act, which transferred the control of atomic energy from military to civilian hands with the intent of fostering peaceful uses for the powerful new technology. On October 31, 1946, the University of Chicago signed the contract, and the nation's first contractor-operated nuclear laboratory was officially in operation.

USS *Nautilus,* the first nuclear sub

Photo courtesy of U.S. Navy Archives

The chief role of Argonne was to develop peaceful uses for nuclear power, specifically the generation of electricity and medical research. In the 1950s, for example, Argonne scientists discovered the medical uses for ultrasound technology. (As the Cold War heated up, Argonne's research was also a boost to the military, including the launching of the USS *Nautilus,* the world's first nuclear submarine, in 1954.) The awards and honors earned by the laboratory's scientists over the years number in the hundreds. Most recently, in 2003, Argonne scientist Alexei Abrikosov was awarded the Nobel Prize in Physics for his theories on extreme-low-temperature effects on matter.

Argonne has enjoyed a colorful history while advancing America's scientific understanding. In 1951, during the height of the Cold War and fears of Soviet espionage, radio-news entrepreneur Paul Harvey attempted to breach Argonne's fences to prove its lax security, but he was apprehended by a patrol on a cold February morning, his coat ensnarled in the barbed wire. Harvey was eventually acquitted of all charges.

The laboratory's latest focus is in the groundbreaking field of nanotechnology, studying the electric polarization of materials as minuscule as three atoms thick.

- APRIL 20 -
1769
PONTIAC'S MURDER LEADS TO LEGEND OF STARVED ROCK

On this day in Illinois history, Chief Pontiac—who had led the fierce Indian uprising against the British rule of 1763–65—was murdered by an Illiniwek near Cahokia, leading to vengeance and legend at Starved Rock.

The four miles of scenic bluffs, canyons, and waterfalls in LaSalle County along the Illinois River, shaped thousands of years ago by melting glaciers, became a state park in 1911. At its center is Starved Rock, steeped in history and myth, a 140-foot sandstone butte rising up from the slow moving waters. Pontiac, a tribal leader of the Ottawa Indians, had formed a broad alliance of Indian nations aimed at expelling the British from the region. After coordinating a series of costly raids on British forts in the region, he finally surrendered, signing a peace treaty first offered in Illinois in 1765. Three years later, while traveling through Illinois Country, Pontiac was murdered at Cahokia by a Peoria Indian—a member of the Illiniwek confederacy that had long been at war with (and largely decimated by) eastern tribes allied with Pontiac. The scene occurred in a cave, after a feast held perhaps for the old chief's honor, with a young, inebriated warrior clubbing and stabbing Pontiac to death after a long night of drinking.

The murder wrought horrible revenge. "The news spread like lightning through the country," recorded one frontier historian. "The Indians assembled in great numbers, attacked and destroyed all the Peorias." A band of Fox and Potawatomi, allies of the Ottawa, descended on the Illiniwek village near "the Rock," as the first French explorers simply called it. (The perfect location for a stronghold, the Rock was the site of the original Fort St. Louis, built here by La Salle and Tonti in 1682–83. By the time the Illiniwek returned to seek refuge from Pontiac's marauding allies, dusk had set on both the dominance of their confederacy and the era of French control in Illinois.) Many ascended the Rock to take refuge from the slaughter. There they were surrounded by the enemy until supplies vanished and the besieged Illiniwek starved to death. The place has been known as "Starved Rock" ever since.

In the 1930s, the Civilian Conservation Corps built a magnificent lodge on a bluff adjacent to the Rock—to this day its popular restaurant keeps visitors to the state park from starving.

- APRIL 21

1861

CHICAGO DRAGOONS DISPATCHED TO CAIRO, ILLINOIS

On this day in Illinois history, seven days after the Confederacy captured Fort Sumter, South Carolina, cavalrymen of the Chicago Dragoons—the state's first troops to enter the field—were dispatched to secure downstate Cairo.

The Dragoons (Company C of the 16th Illinois Cavalry) had an important assignment as Cairo, at the Junction of the Ohio and Mississippi rivers, was a geographical crossroads between North and South. It would become the site of General Ulysses S. Grant's U.S. Army headquarters in the West and a base for the U.S. Navy's Western Flotilla. The Dragoons' recruits all hailed from Cook County; their commander was 38-year-old Captain Charles W. Barker, who had organized the Dragoons in 1856. After falling nearly dormant due to low funding, the Dragoons, under authorization of Governor Richard Yates, reorganized at the onset of hostilities. Within two days, the Captain had more volunteers than he could handle. One hundred men eager to "kill traitors" were eventually provided a mount (at $100 to $115 per horse) and elaborately armed with a Sharpes carbine rifle, two Colt revolvers, and a dragoon's saber. Splendid blue uniforms with orange trimming adorned them.

Three weeks of training in Springfield were followed by about one month in Cairo, and then the Chicago Dragoons were ordered to Clarksburg, West Virginia, on escort duty for General George McClellan, then Union commander of the Army of the Potomac. There, they engaged in a skirmish with Confederate troops in Buckhannon on June 30 and participated in the Battle of Rich Mountain three weeks later—the first actions seen by Illinois cavalry. During their three-month commission (April 19–July 31, 1861) the Dragoons experienced few casualties and no losses. Baker was promoted to major but resigned amid charges of lying, thieving, and drunkenness in 1862; of his 110 men, divided by his detractors and his defenders, an astonishing 56 percent became commissioned officers; three achieved the rank of brigadier general by war's end.

The *Chicago Tribune* covered the Dragoons on an almost daily basis, as one young man in that unit, Private William Medill, was the younger sibling to the newspaper's influential publisher, Joseph Medill.

- APRIL 22 -
1988
MEL PRICE, LONGTIME U.S. REPRESENTATIVE FOR ILLINOIS, DIES

Charles Melvin "Mel" Price, who served 21 successive terms representing the 21st state as a Democrat in the U.S. Congress, died in Camp Springs, Maryland, on this day in Illinois history.

Price was born in East St. Louis, Illinois, on New Year's Day 1905. After graduating from St. Louis University, Mel returned home from across the river to launch a newspaper career as sports editor and news correspondent for the *East St. Louis Journal* from 1925 to 1933. A sports lover, Price once saved his own life by choosing a Cardinals baseball game over an invite by St. Louis Mayor William Becker to join a small group for a daytime excursion in his airplane glider. While at the ballpark, the young sports reporter heard the public-address system announce that the mayor's glider had crashed, with no survivors.

After serving a full decade as secretary to Congressman Edwin M. Schaefer (1933–1943), Price was elected to the U.S. Congress in 1944. He spoke on behalf of Illinois for 43 years—through nine U.S. presidents—in the House of Representatives. Few of Price's campaign challengers ever came close to succeeding; his 16th reelection was won by a margin of 77,728 to 18,802 votes. Price served in Congress through the final days of his 84-year life.

Price was an early advocate of nuclear energy, arguing that the United States must break its dependence on foreign oil. "No one died at Three Mile Island," he would rejoin his critics. "Each new nuclear power plant will save 12 million barrels of oil a year." He pointed out that many in the scientific community strongly disagreed with the antinuclear stand of his own party, and used France's safe and economical nuclear programs as an example of what could be done at home. Also, to the chagrin of some fellow Democrats, Price was a staunch supporter of President Ronald Reagan's military buildup: "In defense, you have to be prepared for what the other fellow might do. . . . I would rather have that weapon or service and not need it, as to need it and not have it."

Price met many distinguished heads of state during his 55 years in government, but he never forgot his roots and returned often to his Belleville, Illinois, home. He was buried at nearby Mount Carmel Cemetery.

- APRIL 23 -
1861

ILLINOIS GENERAL ASSEMBLY CONVENES TO RAISE CIVIL WAR MILITIA

Governor Richard Yates called an emergency session of state legislators on this day in Illinois history, to organize the massive numbers of state volunteers arriving at Springfield to defend the Union in the Civil War.

President Abraham Lincoln had requested 75,000 volunteer militiamen from each Northern state to counter Southern aggression at Fort Sumter, and Illinois's response was overwhelming. The Land of Lincoln supplied more than 250,000 troops to the Union cause, a sum exceeded only by the more populous states of New York, Pennsylvania, and Ohio; 15 percent of Illinoisans joined the war effort, a greater percentage than any other major state, North or South. Illinois provided 177 Union generals. Chief among these were Ulysses S. Grant, John A. Logan, and Richard J. Oglesby, all of whom enjoyed prominent political careers after the hostilities ended. Another notable Illinoisan

Reunion of Illinois Civil War veterans

Photo courtesy of Library of Congress, LC-USZ62-127587

who served the Union was Mary Ann "Mother" Bickerdyke, whose fame as a frontline nurse made her a celebrity. And Illinois cities—Alton, Chicago, and Springfield, all of which held prisons for Confederate soldiers, and Cairo, as a key military encampment—played significant roles in preserving the Union.

At the emergency session, which lasted ten days, the Illinois General Assembly took several significant measures. They issued a $2 million war bond, reorganized the state militia (largely along ethnic lines), and enacted laws forbidding treasonous actions, such as the use of telegraph lines by Southern sympathizers. Senators Stephen A. Douglas and Lyman Trumbull, who represented southern Illinois constituencies where Confederate sentiment was strongest, spoke passionately to preserve the loyalty of southern Illinoisans to the Union.

By war's end, nearly 9,000 Illinois volunteers had been killed on the battlefield, with more than twice that number succumbing to disease.

FATHER AUGUSTUS TOLTON ORDAINED
TO BECOME FIRST BLACK PRIEST IN THE UNITED STATES

Augustus Tolton of Alton, Madison County, was ordained in Rome, Italy, on this day in Illinois history, and would return home as the first known black Catholic priest in the United States.

Born into slavery in 1854 Missouri, Augustus escaped to freedom with his mother and three siblings—two sisters and a brother—across the Mississippi River during the Civil War. His father had already fled the slave state, joined the Union Army, and been killed in battle. The family settled in Quincy, Illinois, and joined the Roman Catholic Church. Young Augustus took immediately to his studies at St. Boniface School, and later St. Peter's, guided by nuns from the University of Notre Dame who staffed the campus. He wished to devote his life to the priesthood.

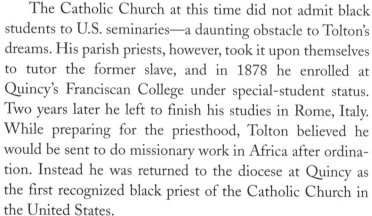

Photo courtesy of Tolton Collection in the University Archives at the Brenner Library of Quincy University

The Catholic Church at this time did not admit black students to U.S. seminaries—a daunting obstacle to Tolton's dreams. His parish priests, however, took it upon themselves to tutor the former slave, and in 1878 he enrolled at Quincy's Franciscan College under special-student status. Two years later he left to finish his studies in Rome, Italy. While preparing for the priesthood, Tolton believed he would be sent to do missionary work in Africa after ordination. Instead he was returned to the diocese at Quincy as the first recognized black priest of the Catholic Church in the United States.

Father Tolton ministered at St. Joseph's Church for two years. His moving sermons grew tremendously popular, and as his reputation spread Tolton attracted a widening flock of parishioners. Local German and Irish Illinoisans also attended the church. But with increasing popularity came increasing persecution. Tolton drew the ire and envy of other area ministers (Catholic and non-Catholic), and St. Joseph's was given the harsh epitaph, "that ni**er church." Tolton, with his mother and sister, was driven to Chicago. There, he established St. Monica's Church—soon to be the center of the city's black Catholic community—and gave Mass without getting quite so much harassment in return.

He died in Chicago of a heart attack at just 43 years of age, in 1897.

- APRIL 25 -
1953
CHICAGO GENETICIST JAMES D. WATSON
PUBLISHES GROUNDBREAKING DNA RESEARCH

On this day in Illinois history, Cook County native James Dewey Watson—winner of the Nobel Prize in Medicine—published his discovery of DNA in the scientific journal *Nature*.

Watson was born in Chicago on April 6, 1928, and was enrolled at the University of Chicago by the age of 15. He had spent his whole childhood in Chicago, where he developed a passion for bird-watching and excelled as a student at Horace Mann Grammar School and, later, South Shore High School. He graduated from U of C in 1947 with a degree in zoology, and followed that up with a PhD in the same field from Indiana University in 1950. In 1952 Watson joined fellow geneticists Francis Crick, Rosalind Franklin, and Maurice Wilkins at the University of Cambridge. There, the quartet explored the basic building blocks of cellular existence and codiscovered the secrets of DNA (deoxyribonucleic acid), the genetic blueprint for life as we know it. DNA—a strand of molecular pairings bonded together in a chemically linked chain—is unique to each and every human being. The four scientists published their groundbreaking findings the following year, and Crick, Watson, and Wilkins were awarded the Nobel Prize in Medicine in 1962 (Franklin, sadly, died in 1958 at age 37).

Watson continued to study and publish. In 1968 he authored *The Double Helix*, an account of the discovery of DNA which has since been listed among the 100 best nonfiction books by the *Modern Library*. He is also credited with devising the format of virtually all modern-day science textbooks. And, of course, his historic discovery of DNA has led to breakthrough investigatory methods in crime labs across the globe.

Watson—an outspoken atheist whose controversial views include advocating genetically modified crops—served as the head of the U.S. government's $3 billion Human Genome Project from 1988 to 1992.

- APRIL 26 -
1927
NBA HALL OF FAMER HARRY GALLATIN BORN IN ROXANNA

Harry "The Horse" Gallatin—seven time all-star in the National Basketball Association and award-winning coach at Southern Illinois University—was born in Madison County on this day in Illinois history.

He was nicknamed "The Horse" for a relentless work ethic and a physical presence on the court matched only by his intense competitiveness. Gallatin starred as team co-captain at Roxanna High School (1940–44) and a leading scorer at Northeast Missouri State College (1946–48), where he was Team MVP and Conference MVP his final year before turning pro. The 6-foot-6 center-forward was drafted in the first round by the New York Knickerbockers and spent 1948 through 1957 with that franchise to become one of the dominant rebounders in the NBA. He spent his final season (1957–58) with the Detroit Pistons and retired having set a then-record 682 consecutive games-played streak. A scrappy player, Gallatin finished in the top 10 for rebounding six times, top 20 for scoring six times, and top 10 for field goal percentage four times. He led the league with 15.3 rebounds per game in 1954, hitting the boards with the theory that, "Most the time, the player who wants the ball more will get it."

After retiring as a player, Gallatin returned home and took over as head basketball coach at Southern Illinois University Carbondale. He led the Salukis to four straight winning seasons (1958–59 through 1961–62) and a third-place finish nationally in his final year. He then coached for four years in the NBA and won Coach of the Year honors in 1963, leading the St. Louis Hawks (1962–65) and New York Nicks (1965–66). Gallatin was then installed as the first director of athletics at Southern Illinois University Edwardsville in 1967. He coached both basketball and golf at SIUE, and led the later team to 17 NCAA Championship tournaments. He retired in 1991.

Gallatin, who also played baseball for the Chicago Cubs organization from 1948 to 1951, was enshrined to the Basketball Hall of Fame on May 13, 1991.

- APRIL 27 -
1790
ST. CLAIR COUNTY—ILLINOIS'S FIRST—ESTABLISHED

On this day in Illinois history, Governor Arthur St. Clair of the Northwest Territory created the future state's first county—named for himself.

The Northwest Territory was organized in 1787 by the U.S. Congress from lands north of the Ohio River, east of the Mississippi, and south of the Great Lakes procured from the British during the Revolutionary War. Virginia held claim to Illinois County in 1778, after George Rogers Clark took control from the British. In addition to present-day Illinois, the territory included the future states of Ohio, Indiana, Michigan, Wisconsin, and parts of Minnesota— in total, more than 260,000 square miles—all of which Virginia, in conflict with claims from rival states, ceded to the federal government in 1784. To administer this vast region, the Northwest Ordinance was passed a few years later, and Revolutionary War hero Arthur St. Clair was appointed the first (and only) territorial governor.

Declaration ceremony for St. Clair County

Photo courtesy of St. Clair County Historical Society

Before an assembly of frontiersmen, clergy, native Indians, and newly arrived settlers, Governor St. Clair declared: "Know ye that, it appearing to me to be necessary . . . a county should be immediately laid out . . . named and hereafter to be called the County of St. Clair, and the said County of St. Clair shall have and enjoy all and singular the jurisdiction, rights, privileges, and immunities whatsoever to a county belonging . . . to the [Northwest] ordinance of Congress before mentioned."

St. Clair County extended across the southwestern third of present-day Illinois, bounded by the Ohio River to the south, the Mississippi to the west, and the Illinois to the north. The county seat, originally Kaskaskia and then Cahokia, was moved to Belleville in 1814, where it remains to this day. By 1827, St. Clair County had been carved into several smaller counties, and comprised less than 1,000 square miles, taking its current form.

No less than 30 of Illinois's current 102 counties, in whole or in part, were carved from the original St. Clair County.

- APRIL 28 -
1901
CHICAGO WHITE SOX SET SINGLES RECORD
EN ROUTE TO AMERICAN LEAGUE PENNANT

At South Side Park, on this day in Illinois history, the Chicago White Sox belted out a record 23 one-base hits off the same pitcher, Bock Baker of the Cleveland Indians, on their way to a 13–1 victory, an 83-53 record, and a first-place finish in the American League.

It was the first year that the AL was considered a major league, and the White Sox's second season in town. They had come from Minnesota in 1900, formerly called the St. Pauls of the minor Western League (1895–99), and adopted an abbreviated form of the original Cubs' nickname, the White Stockings. Under the new ownership of Charles Comiskey, the White Sox put together a solid ball club for the 1901 season. Built on pitching, the team's ace was future Hall of Famer Clark Griffith, who went 24-7 with a 2.67 ERA. (Griffith also managed the team.) Roy Patterson added another 20 wins, and as a team White Sox hurlers led the league with a .298 ERA.

The offense—as evidenced by the 13 runs off 23 singles off Baker (whose major-league career lasted all of two games)—excelled at small ball. Fielder Jones, the first outfielder in American League history to perform an unassisted double play, paced the offense at a .311 clip with a whopping two home runs and 65 RBI. Another player worth noting was outfielder Dummy Hoy, who batted .294 with two round trippers and 60 RBIs despite being deaf, mute, and at full stature a diminutive 5 feet, 4 inches and 148 pounds. (Baseball fans can credit Hoy for major-league umpires' use of hand signals to call balls, strikes, and outs.) They hit just 26 home runs as a team, low even by the standards of the so-called "dead ball" era. But Sox batters led the American League in runs scored (809), and bases stolen (280), and were second on base percentage (.350).

Unfortunately, the World Series had not yet been inaugurated, and the Chicago White Sox could not test their merit against that year's National League champion Pittsburgh Pirates.

- APRIL 29 -
1860
LORADO TAFT BORN IN ELMWOOD

The great sculptor, teacher, and author Lorado Zadoc Taft was born in Peoria County on this day in Illinois history.

Taft's heroic sculptures can be seen throughout the Illinois landscape. Most imposing is the 50-foot monument to the Sauk warrior, Black Hawk, overlooking the Rock River near Oregon, Illinois. The 100-foot long *Fountain of Time,* another majestic work, was erected at the University of Chicago. Visitors to the city's historic Graceland Cemetery cannot miss *The Eternal Silence,* Taft's haunting memorial to Chicagoan Henry T. Graves, or the larger-than-life Crusader he designed for the grave of Chicago newspaperman Victor Lawson.

Lorado attended the University of Illinois in Champaign to study drawing and sculpting in the 1870s, graduating in 1879 and earning a Master's degree the following year. After further studies in Paris, France, he returned to Illinois in 1893 and took positions lecturing on the history of art at the Art Institute of Chicago, the University of Chicago, and back at the University of Illinois in Champaign. Many of Taft's collected lectures were published as titles on American art history. His *The History of American Sculpture* (1903) remained the authoritative work on the subject for decades.

Taft opened his first Chicago studio in 1893 and soon saw tremendous demand for his work. His first major commission was for two sculptural groups—*The Sleep of the Flowers* and *The Awakening of the Flowers*—to be placed prominently at the entrance to the Horticulture Building for the 1893 Columbian Exposition in Chicago. (In 1892, Taft asked the fair's lead architect, Daniel Burnham, if some of his female students could be employed to help complete the sculptures on time. Burnham's reply was to hire anyone, "even white rabbits if they'll do the work." From that exchange was born a group of pioneering women sculptors, "The White Rabbits," among Taft's many other successful students.) Taft's subsequent award-winning works included sculptures for the Pan-American Exposition in 1901, the Louisiana Purchase Exposition in 1904, and the Panama-Pacific Exposition in 1915.

Lorado Taft continued working right up to the final days of his life, and he died on October 30, 1936.

- APRIL 30 -
1983
HAROLD WASHINGTON RESIGNS FROM U.S. CONGRESS TO BECOME MAYOR OF CHICAGO

On this day in Illinois history, Harold Lee Washington resigned from his second term in the U.S. House of Representatives to campaign for mayor of his native Chicago.

Washington, born and raised in Chicago, had served with the United States Air Force Engineers from 1942 to 1946, and was decorated for bravery with the 1887th Engineer Aviation Battalion in the Pacific Theatre during World War II. He graduated from Northwestern Law School in 1952 before commencing a law practice in the city the following year. Washington was an assistant city prosecutor before being elected to the Illinois General Assembly in 1964. His tenure in the state legislature (1965–1976 in the House of Representatives, 1977–1980 in the Senate) launched his election to the U.S. Congress in 1980. He was elected the first African American mayor of Chicago on April 12, 1984, with 52 percent of the general vote. During the Democratic mayoral primary that year, Washington ran against wily incumbent Mayor Jane Byrne and the son of legendary machine boss Richard J. Daley, and then–state's attorney for Cook County, Richard M. Daley. Washington's base was energized, and more than 100,000 new African American voters registered for the city's primaries. It was a tight race. Washington won with 37 percent of the vote, compared to 33 percent for Byrne and 30 percent for the young Daley.

The general election for mayor of Chicago had been an automatic win for the Democratic nominee for generations, but with a racially divided city, Washington faced another tough campaign against Republican Bernard E. Epton. Despite the support of many white Democrats, including "Fast Ed" Vrdolyak, chairman of the Cook County Democratic Party, Epton was defeated by Washington by a 4 percent margin of the vote. Washington assumed office on April 29, 1983, one day prior to officially resigning from Congress, holding his inauguration at Chicago's Navy Pier. Mayor Washington continued to face dissent within his own Democratic party. Opposing him at every turn—refusing to appoint the mayor's nominees or enact his legislation— was a powerful block of 29 (out of 50) City Councilmen called the "Vrdolyak 29." Washington responded by wielding the veto, which the opposition needed 30 votes to override, nearly always falling one vote short.

Washington was reelected in 1987, but that November he died of a heart attack in his office and was buried in the city's Oak Woods Cemetery.

This day in
May

- MAY 1

1893

CHICAGO'S COLUMBIAN EXPOSITION OPENS

The 1893 World's Fair, more splendid than any previous international exposition, opened its turnstiles to the waiting public on this day in Illinois history.

Four times as large as any World's Fair before it, the Columbian Exposition commemorated the discovery of the New World 400 years earlier, by celebrating all manner of human endeavors before and since. The site was Chicago's lakefront, near the South Side neighborhood of Jackson Park. The expo was dubbed the "White City" in reference to architect Daniel Burnham's 200 classically designed buildings, which were "grand, marvelous, and unequalled," as described by one visiting reporter. The Manufacturers and Liberal Arts Building—largest in the world at the time—alone housed 44 acres of floor space. Surrounding it were dozens of other structures crowded with exhibits from floor to ceiling.

Photo courtesy of Library of Congress LC-US262-97300

More than 27.5 million guests passed through those turnstiles over the next six months. Illinoisan George Ferris introduced the world to his 250-foot "wheel." Lorado Taft, who would go on to become one of the state's most famous sculptors, displayed his first major commissioned work at the fair's Horticulture Hall. Other firsts that awaited an awed and eager public included Cracker Jacks, the hamburger, and Pabst Blue Ribbon beer.

Exhibits from 38 states and 46 countries were featured. There was a German village, a Japanese village, and a Chinese opera house. A reproduction of a Viking longship, which had sailed for 28 days across the Atlantic with its Norwegian crew, was anchored beside replicas of Columbus's *Niña*, *Pinta*, and *Santa Maria*. But perhaps most popular was Old Cairo, with an Egyptian bazaar, camel rides, and exotic dancers.

"All at once and out of nothing, in this dingy city of six or seven hundred thousand," wrote Theodore Dreiser, "had now been reared this vast and harmonious collection of . . . the artistic, mechanical, and scientific achievements of the world."

It was said that one in four Americans attended the 1893 World's Columbian Exposition—the pride of Chicago.

- MAY 2 -
1953
BAHÁ'Í TEMPLE DEDICATED IN WINNETKA

On this day in Illinois history, the first-ever Bahá'í House of Worship in America was dedicated in Cook County.

Ground was broken in May of 1912, construction did not begin in earnest until 1920, and in 1953 the serene North Shore landmark was officially dedicated. It took

so long because the Bahá'í are not permitted to accept donations from non-Bahá'ís, including government agencies, and they were at times too low on funds to proceed. An architectural marvel, the temple is now the most identifiable building in Chicago's northern suburbs. Like all Bahá'í Houses of Worship, the Winnetka temple has nine sides topped by a dome, which rises about 150 feet to the sky, and is surrounded by lush gardens and tranquil water fountains. The ashen white walls are decorated with a fine, interwoven relief pattern. One of seven Bahá'í Houses of Worship across the world, it is called "The Mother Temple of the West" because it was the first erected in the Western Hemisphere. In fact, it was the second Bahá'í temple erected anywhere, but the destruction of its forerunner in Russia by an earthquake makes it the oldest standing in the world.

The Bahá'í sect, founded in the 1800s by Bahá'u'lláh—held to be Messenger of God in This Day by followers—believes in the unity of all humanity; the world's religions are a part of the one divine truth. The Bahá'í embrace peace and believe this knowledge of divine unity will one day lead to a promised Kingdom of God on Earth. While they were locked away in dungeons or exiled from their native land of Persia (modern-day Iran) for such blasphemous ranting, they found a far more welcoming home in the Prairie State. The physical beauty of the temple is intended to evoke the spiritual truths it embodies—the oneness of God and all creation.

The Bahá'í House of Worship in Winnetka was named to the National Register of Historic Places in 1978.

- MAY 3 -
1865

LINCOLN'S FUNERAL TRAIN ARRIVES IN SPRINGFIELD

President Abraham Lincoln's funeral train, after traveling two weeks and nearly 2,000 miles on a farewell tour across the nation, reached the state capital, where the body would be interred, on this day in Illinois history.

Lincoln was assassinated on April 15, 1865, by John Wilkes Booth while watching a play at Ford's Theatre in Washington, D.C.—mere days after General Robert E. Lee surrendered to General Ulysses S. Grant at Appomattox Court House, effectively

Photo courtesy of Library of Congress, LC-US262-6942

ending the Civil War. So a grieving nation could pay its last respects, a funeral train carried the president's body back to Springfield, Illinois, retracing most of the route Lincoln had taken as president-elect to the White House in 1861, with an additional stop in Chicago. Also on board was the coffin of Lincoln's son, Willie, who had died at the White House in 1862 and was to be buried with his father in Illinois.

The Lincoln Special, as the train was christened, carried 300 mourners and an honor guard, with a large portrait of the president draped over the front engine. It made several daily stops along the way. Thousands would line up for a glimpse at Lincoln's corpse at designated viewings in major cities—300,000 at Philadelphia's Independence Hall, where the Declaration of Independence had been signed; 500,000 at New York's City Hall the following day—before the coffin was borne back to the train to continue its farewell journey. Smaller towns along the route would be completely empty, as hundreds of rural Americans lined both sides of the track while the Lincoln Special slowly passed them by. The funeral train reached Chicago on May 1, where a grand procession that rivaled New York's in size and splendor carried the coffin from Michigan Avenue to a public viewing at the Cook County Court House on Clark Street.

Lincoln's body was finally buried the day after it arrived in Springfield—with Willie's coffin placed beside his father's in a temporary tomb—at Oak Ridge Cemetery.

- MAY 4 -
1886
EIGHT CHICAGO POLICE KILLED AT HAYMARKET RIOT

A tumultuous week of organized labor demonstrations reached its explosive crescendo at the Haymarket Square Riot, which really took place on Des Plaines Street two blocks from the square, on this day in Illinois history.

Chicago in the 1880s was a hotbed of anarchist activity. German-born labor activist August Spies published the weekly anarchist newspaper, *Arbeiter Zeitung*, which called for open rebellion in its editorial pages. It was just one of several radical journals in the city that spread the anarchist message through Chicago's large immigrant working class. *The Alarm*, edited by Alan Parsons, was the only English-language publication among them. The Black International—a militant labor group from Pittsburgh, Pennsylvania—had centralized in Chicago and instilled its doctrine of violence into Illinois's more mainstream organizations such as the Knights of Labor and the Trade and Labor Assembly.

A general strike was called in 1886 to demand an eight-hour workday. On May 1, about 60,000 workers from affiliated labor unions demonstrated at the McCormick Reaper Works. The rally was peaceful. Two days later, however, a small riot erupted outside the factory. Spies was addressing a gathering of workers when about 200 of his listeners descended upon a group of strikebreakers heading home after the workday. Chicago police who had moved in to break up the scuffle felt threatened enough to open fire. At least one labor activist was killed and several more were wounded.

The following day, an unknown anarchist sought revenge. A rally was called at Haymarket Square to denounce the previous day's atrocity. Spies, Parsons, and others spoke to 3,000 assembled strikers. Rainfall subdued the event, and the crowd numbered only several hundred by the time 200 police marched in from the Des Plaines Street police station to disperse the assembly. It was then that a dynamite bomb was tossed into the police ranks, killing one immediately, fatally wounding seven, and injuring scores of others. (It was reported that several casualties were likely the result of panicked, random police gunfire.)

Though the actual culprit was never identified, Spies, Parsons, and six others were arrested as ringleaders, most of whom were eventually convicted and sent to the gallows without any proof of having thrown the fatal explosive.

- MAY 5 -
1950
GWENDOLYN BROOKS AWARDED THE PULITZER PRIZE

Gwendolyn Brooks won the Pulitzer Prize for her 1949 book of poetry, *Annie Allen*, making her the first African American so recognized, on this day in Illinois history.

Brooks was born on June 7, 1917, in Topeka, Kansas, and as a child came to Chicago, where she lived out the rest of her life. Her first poem, "Eventide," saw print in *American Childhood Magazine* in 1930. She was encouraged by local poets like Langston Hughes and inspired by the works of Ezra Pound, T. S. Eliot, and e.e. cummings. Later poems, echoing the day-to-day struggles in the South Side neighborhood in which she was raised, were published regularly in the *Chicago Defender*, an influential African American–owned city newspaper. Poor inner-city characters and a bluesy, lyrical style define her work and established Brooks as a leading voice of the Black Arts movement.

Her most cited poem is "We Real Cool," about a group of dropouts Brooks noticed one day hanging out at a pool hall:

> We real cool. We / Left school. We / Lurk late. We / Strike straight.
> We / Sing sin. We / Thin gin. We / Jazz June. We / Die soon.

Brooks' first collection of poems, *A Street in Bronzeville*, was published in 1945 and won her immediate acclaim. She won a Guggenheim Fellowship and was named one of *Mademoiselle* magazine's Ten Women of the Year. *Annie Allen*, which tells through poems the story of a black woman growing up among poverty and discrimination in Chicago, was praised for its sense of humor, wit, and use of restrained irony. The poet, who also published one novel, an autobiography, and a series of guidebooks for aspiring black writers, went on to teach at Columbia College Chicago, Northeastern Illinois University, and Elmhurst College. After the death of Carl Sandburg in 1968, Brooks was declared Illinois's second poet laureate.

She died on December 3, 2000, at the age of 93.

- MAY 6 -
1856

STEAMBOAT *EFFIE AFTON* CRASHES INTO NEWLY CONSTRUCTED ROCK ISLAND BRIDGE

On this day in Illinois history, the steamboat *Effie Afton* was destroyed after colliding with the first railroad bridge to cross the Mississippi River, leading to a famous battle in the Illinois Supreme Court.

The Rock Island Bridge had been a bone of contention between the rival railroad and shipping industries since the day it opened, on April 22, 1856. By the 1850s, riverboat companies had established a monopoly on east–west trade, setting prices high, but saw new competition from the burgeoning railroad industry. Rock Island, at the height of the steamboat era, saw nearly 2,000 riverboats dock at its banks per year. The idea of a railroad bridge crossing the mighty Mississippi was especially threatening to the livelihood of these water carriers, not only in business terms but as a dangerous physical barrier as well. So many barges and riverboats had crashed into the Rock Island Bridge that river captains called it "Hell's Gate." Many sank. Finally, after the *Effie Afton* crashed into its piers and subsequently burned, its owners seized upon this all-too-common occurrence to sue the Rock Island Railroad for obstruction of Mississippi River navigation.

A modern bridge spans the Mississippi River at Rock Island

"A distinguished lawyer who is employed by the bridge company to defend that mammoth nuisance," opined a local newspaper, "is expected in a few days . . . for the purpose of examining that huge obstruction to the free navigation of the river." That attorney, Abraham Lincoln, examined the site, prepared his defense (that the steamer's starboard wheel had gone dead, forcing it back downriver to crash into the bridge), and successfully argued the case on behalf of the railroad. Facing a jury deadlock, the owners of the *Effie Afton* dropped the case, which now symbolized a huge victory of the railroads over the shipping industry.

Over the course of the next ten years, hundreds of ships crashed into the bridge, which was eventually torn down to be replaced by a second Rock Island Bridge at a safer location downriver, with slower rapids.

- MAY 7 -
1929
AL CAPONE MURDERS HIS OWN HIT MEN

On this day in Illinois history, in a scene immortalized by the 1987 hit movie *The Untouchables,* Al Capone executed three of his own executioners who had fallen from favor.

Al Capone was a New York thug recruited to Chicago in 1922 by Windy City mob boss Johnny Torrio. Capone's efficient brutality soon caught the notice of Torrio, who promoted him to second in command of the organized-crime racket that ran a vast bootlegging, prostitution, and gambling network in Chicago and supplied speakeasies with illicit booze throughout the northern half of the state. He assumed control of the syndicate when Torrio, narrowly escaping the bullets of rival mobsters in the mid-1920s, fled the city for the safety of Italy. An oddball character, Capone kept a herd of miniature elephants in his desk for good luck, adorned his office with framed pictures of movie stars like Fatty Arbuckle, and carried a business card that dully stated his profession as "Used Furniture Dealer." His nickname, "Scarface," came from scars he earned from a scuffle at a Brooklyn bar as a young man; the man who cut him later became a loyal bodyguard.

Capone abhorred disloyalty. At the peak of his power and celebrity, Capone had gotten word that three of his Sicilian colleagues had betrayed him. In traditional Sicilian style, he granted them great hospitality before execution. The three hit men—named Scalise, Anselmi, and Giunta—oblivious to the fact that they had been exposed, were the guests of honor at a resplendent, bacchanalian feast at Capone's Cicero, Illinois, home. After gorging themselves on course after course of gourmet fare and washing it down with several bottles of wine, the moment of retribution had come. The room fell silent as Capone's bodyguards strapped the three men to their chairs and Chicago's undisputed "King of the Underworld" proceeded to beat each in turn to a lifeless pulp with a baseball bat. It was an acute lesson in loyalty to all present.

Such was the calculated brutality of Alphonse Capone, who would top the Public Enemy list first issued by the Chicago Crime Commission the following April.

- MAY 8 -
1936
JAMES R. THOMPSON, ILLINOIS'S FIRST
FOUR-TERM GOVERNOR, IS BORN

"Big Jim" Thompson, the longest-ever serving governor in the state, was born in Chicago on this day in Illinois history.

Thompson, a graduate of Northwestern Law School, was serving as a federal prosecutor for the Northern District of Illinois when, in 1973, he gained notoriety for winning a high-profile conviction against former state governor Otto Kerner. Kerner, a Democrat who sat in Springfield from 1961 to 1968, had been indicted on charges of perjury, mail fraud, and tax evasion (among other things) in connection with a racetrack

Photo courtesy of Abraham Lincoln Presidential Library

bribery scandal. With his newfound fame, Thompson launched a gubernatorial campaign on the Republican ticket for the 1976 elections. He won that contest—the first of four—with 65 percent of the vote over then Secretary of State Michael Howlett. That landslide victory was followed by another electoral drubbing of a Democratic candidate, Michael Bakalis, in 1978 (recent changes in the state constitution made for the one brief, two-year term). Four years later, Governor Thompson won reelection again in a much closer race against U.S. Senator Adlai E. Stevenson III (son of the former governor and three-time vice presidential candidate), whom he defeated more soundly in a 1988 rematch. His four successive elections were unprecedented in Illinois history.

Thompson's 14 years in office were marked by moderation, pragmatism, and an inimitable personal charisma, which won him allies on both sides of the aisle. In 1986, both business leaders and the AFL-CIO endorsed him. Though dismissed as a "Democrat in disguise" by the more conservative wing of his own party, most Illinoisans recognized Thompson's accomplishments. Media savvy, he once rode a horse into the rotunda of the State Capitol, and helped revive the state's economy by attracting increased foreign investment. Thompson used his diplomatic skills—he was once described as being "like an aggressive sheepdog"—to mend a bitter rift between Illinois's legislative and executive branches and to cooperate with the Democrat-dominated Chicago City Hall. In 1976, he even convinced the Chicago White Sox not to leave town.

Thompson served on the ten-member, bipartisan 9/11 Commission in 2002–03 to assess the nation's preparedness before the Islamist attacks on U.S. soil in 2001, and to make recommendations for preventing further such atrocities.

Joseph Smith, leader of the Church of Jesus Christ of Latter-day Saints—or Mormons—chose an abandoned Sauk village in Hancock County for the new spiritual and political center for his church, on this day in Illinois history.

Smith—"the American prophet"—had founded the Mormon religion in New York after claiming to have received visitations from God and the angels in the early 1820s, and published the (allegedly) divinely inspired *Book of Mormon* in 1830. His many revelations—including one on Christmas Day of 1832 that foretold a coming war between the North and South—along with the church's proclivity for self-governance, raised suspicion and fear among non-Mormons. Political, economic, and religious tensions with neighbors caused the growing sect to move ever westward— first to Kirkland, Ohio, and then to Independence, Missouri. In each case, an irate and distrusting citizenry drove the Mormons off.

Nauvoo from a distance

In 1838, Governor Lilburn W. Boggs of Missouri issued an "Order of Extermination" to expel the group from that state. Three days later a mob of 250 Missourians assaulted the Mormons, killing 20. Joseph Smith was jailed, and the community fled across the Mississippi River to Quincy, Illinois, which welcomed them.

Smith escaped prison that May and joined his flock at Quincy. He soon purchased the nearby hamlet of Commerce on the site of an old Indian village. He renamed it Nauvoo, which means "beautiful place of rest" in Hebrew, and declared it the new Mormon capital: "The place was literally a wilderness. . . . but believing that it might become a healthy place by the Blessing of Heaven to the Saints . . . I considered it wisdom to make an attempt to build up a city." And a city it became. Smith directed the draining of marshland, the building of homes and a great temple, and the creation of an armed militia. Five thousand more Mormons arrived almost immediately, and by 1844 the population peaked at 20,000—surpassing Chicago as the largest city in Illinois—as the usual anxiety once again began to mount among neighboring communities.

Within a few years Nauvoo would become the most volatile city in the state, leading to murder, martyrdom, and the so-called Mormon War.

- MAY 10 -
1861
CAIRO REINFORCED AGAINST CONFEDERATE ATTACK

Cairo, which sits at the southernmost tip of the state, received 2,700 troops with heavy artillery (six- and twelve-inch cannons) from the capital of Springfield on this day in Illinois history.

They joined troops already dispatched in previous weeks. The delta city was a prime piece of real estate in May 1861. Sitting on a narrow peninsula where the Mississippi pours its waters into the Ohio River, Cairo became of huge strategic importance to the Union once the guns had fired at distant Fort Sumter a month earlier. To command Cairo was to command a key intersection of North and South. Across the water to the west was the state of Missouri, and to the east stood the banks of Kentucky—slave-owning Union states with plenty of Confederate sympathy. Cairo's population was 2,200, and perhaps one-third to half its citizenry, which included only about 50 free slaves, were likewise sympathetic to the South. But the peninsula city soon became a formidable Northern stronghold, poking thornlike into the proverbial side of the upstart Confederacy.

By June, more than 12,000 Union troops were stationed in or around Cairo. It also became the headquarters of the Western Flotilla, or Mississippi Squadron, of the U.S. Navy. The massive earthen works and cannons controlled the junction of the rivers, while the stronghold, named Fort Defiance, served as the launching point for Union campaigns up and down the Mississippi that would serve to split the Confederacy in half. This significant buildup of divisions and gunboats attracted the attention of the nation's press. One imaginative *New York Times* reporter likened the city to "the Gibraltar of the West" and referred his readers to "a heavy chain of torpedoes stretched across the Mississippi."

Ulysses S. Grant, colonel of the Illinois 21st Infantry, took command of Fort Defiance that September and established his headquarters at the posh, five-story St. Charles Hotel. It was from here that he began to earn the reputation of a great military leader. His arrowlike offensive from Cairo would capture two major Confederate forts and nearly 14,000 prisoners.

The city was never attacked by the Confederacy.

- MAY 11 -
1894
PULLMAN WORKERS STRIKE

On this day in Illinois history, disgruntled employees of the Pullman Palace Car Company went on strike, setting in motion a tumultuous labor dispute between the American Railway Union and railroad executives across the nation.

George Pullman, who governed virtually all aspects of his employees' lives at the company town at Lake Calumet south of Chicago, had lost profits in the 1893 economic depression. He responded by lowering rail workers' wages by 25–40 percent without lowering their rent. Since rent was deducted directly from pay and workers were at the mercy of prices set for goods at Pullman stores, employees saw a significant cut in what they took home month after month.

More than 3,000 fed-up Pullman workers finally went on strike. They gained the support of Eugene Debs, president of the United Railway Workers, who offered to negotiate on their behalf. The inflexible Pullman refused to so much as meet with Debs, much less recognize the workers' complaints. The strike won popular support from tens of thousands of union members and quickly spread to 27 states; rail workers, in a show of solidarity, simply refused to service any trains that included Pullman cars. This clogged the nation's railways, interfered with interstate commerce, and stopped mail delivery.

Railroad executives went to U.S. Attorney General Richard Olney, a former railroad lawyer, for support. He declared the actions taken by the American Railway Union illegal, issued an injunction for Debs and the union to cease and desist, and persuaded President Grover Cleveland to send 12,000 federal troops to Chicago to break the strike. By the time it all ended in mid-July, hundreds of boxcars would be set ablaze, seven strikers would be killed in clashes with the militia, and Debs would be arrested and eventually imprisoned for violating the injunction.

Pullman died just a few years later. He rests at Chicago's Graceland Cemetery, buried in an asphalt-covered casket sunk into a room-sized block of concrete, overlaid with row upon row of railroad ties—so fearful was the family that embittered workers might return to desecrate his body.

- MAY 12 -
1880
ANTARCTIC EXPLORER LINCOLN ELLSWORTH BORN IN CHICAGO

The first man to navigate a successful trans-Antarctic flight, Lincoln Ellsworth, was born in Chicago on this day in Illinois history.

Ellsworth, who came from a prominent Chicago family, was raised in great wealth and comfort but desired adventure in the most remote corners of the globe. His father was a successful businessman who sponsored one of the city's first skyscrapers, the Ellsworth Building. The family home was adorned with a vast library of treasured first editions, and an art gallery filled with works by such masters as Rembrandt. But Ellsworth was not content with his father's collection of masterpieces; he wanted to explore the places about which none of the greats had ever written or put to canvas. In 1925, during the age of aviation exploration, he joined Norwegian explorer Roald Amundsen in a failed attempt to fly over the North Pole. He completed the mission the following year in another attempt with Italian aviator Umberto Nobile. Several years later, Ellsworth joined a team that attempted yet another journey to the North Pole, this time by submarine—an unsuccessful venture. After that, he turned his ambitions to the as-yet unconquered South Pole. Ellsworth was determined to lead the first aerial exposition to fly the length of Antarctica.

The third time was the charm for Ellsworth's Antarctic adventures. Twice he had attempted to navigate the uncharted airspace, and twice he had been frustrated by inclement weather and inoperable equipment. His exploration party included not only himself, but a several-man crew with pilot, mechanic, radio operator, meteorologist, medic, and others. The ship *Wyatt Earp* (named for another famous Illinoisan whom Ellsworth admired) took them to the advance base and launching point, Dundee Island, off the northwestern coast of the Ronne Ice Shelf. Ellsworth's plane, the Polar Star, was an all-metal monoplane with a 600-horsepower engine capable of reaching 230 miles per hour and a range of 7,000 miles on a full tank of gas. On November 23, 1935, Ellsworth and his copilot took off. After being forced to land several times due to poor visibility, a sputtering engine, and a three-day blizzard that nearly buried the Polar Star in snow, they completed the 2,200-mile first-ever trans-Antarctic flight on December 5.

Ellsworth became the first man ever to fly over both the North and South Poles, and he claimed 380,000 miles of Antarctica for the United States.

- MAY 13 -
1832
MAJOR STILLMAN ORDERED TO CONFRONT BLACK HAWK

Governor John Reynolds ordered Major Isaiah Stillman, with his 300 state militia-men, to engage Black Hawk's band of Sauk and Fox on this day in Illinois history.

In April, the 65-year-old Black Hawk led a band of 400 warriors and their families east across the Mississippi River into Illinois. He tried to recruit additional warriors from among the Kickapoo, Potawatomi, and Winnebago Indians along the way. And Winnebago prophet White Cloud assured Black Hawk that the British, too, would supply men and arms to support the reconquest of Illinois. Black Hawk thus raised a British flag over his Indian camp at present-day Prophetstown. He refused to lower it and disperse after a U.S. envoy and the Sauk and Fox tribal councils advised him to do so. But few Indian allies rallied to his side, and the British never came.

Historical marker and head-stones at site of Stillman's Run

Black Hawk's defiance was met with panic in Illinois. He soon realized his error in judgment and started back toward Iowa in early May. But it was too late. Governor John Reynolds—himself serving in the field—ordered Stillman, with his untrained and poorly disci-plined force, to pursue the Indian party and "coerce them into sub-mission." An Indian truce party was met with futility for lack of an interpreter, and they engaged Black Hawk's warriors in present-day Ogle County the following day. It was a rout. After an initial volley that killed 11 militiamen, Stillman's inexperienced troops fled the skirmish. Hence it was known as "Stillman's Run," the first open engagement in the Black Hawk War of 1832. Black Hawk would see few victories thereafter.

Back home, Stillman's men reported that 2,000 "bloodthirsty warriors were sweep-ing all Northern Illinois," intent on destruction. With hopes of peace destroyed, Sauk and Fox raiding parties killed scores of Illinois settlers from Ottawa to Galena. The bodies of men, women, and children were left scalped and mutilated. A volunteer force of more than 9,000 Illinois militiamen, supplemented by volunteers from Wisconsin, Michigan, and Indiana, soon assembled to hunt down Black Hawk and his followers. More than 1,000 federal troops were also sent from Washington, D.C. Joining the militia were six Illiniwek warriors—last of a dying nation—eager to visit revenge on their old enemies, the Sauk and Fox.

The ensuing conflict, which raged throughout the summer, resulted in the virtual elimination of any native Indian presence in northwestern Illinois.

- MAY 14 -
1804
LEWIS & CLARK EXPEDITION OFFICIALLY LAUNCHED FROM CAMP DUBOIS

Meriwether Lewis and William Clark, on this day in Illinois history, embarked on the most celebrated adventure ever commissioned by the U.S. government.

They had spent 181 days in Illinois preparing for the exploration. The 33-man party, officially named the Corps of Discovery, departed at 4 p.m. before a cheering crowd of Illinois pioneers. Their point of departure was Camp Dubois, a small fort on the Wood River across from the mouth of the Missouri River, near present-day Hartford, Illinois. There, the men had spent the winter stocking provisions and training for the arduous journey to come. A fully functioning military camp, it was the Corps' home since December 12, 1803. Sgt. John Ordway, a 29-year-old volunteer from Kaskaskia, was largely responsible for drilling and disciplining the troops. He wrote his family before they launched: "We are to ascend the Missouri River with a boat as far as it is navigable and then go by land, to the western ocean, if nothing prevents. . . . If we make Great Discoveries, as we expect, the United States has promised to make us Great Rewards. . . ."

In 1803, President Thomas Jefferson had doubled the size of the United States by purchasing the Louisiana Territory from Napoleon—who was cash-strapped from waging constant war on Europe—for the remarkable price of a few cents per acre. Jefferson first approached George Rogers Clark to lead the exploration. George, a hero of the Revolutionary War who had liberated all of Illinois from British control, declined and suggested that the honor instead go to his younger brother, William. The president's secretary, Meriwether Lewis, joined the younger Clark, and the two recruited the bulk of their Corps of Discovery from among the rugged settlers and soldiers of the Illinois frontier.

Reenactment of launching of Lewis and Clark Expedition

The Corps set off into the unknown and dangerous territory on three boats—two pirogues and a 55-foot keelboat. The later boasted a one-pound swivel cannon fixed to its bow. Their mission, as instructed by Jefferson, was to gather information about the western Indians, map the terrain and waterways, and collect all manner of specimens along the way.

After voyaging 8,000 miles over 28 months, across the Rocky Mountains and to the Pacific Coast and back, Lewis and Clark passed their point of departure, Camp Dubois, Illinois, before returning to St. Louis on September 23, 1806.

STANDARD OIL DISSOLVES NATIONALLY
AS THE INDUSTRY SPUTTERS IN ILLINOIS

On this day in Illinois history—when a gas tank could be filled at ten cents per gallon—the federal government broke up John D. Rockefeller's Standard Oil Trust into 34 independent companies, eliminating Illinois Standard in the process.

The U.S. Supreme Court ruled that, according the Sherman Antitrust Act, Rockefeller's oil conglomerate constituted an illegal monopoly. By the 1880s, Standard Oil had control of about 90 percent of the nation's refineries. Illinois Standard, which came to Wood River, Illinois, in 1907, was one of dozens of companies operating under the auspices of a centralized board of directors. Still, the refinery made Wood River one of the fastest-growing cities in America. It had more workers than houses, according to legend, and Standard Oil had to order hundreds of prefab homes from Chicago's Sears, Roebuck and Company just to accommodate the massive influx of families. Illinois Standard at first produced mostly kerosene, fuel oil, and asphalt, but by the time of the Supreme Court decision, with the increased production of automobiles, it was producing gasoline as well. Then it was dissolved and acquired by Indiana Oil, one of the 34 independents to be formed from the breakup of Rockefeller's empire.

Meanwhile, the oil industry was sputtering throughout southern and central Illinois. The state pumped out 33 million barrels of oil in 1910, saw that dip to a mere 5 million by the mid-1930s, and then, owing to new exploration and discoveries, the industry was gushing again at more than 147 million barrels per year by 1940. The Land of Lincoln was one of the nation's leading producers of petroleum. Oil soon supplanted coal as the state's most valuable natural resource, employing 60,000 workers in more than 30 (mostly southern) counties. The rich deposits—pay zones—were struck anywhere from 500 to nearly 4,000 feet beneath the surface, and eventually some 1,200 oil companies had sunk some 150,000 wells in hopes of discovering oil in Illinois.

At one point, Illinois was third in the nation in crude oil production, and continued to pump out 11 million barrels of oil per year into the 21st century.

- MAY 16 -

1860

REPUBLICAN NATIONAL CONVENTION CONVENES AT CHICAGO'S "WIGWAM"

The first-ever Republican National Convention, and the first national convention for any major political party to be held in the state, convened at Chicago's Wigwam on this day in Illinois history.

Since 1860, the Windy City has hosted more national political conventions than any other American city. The first, which lasted for three days in May of that year, nominated Illinois's own Abraham Lincoln as the Republican candidate for the U.S. presidency. Chicago built a special building to host the event, called the Wigwam. At the cost of $5,000, paid for by Chicago businessmen, the wooden hall was erected along the Chicago River at the corner of Lake and Market streets. Construction took six weeks, and the building was furnished with tables and chairs borrowed from Chicago homes just in time for the convention to begin. The two-story Wigwam—meaning "temporary structure"—could seat 10,000. It eventually burned down in the Great Chicago Fire of 1871.

Lincoln won the nomination on the third ballot. The favorite going in was New York senator William H. Seward, but "Lincoln men" put extra effort into persuading the assembled delegates to select the lanky Springfield orator. The Illinois delegation cut deals with their counterparts from key states to secure the nomination. Chicago Mayor John Wentworth packed the hall with boisterous Lincoln supporters. Lincoln received 231 votes on the third ballot, needing 233 to win, before the Ohio delegation transferred its four votes from Salmon P. Chase to Lincoln, making it final. Senator Hannibal Hamlin of Maine secured the vice presidential nomination. Lincoln did not attend, as was the custom for nominees at the time, and had the decision telegraphed to him in Springfield. He was elected to the U.S. presidency that fall.

To date, the Republicans have held 14 national conventions and the Democrats 10 in the City of the Big Shoulders.

- MAY 17 -
1943

WRIGLEY FIELD HOSTS TRYOUTS FOR ALL-AMERICAN GIRLS PROFESSIONAL BASEBALL LEAGUE

On this day in Illinois history, 280 of the best women ballplayers from the United States and Canada, after advancing through regional tryouts, took the field at the Cubs ballpark to earn a spot on one of four rosters in the All-American Girls Professional Baseball League (AAGPBL).

Chewing-gum mogul and Chicago Cubs owner William Wrigley conceived of the AAGPBL as an antidote to the wartime doldrums of professional men's baseball. (With so many top players in the armed services, major-league attendance was in a perceived nosedive, and minor-league teams were folding overnight.) The league was headquartered in Chicago with inaugural franchises in the nearby "small cities" of Rockford, Illinois; South Bend, Indiana; and Kenosha and Racine, Wisconsin. Only 60 women made the final cut that day to realize a dream that many thought impossible just a year earlier: playing professional baseball. Many were still teenagers, and their new salaries ranged from $45 to $85 per week (more than their parents, in some cases, were making back home).

The league was a huge success. The girls, playing with "dirt on their skirts" and always, by league decree, presenting themselves with the best female etiquette, provided an entertaining and highly competitive brand of baseball. League attendance reached 176,612 in 1943 and had passed 450,000 by 1945. The league continued to thrive in the postwar era, with ten teams playing in two divisions by 1948. The AAGPBL existed from 1943 to 1954, finally driven out by the major leagues' revival and an explosion in minor-league baseball teams and leagues across the country.

Illinois was central to the league's history. The Rockford Peaches were one of only two franchises to play all 12 seasons. They dominated the AAGPBL, winning the championships of 1945, 1948, 1949, and 1950. The Peaches were joined by the Peoria Redwings (1946–1951), and the short-lived Chicago Colleens and Springfield Sallies in 1948. The league's only player to play all 12 seasons, Dorothy "Dottie" Schroeder— a fan favorite and the league's all-time RBI leader—was a native of Sadorus, Illinois.

The AAGPBL inspired the hit movie *A League of Their Own,* and former players were honored at the Baseball Hall of Fame in Cooperstown in 1988.

- MAY 18 -

1865

GOVERNOR JOHN REYNOLDS DIES

On this day in Illinois history, the state's fourth governor, John Reynolds—a moderate Jacksonian Democrat—died in his Belleville home.

Reynolds came to Illinois as a 12-year-old boy in 1800, settling with his parents, Irish immigrants by way of Tennessee, at the Mississippi River town of Kaskaskia. There he embraced the French culture and language spoken by the townspeople (Kaskaskia was originally settled by the French almost 100 years earlier), pursued classical studies, and studied law. He was admitted to the bar in 1812. After serving as a scout in western campaigns against native Indians allied with the British in the War of 1812—earning the nickname "Old Ranger"—Reynolds opened a law practice in Cahokia, Illinois. He commenced a long and successful political career by being appointed a justice of the Illinois Supreme Court in 1818, the same year that Illinois was admitted to the Union.

One term in the Illinois House of Representatives (1827–29) launched Reynolds's successful bid for the governor's office, a post he held from 1830 until resigning in 1834 to fill a vacancy in the U.S. House of Representatives caused by the death of Illinois Democrat Charles Slade. The most noteworthy event during Governor Reynolds's term was the Black Hawk War of 1832. It was Reynolds who raised the state militia and called out the federal troops that together pursued and eventually crushed the Sauk warrior's ill-fated Illinois insurgency. Reynolds even took to the field, recognized as Major General by President Andrew Jackson, and led troops into battle.

He served two two-term stints in the U.S. House of Representatives (1834–37, 1839–1843), during which he vigorously sought to procure federal funds for the construction of a canal through the Chicago portage, thus connecting the Mississippi and Great Lakes waterways. This had been a personal goal first articulated during his inaugural address to the Illinois General Assembly in 1830. Thanks in part to his efforts, the Illinois and Michigan Canal opened in 1848 and forever changed the economy and landscape of northern Illinois. Reynolds returned briefly to the Illinois House of Representatives after returning from Washington, D.C.

John Reynolds became an open supporter of secession during the Civil War and died one month after the assassination of President Abraham Lincoln; he is buried at Walnut Hill Cemetery in Belleville, Illinois.

- MAY 19 -
1875
MARY TODD LINCOLN DECLARED INSANE

The former First Lady and widow of President Abraham Lincoln was brought to trial by her son, Robert Todd Lincoln, and pronounced insane by the court on this day in Illinois history.

Years of family calamity, her son believed, had driven Mary Todd Lincoln into madness. After a tumultuous courtship in which Lincoln had once broken off their engagement, the couple was wed in November 1842. Happy at first, they had four children, all boys. In the first of a long succession of personal tragedies for Mary Lincoln, their 3-year-old son, Edward, died in 1850. His death was followed by the death of their second son, Willie, in 1862 of typhoid fever. First Lady at this time, with her husband leading the Union in the Civil War, Mary began to act irrationally and came under growing public scrutiny for her peculiar spending habits on White House furniture and her personal wardrobe. After her husband's assassination at Ford's Theatre in 1865, which she witnessed, Mary suffered from delusions of poverty that forced her to spend even more extravagantly. Rumors that her husband had always loved another woman—Ann Rutledge, who had died at 22 in Illinois before Mary had ever met Abe—further sank the widow into a deep depression.

Photo courtesy of Library of Congress, LC-US262-8341

In 1871, while living in Chicago, Mary's youngest son, Tad, suddenly died. Despite her inheritance and a government annuity of $5,000 granted by Congress in 1870, Mary continued to believe she was impoverished, and began to spend more and more lavishly. Her only surviving son, Robert Todd, concerned about his mother's erratic behavior, literally dragged her to trial, had her pronounced insane, and committed Mary Todd to Bellevue Place, a private, upscale mental institution in Batavia, Illinois, the following day. Convinced of his mother's insanity, Robert Todd wrote a friend two weeks later, stating, "Six physicians in council informed me that by longer delay I was making myself morally responsible for some very probable tragedy, which might occur at any moment." She was released to be looked after by Ninian and Elizabeth Edwards in September of 1875, and officially declared sane the following June.

Mary Todd Lincoln died in 1882 and is buried beside her husband and three sons— all but Robert Todd—at the Lincoln Tomb in Springfield's Oak Ridge Cemetery.

- MAY 20 -

1832

INDIAN CREEK MASSACRE LEAVES 15 SETTLERS DEAD

On this day in Illinois history, a band of Potawatomi warriors—who may not have been connected to Black Hawk's War party—took advantage of the chaos of war to settle old scores and massacred three families of settlers at Indian Creek, in LaSalle County.

With the opening salvo of the Black Hawk War one week earlier, the Illinois frontier was thrown into pandemonium. The recent surge of American settlements in the region had caused great friction among the local Indian tribes. This hearkened back to the Treaty of Peace and Friendship signed in 1795, which set a boundary line along the Illinois River, precluding white settlement in the lands occupied by the Kickapoo, Ottawa, Potawatomi, Sauk, Fox, and Winnebago nations in northwestern Illinois. After the War of 1812—during which local tribes aligned with the British against the Americans—this friendship had soured, and white settlement, previously a trickle, swelled in deference to later treaties that ceded this land to the U.S. government. Some tribal leaders, like the Potawatomi chief, Shabbona, chose to live in peace with the land's new immigrants. Others, however, saw the opportunity provided by Black Hawk's accidental rebellion to visit fierce revenge upon these interlopers to their native lands.

William Davis was a blacksmith who built a homestead along Indian Creek, befriended Shabbona, and held little regard for the other native Indians who protested white encroachment. Davis built a damn on the creek, and a local Potawatomi, Keewasee, complained bitterly that this cut off the supply of fish for his family living upstream. With the outbreak of hostilities, other settlers nearby—four families total—moved in to the Davis compound for protection in numbers; meanwhile, Keewasee was plotting revenge.

On the afternoon of May 20, the young Potawatomi led 50 warriors in an attack on the settlement that ended in minutes. Fifteen people—men, women, and children—were butchered. Two young men escaped, and two young women were taken captive. The girls—Rachel and Sylvia Hall—spent 11 days in Black Hawk's camp, where the Potawatomi had taken them, and were ransomed to U.S. soldiers for ten horses and corn. Unharmed by Black Hawk, the Hall sisters published an account of their dramatic captivity in 1839.

A memorial to the Indian Creek Massacre stands at Shabbona Park, in LaSalle County, with the names of all 15 victims inscribed.

- MAY 21 -
1955

CHUCK BERRY USHERS IN ROCK 'N' ROLL ERA AT CHICAGO'S CHESS STUDIOS

The father of rock 'n' roll, Chuck Berry, cut the genre's first definitive classic, "Maybellene," at Chicago's Chess Studios on this day in Illinois history.

Charles Edward Anderson Berry was a St. Louis–born musician who started performing at East St. Louis, Illinois, nightclubs in 1952. He'd been packing in the crowds with his catchy guitar riffs, witty lyrics, and dynamic showmanship, and was well on his way to becoming the archetypical rock 'n' roller. He played a mix of blues standards and popular "hillbilly" music, accentuated by his personal flair, a singer-songwriter panache that Berry had been perfecting since winning a high school talent contest. Fans screamed when Chuck did his signature "duck walk" across the stage. By 1954, Chuck Berry's trio was the top attraction in the vibrant East St. Louis circuit—Ike and Tina Turner's Kings of Rhythm band was their only rival. In 1955, Berry went to Chicago to see Muddy Waters, and asked the famous bluesman where he might go to cut a record. Waters directed him to Leonard Chess of Chess Records in downtown Chicago.

Berry walked into the recording studio thinking his rhythm and blues numbers would be more to Chess's liking, but it was "Ida Red," an old country and western tune, that really excited the label owner. Recorded and renamed "Maybellene," the first rock 'n' roll classic was thus born. Chuck's electrifying guitar work, "teenybopper" lyrics about a girl and a car, and a solid supporting band—Johnnie Johnson on piano, Fred Below on drums, and the legendary Willie Dixon on bass—epitomized the sound of early rock 'n' roll. "I told Chuck to give it a bigger beat," recalled Chess. "History the rest, you know? The kids wanted the big beat, cars, and young love. It was a trend and we jumped on it." The song sold more than 1 million copies and topped *Billboard*'s Rhythm and Blues chart while reaching number 5 on the Top 100. Berry, who fathered rock 'n' roll in the Land of Lincoln, became an international star.

"It's hard for me to induct Chuck Berry," admitted Rolling Stones guitarist Keith Richards at Berry's 1986 induction to the Rock and Roll Hall of Fame, "because I lifted every lick he ever played!"

- MAY 22 -
1917
CHANUTE AVIATION SCHOOL ESTABLISHED IN RANTOUL

On this day in Illinois history, a new pilot training school named for aviation pioneer Octave Chanute was founded in Champaign County.

In April 1917, when Congress declared war on the Central Powers, the United States's air-combat capabilities were woefully inadequate. The U.S. Army Air Corps had little more than 200 aircraft (as compared, for example, to 1,500 for our allies in France) and only one fully operational aero squadron. The nation was in dire need of trained pilots. Congress appropriated $640 million for the construction and maintenance of 27 flying schools across the country, and the site at Rantoul—conveniently located on level ground near the Illinois Central Railroad—was chosen to train pilots for the war effort. Completed at a cost of $1 million, Chanute Field opened to welcome its first recruits on July 4, 1917.

Photo courtesy of U.S. Air Force Historical Research Agency

Over the course of the war, despite 50 crashes in the first six months, the school graduated some 525 trained pilots. It remained open thereafter and became one of the nation's premier technical training schools for the U.S. Air Force, graduating some 2 million men and women through its closure in 1993. Nearly $14 million in additions and renovations were begun in 1938, funded in large part by President Franklin Roosevelt's Works Progress Administration, including two massive hangars, new barracks and officers' quarters, and a 300,000-gallon water tower. The following year much of this went up in flames, but the ambitious project was nevertheless completed just a few months prior to the Japanese attack on Pearl Harbor. After that, volunteers flocked to Rantoul, and residency at the flying school peaked at 25,000 by 1943. After a brief postwar decline, Chanute Field re-emerged during the Cold War to transform itself from a flying school into a training center for advanced missile-launch and jet-engine technology.

In more recent years a "swords to plowshares" program has completely remade the site, which features restaurants, hotels, private residences, and the Octave Chanute Aerospace museum.

- MAY 23 -
1911
CHICAGO'S CHILD WELFARE EXHIBIT ENTERS ITS FINAL WEEKEND

On this day in Illinois history, the Child Welfare Exhibit, hosted at the Chicago Coliseum from May 11 to May 25, entered its final weekend as one of the largest gatherings ever of its kind.

The Child Welfare Exhibit resulted from the hard work of a broad cross-section of American society—Democrats and Republicans, capitalists and socialists—united by their common concern for the health and well-being of the nation's children. The chief sponsors of the two-week event were Mr. and Mrs. Cyrus H. McCormick, who had amassed a fortune through the manufacture of farm equipment at the city's McCormick Reaper Works. (Their own daughter, Elizabeth, had succumbed to disease at the age of 12 in 1905.) Jane Addams of Hull-House chaired an executive committee of nearly three dozen high-profile organizers of the exhibit. Hundreds of leading citizens—from priests to college professors to politicians—sat on one of nearly 40 separate committees, and 2,000 ordinary Chicagoans volunteered to help out. Up to 45,000

Workshop at Chicago's Child Welfare Exhibit

people flowed into the Coliseum on a daily basis to observe the 72,000 square feet of exhibits, including early research into the sordid living conditions for the children of new immigrants in places like Chicago.

Some of the statistics were startling. The death rate for infants (one year old or younger) in America's 37 largest cities, for example, was between 20 and 25 percent. Another alarming study noted the fact that in Chicago, more than 80 percent of the deaths of children ages 2 years and younger, to disease, could have been prevented. In most cases this came down to a lack of access to fresh air, clean water, and simple sanitation. "There is nothing in all the world so important as children—nothing so interesting," McCormick had avowed in his opening ceremony remarks. "If mankind is to be reformed or improved, we must begin with the child."

And by the final weekend of the Child Welfare Exhibit, nearly half a million visitors had taken his message to heart, many spurred to action by what they had seen and heard there.

- MAY 24 -
1859
ABRAHAM LINCOLN'S FINAL MURDER TRIAL
IN ILLINOIS DISMISSED FROM COURT

The last trial in which Abe Lincoln the attorney was involved, a Woodford County murder stemming from a domestic dispute, was stricken from the court docket on this day in Illinois history.

In the mid-19th century, the courthouse in Metamora, Illinois, seat of Woodford County, was a part of the Eighth Judicial Circuit. This also included Sangamon County, home of Lincoln's Springfield. The future president had argued dozens of routine civil cases there since 1845. Few clients stood out, two of which were George Kerr and Randolph Scott, whom Lincoln defended in 1847 against the charges of aiding a fugitive slave. He won that case by arguing that the black man's status as a former slave could not be proved, and the charges against his clients were therefore baseless. But Honest Abe's most famous client at Metamora Courthouse was also his last—Melissa Goings.

Mrs. Goings had allegedly killed her husband, Roswell, one night after a bitter exchange of words between the couple had turned violent. The man was reputed for having a violent temper. The wife, defending herself, had fractured her husband's skull with two blows from a two-by-four. She posted $1,000 bond and was scheduled to appear in court on October 11, 1857. But when the day of the trial came, Mrs. Goings was a no-show. According to local legend, the Springfield attorney admitted client, "I did not run her off. She wanted to know where she could get a good drink of water, and I told her there was mighty good water in Tennessee." Melissa Goings never returned to town, and the authorities made no attempt to find her since the townsfolk, knowing of her former husband's reputation, were generally sympathetic to her side of the story.

The Metamora Courthouse was placed on the National Register of Historic Places in 1978 and today is a carefully restored museum administered by the Illinois Historic Preservation Committee.

- MAY 25 -
1948
PEORIA MICROBIOLOGIST AWARDED PATENT FOR PENICILLIN

Andrew J. Moyer, a plant pathologist at Peoria's USDA Northern Research Laboratory, was awarded U.S. patent no. 2,442,141 for new methods of fermenting penicillin, on this day in Illinois history.

Moyer's discovery of using corn-steeped liquor in the culture of penicillin, during World War II, had provided the means for mass-producing the much-needed antibiotic. His lab work saved countless lives. Scottish bacteriologist Alexander Fleming first discovered penicillin, a mold that kills off many harmful bacteria in humans, in 1928. British scientists continued experimenting with this "wonder drug" through the 1930s, but could not isolate a natural fermentation method that would produce sufficient quantities for its more general use. With the outbreak of World War II in 1939, however, penicillin was urgently needed to care for soldiers and civilians suffering burn wounds from the bombing raids of the German Luftwaffe. With laboratories in the United Kingdom imperiled by the Battle of Britain, all hope was turned to the United States for further research.

Peoria, Illinois—in the heart of the greatest corn-producing region in the world—was where the United States Department of Agriculture based its Northern Research Laboratory. They had already been exploring new industrial uses for the abundance of corn products when British scientists first visited the Peoria laboratory in 1941. Moyer identified corn-steeped liquor, the liquid leftover from soaking the cob before its kernels are removed, as a new medium for organic fermentation. His revolutionary method would yield a tenfold increase (at least) in the production of penicillin, making possible the commercial manufacture of the desperately sought-after drug. In 1943, Moyer and his Peoria colleagues also discovered a more potent penicillin mold—*Penicillium chrysogenum*—growing on the ripened cantaloupes of a local farmer. This created an even stronger antibiotic.

By the end of the war, 21 plants in the United States produced the drug, and more than 300 billion units of penicillin were made available to Allied forces crossing the channel on D-Day.

- May 26 -
1926
Jazz Great Miles Davis Born in Alton

Miles Davis—"The Father of Cool," one of the most innovative and influential musicians of the 20th century—was born in Madison County on this day in Illinois history.

Born into a well-to-do Alton family—his dad, Miles Davis II, was a successful dentist—one-year-old Miles moved to nearby East St. Louis, Illinois, with his mother and father in 1927. His mother, Cleota, a talented classical musician, wanted Miles to pursue the violin. Instead, he took up the trumpet, a gift from his father on his 13th birthday, and never looked back. Miles became a local phenomenon, playing with East St. Louis bandleader Eddie Randall and studying under the city's most accomplished trumpeters. After graduating from high school, Miles played a stint with the popular Billy Eckstine Band alongside the legendary Charlie Parker.

In 1945, Davis left Illinois on a scholarship to the Juilliard School of Music in New York City. Formal studies were abandoned, however, as he sought out his idols—becoming a sideman to Parker, Thelonious Monk, and Dizzy Gillespie, among others—and established a stage and studio career of his own. Davis' distinctive "cool" sound and experimental compositions won him accolades throughout the jazz scene, and by 1950 Capitol Records signed him. Davis became addicted to heroin while touring the New York jazz clubs. While he was wasting away, his live gigs suffered in the early 1950s. In 1954, Davis returned to East St. Louis and, with the help of his father, kicked the drug habit. He returned to New York with vigor and cut some of the most stunningly complex jazz recordings ever, working with the greatest artists and composers of the era—from John Coltrane and Sonny Rollins to Gil Evans and Dave Brubeck. Davis' most notable recordings include *Birth of Cool* (1948), *Conception* (1951), *Miles Ahead* (1957), *Sketches of Spain* (1960), and *Bitches Brew* (1969). Fellow Illinoisan Ronald Reagan invited Davis to attend a 1987 White House tribute to soul great Ray Charles.

Davis, one of the most prodigious jazz artists ever, died on September 28, 1991, and is buried at Woodlawn Cemetery, in the Bronx, New York.

1837
"WILD BILL" HICKOK BORN IN TROY'S GROVE, ILLINOIS

James Butler Hickok, better known as pistol-slinging, card-playing cowboy "Wild Bill," was born in rural LaSalle County on this day in Illinois history.

Born to William and Polly Hickok, James grew up taking target practice on the open Illinois prairie with his three brothers, and by the age of 17 had become a superb marksman. He left home at 18 for the Wild West. Hickok first drove stagecoaches on the Oregon and Santa Fe trails, and later served as a scout, courier, and spy for the Union Army during the Civil War. His unrivaled skill as a gunfighter earned James a feared reputation and a new nickname; it was said of "Wild Bill" that he could pull and fire both his Colt revolvers before his adversary—often a criminal—had a chance to blink. Colonel George Armstrong Custer called him a "strange character, just the one which a novelist might gloat over . . . whose skill in the use of the rifle and pistol was unerring."

Photo courtesy of Wikipedia

Wild Bill Hickok was interviewed for the lead story of the February 1867 issue of *Harper's Magazine,* and a living legend was born. He returned to Troy Grove in 1869 to see to his mother, who had become ill, but left Illinois again to serve as the sheriff of Ellis County, Kansas, and later as the U.S. Marshal of Abilene, Kansas. In 1876, while playing poker at a Deadwood, Dakota Territory saloon, Wild Bill was shot in the back by a man who claimed his brother had been killed by the Illinois gunslinger in a recent duel. (According to the saloon keeper, Hickok was holding black aces and eights at the time of his murder—thereafter known as a "dead man's hand.") An ad hoc jury at first fell for the man's story, and acquitted him of murder; but a retrial was held when it was discovered that the murderer had no brother, and he soon was hanged. Wild Bill's own brother, Lorenzo Hickok, traveled from Illinois for the sentencing.

Wild Bill Hickok remains an indelible fixture in American folklore, and a memorial to him today stands near his boyhood home in LaSalle County, Illinois.

- MAY 28 -
1917
EAST ST. LOUIS ROCKED BY RACE RIOT

On this day in Illinois history, the city of East St. Louis was the scene of an ugly riot that pitted white workers against their black counterparts.

East St. Louis was a thriving industrial town, dubbed the "Pittsburgh of the West" and one of America's fastest-growing cities—and also a nexus of its racial tensions. In this era of segregation, whites and blacks used separate hospital wards, ate at separate dining halls, and lived in separate parts of the city; races mixing at the workplace proved to be a recipe for disaster. White fears of blacks moving in to take good-paying jobs—most pronounced among labor organizers—were rampant. Aluminum Ore Company was one of the city's top employers, and when blacks were hired at wages that undercut the union's demands, union delegates organized nothing short of a citywide massacre.

Amid circulating rumors of black workers hoarding firearms for a planned riot, a mob of 3,000 descended on downtown, smashing storefronts, destroying buildings, and beating innocent bystanders. A union leader had just exited City Hall after meeting with the mayor, and upon word of a black man being arrested for armed robbery, he organized a throng of iron and steelworkers with the shout "Take the guns away." Nobody was killed that day, but several blacks were severely beaten and the National Guard had to be called in to restore order. Tensions festered for weeks.

Photo courtesy of Library of Congress, Historic American Buildings Survey, HABS, IL-1113-7-1

Aerial view of East St. Louis

Later that summer, an incident involving a black gang firing upon a police car and killing two white officers spurred the worst race riot Illinois has ever seen. Labor leaders encouraged vengeance for the two detectives, and on July 2 another mob of enraged whites descended on the black ghetto in a fit of indiscriminate violence. By the time Governor Frank O. Lowden sent in the state militia, 48 East St. Louis residents—39 blacks and 9 whites—lay dead. During the carnage, a local church rang its bell to warn of the rampaging mob, and hundreds of blacks found refuge in the basements of sympathetic whites.

Twelve blacks and nine whites were convicted of murder or homicide, and a grand jury blamed the riot on agitators on both sides.

ILLINOIS REPUBLICAN PARTY MEETS IN BLOOMINGTON FOR FIRST STATE CONVENTION

On this day in Illinois history, an amalgam of political dissenters from the Whigs, Democrats, and Independents—allied by their opposition to slavery—united to form the state's Republican Party in McLean County.

There had been rumblings for the organization of a new antislavery party in Illinois for years. In 1848, the short-lived Liberty Party, which was staunchly abolitionist, had existed in 13 northern counties. That same year the city of Ottawa hosted a Free Soil convention. The chief issue on its platform was blocking the expansion of slavery, but the Free Soilers, to their loss, refused to band together with like-minded groups. By the early 1850s abolitionists had held similar meetings in Chicago and Rockford, and began to organize in smaller cities as well. In 1854—galvanized by the recent passing of the Kansas-Nebraska Act, which allowed for the expansion of slavery on a state-by-state basis and was championed by Illinois Democratic senator, Stephen A. Douglas—a group of Whigs met in Springfield to join a new coalition, the Republican Party. This new coalition was committed to the banning of slavery in the Old Northwest (Illinois, Indiana, Michigan, Ohio, Wisconsin, and parts of Minnesota). Among the Whig defectors was Abraham Lincoln. But, not wanting to appear too extreme and thus harm his senatorial aspirations, Lincoln declined a seat on the party's central committee.

Two years later, at the Republican's first official statewide convention, Lincoln was ready to play a more prominent role. Two hundred and seventy delegates from 70 Illinois counties convened in Bloomington at Major's Hall, then a teacher's college. There was virtually no representation from the southern counties, however. Leaders included Senator John M. Palmer of Collinsville, who presided over the mass meeting; Owen Lovejoy, the strident abolitionist who orchestrated much of western Illinois's Underground Railroad; and Lincoln, who delivered his so-called "Lost Speech," which strongly denounced slavery but was not to be distributed outside the convention room halls.

That year Illinois Republicans supported the presidential nomination of John C. Frémont—"Free Soil, Free Speech, Free Men—Frémont"—who lost the election to Democrat James Buchanan.

- MAY 30 -
1933
SALLY RAND DEBUTS THE "FAN DANCE" AT CHICAGO'S WORLD'S FAIR

Former silent-film starlet Sally Rand first dazzled spectators at the Century of Progress Exposition with her world-famous "fan dance," on this day in Illinois history.

Rand was born Helen Gould Beck on Easter Sunday 1904, in the Missouri Ozarks. By her teens, she had adopted the stage name Sally Rand—at the suggestion of film-maker Cecil B. DeMille—and was playing vaudeville acts, performing acrobatics for the Barnum & Bailey Circus, and starring in silent movies through her 20s. When the "talkies" arrived, however, the multitalented Rand was denied leading roles because of an inescapable lisp. Rand came to Chicago in 1932 with the show "Sweethearts on Parade" and stayed to take on a regular gig at the Paramount Club, which was looking for "exotic acts and dancers." It was there that she conceived of her ticket out of the Great Depression—the risqué fan dance, with her naked body scarcely concealed by fluttering two large, pink ostrich feathers.

She was commissioned to perform this act at the "Streets of Paris" exhibit during the Century of Progress Exposition, and it was an instant sensation. Thousands—mostly men—flocked to see her. Some were offended, including Chicago Mayor Edward Kelly, and Rand soon found herself in court. Superior Judge Joseph B. David tossed out the charges that Rand's act was "lewd, lascivious, and degrading to public morals." The judge disagreed: "There is no harm and certainly no injury to public morals when the human body is exposed; some people probably would want to put pants on a horse. . . . When I go to the fair, I go to see the exhibits and perhaps to enjoy a little beer. As far as I'm concerned, all these charges are just a lot of old stuff to me. Case dismissed for want of equity." The fan dance thus persevered.

Rand continued dancing, took her act on the road after the exposition, and by virtue of her newfound fame was soon earning $3,000 per week in the midst of the Great Depression.

CHICAGO CUB RON SANTO SETS RECORD
FOR CONSECUTIVE GAMES AT THIRD BASE

Ron Santo, legendary third baseman and current radio broadcaster for the Chicago Cubs, set a National League record for his 364th straight game at the "hot corner," on this day in Illinois history.

Santo's durability became all the more impressive when it was revealed that he had been concealing the fact that he had diabetes, surreptitiously treating himself with medication throughout his career. The streak ended at 390 games when Santo's cheek was fractured by a hit-by-pitch, during a game in which the Cubs and Mets pitchers threw beanballs at opposing batters. He had surgery and was back in the lineup the following week. This all occurred in the midst of an impressive 28-game hitting streak. Santo's career numbers include more than 2,200 hits, along with 342 home runs, 1,331 RBIs, and a lifetime .277 batting average in one of the toughest pitching eras in major-league history. Santo led the National League in walks four times. He added five Gold Glove Awards and nine All-Star Game selections to a stellar baseball career that spanned 14 years (1960–1973) at Wrigley Field, and one last season as a Chicago White Sox at Comiskey Park in 1974. Despite these numbers, Santo has yet to be inducted into the Hall of Fame.

A fan favorite in his playing days, Santo—nicknamed "Pizza" for his favorite concession—continues to be a fan favorite in the radio booth. In November 1973, at the twilight of his playing career, he became the first major-leaguer to invoke the no-trade clause of a contract, refusing to leave his beloved City of the Big Shoulders in a trade that would have landed him in California. A couple of weeks later he agreed to go to Chicago's South Side in a crosstown trade that brought future Cy Young Award winner (and fellow Cub broadcaster) Steve Stone to the Northside. After retirement, Santo joined play-by-play man Pat Hughes in the radio booth, and he has raised more than $50 million for the Juvenile Diabetes Research Foundation since 1974.

In 2003, the Chicago Cubs retired Santo's No. 10 jersey; it joined those of teammates Ernie Banks (No. 14) and Billy William (No. 26) flying high over the bleachers at Wrigley Field, if not yet in Cooperstown.

This day in
June

- JUNE 1 -

1912

DANIEL BURNHAM, FAMOUS CHICAGO ARCHITECT, DIES

On this day in Illinois history, Daniel H. Burnham, visionary architect of the White City at Chicago's 1893 Columbian Exposition, died.

Burnham and his partner, John Wellborn Root, formed Burnham & Root, the preeminent architectural firm of 1880s and 1890s Chicago. Their landmark downtown buildings include the Rookery, the Reliance Building, and the Manadnock Building—at 16 stories, the tallest masonry skyscraper ever built in the United States. The firm of Burnham & Root was in tremendous demand in the burgeoning city. Their Masonic Temple Building—torn down in 1939—stood at 21 stories and over 300 feet, for a time the tallest building in Chicago.

Burnham's credo: "Make no little plans, they have no magic to stir men's blood. . . . Make big plans, aim high in hope and work. . . ." And plan big he did. Grief-stricken by Root's untimely death from pneumonia, Burnham launched himself into planning for the 1893 World's Columbian Exposition, to be hosted by Chicago, for which the firm had recently been commissioned as chief architectural consultants. His grandiose design featured gardens, boulevards, and classical-style buildings awash in white plaster—the so-called White City, a magnificent site built upon what had been marshland on the city's South Side. The only permanent building was the Palace of Fine Arts, today's Museum of Science and Industry. The White City spawned a revival in classical architecture throughout America that would last for decades.

Burnham was commissioned in 1907 to devise the famous Chicago Plan, which was published in 1909. Aimed at the beautification of the city and a moral boost to its citizens, including improved living conditions with increased public park areas, it became the model for comprehensive city planning across the nation. It was designed under the principle that every citizen be within walking distance of a park. Chicago, with its fountains and boulevards, was to become a "Paris in the Prairie." Visitors to the city's beautiful lakefront today owe thanks to Burnham's vision.

He is buried at Chicago's Graceland Cemetery not far from his business partner, John Root, and former competitor and fierce critic Louis Sullivan.

- JUNE 2 -
1845

FUTURE GOVERNOR WILLIAM H. BISSELL VOLUNTEERS FOR WAR

On this day in Illinois history, William Bissell—"Patriot-Statesman-Hero"—answered Governor Thomas Ford's call for volunteer troops to fight in the war with Mexico.

Bissell was a Monroe County schoolteacher and physician before entering politics. He sat in the Illinois House of Representatives from 1840 to 1842. Like so many others of his era, he used his status as war hero to further his political career. President

Polk had requested three regiments from Illinois, and enough men volunteered for nine. (Abraham Lincoln, then a Whig in the Illinois General Assembly, opposed the war as he saw its objective—winning Texas from Mexico—as a boon to slave-owning states.) Bissell, who joined as a private, was elected colonel of the Second Illinois Regiment, scoring the overwhelming confidence of his men, with votes of 807–6. He stood out at the bloody two-day Battle of Buena Vista, where the Americans were outnumbered nearly five to one. "Colonel Bissell, the only surviving colonel of the three [Illinois] regiments," commended General Zachary Taylor, "merits notice for his coolness and bravery on this occasion."

Bissell rode that meritorious service straight to the U.S. House of Representatives, where he was easily elected to two terms (1850–54) as a Democrat. It was there that he famously called out Southern veterans of the Mexican War on their hollow boasting of great feats performed in battle. For this, Bissell was challenged to a duel by Jefferson Davis, a Congressman from Mississippi and future president of the Confederacy. Bissell accepted—Army muskets with ball and buckshot being his chosen weapons—but President Taylor intervened to stop the bloodshed. Bissell then ran for and won the governorship of Illinois in 1856. Switching parties, he became the first Republican, the first Catholic, and the first invalid (a result of illness, not a war wound) to be elected to that office. During his single term, Governor Bissell was at the center of a controversial 1855 reapportionment bill—an attempt to gerrymander Illinois's voting districts—which he at first signed but ultimately vetoed.

On March 18, 1860, William H. Bissell became the first governor of Illinois to die while in office, succumbing to pneumonia at the age of 49 and then buried at Springfield's Oak Ridge Cemetery.

- JUNE 3 -
1861
STEPHEN A. DOUGLAS DIES IN CHICAGO

Stephen Douglas, famous for his 1858 debates with Abraham Lincoln, succumbed to typhoid fever at the age of 48 on this day in Illinois history.

Douglas came to Jackson, Illinois, in 1833 from Vermont and opened up his law practice the following year. He immediately threw himself into politics. The young attorney was elected public prosecutor in 1835 and a member of the state legislature in 1836. Continuing his rapid rise in state government, Douglas served as a judge of the Illinois Supreme Court from 1841 to 1843. The 5-foot-tall Douglas was a commanding orator with few equals in debate—those who saw him speak were soon calling him "The Little Giant." In 1843, those skills took him to the U.S. House of Representatives, and to the Senate in 1847. In 1858, following the legendary Lincoln-Douglas debates, he was elected to his third Senate term.

Photo courtesy of Library of Congress, LC-DIG-cwpbh-00880

In Congress, Douglas distinguished himself as a champion of westward expansion. As chairman of the committee of territories, he introduced bills for admitting eight states to the Union, which forced him to wrestle with the contentious issue of slavery—should these new states be admitted as slave or free? In 1854, he supported the fiercely debated Kansas-Nebraska Act—to garner Southern support for his presidential ambitions, his opponents charged—which established the principle of Popular Sovereignty. Each new state was "free to form and regulate their domestic institutions in their own way." In other words, the federal government could not check the westward advance of slavery. Lincoln disagreed.

In 1852 and 1856 Douglas ran for the Democratic nomination for the presidency, losing both times. In 1860 he won the nomination of a divided Democratic party but lost the general election to Abe Lincoln, whom he had narrowly defeated for Illinois's U.S. Senate seat two years earlier. After the election he campaigned vigorously on Lincoln's behalf to save the Union. Douglas considered secession a crime and advocated preservation of the Union at all costs. At his final speech in early May, "Preserve the Flag," before the state General Assembly, Douglas urged his Illinois followers to remain loyal to the new president.

President Abraham Lincoln called for 30 days of mourning at the death of his former adversary.

- JUNE 4 -

1944

GERMAN U-BOAT 505
CAPTURED BY CHICAGO CAPTAIN

On this day in Illinois history, Chicagoan Daniel Vincent Gallery, captain of the USS *Guadalcanal,* captured German U-Boat 505—the only Nazi submarine ever seized by the U.S. Navy during World War II.

D. V. Gallery was born and raised in Chicago. He graduated from the U.S. Naval Academy in Annapolis, Maryland, in the 1920s, devoted his life to the Armed Forces, and in 1942 was assigned to command Fleet Air Base in Reykjavik, Iceland. There, he won the Bronze Star for combat operations against the dreaded U-Boats. German U-Boats were a major hindrance to Allied war efforts; victory depended on the ability of the U.S. Navy and Merchant Marines to safely transport men and supplies to the European battlefronts, and U-Boats were wreaking havoc on those efforts. In 1943, Gallery was appointed Commanding Officer of Task Group 22.3—with its escort carrier, the USS *Guadalcanal,* and four destroyers—and ordered to hunt down U-505, which had been tracked by American and British code breakers who intercepted German radio transmissions.

After a persistent cat-and-mouse chase off the Atlantic coast of Africa, the American battle group finally caught the German U-Boat. U-505 had sunk 47,000 tons of Allied shipping, including three American boats, up to that day. One ship, the USS *Chatelain,* disabled it with a depth charge, and crewmen from another, the USS *Pillsbury,* boarded the defenseless sub as it surrendered at the surface. (It was the first time since the War of 1812 that an American crew had boarded and captured an enemy vessel.) Aboard U-505 was a special prize: The Enigma Machine. This enabled Allied intelligence officers to systematically break the Nazi code, turning the tide of the war at sea—and land—irrevocably in the Allies' favor from that point forward.

In 1954, the captive U-505 found its permanent home as a National Historic Landmark at Chicago's Museum of Science and Industry, in the hometown of the U.S. Navy captain who captured her.

- JUNE 5 -
1929
CHICAGOAN GLORIA SWANSON FILMS HER FIRST "TALKIE"

On this day in Illinois history, Gloria Swanson, silent-film star who emerged from the city's Essanay Studios, began filming her first "talkie," *The Trespasser*.

She was born in Chicago on March 27, 1899. Gloria May Josephine Svensson was raised an Army brat, living between the Windy City and U.S. Army bases from Puerto Rico to Key West, Florida. She loved theater—singing, dancing, and acting in school plays—and was working at a department store in Chicago when, at the age of 15, an aunt cajoled her into visiting Essanay Studios. (Essanay was considered the "Hollywood of the Prairie," launching the career of Charlie Chaplin, among others.) The attractive teenager was thus discovered and found immediate work. She debuted in "bits," or supporting roles for short films called two-reelers, in 1913. At Essanay, Gloria Swanson met and later married actor Wallace Beery, who took her away to Hollywood in 1915. Their marriage (the first of six for the fashionable starlet) lasted just three years; her movie career endured considerably longer.

She was a Hollywood natural. After Swanson played leading roles in silent movies throughout the Roaring Twenties (most notably with filmmaker Cecil B. DeMille), her voice finally broke on to the silver screen. *The Trespasser,* which she filmed for three weeks in June 1929, was a resounding success. Audiences were happy to discover that she could not only speak but also sing. Swanson, who played a divorcee fighting for the custody of her child, was nominated by the Academy of Motion Picture Arts and Sciences for Best Actress in a Leading Role. (It was also around this time she had a fling with Joe Kennedy, father of the future U.S. president.) More performances followed, some fairly popular and some flat-out bombs. But Swanson—who once declared, "I won't be a second anyone!"—reclaimed the pinnacle of stardom with the 1950 box-office hit *Sunset Boulevard*. She was then between husbands number five and number six, William F. Dufty, whom she did not marry until 1976. She transformed into a TV star in the 1960s and appeared as herself in her final film, the forgettable *Airport '75*, in 1974.

Gloria Swanson died in 1983 with two stars—one each for movies and for TV—on the Hollywood Walk of Fame.

- JUNE 6 -
1924
"TRIAL OF THE CENTURY" BEGINS IN CHICAGO

The sensational trial of Nathan Leopold Jr. and Richard Loeb, two young Hyde Park, Chicago, adults accused of the heinous murder of 14-year-old Bobby Franks, began amid national attention on this day in Illinois history.

The 18-year-old Leopold and 19-year-old Loeb, children of privilege both, had for months been planning the perfect crime. It was carried out on May 21, 1924. They were serial criminals, from petty theft to arson, who believed their affluence and social status made them immune to the law. The kidnapping and murder of Franks was a sort of macabre test of that theory. On that summer morning after class—the partners attended the University of Chicago part time—they came upon their prey. The Hyde Park murderers lured the innocent child, a neighbor who recognized and trusted them, into a rental car, bludgeoned him with a chisel, and suffocated him to death with a cushion. They dumped acid on the boy's face to obscure his identity and dumped the body in a drainpipe at a south Chicago swampland where Leopold, an expert ornithologist, often went to bird-watch.

The supposed gifted intellects of Leopold and Loeb were belied by the carelessness of the crime. It was a sloppy job. A ransom note demanding $10,000 from Franks's wealthy parents, created as a diversion, was traced back to a typewriter Leopold had used in college; eyeglasses left at the scene were likewise identified as belonging to Leopold; and both suspects, without a solid alibi, caved quite easily under questioning. On May 31, just ten days after the crime, they confessed to the murder of Bobby Franks. What followed was "The Trial of the Century." Leopold and Loeb, on the advice of their attorney, Clarence Darrow, shocked all by pleading guilty rather than not guilty by insanity. Mobs formed outside the Chicago criminal courtroom while from inside Cook County Jail, the defendants joked with their guards, mocked reporters, and delighted in retelling the ghastly details of the crime. Darrow, in a spellbinding two-hour oration (immortalized in the 1956 film *Compulsion* by Orson Welles) spared the two from the death penalty by blaming their behavior on the philosophy of Nietzsche—his concept of the "superman"—which the boys had embraced in college, filling their minds with notions of self-invulnerability.

The duo was sentenced to life plus 99 years, but Leopold was murdered in prison in 1936 and Loeb released on parole in 1958.

- JUNE 7 -
1969

ROCK ISLAND ARSENAL DESIGNATED
NATIONAL HISTORIC LANDMARK

On this day in Illinois history, Rock Island Arsenal—at what was once Saukenak, capital of the Sauk and Fox Indian nations—became a National Historic Landmark.

The 946-acre island in the Mississippi River between the Quad Cities (Rock Island and Moline, Illinois, and Davenport and Bettendorf, Iowa) was recognized early on by the United States government for its strategically important location. An 1809 Act of Congress secured the island as a federal military reservation.

Photo courtesy of Library of Congress, Historic American Buildings Survey Collection, Haer IL 20T-1

Fort Armstrong was built there in 1816 and served as the Army's headquarters during the Black Hawk War of 1832. It saw limited use and even neglect over the next few decades of peacetime, but in 1862, with the nation embroiled in civil war, construction began on what would become the nation's largest government-owned manufacturer of arms and ordnance. General Thomas J. Rodman—"Father of Rock Island Arsenal"—oversaw construction of the facility from 1865 to 1871. He is credited with designing the buildings known as Arsenal Row, Armory Row, and the 50-room Commander's Mansion, which stands as the second-largest government-owned private residence in the nation (after the White House).

Rock Island Arsenal quickly became the region's number-one employer as America entered 20th-century conflict after 20th-century conflict. Workers there produced the equipment—everything from canteens to saddlebags to howitzer cannons—necessary for defending the nation. The arsenal produced more than 15,000 sets of cavalry and 50,000 sets of infantry equipment during the Spanish-American War; more than 110,000 .30 caliber bolt-action rifles during World War I; and millions of artillery components during World War II. This production continued through the Vietnam and Gulf wars. Today, Rock Island Arsenal has about 2,000 civilian employees and houses one of the largest and oldest military museums in the country.

- JUNE 8 -
1831
BLACK HAWK'S BAND RECLAIMS SAUKENUK

On this day in Illinois history, after having returned over the spring, Black Hawk and his Sauk and Fox followers refused to follow tribal orders and return to Iowa, claiming their right to remain at their "ancestral" home in present-day Rock Island County.

Though the Treaty of 1804 and subsequent agreements did not call for the immediate removal of Indians, they did grant the United States title to all land east of the Mississippi River, and white settlements had begun to spread across northwest Illinois throughout the 1820s. In 1829, in response to settlers' demands for more land, tribal chiefs in Illinois were warned to vacate all farms and villages—including their capital of more than 100 years, Saukenuk, on the Mississippi River. This caused great tension among the Sauk and Fox, who denied they had ever ceded their homeland and considered all past treaties nothing more than trickery by the U.S. government. But those who saw the folly of standing to fight, led by the influential Sauk chief Keokuk, acquiesced to relocating across the Mississippi River as unwelcome but necessary. He led his people peacefully to Iowa in the fall of 1829 and warned that "any Indians who attempted to return to reside at Rocky River . . . must take their own chances."

Lorado Taft's Black Hawk overlooking the Rock River

Black Hawk took his chances. "My fathers were great men," he said in response to Keokuk, "and I wish to remain where the bones of my fathers are laid." He and his faction refused to cede their homes to the new settlers. Hundreds of warriors and their families had returned that spring to find their villages occupied, their burial grounds plowed, and their corn fields planted by whites. Governor John Reynolds declared this a "state of actual invasion" and demanded Black Hawk's immediate departure. General Edmund Gaines, commander of the Western Division of the U.S. Army, had moved his headquarters to nearby Rock Island, Illinois, in response to Black Hawk's defiance. Reynolds called up a volunteer militia of 1,400 men and, with Army troops dispatched from St. Louis, marched on Saukenuk. One unit was led by a young Abraham Lincoln. Outnumbered and outgunned, Black Hawk escaped with his people in the middle of the night on June 26, 1831, without conflict, back across the Mississippi River.

Within days Black Hawk signed yet another treaty and promised never to return to Illinois; yet he would return within a year.

- JUNE 9 -

1915

ILLINOISAN WILLIAM JENNINGS BRYAN RESIGNS AS U.S. SECRETARY OF STATE

Over disagreement with President Woodrow Wilson's perceived militarism, U.S. Secretary of State William Jennings Bryan—opposed to U.S. involvement in the Great War—resigned his post on this day in Illinois history.

William Jennings Bryan—nicknamed "The Great Commoner"—was born in Salem, Illinois, on March 19, 1860. He graduated from Illinois College in Jacksonville in 1861. After studying law at Northwestern University in Evanston, Illinois, Bryan relocated to Nebraska, where he represented that state in the U.S. Congress from 1891 to 1895. In 1896 he returned to Illinois to deliver his triumphant "Cross of Gold" speech, in support of the silver standard, at the Democratic National Convention in Chicago. He won his party's nomination, as he would again in 1900 and 1908—falling short of winning the general election all three times. Bryan supported Woodrow Wilson at the 1912 Democratic Convention, breaking a 46-ballot deadlock that finally delivered Wilson the presidential nomination. He then served as secretary of state under President Woodrow Wilson from 1913 to 1915, but he resigned in protest of the administration's militant response to the sinking of the ship the *Lusitania* by a German U-Boat, and the subsequent buildup for war. Yet, once war was declared in 1917, Bryan—then approaching 60 years of age—tried to enlist in the Army.

Photo courtesy of Library of Congress, USZC2-6259

Bryan never strayed from his Midwestern values and his Christian convictions. He championed women's suffrage and prohibition, and was a leading critic of the theory of evolution. He had volunteered for the Spanish-American War in 1898, and though he never saw combat personally, he grew to embrace pacifism and warn constantly of the ill consequences of imperialism. It is said that this pacifism hurt him politically. In 1924, having retired from the political arena, Bryan re-emerged on the national stage as he led the prosecution in the famous Scopes Monkey Trial, in which he prevailed over fellow Illinois attorney Clarence Darrow.

Bryan, exhausted, died five days after the close of the trial, on July 26, 1925, and was interred at Arlington National Cemetery in Virginia.

In a brilliant publicity stunt at the closing gala of the annual American Institute of Architects Convention, the Chicago Tribune Company announced a competition to design its new headquarters, on this day in Illinois history.

The 462-foot Gothic skyscraper—home of WGN Radio and the *Chicago Tribune*—was the result of an open challenge to design the "world's most beautiful office building" in downtown Chicago. The contest drew more than 200 submissions—most serious, some less so—and plenty of worldwide hype. Winner of the competition and its $50,000 prize was the architectural partnership of Raymond Hood and John Howells. (Engraved figures of the fabled Robin Hood and a howling dog grace the tower's entrance in commemoration to the architects.) However, this choice proved controversial as its Gothic design contrasted sharply with the more modern, forward-looking style of the Chicago School of Architecture. In fact the top two runners-up, architects whose designs ultimately had more influence on the future of skyscrapers, were deemed far more innovative by many public and private critics at the time.

Construction of the highly decorative landmark took three years (1922–25) to complete. The medieval buttresses, which crown the tower, once dominated the Chicago skyline and for years stood out radiantly above lesser skyscrapers when illuminated at night. Embedded at the lower levels of Tribune Tower are more than 120 fragments—bricks and stones—brought to the construction site from the world's most famous landmarks by *Chicago Tribune* correspondents. These include national sites such as Bunker Hill, Mark Twain's "Injun Joe Cave," and Lincoln's Tomb; and international sites such as the Taj Mahal, the Pyramids of Egypt, and the Great Wall of China. Each is labeled by source. A piece of moon rock was added to the mix in later years.

With its decorative spires and buttresses and unique relief work, Tribune Tower remains one of Chicago's most identifiable buildings to this day—though it still has its detractors.

- JUNE 11 -
1913
ILLINOIS SUFFRAGISTS BILL PASSES THE GENERAL ASSEMBLY

On this day in Illinois history, a bill granting women the right to vote in presidential elections, which had already passed the state senate, received an 83–58 stamp of approval—with six votes to spare—in the House of Representatives.

Governor Edward Dunne signed the Illinois Municipal Voting Act into law on June 26. "The effect of this victory upon the nation was astounding," wrote Carrie Clinton Chapman Catt, a leading women's-rights advocate. "When the first Illinois election took place in April . . . Illinois, with its large electoral vote of 29, proved the turning point beyond which politicians at last got a clear view of the fact that women were gaining genuine political power." That power was born with the Illinois Women's Suffragists Association (IWSA) at a Chicago ballroom in 1869, and fostered by two generations of Illinois suffragists.

In 1870, a 33-year-old member of the IWSA and a former teacher at a one-room school, Frances Elizabeth Caroline Willard, had implored, "The idea that boys of 21 are fit to make laws for their mothers, is an insult to everyone." Two years later the IWSA joined some 500 national suffragists who were arrested for attempting to crash the polls during that year's presidential election. Most prominent was Susan B. Anthony, who declared famously when refusing to pay her $100 fine: "Resistance to tyranny is obedience to God." Lesser known is Lombard, Illinois's "Lady Lawyer," Ellen Martin, who, through a successful court hearing based on a technicality (the city charter that allowed "all citizens"—not specifying gender—the right to vote in all elections), led 15 local women in casting Illinois's first female votes to be tabulated for a presidential election.

Progress continued in incremental steps, such as the landmark victory in June 1891, when the Illinois General Assembly passed a bill that entitled women the right to elect local school officials—the first such piece of legislation across the states. Through organization, constant petitioning, and focus on changing local laws, the movement gained momentum, culminating in the legislative victory of 1913.

Six years later, Illinois became the first state to ratify the 19th Amendment to the U.S. Constitution, granting universal women's suffrage across the Union.

- JUNE 12 -

1924

AMERICA'S BOLDEST TRAIN ROBBERY
TAKES PLACE IN ROUNDOUT

On this day in Illinois history, a dramatic train robbery in Lake County netted one of the largest booties of any such heist to ever be pulled off in the United States.

The Roundout, Illinois, train depot, at the junction of the Chicago, Milwaukee, and St. Paul and Pacific Northwest railroads, was a relatively remote, uneventful station about 32 miles north of Chicago's Union Station. The scheming Newton Gang—

brothers Jessie, Willis, Doc, and Joe—would change all of that. Around 1919 the four siblings grew tired of working on their father's Texas farm. They chose a new vocation—mass larceny—and set off on a crime spree that took them from Canada throughout the American Midwest. Their efforts were spectacular, often involving more explosives than were necessary for the job, and for years they eluded capture, always on the move. And though they carried firearms, and employed tear gas as well as nitro, the boys bragged about never having killed anyone. In the early summer of 1924 the Newton boys turned their sights on northern Illinois, and they planned the biggest train holdup to date. It would be their downfall.

The plan was simple. Two of the men boarded a northbound train in Chicago, disguised as postal employees, and forced clerks on board to hand over $2 million in cash and securities. Once at Roundout, they waited until just beyond the busy junction and leapt to the getaway car, where the rest of the gang waited. It worked—for a few days. The Newton Gang was apprehended by local authorities within the week, and they—along with accomplices who had worked for the U.S. Postal Service—were found guilty and sentenced to long prison terms. Much of the loot, however, was never discovered. Upon release, several years later, the brothers retired comfortably back in Texas, with no explanation for their apparently substantial income.

In 1972, Steve McQueen and Ali MacGraw starred in the hit movie *The Getaway*, based on the exploits of the Newton Boys and the Roundout Train Robbery.

- JUNE 13 -

1903

ILLINOIS FOOTBALL STAR RED GRANGE BORN

Harold Edward Grange—nicknamed "Red" for his hair—was born in Forksville, Pennsylvania.

Arguably one of the most dominant football players ever, Grange starred at the high school, collegiate, and professional levels in Illinois, earning national fame. He moved to Wheaton, Illinois, with his dad at the age of 5 after his mother died. There, despite warnings from a local doctor that he suffered heart tremors, young Red embraced sports. He lettered in football, baseball, basketball, and track all four years at Wheaton High School—finding the end zone 75 times for the football squad. Grange was recruited by the University of Illinois in Champaign in 1922, and became an overnight phenomenon. He scored three touchdowns against Nebraska in his first college game. As a sophomore he led the Fighting Illini to an undefeated season and the team's first national championship. In 1924, he executed the greatest single-game performance ever, racking up 402 yards and seven touchdowns against the mighty Michigan Wolverines. Famous sports writer Grantland Rice was inspired to name Grange "The Galloping Ghost" for his elusive, ghostlike dashes to the end zone. He appeared on the cover of *Time* magazine in October 1925, after having been voted collegiate All-American for three years running.

Photo courtesy of Chicago Historical Society

After college, Grange was signed by George S. Halas of the Chicago Bears to star on a football barnstorming tour. Grange continued to dominate on the field, and took in over $100,000 in salary and gate receipts over 19 weeks, at a time when the average player earned less than $100 per game. It was this 67-day tour, highlighted by the Galloping Ghost from Wheaton, Illinois, that put Halas's Bears and the NFL on the map. Grange retired from football in 1934, having scored 87 touchdowns, carried the ball 4,103 times, gaining 33,920 total yards, and averaging 8.4 yards per try throughout his Illinois high school, college, and pro careers. He died on January 28, 1991, after being inducted into both the college and professional football halls of fame.

Red Grange, who stood 5-foot-11 and just 175 pounds, espoused a simple philosophy of the game he loved: "If you have the football and 11 guys are after you, if you're smart, you'll run."

- JUNE 14 -
1671
FRANCE CLAIMS ILLINOIS COUNTRY

On this day in Illinois history, the French claimed the rivers, prairies, and bluffs—yet unseen—that would a century and half later become the 21st state of the Union.

France claimed title to Illinois Country at an imperial ceremony held at Sault Ste. Marie, Canada, attended by government officials, Jesuit priests, and representatives from more than a dozen scattered Indian nations. Based largely on tales told by local

Restored powder magazine at Fort de Chartres

Algonquin Indians about a great river called "Misi Sipi"—meaning big river—to the west, the French were anxious to explore their new lands, hoping to discover the ever-elusive Northwest Passage to the Orient. Almost two full years later, a vigorous young explorer named Louis Jolliet, handpicked by the governor of New France, set off with Father Jacques Marquette to survey King Louis XIV's latest acquisition. During their historic journey, one of the sites that left a lasting impression was that which has since been dubbed the "Piasa Bird" outside present-day Alton.

This larger-than-life Indian pictograph, a storm-spirit of the Illiniwek with the scaled body of a swamp beast, with taloned feet and monstrous wings, had been painted high on the bluffs overlooking the Mississippi River. Its human face was adorned with a tiger's beard, a bear's fangs, and the antlers of a buck. Legend said it had once lived nearby and preyed on the flesh of men.

It was just south of that site, in the fertile flood plain called America Bottom, that France would establish its key forts and trading posts, links in a long and thin line connecting New France to the Gulf of Mexico via the Mississippi and Illinois rivers. Kaskaskia, Cahokia, and Prairie du Rocher became the first European settlements in Illinois. In 1720, they built Fort de Chartres, the most imposing stronghold in the West. They built it too close to the riverbank—the fort suffered regular flood damage and had to be upgraded three times by the 1750s. That same year a Frenchman named Renault arrived to mine for gold. When he found none, he sold to Illinois its first African slaves, laborers for whom he now had little use. They were purchased by the French families who had formed semi-communal farms at these early frontier settlements.

The name *Illinois*, in fact, derives from the explorers adding a French ending to the Indian word *Illini*, the land of the Illiniwek.

1805

WILLIAM OGDEN BORN

William Butler Ogden, Chicago's first mayor (1837–1841), was born on this day in Illinois history in western New York. He came to Chicago 30 years later.

"I was born close to a sawmill, was cradled in a sugar trough, christened in a mill pond, early left an orphan, graduated from a log schoolhouse and, at 14, found I could do anything I turned my hand to and that nothing was impossible," Ogden wrote. And in Chicago he indeed turned his hand to many things. He came to Chicago in 1835 to plat land purchased by his brother-in-law. Unimpressed by the boggy, unsettled terrain, Ogden informed his sister that the land grab had been an act of "great folly." But once the land was drained and divided into lots, and began to sell at three times the original purchase rate, the young New York land speculator decided to stay in Illinois.

Ogden immediately became one of the prime movers of the fledgling city. He helped coordinate the digging of the Illinois & Michigan Canal, worked to draft and submit a city charter to the Illinois General Assembly, and, in 1837, once that charter was granted and Chicago became a city, William B. Odgen was elected its first mayor. He ran as a Democrat and defeated Whig candidate John Kinzie, another important city founder.

Ogden, whose term lasted two years, was a shrewd and generous mayor. He taxed citizens heavily to improve the city's appearance. He designed the first swing bridge over the Chicago River, funded city institutions like Rush Medical Center and the McCormick Reaper Works, and donated the land on which Holy Name Cathedral was built—securing Catholic support for his civic projects. When told by his secretary that he was worth $1 million, Mayor Ogden responded amusingly, "By God . . . that's a lot of money!" He later turned to the transportation industry and built the first railroad out of Chicago, the Galena & Chicago Railroad, in 1848. He eventually became the first president of the Union Pacific and played a key role in Chicago's becoming the transportation hub of a nation.

Ogden lost nearly all his possessions in the Great Chicago Fire of 1871 and died six years later on August 3, 1877.

- JUNE 16 -
1858
LINCOLN DELIVERS HIS "HOUSE DIVIDED" SPEECH

Abraham Lincoln delivered his momentous "House Divided" speech in Springfield on this day in Illinois history, while accepting the nomination for U.S. Senator at the Republican State Convention.

More than 1,000 delegates gathered at the old statehouse to select Abe Lincoln as their challenger for the U.S. Senate seat held by Illinois Democrat Stephen A. Douglas. Lincoln was chosen at around 5 p.m., and he addressed the assembled crowd as their official nominee three hours later. His speech was titled "A House Divided Against Itself Cannot Stand," paraphrasing the New Testament. Lincoln spoke directly and bluntly to the issue of the day—slavery:

> I believe this government cannot endure permanently half slave and half free. I do not expect the Union to be dissolved—I do not expect the house to fall—but I do expect it will cease to be divided. It will become all one thing or all the other. Either the opponents of slavery will arrest the further spread of it, and place it where the public mind shall rest in the belief that it is in the course of ultimate extinction; or its advocates will push it forward, till it shall become alike lawful in all the States, old as well as new—North as well as South. Have we no tendency to the latter condition?

He then spoke of the threat posed by Senator Douglas, together with his allies in the Supreme Court, to nationalize slavery. Many in the hall felt that Lincoln's words were too radical, inappropriate for the occasion. William H. Herndon, Abe's law partner, felt Lincoln was being courageous but premature by taking such a bold and public antislavery stance. Others said that he lost the Senate race then and there; in fact, Lincoln did lose to Douglas, however narrowly. Nevertheless, it was this speech and the historic series of Lincoln-Douglas debates it spawned that would launch Abraham Lincoln into national prominence.

He was elected to the United States presidency two years later.

- JUNE 17 -
1931
PRESIDENT HERBERT HOOVER REDEDICATES LINCOLN'S TOMB

President Herbert Hoover led a rededication ceremony at Lincoln's Tomb, at Springfield's Oak Ridge Cemetery, on this day in Illinois history.

The 117-foot granite tomb, first dedicated on October 15, 1874, is the final resting place for Abraham Lincoln; his wife, Mary; and three of their four sons—Edward, William, and Thomas. (Robert Todd, the eldest and only of Lincoln's children to survive into adulthood, is buried at Arlington National Cemetery in Virginia.) After the president's assassination, a committee of prominent Springfield citizens fronted by Governor Richard Oglesby raised nearly $250,000 in private contributions to fund the tomb's construction, and held a contest in which the winning design would be awarded a $1,000 prize. That design—submitted by Vermont sculptor Larkin

Photo courtesy of Library of Congress, LC-US262-132051

Mead—featured a 100-foot obelisk, a series of bronze statuary (representing Lincoln, along with the military themes of infantry, artillery, cavalry, and navy) on the exterior, and a granite interior where can be found the famous words of Secretary of War Edwin M. Stanton: "Now He Belongs to the Ages."

The interior was redesigned in 1930–31, which occasioned the rededication address delivered by President Hoover. The rotunda features a small model of the Lincoln Memorial in Washington, D.C., along with famous quotes and scenes from Lincoln's remarkable life and times. Mary Todd Lincoln and three of the children rest in a vault in the southern wing; the president is entombed beneath in a reinforced-steel vault, the response to an attempted grave robbery in 1876. (Hoping to gain a $200,000 ransom, the gang of thieves had planned to bury Lincoln at the Indian Dunes until they were paid. They were caught by the Secret Service in the middle of the act, with the casket halfway removed from the tomb.)

The city of Springfield had originally planned to bury Lincoln at the site of the current Illinois Statehouse—then a large wooded area called the Mather Block—but was overruled by hiss widow, who preferred the recently dedicated Oak Ridge Cemetery.

- JUNE 18 -
1924
BASKETBALL GREAT GEORGE MIKAN BORN IN JOLIET

On this day in Illinois history, the NBA's first great "Big Man," George Mikan, was born in Will County.

The 6-foot-10-inch center, not exceptionally tall for the game by today's standards, stood far above the competition throughout his basketball career. Mikan never made the cut for his Joliet Catholic High School basketball team. Big men, awkward and slow, did not dominate the game back then. But at Chicago's DePaul University, under the tutorship of legendary coach Ray Meyer (who guided the Blue Demons for an amazing 42 seasons) the "Gentle Giant" not only made the starting five, but became the team's MVP, dominated the NCAA, and single-handedly revolutionized the game of basketball. Meyer directed Mikan in a tireless series of drills—shooting baskets, jumping rope, shadow boxing—to improve both his basketball skills and his coordination. A dance instructor was even hired to improve the big man's footwork. Mikan proceeded to lead the Blue Demons to an 87-17 record from 1942 through 1946, an NCAA Final Four appearance in 1943, and an NIT championship title in 1945. Mikan, who had been snubbed by Notre Dame, was a three-time College All-American at DePaul. The era of the "Big Man" had arrived.

He continued to dominate as a professional. In 1946, Mikan launched his pro career with the short-lived Chicago Gears of the National Basketball League, earning a $12,000-per-year salary. When that league folded he went to the NBA's Minnesota Lakers (later the Los Angeles Lakers) and was that franchise's marquee player for nine seasons. He led the L.A. Lakers to five championship titles, retired as the league's all-time leading scorer (with 11,764 points) in 1956, and was declared among the 50 greatest players in NBA history in 1996. To accommodate Mikan's inimitable presence on the court—always wearing his trademark wire-rimmed glasses—the NBA officially doubled the width of the free-throw line, instituted the goaltending rule, and started using a 24-second shot clock. In 1959 he was enshrined in the basketball Hall of Fame.

George Mikan, basketball's first true superstar, died on June 2, 2005. The 91-year-old Ray Meyer recalled Mikan as being "the greatest competitor I ever coached."

- JUNE 19 -
1974
MOB BOSS SAM GIANCANA
GUNNED DOWN AT HIS OAK PARK HOME

On this day in Illinois history, Sam "Momo" Giancana—head of the Chicago crime syndicate "The Outfit"—was gunned down at his Cook County home just days before a scheduled testimony before a federal grand jury.

Giancana, born on May 24, 1908, in the city's Little Italy neighborhood, led a life of crime and rumor. He joined the local "42 Gang" early and made his mark as an unhinged and sadistic street thug with ambitions to make it big in the city's underworld. He was soon recruited by Frank "The Enforcer" Nitti, successor to Al Capone, and earned a spot as one of the mob's top getaway drivers. His fearlessness and reckless skill behind the wheel—and unflinching willingness to kill—earned Giancana the nickname "Mooney," as in a bark-at-the-moon madman. He shortened it himself to "Momo." As Momo progressed through the ranks of organized crime, all the way to the top of the Chicago Mafia, he made some powerful acquaintances. Among the more wild (but believable) speculations about him were that he had been contracted by the CIA to take out Cuban strongman Fidel Castro; or that, later, he worked in cahoots with President John F. Kennedy on a number of secretive deals, their famous go-between being a shared lover, Hollywood socialite Judith Campbell.

No Capone-like "godfather," Giancana was forced to step down as mob boss in 1966. Though he did expand the power of The Outfit by taking over operations—via a few well-placed assassinations—of the city's "Black Belt," he proved himself too selfish and unpredictable for the position of Chicago's top criminal. (At one point he had contracted a hit on Desi Arnaz for producing the antimob television series *The Untouchables*.) Under increasing heat from the FBI, he spent 1967 through 1974 in Mexican exile, finally extradited back to the United States in 1975. While scheduled to appear before a Senate committee to answer questions pertaining to the old Castro assassination plot, Giancana was on the receiving end of seven slugs from a .22 caliber handgun. The murder took place in his basement kitchen with heavy surveillance, by both the FBI and local authorities, just outside his home. His killer is still unknown.

Giancana, who was arrested 70 times during his colorful career, had mumbled many times his favorite motto: "Live by the sword, die by the sword."

- JUNE 20 -
1673
MARQUETTE AND JOLLIET ARRIVE
TO EXPLORE ILLINOIS COUNTRY

On this day in Illinois history, Father Jacques Marquette and Louis Jolliet, an explorer and land surveyor, arrived via the Mississippi River on the first recorded European voyage into the future 21st state of the Union.

They left from Mackinac Island, site of a Jesuit mission in northernmost Lake Michigan, on May 17. Two narrow birch-bark canoes packed with food, supplies, and gifts for local Indians carried the small expedition to the uncharted wilderness beyond. Marquette and Jolliet were accompanied by five French oarsmen and two Indian guides from the Miami nation. They paddled hundreds of miles down the length of the Mississippi to its confluence with the Arkansas before turning back, surmising that the great river was not, indeed, the ever-elusive Northwest Passage to China. Meanwhile, Illinois Country—as the region was commonly called—was left unexplored on their eastern bank.

On the return trip, near present-day Peoria, Marquette and Jolliet took a detour up the Illinois River. Theirs are the first impressions we have of the Illinois landscape: "We have seen nothing like this river for the fertility of the land, its prairies, woods, and wild cattle [buffalo]. . . . The Illinois River valley is the most beautiful and most suitable for settlement. . . . We have seen nothing like this in all our travels."

They met and befriended a tribe of Kaskaskia Indians along the way. The French explorers learned that the Kaskaskia called themselves "Illiniwek," which translated roughly to "superior men," and were at war with the "inferior" Iroquois to the east and Sioux to the west. They treated the French exploration party, not being Iroquois or Sioux, with great kindness, and seemed more amenable to Christianity than the other tribes. The Frenchmen took note of the Illiniwek's more notable practices: They ate dog meat, made slaves of captured women and children, and devoured the raw hearts of fallen enemy warriors; they covered themselves in tattoos, placed their dead to decompose in tree branches, later placing the fallen bones in a sepulcher, and played a fiercely competitive ball-and-stick game called lacrosse.

So impressed was Father Marquette that he promised to the Kaskaskia a return voyage to build Illinois's first Jesuit mission—a promise he kept.

- JUNE 21 -
1908
VIRGINIA MARMADUKE BORN IN CARBONDALE, ILLINOIS

On this day in Illinois history, Virginia Marmaduke—the "Grand Duchess of Journalism"—was born in Carbondale.

Marmaduke covered, in her own words, the "blood, guts, and sex—not necessarily in that order," of the news at a time when most women reporters were stuck writing for the entertainment or fashion columns. She got her start at the *Herrin Daily Journal,* proving as a young journalist that she could compete with anyone in the business. Marmaduke covered the same stories, but from a woman's perspective. One local casino was driven out of town after she exposed the deleterious effect it had on the local community by interviewing the wives of coal miners who had blown their pay drinking and gambling.

Her break into the big time came in 1943 when she was hired to the crime beat for the *Chicago Sun.* The newspaper editor, who admired Marmaduke for her spunk and assigned her to report on all the city's flamboyant underworld, nicknamed her "Duchess." The name stuck as her reputation flourished, and the Grand Duchess of Journalism not only survived the *Sun*'s merger with the *Times* but signed a larger contract with the *Chicago Tribune* and went on to become one of the city's most notable columnists. She even hosted her own radio program, *A Date with the Duchess,* on WGN.

Her 35-year newspaper career was marked by a number of firsts. She was the first woman on the editorial staff of a major Chicago daily; the first woman reporter to cover sports (harness racing) in the city; and, in 1979, the first female columnist declared Press Veteran of the Year by the Chicago Press Veterans Association. But Marmaduke, despite all her big-city success, always returned to her southern Illinois home. She spoke of the campus at Southern Illinois University in Carbondale as the "loveliest university in the whole state," and devoted much of her retirement to fund-raising for SIU. She became the school's official ambassador in 1970, founded four scholarships for aspiring journalists, and could regularly be found offering advice to students on the university grounds.

Virginia Marmaduke, whose proudest moment came as hostess for the Land of Lincoln pavilion at New York's 1964 World's Fair, died on November 8, 2001, at the age of 93.

- JUNE 22 -

1922

HERRIN COAL-MINER RIOT ENDS IN MASSACRE

Nineteen nonunion coal miners were slain in the Herrin Massacre after 24 hours of violence, in downstate Williamson County, on this day in Illinois history.

The United Mine Workers of America, who in Illinois had won the eight-hour workday and higher wages along with other key demands in previous strikes, had the entire country gripped in the midst of a nationwide coal strike in the summer of 1922. Miners at Herrin, Illinois—located in the middle of the second-largest coal field in America—dutifully followed the orders of the national union. The Southern Illinois Coal Company attempted to break the strike by firing its unionized workers, hiring scabs from Chicago, and resuming mining at the nearby Lester strip mine, under the protection of armed guards. The Herrin members of the UMWA felt threatened at the sight of $250,000 worth of coal being shipped out by nonunion workers—a scene that could undermine everything they had achieved through previous labor disputes. Tensions arose, leading to a series of calamitous events that gained national attention.

On June 21, a report of a busload of scabs en route to Herrin being attacked by a UMWA mob outside Carbondale reached town. The sheriff of Herrin left town to investigate the incident—in his absence, the union miners attacked. The gunmen hired to defend nonunion workers at the Lester strip fired upon the attackers, taking the lives of three union miners in the ensuing mayhem. This riled the UMWA belligerents to regroup and lay siege to those inside the mine. They looted Herrin hardware stores for guns and ammo and returned on the offensive. The Lester strip was surrounded, phone lines cut, and the nonunion workers and gunmen agreed to surrender for the promise of safe return to Chicago.

But a peaceful retreat was not allowed to the mine's defenders. After laying down their arms, many were hoarded together and told to make a dash for Chicago—they were shot in the back as they ran. One group of six was taken to a nearby school, where they were tortured and murdered by union thugs. The *St. Louis Globe-Democrat* called the massacre "the most brutal and horrifying crime that has ever stained the garments of organized labor."

The UMWA miners involved were cleared of all murder, conspiracy, and rioting charges, and sympathetic Herrin, Illinois, residents raised their full $410,000 bail.

- JUNE 23 -

1911

JOHN MCDERMOTT WINS U.S. OPEN AT CHICAGO GOLF CLUB IN WHEATON

On this day in Illinois history, 19-year-old John McDermott became the youngest ever champion of the U.S. Open, and the first native-born American to win the prestigious golf tournament.

The U.S. Open, one of the four major championships of golf (the Masters, British Open, and PGA Championship round out the list), was held in 1911 for the third time since the traveling tourney's 1895 inception at the Chicago Golf Club. (The previous two were held in 1897 and 1900.) The Chicago Golf Club, actually located in Wheaton, Illinois, the seat of DuPage County, was established in 1892 by a group of Chicago businessmen. Inspired by the legendary Royal and Ancient Golf Club

of St. Andrew's in Scotland, architect Charles Blair Macdonald designed the nine-hole course on 60 acres of farmland donated by A. Haddow Smith, a recent Scottish immigrant and devoted golfer. Macdonald and 30 of his colleagues pitched in $10 apiece to construct the course, the first in the United States west of the Alleghenies. Nine more holes were added the following year, making Chicago the home of the first 18-hole golf course in America.

The U.S. Open had been dominated by golfers from the United Kingdom for the first 16 years of its existence, but a young American upstart from Philadelphia, Pennsylvania, was about to make history. Johnny McDermott—who according to legend was able to knock three dozen golf balls in a row into a rolled-up newspaper—had dropped out of the tenth grade to study golf. His pinpoint accuracy was unrivaled in the golf world. McDermott shot 307 in 72 rounds, forcing a three-way playoff between himself, British pro George Simpson, and fellow American Mike Brady. In the end, McDermott prevailed, becoming the first American-born U.S. Open champion.

The U.S. Open has returned to Illinois several times since: at Medinah Country Club in DuPage County (1949, 1975, and 1990), Midlothian Country Club (1914), North Shore Golf Club in Glenview (1933), Olympia Fields Country Club in Matteson (1928, 1935, and 2003), and Skokie Golf Club in Glencoe (1922).

- JUNE 24 -
1832

BLACK HAWK LEADS 200 WARRIORS IN A SIEGE OF APPLE RIVER FORT

On this day in Illinois history, the veteran Sauk warrior Black Hawk personally led a large war party against the sparsely defended Apple Rover Fort at present-day Jo Davies County.

It was one of the most remarkable skirmishes of a 16-week war, and the only military stronghold engaged directly by Black Hawk's forces. Apple River Fort, near the lead mines of Galena, was hastily erected that May as Illinois's northernmost outpost. It was garrisoned at the time by only 13 militiamen, under the command of Captain Clack Stone. They were joined by several of their wives and a number of local settlers seeking protection. This modest force was far outnumbered by more than 200 Sauk and Fox warriors under Black Hawk's command. Four soldiers, dispatched from Galena en route to deliver a message to General Henry Atkinson at Dixon's Ferry

Photo courtesy of Abraham Lincoln Presidential Library

(present-day Dixon), had just left the fort when, about 300 yards outside its gate, they were fired upon by Black Hawk's band. Three soldiers withdrew back into the fort, and the fourth, Frederick Dixon, made a speedy retreat back to Galena to alert the colonel there of the assault.

For 45 minutes the fort's defenders held off the advancing Sauk and Fox warriors. Captain Stone and Elizabeth Armstrong are credited with rallying those inside against the overwhelming odds; Stone positioned all available men and rifles along the stockade walls, while Armstrong organized the women into two squads—one to stockpile ammunition, another to reload the rifles after being discharged. Thinking the fort better defended than it actually was, and having lost several warriors, Black Hawk called off the attack and was content to pilfer the nearby settlement cabins, which had been abandoned. The garrison suffered only two casualties. A relief column arrived from Galena the following day, and soon no less than 400 federal cavalry and 2,600 mounted Illinois militia under Atkinson's command pursued Black Hawk's band.

Apple River Fort was spared, and Black Hawk, from that point forward, fought a defensive and ultimately disastrous campaign against superior numbers.

- JUNE 25 -
1862
UNION LEAGUE OF AMERICA FORMED IN PEKIN

On this day in Illinois history, the Union League of America was formed in Tazewell County to promote loyalty to the Union during the Civil War.

The original secretive society had just 11 members, who vowed to "support, maintain, protect, and defend the civil liberties of the Union of these United States against all enemies either domestic or foreign." They were motivated to challenge local Copperheads, northern Democrats who sympathized with the South, and to stem growing discontent in southern Illinois after several early Union defeats to the Confederacy in the early months of the war. Membership soon swelled, spreading patriotism across the state, and in late September the first statewide council was held in Bloomington, Illinois, at which a dozen county chapters of the Union League were represented. Joseph Medill, a staunch Republican and publisher of the *Chicago Tribune,* was appointed chair of the executive committee. The following March the Grand Council met in Chicago, representing 404 chapters throughout the state—complete with secretive handshakes and unwritten agendas—and by this time the Union League had sprouted up in Ohio, Indiana, Michigan, Minnesota, Wisconsin, and Iowa as well. Membership in Illinois alone was in the tens of thousands.

The Union League supported local candidates who were "true and reliable men" and, in turn, supported the war effort. Quietly, they also raised money and supplies for Union troops. More than $25,000 in cash raised by Union League officers, for example, reached the Sanitary Bureau of Springfield in 1864, to care for wounded soldiers. Another of their silent but effective contributions to the war effort was providing protection to Illinois Governor Richard Yates after assassination threats. Postwar operations focused on securing the loyalty and protecting the rights of emancipated Southern blacks.

The presence of the Union League spurred the creation of a rival secret society in the South, the Ku Klux Klan, which eventually drove off the league's influence in the South after radical Reconstruction in the late 1870s.

ABRAHAM LINCOLN SPEAKS OUT
AGAINST DRED SCOTT DECISION

Abraham Lincoln, who had made his first public speech opposing slavery in March 1837, spoke out vehemently against the Dred Scott Decision on this day in Illinois history.

Dred Scott and his wife, Harriet, were slaves who unsuccessfully went to court to sue for their freedom. Scott's owner, Dr. John Emerson, traveled extensively in his capacity as a U.S. Army doctor. He brought much of his property—human or otherwise—along on his journeys. The basis of the couple's claim, after having resided with their owner for several months in Rock Island, Illinois—upon free soil—was the principle of "once free, always free." Scott went to court in 1847, financed by his original owners, the Blow family of Virginia, who wanted to see the aging couple freed. In a long, drawn-out case that escalated to ever-higher courts, the U.S. Supreme Court in 1857 ultimately decided against the Scotts, with a vote of 7–2. Delivering the majority opinion that slaves—as property—cannot be interfered with by the federal government, Chief Justice Roger B. Taney condemned Dred and Harriet back into bondage.

Photo courtesy of Library of Congress, LC-US262-5092

Dred Scott

Lincoln in turn condemned that decision. "The Dred Scott decision is erroneous," he addressed the crowd, and in so doing directly hectored those, like his chief political opponent, Steven A. Douglas, who supported the court's opinion. "Chief Justice Taney, in delivering the opinion of the majority of the Court, insists at great length that Negroes were no part of the people who made, or for whom was made, the Declaration of Independence, or the Constitution of the United States," Lincoln said, driving home the historical facts. "On the contrary . . . in five of the then thirteen states, to wit, New Hampshire, Massachusetts, New York, New Jersey and North Carolina, free Negroes were voters, and, in proportion to their numbers, had the same part in making the Constitution that the white people had."

Thus Lincoln argued that the two dissenting justices of the Supreme Court were correct, and their opinions, not that of the majority, ought to thereafter be used as the legal precedent.

- JUNE 27 -
1844

MORMON LEADER JOSEPH SMITH KILLED BY MOB AT CARTHAGE, ILLINOIS, PRISON

Joseph Smith, leader and prophet of the Mormon Church based in Nauvoo, Illinois, met his fate at the hands of a hysterical mob while imprisoned in Hancock County on this day in Illinois history.

Nauvoo was in essence an autonomous city. The Mormons there had garnered a favorable charter through the sympathy of state legislature; they were allowed their own courts and university, and they passed their own laws and raised their own militia. Joseph Smith's Mormon Legion numbered 4,500 men at arms—the largest militia in Illinois and second in size nationally only to the U.S. Army. Local opposition among Gentiles—as the Mormons called nonmembers—grew as the city exerted more and more influence over Illinois politics. Residents in nearby Carthage and Warsaw feared the political activism coming out of Nauvoo. They accused Smith and his followers of plotting to establish a religious oligarchy, and rumors began to spread of the practice of polygamy—which turned out to be true—further alienating Smith's flock from their Illinois neighbors. (Smith, after claiming to have received a revelation from God in 1833 that encouraged the practice, himself took at least 33 wives.)

Joseph and Hyrum Smith statue outside Carthage jail

In 1844, the prophet announced his candidacy for president of the United States. A schism in the church soon followed, with Smith's detractors criticizing his political aspirations as tyranny, and denouncing the practice of polygamy. *The Expositor,* a Mormon paper established to give voice to the opposition, never published again after Smith promptly ordered the press destroyed and burned all remaining copies of the newspaper. A warrant for Smith's arrest on the charge of causing a riot was issued in the Hancock County seat of Carthage, and the prophet, along with his brother, Hyrum, turned himself in. The very evening Governor Thomas Ford was in Nauvoo assuring the Mormon community that Joseph Smith would be treated fairly, an anti-Mormon mob stormed Carthage Jail—with the collusion of the guards—and murdered the prophet and his brother before a trial could be held.

Smith became a martyr, more violence would follow, and Nauvoo would be nearly emptied of Mormons within a couple of years.

- JUNE 28 -
1989
ARLINGTON PARK REOPENS AFTER FIRE

On this day in Illinois history, Arlington Park in suburban Arlington Heights, the most beautiful horse-racing park in the Midwest, reopened its grandstand after rebuilding from a devastating 1985 fire.

Arlington Park—showcase for "The Sport of Kings"—first opened on October 13, 1927, and soon took the lead in setting trends for horse-racing venues across America. It installed the nation's first totalizator (an electric "tote board" for tracking races and wagering) in 1933, and not long thereafter became one of the earliest parks to utilize turf racing, electric starting gates, and a photo-finish camera (the "Eye in the Sky"). In 1967, it installed the largest closed-circuit color-TV system of any sports arena in the world. In 1971, Arlington Park held the nation's first commercially funded, $100,000 horse-racing event—the Pontiac Grand Prix—and ten years later inaugurated the world-renowned Arlington Million. That first big race saw Bill Shoemaker jockeying his Thoroughbred John Henry to pass the 40-1 underdog, The Bart, along the final stretch to claim the purse.

The thrilling moments looked to be over when fire swept through the clubhouse and devoured the grandstands on July 31, 1985. But while some meets were relocated to nearby Hawthorne Racetrack, the 1985 Arlington Million was held later that summer at its namesake, with 35,000 spectators filling the temporary bleachers that around-the-clock crews had worked tirelessly to construct. At what was dubbed the "Miracle Million," because so many had doubted it could be pulled off, Teleprompter defeated Greinton by less than a single length in one of the most thrilling races in the track's history. After the marvelous new six-story grandstand reopened as Arlington International Racecourse in 1989, the park continued to make history, including the unstoppable Cigar winning his 16th consecutive race at the 1996 Arlington Citation Challenge. (In 2000, the course's name reverted to Arlington Park after Churchill Downs Inc. bought the property.)

The world's top Thoroughbreds, jockeys, and trainers—following in the footsteps (or hoof marks) of Secretariat, Eddie Arcaro, and Ben Jones—come to Arlington Park every summer in hopes of claiming horse racing immortality.

- JUNE 29 -
1841
OGLE COUNTY REGULATORS SEEK VIGILANTE JUSTICE

A group of more than 100 Ogle County citizens took the law into their own hands and served as judge, jury, and executioner for two notorious local outlaws, on this day in Illinois history.

The Rock River Valley of the 1830s and 1840s was still very much a lawless frontier. Organized bands of rogues preyed on new settlers. Law enforcement was feeble, so much so in Ogle County that Governor Thomas Ford, then a sitting circuit judge in Oregon, Illinois, reflected that bandits were "so numerous, strong, and organized that they could not be convicted for their crimes." Foremost among the outlaws operating in and around Oregon were the so-called Banditti of the Prairie.

Leading the Banditti was the Driscoll family. A dreadful lot, John Driscoll and his four sons (David, Pierce, Taylor, and William) were notorious arsonists and horse thieves whose dubious exploits drew the ire—and vengeance—of the fledgling settlement community. A group of citizens, perhaps led by Ford, formed a vigilante group called the Regulators, intent on driving Driscoll and his breed from the region.

The Regulators issued a decree to the Banditti to get out of town or be horsewhipped. While some outlaws fled, the Driscolls responded by burning down the home of W. S. Wellington, first captain of the Regulators, and killing his horse. Wellington was sufficiently intimidated and resigned, but John Campbell, a neighbor of Driscoll's, took his place. Campbell and another Regulator leader were then ambushed and killed. News of the murders spread, and bands of Regulators organized the following morning to apprehend the murderous Driscolls. David and Taylor had fled, but John was taken in by a group of Oregon vigilantes and his two remaining sons—Pierce and William—by a group from nearby Rockford.

The next day at a nearby clearing called Washington Grove beside the Rock River, the Driscolls faced a jury of Regulators. Pierce was declared innocent (spared perhaps for his young age of only 13), but John and William were judged guilty and sentenced to death. Their final request was to be shot, rather than "hanged like dogs." Lined up before a firing squad of 111 rifles—56 for John and 55 for William—the father-and-son Banditti duo were executed on the spot. After some muted indignation in the *Rockford Star* for this vigilante justice, Judge Ford held a rigged trial in which 100-plus Regulators were summarily acquitted of murder.

Outlaw bands thereafter steered fairly clear of operating in Ogle County.

- JUNE 30 -
1932
DNC DELEGATES DEBATE THE NATION'S FUTURE IN CHICAGO

The 26th Democratic National Convention was in day four of debates on nominees for the U.S. presidency—including Franklin D. Roosevelt—on this day in Illinois history.

After a 12-year drought, both the Republican and the Democratic national conventions returned to Chicago in the summer of 1932. The Great Depression was approaching its nadir, and both political parties were scrambling for a solution to the nation's economic woes. But Chicago was in a celebratory mood. Preparations for the upcoming Century of Progress Exposition and the city's centennial had begun, and Governor Henry Horner had dedicated a group of "Lincoln" buildings on Chicago's lakefront, including a replica of the Wigwam, which had hosted the 1860 RNC nomination of the 16th president of the United States. The Republicans came first (June 14–16 at the Chicago Stadium), argued mostly over the continuation of Prohibition, and renominated sitting President Herbert Hoover. The Democrats followed (June 27–July 2), adopted a decidedly "wet" platform calling for the repeal of Prohibition, and nominated New York Governor Franklin Delano Roosevelt.

FDR would break with decades of convention tradition by boarding a plane to accept his nomination in person—the first presidential candidate ever to do so. He won the nomination on the fourth ballot, defeating fellow New York politician Al Smith by virtue of a backroom deal whereby a third contender, Speaker of the House John Nance Garner from Texas, allocated his votes to FDR in exchange for the vice presidency. Arriving on July 2, FDR famously addressed the assembled delegates: "These are unprecedented and unusual times. . . . I pledge you, I pledge myself, for a New Deal for the American people." He called for new order of "confidence" and "courage," and beat the beleaguered Hoover in a landslide, winning 89 percent of the electoral votes and all but five states. FDR was elected to an unprecedented four terms, and his New Deal agency, the Work Progress Administration, employed thousands of out-of-work Illinoisans, funded dozens of Illinois museums and historical societies, and was instrumental in renovating numerous state parks such as Starved Rock and Massac.

President Franklin Delano Roosevelt was renominated for his third term in Chicago at the 1940 DNC, and again—"reluctantly but like a good soldier"—a fourth time in 1944.

This day in

July

- JULY 1 -
1911
OPENING DAY CEREMONIES AT
GREAT LAKES NAVAL TRAINING CENTER

The United States Naval Training Station at North Chicago—later renamed the Great Lakes Naval Training Center—officially opened at high noon, after six years of construction, on this day in Illinois history.

The *Chicago Record-Herald* described the moment: "Suddenly a siren whistle sounded, a gun was fired, the admiralty flag mounted to the top of the building flagpole, and the Stars and Stripes sailed upward in the presence of the audience. The band was playing 'The Star-Spangled Banner.' " Pomp and circumstance abounded at the founding, and the first recruits, who would form the inaugural graduating class of 300 sailors, started coming through the gates two days later.

Photo courtesy of Great Lakes Naval Museum Association

The base was inspired by President Theodore Roosevelt and made a reality thanks to the efforts of Illinois politicians and Chicago businessmen. It was an unconventional idea, training the U.S. Navy so far away from any ocean, but Teddy Roosevelt, former assistant secretary of the Navy, had observed that many of the best sailors had come from the Midwest—why not train them closer to home? Cost was a huge obstacle, though: The 137-acre lakefront site in Lake County carried a price tag of almost $1,000 per acre—an insurmountable fee during peacetime. Illinois Congressman George E. Foss, who had been lobbying for the base, announced that a consortium of wealthy businessmen, organized by the Merchants Club of Chicago, would purchase the site and sell it to the U.S. Navy for the price of $1. The deal was quickly made.

Chicago architect Jarvis Hunt was hired to design the base. The centerpiece of the 39-building complex was the towering Romanesque-style Building One, which had the bow of a sailing ship installed over its main entrance. Six years and $3.5 million in appropriations later, the training station was complete. Designed for 1,500 people, it saw little activity for several years, but in April 1917, 9,000 recruits arrived for boot camp as the United States entered World War I.

Great Lakes Naval Training Center has been training sailors ever since, and with a recent multimillion-dollar investment for new buildings and upgrades, it looks to be safe from lists of base closings in the foreseeable future.

ILLINOIS STATEHOUSE FINALLY COMPLETED

After 20 years of construction, and $4.5 million in expenditures, the state capitol building in Springfield was finally completed on this day in Illinois history.

Governor Richard James Oglesby was serving his first term in 1868 when construction began, and was in his third (nonconsecutive) term when the building was finished. It was Illinois's sixth statehouse—after the original in Kaskaskia, three more in Vandalia, and a lone predecessor in Springfield, now the Old Capitol Building. The General Assembly had first moved into the unfinished sixth Illinois statehouse in 1876, eight years before completion.

It is an impressive structure. The base, designed in crucifix form—379 feet from north to south and 268 feet from east to west—sits on a landscaped nine-acre plot. The site, called the "Mather Block," is the highest point in Springfield. The statehouse features a classically styled facade, Romanesque roof, four matching sets of Corinthian columns at the base of the dome, and a central rotunda illuminated by 20 large circular windows. The immense dome, supported by 17-foot solid limestone walls sunk more than 25 feet into the ground, towers 362 feet aboveground. The flagstaff rises an additional 40 feet from its summit. (An airplane beacon atop the capitol also once served, in the days before communication by radio, as a police signal.) The six-floor interior, hosting government offices, spirals upward, decorated by bas-relief sculpture, depicting Illinois history and statues of prominent Illinois statesmen, and capped with an elaborate display of stained-glass windows. The building's centerpiece is a statue titled *Illinois Welcoming the World*, situated on the ground-floor rotunda directly beneath the dome's apex.

The statehouse has survived several fires over the decades. A few occurred during construction, as workmen's lanterns ignited parts of the dome. The first major fire was in 1886, as "dense volumes of black, stifling smoke" caused great damage to the "handsomely frescoed walls and ceilings," according to an account in the *Illinois State Register*. The worst blaze caused $100,000 in damage in 1933 before the fire department, with some hands-on help from Governor Henry Horner, put out the flames.

A number of memorials to former governors, senators, and groups of individuals, such as coal miners and firefighters who helped build and preserve the state of Illinois over the years—surround the statehouse building.

- JULY 3 -
1904
CHICAGO'S RIVERVIEW AMUSEMENT PARK OPENS

"The World's Largest Amusement Park" opened its gates on Chicago's Northwest Side on this day in Illinois history. "Let's All Go to Riverview" was its motto.

Riverview Amusement Park was built on 22 acres of shooting range-turned-picnic grounds bounded by the Chicago River and Western and Belmont avenues. The land was owned by Wilhelm Schmidt and George Goldman, two former members of a defunct German gun club, who decided to build a more family-friendly venue on the site after Schmidt's son, George, returned home with tales of the amusements parks he'd visited in Europe. This was just one decade after Chicago's Columbian Exposition. The city was nostalgic for the rides, games, and amusements that had been the envy, and playground, of the world ten years earlier. Schmidt and Goldman secured investors and built the park.

Riverview Sharpshooters Amusement Park opened its gates to 25,000 excited Chicagoans that July morning. The park's top attractions included a toboggan slide, a giant swing, a tunnel of love, a carousel, and a miniature railroad. Riverview also featured a midway promenade—in the tradition of the 1893 World's Fair—with food, games, and live musical performances. The foot-long hot dog was introduced at Riverview in the 1930s and was soon an established Depression-era favorite.

The owners continually expanded and improved Riverview. In 1907, half a million dollars were invested on several new attractions, including the Top roller coaster and Shoot-the-Chutes water ride. The Bobs, a famous roller coaster was built in 1926 for $80,000. Its high speeds, 85-foot drop, and screeching gears thrilled riders like no ride ever had before. Riverview Amusement Park by then covered more than 150 acres, and included an ostrich farm, a river walk, and an 18-story Ferris wheel. The 1950s saw the addition of three new roller coasters and the popular Hot Rods racing cars. The Space Ride was added in 1963, so patrons could ride across the sky and survey the magical world below.

After the 1967 season, Riverview Amusement Park closed its gates forever because of financial losses, and three generations of Chicagoans were crushed.

- JULY 4 -
1778
GEORGE ROGERS CLARK CAPTURES KASKASKIA FROM BRITISH

George Rogers Clark captured the British fort at Kaskaskia without firing a shot on this day in Illinois history.

Clark, elder brother of the more famous William of Lewis and Clark fame, is called the "George Washington of the West" for his Illinois campaign against the British during the Revolutionary War. It was learned that the British were paying Illinois warriors for the scalps of Virginia settlers. A major in the Virginia militia, Clark was commissioned as lieutenant colonel and authorized to command up to 350 men. He then received secret orders from Governor Patrick Henry of Virginia, which held claim to the Illinois territory, to raise these troops and secure the frontier by capturing Kaskaskia and other British strongholds.

Photo courtesy of Abraham Lincoln Presidential Library

Garrison Cemetery at Fort Kaskaskia

With most American troops engaged in the East, Clark was able to muster only 175 frontiersmen. Nevertheless, he set out in June of 1778 to oust the British from Illinois. He sent spies forward and won the neutrality of local Indians. Then he and his men marched for six days, at times in single file and disguised as Native Americans to avoid detection by British scouts, and surrounded Kaskaskia on the evening of July 4. Clark's meager force occupied the town without a fight, capturing the weakly fortified Fort Gage by surprise and its unsuspecting commander, Philippe de Rocheblave, in his sleep.

Clark and his men were embraced by the French residents, who were promised American citizenship in exchange for allegiance to the Commonwealth of Virginia. Father Pierre Gibault, the local pastor and a great influence on the locals, was promised religious freedom. The town celebrated its liberation from British rule by ringing what has come to be known as "The Liberty Bell of the West."

Word spread throughout the region of Clark's generosity, and soon the Illinois towns of Cahokia, Prairie du Rocher, and St. Philippe—all originally French settlements—likewise surrendered without a struggle. This base of support set the stage for General Clark's heroic capture of the key British fort at Vincennes, at the present-day Illinois and Indiana border, later that winter.

Were it not for Clark's campaign, the states of Illinois, Indiana, Michigan, Ohio, and Wisconsin might well be Canadian provinces today.

- JULY 5 -
1918

STEAMER *COLUMBIA* SINKS IN ILLINOIS RIVER NEAR PEKIN

On this day in Illinois history, 85 lives were lost when the excursion steamer *Columbia* split in two and sank in 20 feet of water in Tazewell County.

Having departed Peoria earlier that evening, many of the approximately 500 passengers on board the Columbia were gathered on a lower-deck dance floor. Mostly members of the South Side Social Club of Pekin, they were returning from a family day-trip to a carnival. The 125-foot vessel was, as were most steam-powered riverboats of the day, very broad with a flat-bottomed hull that made it virtually impossible to capsize. But it did not capsize—that is, keel over side-to-side—it split in two. Close to midnight the *Columbia,* navigating through thick fog and too close to the shore, struck a submerged stump. The jolted ship broke through the center, causing chaos in the rapidly submerging dance hall. "Everybody upstairs!" the captain hollered, "She's going down!" Within three minutes the *Columbia* was in splintered, sinking ruins.

The *New Excursion Steamer*
COLUMBIA.
"GEM OF THE OCEAN."

The carnage would have been much worse if it had not been for a quick-thinking ship's engineer by the name of Davis. By opening up the safety valve to the boiler room, he prevented a likely explosion that would have claimed many more lives. (In 1865, a steamboat bound for Cairo, Illinois, exploded, killing nearly 2,000 passengers.) Tossed about the lower deck—along with a piano, a soda fountain, and a multitude of decorative fixtures—men and woman scrambled toward the upper deck or escaped through the shattered plate-glass windows. Fortunately, most of the children survived, having remained upstairs in the late evening hours.

Rescue workers eventually pulled 83 bodies from the river, and two remained missing. The sinking of the steamer *Columbia* became one of the worst inland-water tragedies in Illinois history.

- JULY 6 -

1933

CHICAGO'S COMISKEY PARK HOSTS FIRST MAJOR LEAGUE ALL-STAR GAME

National League All-Stars squared off against their American League counterparts for the inaugural Major League All-Star Game, at the home of the Chicago White Sox, on this day in Illinois history.

Roughly 49,200 baseball fans packed Comiskey Park to witness the 4–2 American League victory and were delighted at the sight of a third-inning two-run homer by Yankee great Babe Ruth—the first home run in All-Star Game history. The St. Louis Cardinals' Frankie Frisch belted out the National League's first long ball in the sixth inning, but it was not enough to overcome the final two-run deficit. Hall of Famers Connie Mack and John McGraw managed the American and National League teams, respectively. The Cubs were represented by shortstop Woody English, catcher Gabby Hartnett, and pitcher Lon Warneke. The Sox sent third baseman Jimmy Dykes—the only Chicago ballplayer chosen as a starter by the fans—and outfielder Al Simmons. Former White Sox superstar second baseman Eddie Collins also coached from the American League bench.

The historic matchup was conceived by *Chicago Tribune* sports editor Arch Ward (who also dreamed up the college football all-star games played for so many years at Wrigley Field). Billed as "the game of the century," it was scheduled to coincide with Chicago's Century of Progress World's Fair. Starting a tradition that exists to this day, the fans selected which players would represent the two leagues. American League players took the field in their respective team's home jerseys while the National League team wore specially designed matching uniforms.

Aging slugger Ruth—"the Bambino"—went two for four and made a game saving eighth-inning catch in the outfield.

- JULY 7 -
1946

CHICAGO'S MOTHER CABRINI CANONIZED
AMERICA'S FIRST SAINT

On this day in Illinois history, Mother Frances Xavier Cabrini—who became a miracle worker to the state's immigrant poor—was canonized Patron Saint of Immigrants by Pope Pius XII.

Maria Francesca Cabrini was born on July 18, 1850, on the family farm near San Angelo, Italy. She had 12 older siblings. Drawn to missionary work as a young child, she took religious vows in 1877 and taught at a local Catholic orphanage. Always wanting to establish a missionary in China, Mother Cabrini was asked by Pope Leo XIII to care for the masses of immigrants arriving in America from the old countries. "Not to the east, but to the west," he told her. "You will find a vast field for labor in the United States." She arrived in New York City in 1889 and immediately began raising money for a new orphanage, eventually founding 67 institutions (one for each year of her life on earth) spanning the country from New York to Chicago, Seattle to New Orleans.

Naturalized as a U.S. citizen in 1909, the frail little foundress was embraced as a worker of great miracles by her fellow immigrants and citizens. Beginning with empty pockets but full of dreams, Mother Cabrini founded four large hospitals, two of which were built in Chicago, as well as schools, charitable houses, and nurses' homes—all serving the needy urban areas of America. Surviving on pure charity, her institutions were always open to non-Catholics, and the contributions came flowing in from Catholics and non-Catholics alike. She could be a shrewd businesswoman, too. Once, while negotiating the price of a Chicago property, Mother Cabrini felt uneasy about the sellers' promises and sent two sisters out with tape measures to double-check the lot size. Her miracles included the restoration of sight to a young boy and the healing of a nun afflicted with terminal illness.

Mother Cabrini died of malaria on December 22, 1917, at a Chicago hospital.

On this day in Illinois history, William Jennings Bryan delivered the most triumphant speech in the annals of national conventions at the 1896 Democratic National Committee, held at the Chicago Coliseum.

The 36-year-old Bryan, a native of Salem, Illinois, was at best a dark-horse candidate going in but maneuvered to win over a majority of delegates with what he promised the night before would be "the greatest speech of my life." And it was. Bryan was polling seventh in a pack of candidates led by Richard Parks Bland—or "Silver Dick"—of Missouri. Silver, indeed, was the buzzword of the convention; most Democrats championed the free coinage of silver to lift the nation, and in particular the nation's farms, out of the economic woes of the 1890s. Their opponents, the "Gold Bugs," represented the northeastern banks, business trusts, and railroads that advocated for the gold standard. President Grover Cleveland, a Democrat, likewise supported gold and therefore lost any chance of renomination among his own party.

Photo courtesy of Library of Congress, LC-US262-86705

The contest was wide open. Bryan, knowing he'd need to preserve his booming voice to reach the packed hall, declined an early invitation to be chairman of the convention (which would require constant shouting over crowds). He also declined the keynote address, instead choosing the final slot on the speaking schedule.

His closing speech drove the assembled delegates into a frenzy. "If they dare to come out in the open field and defend the gold standard as a good thing, we will fight them to the uttermost," Bryan invoked. "We will answer their demands for a gold standard by saying, 'You shall not press down upon the brow of labor this crown of thorns; you shall not crucify mankind on a cross of gold.'" Once finished, he held his arms outstretched like a crucifix and faded backward from the stage. A spellbound group of supporters carried Bryan upon their shoulders around the convention hall. Bryan ultimately defeated Bland in a unanimous landslide.

Owing largely to an incessant Republican smear campaign by the East Coast newspapers and the defection of the National Democrats, who formed their own ticket, Bryan lost the 1896 presidential election to GOP nominee William McKinley.

- JULY 9 -
1893
FIRST SUCCESSFUL OPEN-HEART SURGERY
PERFORMED IN CHICAGO

Dr. Daniel Hale Williams successfully operated on a stab victim, in what may be the first successful open-heart surgery, at his Provident Hospital on Chicago's South Side, on this day in Illinois history.

Williams graduated from Chicago Medical School, now Northwestern University Medical School, in 1883. One of only three African American physicians in Chicago at the time, he secured a position at the South Side Dispensary where he would practice medical surgery for several years. Most of his patients came from City Railway Company and the Protestant Orphan Asylum. He concurrently taught anatomy at Northwestern University through the late 1880s. Despite personal success, Williams was keenly aware of the limited opportunities available to African American physicians and nurses, as well as the generally inferior treatment provided to blacks at city hospitals.

He founded the interracial Provident Hospital and Training School Association, as a remedy to social inequities in the field of medicine, in January 1891. The three-story building, with just 12 beds, trained black nurses and doctors and achieved an exceptional 87 percent recovery rate for its 189 patients, during its first year. Williams's insistence on sanitation and embrace of the most innovative surgical procedures were largely responsible for this success. It was in this setting that a local man, James Cornish, was carried to the Provident Hospital emergency room with a life-threatening stab wound to the chest. Williams, assisted by six physicians, opened the man's chest, exposed the beating heart, and sewed up the near-fatal gash. With a prayer, Williams closed and sutured the incision, and the world's first open heart surgery was complete. Cornish walked out of the hospital one month later, fully healed.

After this amazing feat, President Grover Cleveland appointed Williams surgeon-in-chief of the Washington, D.C., Freedmen's Hospital.

- JULY 10 -
1925
WGN RADIO, CHICAGO, BROADCASTS THE SCOPES MONKEY TRIAL

WGN's Ryan Quinn became the first announcer to broadcast a live trial on American radio, the landmark Scopes Monkey Trial, which began on this day in Illinois history.

Radio was still in its infancy. The highly sensationalized trial from the small town of Dayton, Tennessee, had ignited controversy across the nation and provided the perfect opportunity for a media revolution. John T. Scopes, a local teacher born in Salem, Illinois, was accused of violating Tennessee's recently passed Butler Act, which prohibited the teaching of the evolution of man, as opposed to biblical creationism, in the public schools. (Scopes's textbook was not Darwin's *The Origin of Species,* but George Hunter's *Civic Biology,* which also featured the now-discarded theory of eugenics and advocated quite explicitly for white supremacy. But it is unlikely that Scopes actually taught either theory in the classroom.) The courtroom devolved into an exercise in oratorical grandstanding. The trial pitted modernists who dismissed the Bible as pure superstition, with Scopes as their hero, against Christian fundamentalists who embraced a literal interpretation of the sacred texts.

Two Illinois attorneys played prominent roles in the drama. Clarence Darrow, Chicago's preeminent defense attorney and nationally famed agnostic, argued in Scopes's defense. William Jennings Bryan, four-time Democratic presidential nominee from Salem, Illinois, and an outspoken advocate of Christianity, represented the prosecution. In a bold move, the two lawyers challenged one another to cross-examination, and each in turn was held in contempt of court for exchanging insults. A more thrilling made-for-radio scenario could not have been scripted.

WGN was there to bring the unfolding drama to millions. The effort, with four microphones placed in the courtroom and hundreds of miles of AT&T cable extending up to Chicago, cost the one-year-old radio station $1,000 dollars a day. Quinn, who kept his commentary colorful but tastefully brief, observed, "We're like moon men here. . . . the radio guys from outer space." After an eight-day trial, the jury ruled against Scopes—a decision eventually overturned by the Tennessee Supreme Court—and the WGN radio crew packed up and returned home.

The Scopes Monkey Trial was a watershed event in the history of law, education, and the media in the United States, and Illinoisans played central roles in each instance.

- JULY 11 -
1886
CHICAGO'S STREETERVILLE NEIGHBORHOOD BORN

On this day in Illinois history, Captain George Wellington Streeter ran his steamboat, the 35-ton *Reutan*, aground on a sandbar just off Chicago's north shore—and refused to leave.

The "Cap," as he was called, declared that the land belonged to him and dubbed it the "District of Lake Michigan," beyond the jurisdiction of the state of Illinois. There, upon the stranded wreck, he and his crew—consisting of his common-law wife, Maria—made their home. Mayor John Wentworth had recently cleared the area of squatters, but Streeter argued—convincingly—that this was "built land," and no legal documentation existed to prove that is was indeed a part of Chicago. After the Great Chicago Fire of 1871, Streeter invited local contractors to dump their debris on and around his island. What resulted was 186 acres of landfill now known as Streeterville. Though the police forcibly removed Streeter at one point and the courts finally declared his claims to be without merit in 1918, he returned to defend his land with a shotgun until his death in 1921.

While Streeter, his wife, and the *Reutan* are long gone, Streeterville is now the site of some of the city's most celebrated landmarks. After Streeter's death, what the *Chicago Daily News* described as "a program of building activities unsurpassed by any district of similar size in the world" ensued on the formerly contested acreage. On the site today can be found the art deco Palmolive Building; the high-class Drake Hotel; and the North Lakeshore Drive Apartments, designed by the world-renowned architect Mies van der Rohe. Water Tower Place, the Museum of Contemporary Art, and, of course, the John Hancock Center—the city's signature skyscraper—were later additions to Streeterville.

Streeter's heirs continued to sue for the land until Maria Streeter was declared ineligible, because they had never legally married, and a Cook County court ruled against a group of nieces and nephews in 1928.

- JULY 12 -

1995

CHICAGO HEAT WAVE BEGINS

A brutal five-day heat wave that claimed several hundred lives in Chicago started on this day in Illinois history.

The heat wave began on July 12 and peaked the following day at 106° F. Unrelenting temperatures in the mid-90s to low 100s continued to punish the city until the heat finally broke at 89° F on July 17. The city was one big heat trap, brick and concrete buildings baked like ovens, and residents set their air-conditioning units and fans on high, taxing Chicago's power supply beyond its limits. An energy surge led to the failure of several power grids, and at one point 49,000 households were without electricity. The power outage led to a worst-case scenario.

The heat wave caused up to 739 deaths over the five-day span. It was the worst natural disaster in the state since the Great Tri-State Tornado of 1925, and the second highest death toll in Chicago after the *Eastland* disaster of 1915. The intense heat, accompanied by record levels of humidity, caught the city off guard. An official heat warning was not issued until July 16, four days after the heat wave began. Some expressed denial. "It's hot," Mayor Richard M. Daley told the press. "But let's not blow it out of proportion. . . . Every day people die of natural causes. You cannot claim that everybody who has died . . . dies of heat. Then everybody in the summer that dies will die of heat." The media echoed the mayor's somewhat convoluted skepticism, asking if the heat-related deaths were "really real." Federal relief was nowhere in sight.

But by the end of the week, with the city morgue full, Cook County had to use refrigerated trucks to hold the bodies. Fire engines substituted for ambulances and, in at least one instance, were used to hose down sweltering schoolchildren whose bus had broken down. Most of the victims were elderly citizens who lived alone in the inner city, isolated from their neighbors and neglected by their families. They refused to open their windows or sleep outdoors (as Chicagoans had done in earlier eras during hot summer months) for fear of crime.

The heat wave of 1995 was not the first or worst suffered by the state, as the summer of 1936 (during the hottest decade on record) saw nine straight days of 100° F—plus temperatures in Rockford—with nowhere near the toll in human life however.

- JULY 13 -
1911
FALL OF SENATOR LORIMER

On this day in Illinois history, William H. Lorimer, who had been elected to the U.S. Senate in 1909, lost his seat after Congress declared his election victory invalid based on "corrupt methods and practices."

Lorimer was a self-educated son of English immigrants who was elected by Illinois voters to the U.S. House of Representatives for the first time in 1894. He served two three-term stretches (1895–1901, 1903–09) before leaving that office to claim his Senate seat. The "Blond Boss," as he was nicknamed, worked his way to the Senate floor by way of a kaleidoscope of deals dating back to his days as a West Side Chicago ward boss, and continuing through his maneuvering for votes in the Illinois General Assembly.

Photo courtesy of Library of Congress, LC-DIG-ggbain-03644

U.S. Senators were yet to be popularly elected. Though advisory elections or primaries were held—and often ignored—where voters could show their support for the candidates, the two houses of the state legislature ultimately decided who would hold Illinois's two Senate seats. When Republican incumbent Albert J. Hopkins failed to establish a clear majority of support in the 1908 primaries, Congressman Lorimer blocked his re-election. He then initiated an 18-week debate during which congressmen clamored over dozens of potential replacements, and finally won support of 53 Democrats and 55 Republicans for himself to assume Hopkins's seat.

Within a year, Senator Lorimer was in trouble with the public eye, and his downfall was imminent. Charles A. White, a Democrat from O'Fallon, Illinois, told the *Chicago Tribune* about payoffs made to get Lorimer elected. Direct payments of up to $1,000 had been added to a general slush fund of $100,000 and divvied up between legislators in return for their votes. Lorimer had won his Senate seat by bribery. The scandal had national repercussions, splitting the Republican Party and precipitating a surge in the Progressive Movement that demanded, among other things, an end to such political corruption. After a lengthy investigation and weeks of harsh debate, the U.S. Senate expelled William Lorimer from his seat by a vote of 55–28.

Lorimer was a prosperous Chicago businessman until his death on September 13, 1934, and he was interred at the city's Catholic Calvary Cemetery.

- JULY 14 -
2001
FINAL TV BROADCAST OF *BOZO'S CIRCUS*

WGN-TV, on this day in Illinois history, aired its last episode of the children's daytime classic that was adored by millions and featured Bozo the Clown.

Bozo's Circus debuted on September 11, 1961, and became the longest-running children's show in American television history. The Bozo character was actually born in California (much like that other clown, franchised to become famous in Illinois, named Ronald McDonald), appearing on a series of children's records for Capitol Records. WGN purchased the rights to feature Bozo in their programming, and in 1959 Bob Bell first donned the clown suit to host a half-hour animated series. That show was soon dropped and Bozo briefly forgotten. But Bell returned with the orange hair, red suit (changed to blue in later years), and ridiculously oversized shoes in *Bozo's Circus* two years later. The concept was changed to incorporate old vaudeville skits and feature live performances, and a new phenomenon was born. Every day at lunchtime schoolchildren would rush home to catch the one-hour bonanza. It became the most popular program of the 1960s and 1970s, was syndicated (or imitated) throughout the country, and Bell remained the show's ebullient anchor for another 23 years. He was replaced by comedian Joey D'Auria, who played Bozo the Clown from 1984 through 2000.

The show was full of unforgettable characters and thrilling games for those lucky enough to be chosen to participate from the live studio audience. There was Cooky the Cook, Ringmaster Ned, and Mr. Bob the Bandleader with his three-piece orchestra. The Grand Prize Game, with one boy and one girl drawn daily by the "magic arrow," was the highlight of every show, and millions dreamed of landing that ping-pong ball in bucket number six to win the brand-new Schwinn bicycle and pail full of silver dollars. But the beginning of the end came in 1994, when the FCC stipulated that all children's programming must adopt an educational format. It was no longer pure entertainment: Gone were the magic arrows, silly cartoon segments, and the soul of a children's show that had made a legend of Bozo the Clown.

Bozo's Circus achieved such astounding popularity in its heyday that at one point there was a ten-year waiting list for tickets, and young couples submitted the names of children yet to be born.

- JULY 15 -
1900
ZION CITY FOUNDED AS CHRISTIAN UTOPIA

On this day in Illinois history, world-renowned evangelist Dr. John Alexander Dowie founded a city in Lake County in hopes that it would become a Christian utopia.

Dowie—a religious zealot whom many have claimed to be a fraud—was a Scottish clergyman who immigrated to the United States by way of Australia and established the Christian Catholic Church in Zion in 1896. He declared himself the First Apostle and promised to build a city to serve as a refuge from the "reign of lawlessness" in the big city. His motto: "Where God rules, man prospers." He won followers via seemingly miraculous acts of faith healing, the most notable being Sadie Cody, niece of Buffalo Bill, during the 1893 World's Columbian Exposition. Followed by about 5,000 adherents, Dowie built Zion City on Lake Michigan's shores in the northeasternmost corner of the state, 41 miles north of downtown Chicago. There, he set some strict laws to govern the town. Alcohol, tobacco, and pork were all banned; likewise, citizens were forbidden to wear cosmetics, attend the theater (none existed in town), or even whistle a tune in public. Dowie believed the world was flat and refused to allow trains to stop in Zion on Sundays. Politicians were also banned.

Zion, named for the hill upon which Jerusalem sits, was to become a place of interracial harmony, a Christian theocracy free of crime and vice, and a moral beacon for the rest of the world. But when Dowie started identifying himself as Elijah the Restorer—after the prophet of the Old Testament—his star began to fall. In spite

City of Zion, 1904

of Dowie's baptizing 10,000 converts, circulating his *Leaves of Healing* Zionite newspaper to 40,000 subscribers, and having reportedly healed thousands under his ministry, the claim was too wild for many church members to handle. By 1906 Dowie was deposed from power and denounced by most contemporary religious leaders. His ministry was gone and Zion fell into economic depression, but a successor, Wilbur Voliva, helped revive the church and town and in 1922 established the nation's first Christian radio station (WCBD).

John Alexander Dowie died a miserable man amid increasing criticism, fallen from the path but still believing he was Elijah, on March 9, 1909, and was buried in Zion.

- JULY 16 -

1915

FIRST STATE FLAG BECOMES OFFICIAL

Legislators in Springfield, after a three-year contest, adopted the winning design for a state flag on this day in Illinois history.

Photo courtesy of Jeff Ruetsche

In 1912, Ella Park Lawrence of Galesburg, Illinois, launched a campaign to design the official state banner. As the fourth Illinois Regent of the Daughters of the American Revolution (DAR)— a national organization of patriotic women descended from Revolutionary War heroes—Lawrence had traveled to Washington, D.C., where she noticed that Illinois had no official banner displayed alongside those of the other states at Memorial Continental Hall, a DAR war memorial, beside those of the other states. To remedy this, she commissioned a competition, inviting all chapters of the DAR across Illinois to submit designs for a long-overdue state flag. The winning chapter would receive $25.

Thirty-five banners were submitted between 1913 and 1914, and in the end of the judging, the design of Lucy Derwent from the Rockford DAR chapter was chosen above all others. Based on the official state seal, it featured a bald eagle perched on a rock above rich prairie soil. Emblazoned on the rock are the years 1818, for Illinois statehood, and 1868, when the state seal was originally created by then–Secretary of State Sharon Tyndale. Clutched in the eagle's beak is a red ribbon marked with Illinois's motto: "State Sovereignty, National Union." (Interestingly, this is phrased in reverse order atop the dome at the state capitol in Springfield—no doubt the result of endless debates over which has preeminence.) A red, white, and blue shield, consisting of 13 stars and stripes to represent the original 13 colonies, rests against the rock.

This flag flew for 55 years, before the letters I-L-L-I-N-O-I-S were added in blue beneath the design in 1970.

- JULY 17 -

1917

BASEBALL HALL OF FAMER LOU BOUDREAU BORN IN HARVEY

Louis Boudreau, who returned home to both manage and work the radio booth for the Chicago Cubs after his stellar player-manager days in Cleveland, Ohio, was born in Cook County on this day in Illinois history.

Boudreau was captain of the baseball team at the University of Illinois in Urbana-Champaign when he signed a contract to play professionally for the Cleveland Indians organization after graduation. He debuted in the majors in 1940, making the All-Star team in his first season (seven times total) and quickly establishing himself as a solid hitter and "slick-fielding" shortstop. In 1941, Boudreau—who topped all American League shortstops in fielding percentage eight times—earned the distinction of putting the final out to Joe DiMaggio's 56-game hitting streak. The following season, the 24-year-old Boudreau became player-manager of the Indians, the youngest to skipper a ball club from opening day in major-league history. In 1948, he experienced his dream season, winning the World Series as manager while contributing a .355 batting average, 18 home runs, and 106 RBIs at the plate, as well as being named the league MVP. After ending his playing career in Boston in 1952, Lou retired from the field to become a full-time manager in the American League through 1957.

He returned to Chicago, as a broadcaster—or so he thought. In 1960, erratic Cub owner Philip K. Wrigley, unhappy with the team's performance, swapped Boudreau's role with that of loquacious team manager Charlie "Jolly Cholly" Grimm. The lackluster Cubs went 54-83 from that point on in the season, after which Grimm retired and Boudreau was returned to the radio booth in 1961. There, he would remain as color commentator for the better part of three decades, even working occasionally with the legendary Jack Brickhouse on WGN-TV. While known to butcher players' last names from time to time—an endearing quality shared by fellow Chicago play-by-play man Harry Carry—Boudreau's game-play analysis was second to none. He was elected to the National Baseball Hall of Fame in 1970.

Lou Boudreau died on August 10, 2001, after resettling in Chicago's south suburbs, and is buried at Pleasant Hill Cemetery in Franklin, Illinois.

- JULY 18 -

1940

FDR NOMINATED AT CHICAGO STADIUM FOR UNPRECEDENTED THIRD TERM

President Franklin Delano Roosevelt, on this day in Illinois history, was nominated for an unprecedented third term to the White House during the Democratic National Convention in Chicago.

FDR had served two terms, since 1933, during one of the most trying decades in American history. The Great Depression was not yet a thing of the past, though the

worst of it was over. The United States sat on the unwelcome precipice of entering another world war as the totalitarian juggernauts of Nazi Germany and imperial Japan visited death and destruction upon both hemispheres. During a time when most Americans were not looking for change in the White House, the nomination was all but a foregone conclusion before the convention even began. It was like a Joe Louis fight, opined the *Chicago Tribune*, "over before the crowd got settled." Meeting July 15–18, 1940, that crowd cast its unanimous vote for the sitting president, hoping he could deliver a knockout punch to the troubles that threatened America and the world.

What the 1940 DNC in Chicago may have lacked in political drama, it made up for in setting a number of precedents. For the first time, the Democrats adopted a simple majority vote, replacing the long-standing two-thirds rule required for a winning nominee. For the first time, the convention was scheduled around a national radio audience, with the marquee speeches and events occurring during prime-time evening hours to ensure greater numbers of listeners. And for the first time, owing to the recently passed Hatch Act, a far smaller percentage of government workers served as delegates (with the goal of cutting down on election fraud). In full force were the League of Women Voters and the National Colored Democratic Association, both advocating a platform that championed equal rights. Many of the record 1,849 delegates in town also attended the third annual Chicago Police and Fire Show at Soldier Field, and bought out the vendors' souvenirs labeled "F. D." It stood for "Fire Department," but the enthusiastic Democrats mistook it for Franklin Delano's initials.

FDR went on to defeat the Republican nominee, Wendell Willkie, 449 to 82 electoral votes in the November election.

CAHOKIA MOUNDS DESIGNATED NATIONAL HISTORIC LANDMARK

The Cahokia Mounds—immense remains of an ancient Native American civilization near present-day Collinsville—were designated a National Historic Landmark on this day in Illinois history.

Covering 2,200 acres off the eastern banks of the Mississippi River, the network of earthen mounds was once a city of 10,000–20,000 inhabitants that thrived from the 8th through the 15th centuries. The central mound (called Monks Mound for the community of French Trappist monks who settled there in the early 1800s) is the largest prehistoric earthwork in the United States; a truncated pyramid some 100 feet high and 700 by 1,000 feet at the base, it consists of more than 20 million cubic feet of compacted soil. The pyramid is surrounded by more than 100 smaller mounds, each likewise built by hand, suggesting slave labor, fanatic religiosity, or both. Each mound served as the platform for ceremonial buildings, residences, and—for the elite—burial

Domestic scene at ancient Cahokia

Photo courtesy of Illinois Historic Preservation Agency

sites. Atop Monks Mound stood a palace for the city's ruler that was approximately (archaeologists suggest) five stories high. Four large wooden solar calendars called "woodhenges" align at the equinoxes, marking the start of summer and winter with the rising sun to the east at dawn.

With the original inhabitants long gone, the site was occupied by the Cahokia Indians, a tribe of the Illiniwek Confederacy, when French explorers arrived in the late 17th century. But archaeologists have been able to discover plenty about those who built the fascinating site. Called the Mississippian Culture, the civilization peaked around 1100–1200 AD—long before Europeans or even the Illiniwek arrived in Illinois. The Mississippians developed an agricultural economy with sophisticated governmental, religious, and social organizations. Cahokia Mounds was their capital, with major satellite cities at East St. Louis and Lebanon, Illinois, and St. Louis, Missouri, and numerous outlying hamlets in the region. It was, at the time, larger than most major European metropolitan areas.

In the mid–15th century, perhaps because of deluge, disease, war, or the depletion of natural resources—their true fate is unknown—the Mississippian people suddenly disappeared.

- JULY 20 -
1888

CHICAGO ATTORNEY BECOMES
CHIEF JUSTICE OF U.S. SUPREME COURT

On this day in Illinois history, one of the state's most prominent attorneys, Melville Weston Fuller, had his nomination as chief justice of the U.S. Supreme Court confirmed by the U.S. Senate.

Fuller was born and raised in the state of Maine, the son of a lawyer and grandson of a judge, and started his own law practice there in 1855 at the age of 22. The following year he left for Chicago. There, he became a prominent attorney and was deeply involved with the Illinois Democratic Party. Within two years, Fuller was arguing

before the Illinois Supreme Court, and about two decades later he appeared before Judge Morrison Waite, chief justice of the U.S. Supreme Court, whose robes he would don in 1888. In 1860, Fuller managed Illinois Senator Stephen A. Douglas's presidential campaign against Abraham Lincoln, and he was later elected as a Democrat to the Illinois House of Representatives, where he served for one term (1864–66). Fuller was sent five times as state delegate to the Democratic National Convention between 1864 and 1880, delivering the nomination speech of Indiana governor Thomas Hendricks for vice president in 1876. The Democrats lost that election, but returned with a ticket of Grover Cleveland and Hendricks again as the vice presidential candidate to retake the White House in 1885, and Fuller thereafter had a good friend in a very powerful position.

When Fuller was nominated to the highest position in the federal court system by President Grover Cleveland, after the death of Justice Waite in March of 1888, he may have been well known in Illinois, but was a relatively obscure figure nationally. After a lukewarm reception in the U.S. Senate, he was confirmed by a 41–20 bipartisan majority. Chief Justice Fuller was sworn in on October 8, 1888, and served until his death on July 4, 1910. Major cases during his judgeship included *Kid v. Pearson* (1888), which upheld the illegality of manufacturing liquor in states with temperance laws, and *Plessy v. Ferguson* (1896), which would infamously be used in later years to establish the legal precedent for separate but equal facilities based on race.

It was Justice Fuller, the jovial leader of the Court, who started the custom whereby each justice greets the others with a handshake at the start of each session.

Photo courtesy of Library of Congress, LC-US262-90767

- JULY 21 -
1899
ERNEST HEMINGWAY BORN IN OAK PARK

Hemingway, member of the so-called Lost Generation of American writers who came of age in post–World War I France, was born in suburban Cook County on this day in Illinois history.

He lived a life greater than any fiction. Hemingway—best known for the use of rugged imagery and machismo in his semi-autobiographical prose—had a peculiar childhood. His mother dressed him as a girl in his early years, calling him Ernestine; later, as a preteen, he embraced the more masculine pastimes of hunting, boxing, and football with his father. After graduating from Oak Park High School, where he edited the school paper, Ernest served a three-month stint as a reporter in Kansas City, Missouri, before setting off on a life of adventure.

Hemingway first went to Europe to serve as a volunteer ambulance driver in France and Italy during the Great War. There, he immediately witnessed the brutality of armed conflict and was wounded on the Italian front by mortar fire in July 1818. His own leg torn by shell fragments, Hemingway saved a soldier's life by carrying the wounded man to safety on his back, and for this he was awarded the Italian Silver Medal of Valor. Hospitalized in Milan, he fell in love with a nurse from Washington, D.C. She, however, fell in love with another wounded soldier, thus inspiring the failed romances and broken hearts of Hemingway's popular novels. He would have four marriages and three divorces in his life.

After the war, he settled in Paris and became close friends with fellow expatriates Gertrude Stein, Ezra Pound, and James Joyce. (He later smuggled copies of Joyce's banned *Ulysses* into the United States.) During this time he composed some of his greatest works: *The Sun Also Rises, Men Without Women,* and *A Farewell to Arms.* Further adventures for "Papa"—Hemingway's nickname—included an African safari, raising funds to fight the fascists in Spain, and confronting German SS officers as a war correspondent in World War II France. He was an ardent fan of bullfighting, which, too, became a recurrent theme in his writings. Hemingway published his masterpiece, *The Old Man and the Sea,* in 1952, which earned him both the Pulitzer Prize and the Nobel Prize for literature.

Haunted by personal demons, Ernest Hemingway—like his father before him—took his own life with a gun on July 2, 1961.

- JULY 22 -
1934
JOHN DILLINGER SLAIN OUTSIDE CHICAGO THEATER

Notorious bank robber John Dillinger—the Federal Bureau of Investigation's "public enemy number one"—was gunned down outside Chicago's Biograph Theater on this day in Illinois history.

He had a $10,000 bounty on his head and hundreds of federal agents on his trail after three months on the lam at the time of the ambush. Dillinger, an embittered 30-year-old ex-con from Indianapolis, Indiana, turned to a life of crime in 1933. Within

a year he had led his flamboyant gang (several of whom ended up on Chicago's Most Wanted list) in several high-profile bank heists, netting more than $300,000 and capturing the imagination of Depression-era America. After being caught in March of 1933 but sprung by his gang from an Ohio prison, Dillinger was finally captured again in Arizona in 1934. A charismatic thug whose exploits dominated the nation's headlines, Dillinger told reporters, "I'm innocent, but I'll probably get the works. They got me charged with everything from strangling a goldfish to stealing the socks off a blind man." While awaiting trial for the January murder of a police officer during a bank job in Chicago, Dillinger again escaped from behind bars at the "escape-proof" Crown Point Prison in Indiana.

Narrow escape followed narrow escape, and he finally had minor plastic surgery in Chicago to conceal his identity. But Dillinger's downfall would come through his one weakness: women. Confident of his relative obscurity in the big city, Dillinger took his latest in a long string of girlfriends, Polly Hamilton, out for a night on the town. But Hamilton's landlord, a Romanian brothel owner named Anna Sage, had Polly's new boyfriend pegged, and she offered to help nab him in exchange for not being deported. The famous Lady in Red (her dress, the signal to mark Dillinger, was actually orange), Sage accompanied the couple to the upscale Biograph Theater that night. When the three exited after viewing *Manhattan Melodrama*—the fabled outlaw with one lady on each arm—Dillinger was shot four times by federal agents who lay in ambush. He died before hitting the ground. Sage, despite the tip-off, was deported to Romania, but with $5,000 in reward money from the FBI.

Crowds gather at site of Dillinger's slaying

- JULY 23 -
2003
EVANSTON NATIVE CHARLTON HESTON
AWARDED PRESIDENTIAL MEDAL OF FREEDOM

Charlton Heston, the Evanston-born actor known for portraying Moses, Ben-Hur, and astronaut George Taylor from the sci-fi classic *Planet of the Apes*, was awarded the Presidential Medal of Freedom on this day in Illinois history.

Heston's acting career began at Winnetka High School in the early 1940s, where he won a full drama scholarship to Northwestern University in Evanston. He left college in 1944 to join the U.S. Air Force and served for three years before launching an acting career. In 1947, he debuted to wide critical acclaim on Broadway in a presentation of the Shakespearean-based classic *Antony and Cleopatra*. Heston moved to Hollywood in 1950 and got his big break starring in 1952's *The Greatest Show on Earth*. He achieved superstardom in Cecil B. DeMille's *The Ten Commandments*. Thereafter Heston was one of the nation's most identifiable stars on the big screen. Coming of age in Hollywood in the era of epic film making, he is considered one of the greatest leading men in movie history. He won the Academy Award for Best Actor in 1959 for his leading role in *Ben-Hur*.

Heston has also been politically active throughout his acting career. In the 1960s, Heston was a highly visible supporter of the civil rights movement. He marched with Dr. Martin Luther King Jr., on Washington, D.C., in 1963. He also served as president of the Screen Actors Guild, a labor union for film actors, stars and nonstars alike, from 1966 to 1971. The Democratic Party encouraged him to run for California's seat in the U.S. Senate in 1969, but he declined. In later years, Heston became a staunch advocate of the Second Amendment—the right to bear arms—and was elected president of the National Rifle Association in 1998. His activism has at times been grossly distorted by critics. Heston was diagnosed with prostate cancer in 1998 and announced in the summer of 2002 that he suffers from Alzheimer's Disease as well. He retired as the NRA's chief spokesman later that year.

President George W. Bush presented the award, introduced by President John F. Kennedy in 1963 and given annually in recognition of meritorious civilian service to the country. It is the highest nonmilitary honor awarded by the U.S. government.

- JULY 24 -
1915
USS *EASTLAND* CAPSIZES IN CHICAGO RIVER

Eight hundred and forty-four people drowned in the worst maritime disaster ever to strike the Great Lakes region on this day in Illinois history.

The *Eastland,* a 269-foot luxury steamer known as the "Speed Queen of the Great Lakes," was docked at a wharf near the Clark Street Bridge when tragedy struck. More than 2,500 guests of the Cicero-based Western Electric Company started boarding at 6:30 a.m. for what was to be a company picnic and day cruise to Michigan City, Indiana. The ship had recently added several lifeboats that allowed it to increase its capacity; the largest load it had ever carried before this fatal morning was slightly more than 1,100 passengers. The *Eastland,* a ship already reputed as unstable, was made only more top-heavy by the new lifeboats and greater occupancy.

When several hundred passengers rushed to the starboard side of the upper deck to wave goodbye to friends on land, the Eastland began to list gradually from side to side. Captain Joseph Erickson and his crew attempted to right the ship, but the dan-

gerous listing continued as most passengers remained oblivious. The side-to-side rocking of the ship continued to gradually increase by degrees. Feeling secure, some passengers even began cracking jokes, rather than panicking, at the *Eastland's* subtle swaying. By 7:30 a.m., however, while still at the wharf, with the band playing and guests dancing, the *Eastland* finally rolled portside into the shallow, muddy river.

Hundreds died, including 22 entire families, despite desperate attempts to save those trapped in the lower deck. All but three of the ship's crew members were fortunate enough to survive. Another lucky fellow was a young summer hire at Western Electric who would go on to change Sunday afternoons in America forever; George S. Halas—future cofounder of the National Football League and legendary coach of the Chicago Bears—arrived too late that morning to join his fellow employees aboard the doomed *Eastland.*

The *Eastland* itself was salvaged, renamed the *Wilmette* in 1920, and used for training at Lake County, Illinois's Great Lakes Naval Training Center before finally being turned to scrap metal in 1947.

- JULY 25 -
1952

ILLINOIS GOVERNOR RELUCTANTLY ACCEPTS NOMINATION FOR U.S. PRESIDENCY

On this day in Illinois history, Adlai Stevenson, while serving the state's 34th governorship, was nominated for the nation's highest office at the Democratic National Convention in Chicago.

The 1952 DNC was held at Chicago's Amphitheater from July 21 to 26. Stevenson, who earlier that month had requested he be left off the ticket, would by the end of the week be the first Illinoisan to run for the U.S. presidency since Lincoln and Douglas—Illinoisans both—squared off in 1860. Stevenson was elected governor of Illinois in 1948 on a reform platform. He'd broken up organized crime rackets in Rock Island, Peoria, Joliet, Springfield, Decatur, and East St. Louis as well as moving forward with major education, welfare, and state highway construction projects. In short, Governor Stevenson had made (and was making) things happen. Despite his own wishes, the national party felt Stevenson's intellect, wit, and charm was just the elixir needed by Democrats to hold onto the White House from as President Harry S. Truman departed.

On July 26, 1952, Stevenson delivered his eloquent acceptance speech. "I would not seek your nomination for the Presidency, because the burdens of that office stagger the imagination. Its potential for good or evil, now and in the years of our lives, smothers exultation and converts vanity to prayer," he intoned. "I have asked the Merciful Father—the Father of us all—to let this cup pass from me, but from such dreaded responsibility one does not shrink in fear, in self-interest, or in false humility. So, 'If this cup may not pass from me, except I drink it, Thy will be done.'" And then, invoking the challenges of a tumultuous 20th century, Stevenson added, "more important than winning the election is governing the nation. That is the test of a political party, the acid, final test." That test never came for Stevenson, who was defeated in the general election by the Republican candidate, World War II hero of the European front, General Dwight D. Eisenhower.

Stevenson made another failed attempt at the presidency in 1956, losing to the incumbent "Ike," and was appointed U.S. Ambassador to the United Nations by President John F. Kennedy in 1961.

- JULY 26 -
1948
BERNIE SHELTON MURDERED

On this day in Illinois history, Bernie Shelton of the infamous Shelton Brothers Gang, kingpins of downstate organized crime, was gunned down by a hit man sent by rival mobsters.

Bernie, along with his brothers, Earl, Roy, and "Handsome" Carl, was a law-abiding Herrin coal miner before mixing it up with the East St. Louis underworld during Prohibition. Before long, the brothers had assembled a cadre of loyal thugs and muscled their way to the top of southern Illinois crime. They controlled an illicit web of bootleggers, bordellos, and blackjack tables that spanned from Peoria to Metropolis and brought them terrific profits. They warred for years against the local Ku Klux Klan, who raided local stills and speakeasies under the guise of prohibition agents, as well as fellow mobsters, the Charlie Birger Gang, all the while respecting the northern territories of Al Capone and the Chicago syndicate. So audacious were the Sheltons that at one point they modified a gasoline truck into a fair resemblance of a Sherman Tank—with armor plating, gun ports cut into the sides, and a machine gun mounted to the rear—inviting all-out war with their rivals.

Even after the repeal of Prohibition, the Sheltons continued to run illegal gambling and prostitution rackets, and enjoyed a renewed heyday in the "open" city of Peoria during the early 1940s. That era ended, however, with the election of that city's reform-minded mayor, Carl Triebel, in 1945. Soon after, Handsome Carl was assassinated by an old gangland foe, Charles "Blackie" Harris, but Bernie Shelton refused to slow down. He was determined to be the sole kingpin of the region. After snubbing an offer of amity from the Chicago syndicate—a big mistake—the power-obsessed Bernie Shelton was taken out by a single, well-marked shot from an assassin's rifle in front of his Parkway Tavern in Peoria. The following summer, Roy Shelton, who had long since settled down to become a farmer, was similarly gunned down while out plowing his fields. Only Earl lived to see old age.

The murder of Bernie Shelton made big headlines and resulted in underdog Adlai Stevenson—a man who promised, if elected, a fierce crackdown on organized crime—moving into the governor's mansion in 1949.

- JULY 27 -
1970
PLAN UNVEILED FOR CHICAGO'S SEARS TOWER

Mayor Richard J. Daley held a joint press conference with Sears, Roebuck and Company's chairman, Gordon Metcalf, on this day in Illinois history, to announce that the world's largest retailer would build the world's tallest building in downtown Chicago.

Sears was a Chicago institution, and convincing the company to stay in the city during an age when major corporations across America were fleeing to the suburbs was, in itself, a major coup for Daley. But the plan released that day for the 1,454-foot behemoth of glass and steel was the mayor's greatest triumph in building up the city's skyline—it was the exclamation point to all his efforts since taking office in 1955. The building would soar 104 feet higher than New York's World Trade Center, and its 4.4 million square feet of interior space was to be exceeded only by the Pentagon in Washington, D.C. It would be the perfect symbol towering above the City of the Big Shoulders.

Chief architect Bruce Graham was encouraged by Sears to: "Go as tall as the Federal Aviation Administration will let us go." He was a practitioner of the Miesian style—made famous in Chicago by architect Ludwig Mies van der Rohe—and employed it magnificently in designing a structure composed of nine tubular buildings, bundled together, each rising up together from a central core. This innovation created more corner offices with greater views than the standard high rise with just four equivalent sides.

Sears Tower was completed three years later—notably, on time and on budget. Final costs reached $150 million. It is a building of truly Chicagoan proportions: more than 76,000 tons of prefabricated steel; 16,000 bronze-tinted windows; the world's fastest elevator (first to 110th floor in less than a minute); and enough internal wiring to cover the globe nearly twice over. Automated window-washers address the needs of the upper floors, from which on a clear day, can be seen the states of Illinois, Indiana, Michigan, and Wisconsin. There were 1,600 workers on site at the tower's completion.

Excluding decorative spires, Chicago's Sears Tower is still the world's tallest building—despite rival claimants.

JOHN KINZIE MADE CHICAGO'S FIRST JUSTICE OF THE PEACE

On this day in Illinois history, John Kinzie—"Chicago's First Citizen"—was appointed justice of the peace by territorial governor William Henry Harrison, to help adjudicate the small settlement outpost.

Kinzie was a Quebec-born trader from Detroit, Michigan, who had moved west along with the American frontier and become one of Chicago's earliest and most prominent settlers. He came to te Illinois Territory in 1804, just one year after Captain John Whistler had arrived with federal troops to secure the Chicago portage by building Fort Dearborn. The 40-year-old trader made a fast impression both on the local Indians and the garrison's soldiers. He befriended all, traded with all, and prospered at the mouth of the Chicago River in his home and trading post, which was originally built by the area's first permanent settler, Jean Baptiste Pointe DuSable, in the 1770s. Clearly the civilian leader of the area (though some officers at the fort later begrudged his selling of whiskey to the Native Americans) Kinzie was an obvious choice for justice of the peace, and he performed Chicago's first marriage ceremony for James Abbott and Sarah Whistler (the captain's daughter) in November 1804. Kinzie, owing to his popularity among the Potawatomi, was spared along with his wife, Eleanor, son, John H., and daughter, Ellen, during the ghastly Fort Dearborn Massacre of 1812. More than 60 soldiers and settlers were not so lucky.

After abandoning Chicago during the War of 1812, the Kinzie family returned to find their home—like themselves four years earlier—spared by the Native Americans, who had burned Fort Dearborn to the ground. Other settlers arrived, the fort was rebuilt, and John Kinzie resumed his prosperous business in the burgeoning hamlet of Chicago. His wealth and influence grew, and Kinzie eventually established posts along the Rock, Illinois, and Kankakee rivers, exuding considerable influence in the economic and social development of the region. He remained in Chicago until his death. His son ran in but lost the city's first mayoral election in 1833, and his daughter-in-law, Juliette Kinzie, later published *Wa'Ubam, or the Early Days in the Old Northwest*, one of the first histories of Chicago.

Kinzie died on January 6, 1828, and was first buried at Fort Dearborn, later moved to the original City Cemetery on the North Side, and finally relocated to Graceland Cemetery when the old cemetery became Lincoln Park.

- JULY 29 -
1858
LINCOLN AND DOUGLAS MEET AT THE
BRYANT COTTAGE TO PLAN DEBATES

On this day in Illinois history, Abraham Lincoln and Stephen A. Douglas met at the home of Francis E. Bryant, in the town of Bement, Piatt County, to discuss the celebrated series of one-on-one debates to be held for the 1858 U.S. senatorial campaign.

Douglas, the two-term incumbent, was a close friend of Bryant, who as a banker, merchant, and recently elected mayor of Bement had helped to organize a network of small-town businessman in support of the senator's reelection. Illinois Republicans

Photo courtesy of Library of Congress, HAEB Collection

had nominated Lincoln, their rising star, to oust Douglas from one of Illinois's two U.S. Senate seats (Lyman Trumbull held the other). Party strategy was to send Lincoln traipsing across the state after Douglas, speaking wherever the Democrat had spoken. While campaigning in Piatt County in late July, Douglas was visiting his friend Bryant when he encountered his opponent on the road between Bement and Monticello, Illinois.

The two men agreed to dine later that night and plan a series of debates rather than continue to address crowds individually. Seven debates would take place in seven towns representing seven of Illinois's nine legislative districts—both candidates had already spoken in Chicago and Springfield. (U.S. Senators were still elected by state legislators at this time.)

The Lincoln-Douglas Debates remain among the most momentous events of their kind in the nation's history. At issue was the expansion of slavery; Douglas supported popular sovereignty, that is, allowing individual territories to decide whether to allow the practice, while Lincoln called for Congress to halt its advance outright.

Douglas won the election, but the debates launched Lincoln to national prominence.

- JULY 30 -
1880
ROBERT McCORMICK BORN IN CHICAGO

On this day in Illinois history, Colonel Robert R. McCormick, publisher of the *Chicago Tribune*, was born to the city on which his life would leave an indelible imprint.

McCormick's grandfather, Joseph Medill, was the *Chicago Tribune*'s founder and a former mayor of Chicago. His father, Robert S. McCormick, served as secretary to U.S. Ambassador to the United Kingdom Robert Todd Lincoln, from 1889 to 1903. After graduating from Northwestern Law School, McCormick assumed the presidency of the Chicago Tribune Company in 1911, and was publisher and editor-in-chief of the *Chicago Tribune* from 1914 until his death in 1955. He, like his father and grandfather, was a staunch Republican and often used the influential paper to voice his political views, defending freedom of speech and freedom of the press while excoriating political opponents. McCormick expanded the scope of the Tribune Company in 1924 when he purchased a radio station, WGN. He had served as a colonel in the U.S. Army during World War I and brought home from his many travels bits and pieces of famous sites from across the globe. These eventually made their way into exterior walls of the Tribune Tower in downtown Chicago, from where WGN continues to broadcast to this day.

A passionate foe of Franklin Delano Roosevelt's, McCormick was a leading member of the isolationists' movement, America First Committee (AFC), which fiercely opposed U.S. entry into World War II. The AFC, in fact, had several core members in the city of Chicago; foremost among them were General Robert Wood, CEO of Sears, Roebuck and Company; Robert Maynard Hutchins, president of the University of Chicago; and William Regnery, director of Hull-House. McCormick—himself a hero of the First World War—assured his readers that "four hundred billion dollars, a million deaths, and several million ruined lives," would be the price to pay for FDR's warmongering. On December 4, 1941, he sent to press secret U.S. government war plans he'd acquired in hopes of exposing President Roosevelt's militancy. But whatever public passions these articles may have stirred were soon wiped put by headlines regarding the surprise attack on Pearl Harbor three days later. It is said that when FDR died in 1945, McCormick hosted a dinner party but refrained from serving Champagne for fear that those in attendance might think he was too brazenly celebrating the passing of an old adversary.

Colonel McCormick died on April 1, 1955, and his 35-room estate, Cantigny, in Wheaton, Illinois, is now a military museum.

- JULY 31 -
1848
JOHN DEERE PLANT OPENS IN MOLINE

John Deere, inventor of "self-polishing" steel plows, opened up a large manufacturing plant in Rock island County for the mass production of farm equipment on this day in Illinois history.

An apprentice to a Vermont blacksmith, Deere came to Illinois in search of greater opportunity in 1836. He set up a forge in the village of Grand Detour, on the Rock River, and had no competition in the small town. He soon learned that local pioneers had become frustrated by the rich, hard-to-plow Illinois soil. It clung to their wooden and cast-iron plows. Farmers needed to stop and clean off the blade every several feet before work could continue. Deere designed an improved self-cleaning plow, fashioned from an old steel-mill saw blade and specially suited for the "gummy" soil of the Illinois prairie. The polished steel handled the soil conditions superbly. Deere began selling handmade models from his small shop in Grand Detour—"10 miles from nowhere."

With increasing demand for his innovative plows, Deere relocated his business to Moline. The Mississippi River offered readily available steel arriving by boat from St. Louis, plenty of water power to operate his mills, and a more accessible distribution route to consumers. By the mid-1850s, John Deere's Moline plant had sold more than 10,000 plows and attracted hundreds of employees and their families to the city. In 1868, his business was incorporated as Deere & Company and began to expand internationally. Still based in Moline, Deere & Company is today one of the world's leading manufacturers of farm equipment, distinguished by its quality products—and green-and-yellow color scheme. Deere once exclaimed, "I will never put my name on an implement that does not have the best that is in me."

He died in Moline on May 17, 1886, having served two years as mayor of Moline and becoming one of the city's leading citizens.

This day in August

- AUGUST 1 -
1843
ROBERT TODD LINCOLN BORN IN SPRINGFIELD

Robert Todd Lincoln, the first and only son of Abraham Lincoln and his wife, Mary Todd, to reach adulthood, was born on this day in Illinois history at the Globe Tavern in Springfield, where the newlyweds rented a room for $4 per week.

In the shadow of his great father, Robert himself established a distinguished career in Illinois business and U.S. politics. He attended Harvard Law School but left without graduating in 1865 to serve in the Union Army. As a captain under Ulysses S. Grant, he was present at Appomattox Court House when Robert E. Lee surrendered. After the war and his father's assassination, Robert moved to Chicago with his mother and younger brother, Thomas. There he completed his studies and was admitted to the bar in February 1867. Robert's most famous case as an attorney was the proceeding he brought against his own grieving mother in 1875, to have her declared insane. The trial resulted in her being committed to a Batavia, Illinois, asylum, and the two remained estranged for the rest of her life.

Photo courtesy of Wikipedia

Robert's meteoric rise to success in both the business world and the political arena is impressive—of course, pedigree was hardly a hindrance. He served as U.S. Secretary of War under presidents James Garfield and Chester Arthur from 1881 to 1885. In 1889, he was appointed U.S. minister to Great Britain by President Benjamin Harrison and held that position until 1893. He returned to his Chicago law practice in 1897 and then served as the president and chairman of the board for the Pullman Company until 1922.

Through bizarre coincidences of history, Robert narrowly missed witnessing the assassination of one U.S. president and was present (though not an eyewitness) for two others. He was invited, but declined, to join his parents at Ford's Theatre the night his father was shot and killed. In 1881, he was in attendance by invitation at the Washington, D.C., train station when President Garfield was gunned down. Again by invitation, Robert was present when President William McKinley was assassinated at the 1901 Pan-American Exposition in Buffalo, New York. He thereafter accepted no further invitations from sitting presidents.

Robert Lincoln died July 26, 1926, in Vermont and is buried at Arlington National Cemetery. He is only member of his immediate family not resting at Oak Ridge Cemetery in Springfield.

- AUGUST 2 -
1832
BATTLE OF BAD AXE RIVER ENDS THE BLACK HAWK WAR

The Black Hawk War ended at the Battle of Bad Axe River—more a massacre than a battle—on the banks of the Mississippi River on this day in Illinois history.

Black Hawk, with hundreds of Sauk and Fox, had been on the run but cut off from escape in Illinois since the Battle of Stillman's Run in May 1832. In pursuit were several thousand volunteer Illinois militia, more than 1,200 federal troops, and hundreds of Potawatomi and Winnebago that Black Hawk had originally hoped to rally to his side. The ensuing summer months were brutal, for both Black Hawk and his band, who were weary of flight and desperate for food, and for white settlements throughout northwestern Illinois, which suffered sporadic raids and at times outright slaughter.

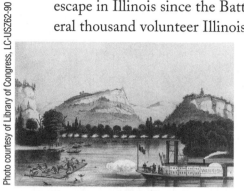

Chaos and carnage at Battle of Bad Axe

Colonel Henry Dodge, commander of a 750-man contingent of volunteers, vowed: "Be assured that every possible exertion will be made to destroy the Enemy crippled as they must be with their wounded and families as well as their want of provision and supplies." And in late July, Dodge and his men finally found Black Hawk's trail. They caught up with the limping band of Sauk and Fox on August 1, 1832, and with federal troops under General Henry Atkinson set out to destroy the tribe utterly.

Black Hawk was pinned down at the banks of the Mississippi, several miles north of his birthplace of Saukenuk (Rock Island, Illinois) in present-day Wisconsin. Dodge was approaching to the east and a U.S. gunship, the *Winnebago,* which had been sent to patrol the river, prevented his escape to the west. He was not allowed to surrender but managed to escape north with a small war party. The remainder of Black Hawk's band was attacked early the following morning, while attempting to flee across the river in hurriedly built canoes and rafts. They were cut down by militiamen firing from the banks and by the gunboat opening up its cannons from 50 yards offshore—warriors, women, and children were indiscriminately slaughtered over an eight-hour period. (Most women and children had previously split off from the main party and found refuge back in Iowa.)

Most of the 100 to 150 who made it across the river were finished off by a hostile band of Sioux waiting on the other side.

- AUGUST 3 -
1839
CORNERSTONE LAID FOR SHAWNEETOWN BANK

On this day in Illinois history, the cornerstone was laid for the first building in the state to operate exclusively as a commercial bank.

Photo courtesy of Library of Congress, HABS, ILL, 30-SHAWT,2-

Shawneetown—along with Washington, D.C., one of only two cities to be platted by the federal government—was the financial capital of Illinois through the early 1800s. As the gateway to Illinois along the Ohio River, the city prospered from the commercial activity generated by the influx of settlers, a local land-grant office (established in 1812, and one of only ten in all Illinois), and the highly profitable nearby salt mines. A Shawneetown merchant, John Marshall, took advantage of this happy confluence of economic factors and established the first bank in Illinois Territory in 1816. He operated it from his home, with his wife and seven children. With a charter from the territorial legislature in Kaskaskia, Marshall issued crude money and offered easy credit to settlers. He often slept at night with a gun atop the trapdoor that led to the bank's safe in the cellar.

The bank closed during a financial panic that swept Illinois in the 1820s, but it reopened in 1834. Times were so prosperous that the directors not only chartered four southern Illinois branches (Jacksonville, Alton, Lawrenceville, and Pekin) but also planned a new permanent bank building designed in the fashion of the day—Greek Revival style. (It was about this time, according to local legend, that the bank declined a $1,000 loan to a group of northern Illinois investors who had traveled more than 300 miles seeking financial backing for their fledgling settlement; it was decided, after much consideration, that the tiny lakeside village—Chicago—was too far away from Shawneetown to ever amount to anything.) The Bank of Illinois at Shawneetown opened its new building—a solid four-story structure fronted by five massive Doric columns—in 1841. The first building in Illinois designed specifically for commercial banking, it emanated the American ideals of dignity and strength but stood vacant for a decade as Illinois suffered another economic depression.

The building reopened in 1854 as the State Bank of Illinois and operated through 1942, by which time Shawneetown, owing to a number of factors—not the least of which was a disastrous 1837 flood—was no longer the commercial hub it had once been.

- AUGUST 4 -
1911
AVIATOR JIMMY WARD DAZZLES 20,000 SPECTATORS AT ROCKFORD AIRSHOW

Flight pioneer Jimmy Ward piloted his Curtis Model D biplane, Shooting Star, over downtown Rockford at one of the nation's earliest aviation exhibits, on this day in Illinois history.

The Rockford & Interurban Railway Co. Flying Exhibition, from August 4 to 6, 1911, was one of a number of such exhibits organized to promote and encourage the nation's fledgling aviation industry. Airplanes may have first taken flight in America, but it was in Europe where governments, spurred by the anticipation of war, more seriously invested in getting manned flight off the ground in the early 20th century. The U.S. government did not purchase its first airplane—the Wright Military Flyer—until 1909 and even then expressed little interest in funding airplane technology. It was left to courageous individuals and entrepreneurial companies advanced aviation in America. The American people were captivated by the notion of manned flight, so aero clubs formed to help fuel public interest and raise funds.

The Rockford show was intended to jump-start commercial aviation in the area. Jimmy Ward, a Chicago taxicab driver who gained fame across the nation as a dauntless aviator, arrived with other famous pilots of the Curtis Exhibition Team to prove the "practicability of aviation." He took off from Loves Park on a 12-mile round-trip flight to South Rockford Park. An estimated 20,000 spellbound spectators observed the ten-minute excursion, as Ward skirted the rooftops of downtown buildings like a "daring birdman" in his Shooting Star airplane.

Nearly 40 years later, the Greater Rockford Airport Authority was created, and soon after RFD Airport—now Northwest Chicagoland International Airport—was built on the site of Camp Grant, where the U.S. Cavalry was trained.

- AUGUST 5 -

1983

OPERATION GREYLORD ROCKS CHICAGO POLITICS

On this day in Illinois history, Operation Greylord—a three-year undercover investigation into widespread corruption in the Cook County court system—went public.

The crookedness of dozens of judges, lawyers, and even police officers and sheriff's deputies, was exposed when news of the Federal Bureau of Investigation operation broke on television and radio airwaves on a Friday afternoon. The agency's man on the inside—their mole—was a disillusioned young attorney named Terrence Hake. Disgusted with the dishonest dealings he had been witnessing, Hake became the key undercover operative to expose those lawyers and judges who were accepting payoffs from litigants in exchange for favorable decisions in court. He wore a wire and planted a bug in the judges' chambers to collect evidence. Hake was joined by other concerned judges and lawyers who had sickened of the rampant corruption of their peers. Everything from parking violations to drunk driving was open territory, depending on the price. "Even a murder case can be fixed," one lawyer was caught on tape saying, "if the judge is given something to hang his hat on."

The massive sting operation led to more than 90 indictments. The first of the accused were named four months later, and by 1990, dozens of guilty officials had been convicted. Most pleaded guilty. They included 17 judges—whom one commentator referred to as "$200 whores in black robes"—48 lawyers, and several Chicago police officers. Most notable, perhaps, was judge Richard F. LeFevour, sentenced to a 12-year prison term for accepting thousands in bribe money. After the investigation, the FBI cited the words of President Theodore Roosevelt: "No man who is corrupt, no man who condones corruption in others, can possibly do his duty by the community."

Operation Greylord was revolutionary in its use of federal agents to address a local problem, setting up an insider as a mole, and employing hidden eavesdropping devices in exposing judicial corruption and the hustling of clients by lawyers. It spawned a whole host of related federal investigations in Chicago. Endemic graft at Chicago City Hall was targeted in Operation Silver Shovel, for example, in the late 1990s. And Operations Lantern, Gambat, and Safebet have likewise landed a number of corrupt politicians and public officials in prison over the past two decades.

Greylord, named for the wigs worn by British judges, may have helped to remedy the so-called Conspiracy of Silence, the intimidation of potential whistleblowers in City Hall and the courts—but some say it's just a start.

- August 6 -

1998

Illinois Loses a Legendary Broadcaster

Jack Brickhouse, a Peoria native who for five decades was the voice of the Chicago Cubs, Bears, and White Sox, died on this day in Illinois history.

Born on January 24, 1916, Brickhouse grew up in the age of radio and got his start in the industry as an 18-year-old sportscaster for WMBD in Peoria. According to the National Radio Hall of Fame, Jack was then the youngest broadcaster in the nation. Not limited to sports, he was assigned to cover just about everything from natural disasters to holiday parades for a take home pay of $17 per week. In 1940, he moved to Chicago's WGN to cover Cubs and White Sox baseball, first on radio and also as a pioneer during the infancy of television sports. He became WGN's first sports telecaster in 1948. In an odd pairing, he even worked with fellow broadcasting legend and *Chicago Sun-Times* columnist Irv Kupcinet on radio broadcasts for Chicago Bears football. It was Brickhouse who coined the oft-repeated phrase, in reference to the "lovable losers" of Wrigley Field, "Any team can have a bad century." After calling more than 5,000 baseball games, Brickhouse retired from play-by-play duties after the 1981 season.

He was the quintessential "homer" who wore his loyalties on his sleeve, always rooting for the home team, at times like a child. Into the microphone he would holler "Whew, boy!" when a play went the right way, "Oh, brother," when one went the wrong way, and his trademark "Hey-Hey!"—now emblazoned on the Wrigley Field foul poles—whenever something great happened. His most famous call, perhaps, was Ernie Banks's 500th home run, coming against Atlanta pitcher Pat Jarvis on May 12, 1960: "Jarvis fires away. . . . That's a fly ball, deep to left . . . back . . . back—HEY-HEY!—He did it! Ernie Banks got number 500!" Always versatile, he also reported from Democratic and Republican national conventions, interviewed seven sitting presidents, and was on the scene for such historic events as Winston Churchill's funeral in London and an audience with Pope Paul VI.

Jack Brickhouse was awarded the Ford C. Frick Award for excellence in broadcasting by the National Baseball Hall of Fame in 1983, and he was inducted into the Radio Hall of Fame in 1998.

THEODORE ROOSEVELT ADDRESSES THE PROGRESSIVE PARTY PRIMARY AT CHICAGO

The former U.S. president famously declared "I feel fit as a bull moose" to newspapermen while accepting the Progressive nomination for U.S. president at Chicago's Orchestra Hall, on this day in Illinois history.

The Progressive Party—nicknamed the Bull Moose Party after Roosevelt's robust comment—was born from the near-riotous Republican National Convention held at the Chicago Coliseum that past June. Supporters of Roosevelt broke from the Republican ranks after party insiders who favored incumbent President William Howard Taft snubbed Roosevelt in spite of his overwhelming victory in the state primaries. Taft had been Roosevelt's handpicked successor four years earlier but had refused to implement his predecessor's agenda; he was accused by the Progressives of stocking the convention with sympathetic delegates in order to capture the nomination. Imitating the sounds of a steamroller, Roosevelt supporters greeted Taft's nomination by blowing horns and chafing sandpaper before storming out of the Chicago Coliseum in protest.

The rank and file were drawn to the Bull Moose Convention as if, in the words of one *Chicago Tribune* reporter, "inspired with something of the spirit of the crusaders." Five hundred suffragettes marched on opening day, from the Art Institute of Chicago to Orchestra Hall; appropriately, none other than Jane Addams had the honor of seconding Roosevelt's nomination, and University of Chicago football coach Amos Alonzo Stagg was assigned "election coach" to help coordinate the massive gathering. Roosevelt, delighted at the show of support, proclaimed: "The main purpose of the Progressive movement is to place the American people in possession of their birthright. . . . the foundations of measureless prosperity, which their Creator offers them."

In a three-way contest, with the Republican vote divided, Democrat Woodrow Wilson emerged the victor, but Roosevelt won seven states and outpaced Taft by a measure of 80 electoral and nearly 700,000 popular votes.

- AUGUST 8 -
1908
SUPREME COURT JUSTICE ARTHUR GOLDBERG
BORN IN CHICAGO

Arthur Joseph Goldberg, future associate justice of the U.S. Supreme Court, was born in Cook County on this day in Illinois history.

Goldberg was born to poor Jewish immigrants who arrived at Chicago's West Side around the turn of the century. His father, who sold fruits and vegetables at Chicago street markets, died young, and the 10-year-old saw his older siblings drop out of school

Photo courtesy of Wirtz Labor Library

to help support the family. Though he was encouraged to stay in school, Goldberg also took on such jobs as wrapping fish at a North Side wharf and selling coffee to baseball fans outside Cubs Park (later Wrigley Field). Inspired by the media frenzy over the 1923 trial of Leopold and Loeb, Goldberg graduated from high school at age 16 determined to become a famous attorney. He had earned a law degree from Northwestern University School of Law by the age of 19, having been editor-in-chief of the prestigious *Northwestern Law Review,* and immediately joined a local law firm as a junior associate. He became a well-known labor lawyer, representing the Chicago Newspaper Guild in the late 1930s. Goldberg was appointed general counsel to the CIO (a major U.S. trade union) in 1948 and helped to orchestrate that organization's merger with the American Federation of Labor in 1955.

Deeply involved with the Democratic Party and labor union politics, Goldberg was appointed Secretary of Labor by President Kennedy from 1961 to 1962. He then filled the robes of Associate Justice Felix Frankfurter, who resigned because of illness, in the fall of 1962. Justice Goldberg was ratified by an up-and-down vote in the U.S. Congress within four weeks of his nomination. Once seated, he blazed a trail of landmark judicial decisions that included *Griswold v. Connecticut* (1965), upholding a citizen's Ninth Amendment right to privacy; and *Furman v. Georgia* (1972), which—temporarily—prohibited the death penalty as an infringement of the Eighth Amendment (forbidding "cruel and unusual punishment"). Justice Goldberg's time on the U.S. Supreme Court lasted only three years, as he accepted President Lyndon B. Johnson's invitation to become U.S. Ambassador to the United Nations in 1965.

He died on January 18, 1990, and his body rests at Arlington National Cemetery in Virginia.

1922

JAZZMAN LOUIS ARMSTRONG MOVES TO CHICAGO

On this day in Illinois history, Louis Armstrong arrived on the budding Chicago Jazz scene to launch a career that would establish him among the elite musicians and entertainers of the 20th century.

He spent fewer than eight full years in Chicago, but it was in the City of the Big Shoulders that Armstrong, "Satchmo" to millions of fans, would set the style and tone for generations of jazz players to come. Born in New Orleans, Louisiana, Armstrong was inspired as a child by that city's colorful marching bands and started performing at the age of 7. He decided to pursue the life of a musician. Playing on Mississippi riverboats as a youth was like "going to University," he'd recall in later years. Armstrong followed his mentor, bandleader Joe "King" Oliver, to Chicago in 1922, seeking a steady gig in the city's vibrant jazz scene. He was 21 years old. In Chicago, the young Armstrong started with the hugely popular King Oliver's Creole Jazz Band almost immediately and cut his first record with the group in April 1923. (The following year he married the band's pianist, Lil Hardin, the first of his three wives.)

Armstrong's playing was creative, melodic, and defined by a dynamic range of tone and far-reaching rhythms. He is credited as being jazz's first great soloist. His personal style—an infectious likeability, affectionate grin, and deep, granular vocals—won warm responses from the crowds, and by 1925, he was fronting the hottest band in Chicago, Louis Armstrong and the Hot Five. His "West End Blues," recorded in 1928, was the jazz standard of the era. Those early Chicago recordings feature some of the most ingenious trumpet solos Armstrong ever produced. Satchmo left Chicago the following year, having established himself in the national spotlight, and began to tour U.S. and European cities. His globe-trotting peaked at the breakneck pace of 300 gigs per year. During a versatile career, he performed with the greatest stars of the day—from Benny Goodman, Bessie Smith, and Ella Fitzgerald (jazz and blues performers), to Mae West and Bing Crosby (in the movies), and even Jimmie Rodgers (the "Father of Country Music").

He died at age 70 in 1971, having transformed jazz from folk music to a truly original American art form that stressed individual expression.

- AUGUST 10 -
1907
ESSANAY MOVIE STUDIOS OPEN IN CHICAGO

Essanay Studios—the early "Hollywood of the Prairie"—was formed in Chicago on this day in Illinois history.

The name derived from the last names of the company's cofounders, George K. Spoor and Gilbert M. Anderson (below)—S and A. Spoor had been the operator of an opera house in Waukegan, Illinois, and Anderson would become famous as "Broncho Billy," the nation's first movie-star cowboy, in hundreds of silent films, or "shorts." Together for ten brief years, they made Chicago the movie capital of the world. In 1909, Essanay joined Edison Studios, and seven other top national movie studios to form the Motion Picture Patents Company. It was an attempt to force smaller competitors out of business, and a trust called the General Film Company was also formed for the exclusive distribution of MPPC films.

Photo courtesy of Library of Congress, LC-USZ62-127541

Essanay employed a staff of 80 and at one point was turning out an average of eight 15-minute silent films each month, featuring the likes of cross-eyed Ben Turpin, Francis X. Bushman, and Gloria Swanson. But an ingenious young Englishman by the name of Charlie Chaplin was Essanay's brightest star. Chaplin starred in two comedies per month. They were short, formulaic, and boasted simple titles such as *The Bank, By the Sea,* and *A Woman.* His most famous Essanay film is *The Tramp,* costarring Edna Purviance as the damsel in distress who would invariably be the cause of a broken heart. It was in the closing scene of that film that moviegoers first saw his trademark ending: a lone Chaplin wandering off slowly down the road, then quickening his pace cheerfully before the screen goes black. At the time, a *Chicago Tribune* editorial denounced as "facilitators of juvenile delinquency" the city's 116 five-cent movie houses (called nickelodeons) that featured Chaplin's films.

By 1917, Essanay Studios, seeking more accommodating weather for its year-round movie operations, had packed up shop and moved to Niles, California.

- AUGUST 11 -

1887

CHATSWORTH TRAIN WRECK LEAVES 100 DEAD

On this day in Illinois history a train full of vacationers headed for Niagara Falls, New York, met disaster in Livingston County, killing 100 passengers.

The Niagara, an excursion train carrying 600 passengers en route to vacation in New York, was heading east just before midnight August 10. It passed through Illinois on the Toledo, Peoria, & Western Railroad. Rolling along at 35 miles per hour, the two-engine, 12-car train approached the small wooden bridge spanning a 15-foot gulch about 2 miles outside Chatsworth and ten minutes east of Peoria. The bridge was on fire, but the engineer failed to see the flames, and the train hit the overpasses at full speed. Timbers crumbled under the weight of the front engine. All five wooden passenger coaches—each at full occupancy—spilled into the small gorge; one crashing on top of the next, compelled by their own momentum to leap from the railroad tracks. Six sleeper cars were badly shaken but fatefully stopped before reaching the ruined bridge. One private car, that of General Superintendent G. E. Armstrong, was spun about and landed perpendicular to the east–west tracks; miraculously, nobody in that car was seriously injured.

The wreck was a scene of indescribable horror. Scores of dead and dying lay strewn about the gorge, a pile of twisted steel and splintered wood all about them. The numbers—85 hundred dead and more than 200 injured—overwhelmed relief efforts; worse, the flames spreading amongst the carnage hampered the work of the Chatsworth Fire Department and the many volunteers who had been shaken from their slumber by the terrible sounds of the crash. The injured were taken to Chatsworth's Grand Ballroom and private residences, a nearby school was turned into a morgue, and survivors packed the town's telegraph office to contact loved ones back home. From the first coach car, only four survived.

It was one of the worst train wrecks in the country's history.

- AUGUST 12 -

1818

ILLINOIS'S FIRST CONSTITUTIONAL CONVENTION AT KASKASKIA

On this day in Illinois history, the recently convened inaugural Constitutional Convention debated the future form of governance for the soon-to-be 21st state of the Union.

Thirty-three representatives from Illinois's 15 counties, elected by male land-holding residents over the age of 21, met at Bennett's Tavern in Kaskaskia to hammer out the details. The contingent included lawyers, physicians, sheriffs, ministers, store-keepers, a flatboat navigator, and a land-grant officer. Those assembled quickly elected Judge Jesse B. Thomas as chairman; chief architect of the state constitution was a Randolph County man named Elias Kent Kane. Kane studied the constitutions of New York, Ohio, and Kentucky, composed an Illinois draft based on his research, and continued to rewrite and revise the document as debate over its content progressed. On August 16, 1818, a final revision—consisting of a preamble and eight basic articles—was accepted and ready to be presented to the U.S. Congress for adoption.

Slavery was the main sticking point among the 33 representatives. Kent, a slave owner himself, knew that inserting language too open to slavery would preclude any chance of the Illinois Constitution being ratified in Congress. The antislavery faction was led by Ninian Edwards, the governor of Illinois Territory; they at first advocated outright prohibition but eventually bowed to compromise. As a result, slavery was banned—sort of—as a number of time-sensitive loopholes allowed for its lingering presence in parts of the state. French settlers along the America Bottom (southwest along the Mississippi River) were permitted to keep slaves brought in during the territorial period. The Saline salt mines (southeast near the confluence of the Wabash and Ohio rivers) were likewise allowed to continue the use of "indentured servants" through 1925 so they would not go bankrupt for want of a workforce. And the children of current slaves were to remain in bondage until they reached age 18 (if women) or 21 (if men).

Nevertheless, the first Illinois constitution was relatively democratic in nature for the times. There were no voting restrictions based on land ownership, and power was concentrated in the bicameral legislature—a senate and house of representatives. A majority of officials were to be popularly elected. On April 14, 1818, the U.S. Congress passed the bill, with slight opposition from representatives from New England and New York who were uneasy with the loopholes to slavery, and Illinois became the 21st state of the Union later that year.

Subsequent state constitutions have been adopted in 1848, 1870, and 1970.

- AUGUST 13 -
1803
ILLINIWEK CEDE ILLINOIS TERRITORY
IN THE TREATY OF VINCENNES

The beleaguered Illiniwek ceded more than 9 million acres of land to the U.S. government on this day in Illinois history.

Illinois was then a part of Indiana Territory, with its capitol in Vincennes. Territorial Governor William Harrison unabashedly sought Indian lands for American settlers, and Illinois, owing to the Louisiana Purchase, was no longer the western frontier of the nation. It offered prime land for settlement. A few weeks earlier, representatives from five tribes had sold 2 million acres in southeastern Illinois.

By this time, the Illiniwek had been in decline for decades. When the earliest French explorers contacted them in the 1670s, the Illiniwek numbered 10,000 to 12,000—possibly more. They were reeling from Iroquois invasions that began in the 1650s and quickly embraced the French for protection. That protection was negligible. In 1680, for example, an Iroquois war party descended the Illinois River and killed or enslaved 600 Tamora, members of the Illiniwek Confederacy. The Iroquois were not the only problem; Illiniwek enemies included the Fox and Sauk to the north, the Osage and Sioux to the west, and the Chickasaw and Shawnee to the south. By aligning themselves with the French, the Illiniwek made a new adversary in the British Empire. War continued to deplete the Illiniwek through the 18th century, and in 1802 a final series of skirmishes with the Shawnee of southern Illinois left them virtually defenseless.

American troops had defeated a fierce uprising by an alliance of tribes called the Wabash Confederacy, in the 1790s. The Treaty of Greenville in 1794 led to the secession of all Native American lands east of the Mississippi River and south of the Great Lakes to the U.S. government. The weakened Illiniwek played little to no role in this conflict, the major actors being the eastern tribes of the Iroquois, Shawnee, and Miami. Nevertheless, their lands were affected. By the early 1800s, the Illiniwek were powerless to resist, with waves of new settlers crossing the Ohio River into Indiana Territory. A delegation of Kaskaskia, Cahokia, Michigamea, and Tamora led by Ducoigne, a Kaskaskia chief, met Governor Harrison at Vincennes and agreed to sell 9 million acres in exchange for $12,000. The Illiniwek were allowed to keep 1,500 acres, 100 of which went personally to Ducoigne. The Peoria nation was not represented and did not agree to the treaty until 1818.

Kaskaskia, Illinois, became the site of the first land office in 1804, just as Lewis and Clark were launching from nearby Wood River to explore the new frontier.

- AUGUST 14 -
1939
ILLINOIS CELEBRATES THE END OF WORLD WAR II

On this day in Illinois history, Illinoisans received—with a mixture of enormous relief, delight, and sense of triumph—word that Japan had surrendered and World War II was over.

The headline of the *Chicago Tribune* read: "GREAT WAR ENDS: Japs Will Surrender to M'Arthur" as half a million people—in a scene repeated on a smaller scale from Cairo to Zion—flooded downtown Chicago in wild, spontaneous celebration. Soldiers, sailors, and marines were there too, and a group of 30 lipstick-smeared Navy men formed a line, "grabbed pretty girls as they passed, kissed them, and passed them on to one another." Not far away, 5,000 celebrants aggregated at the Evanston fire-

Naval air base, Corpus Christi, Texas

house and burned Japan's Emperor Hirohito in effigy. Illinoisans had mobilized for war in the immediate hours after the Pearl Harbor attacks of December 7, 1941, and had eventually contributed 987,000 men and woman to serve in the conflict. More than 22,000 made the ultimate sacrifice.

The Illinois home front also played a huge role in the war effort. Scott Field, Chanute Air Force Base, Glenview Naval Air Base, Fort Sheridan, Great Lakes Naval Training Center, and Camp Grant trained and disbursed thousands of soldiers, sailors, and marines to the war front. The Rock Island Arsenal produced tons of weaponry and ammunition. The Douglas Aircraft Corporation built a plant in Chicago, producing thousands of transport planes. Western Electric in Cicero expanded to nearly 30,000 employees, and the Buick factory in Melrose Park switched its operations to building water-cooled airplane engines. The town of Seneca, in La Salle County along the Illinois River, swelled from 1,200 to 6,600—a more than 500 percent increase in population—by 1943, as its workers constructed tank landing ships for the U.S. military. The state's situation was ideal, away from the coasts and therefore beyond the range of enemy air strike, yet with the transportation infrastructure and industrial capacity to host large numbers of servicemen in a constant state of flux. Its open land and the vast waters of Lake Michigan offered perfect conditions for military training and exercises.

On December 4, 2004, the World War II Illinois Veterans memorial was dedicated in Springfield to honor those Illinoisans who served their country.

- AUGUST 15 -
1967
PICASSO STATUE UNVEILED AT CHICAGO CITY CENTER

A controversial Picasso sculpture—now among the most famous of Chicago land-marks—was dedicated at City Center Plaza on this day in Illinois history.

The 50-foot, 162-ton sculpture of uncertain resemblance was built after a 42-inch steel model, designed by the great Spanish artist Pablo Picasso, then 84 years old, who presented it as a "gift to the people of Chicago" in 1965. He refused to accept the $100,000 payment, but did receive a Chicago White Sox jacket offered by the Public Building Commission of Chicago. The sculpture was erected at the foot of the 31-story Chicago Civic Center. Constructed of the same Cor-Ten steel used on the skin of the skyscraper, the Chicago Picasso, too, has weatherized over time to take on the same rust-colored patina.

The sculpture to this day evokes varied responses. People gasped at the unveiling—is it a horse, a bird, a monster? Some said it was a portrait of Picasso's wife, others figured it was his Afghan dog; many called the sculpture an eyesore at the time. But the city did receive congratulations for its acquisition from such a noted artist. *Time* magazine praised the Chicago sculpture as "one of the most important windfalls" in the city's history. And to this day it remains a favorite photo op for tourists.

Mayor Richard J. Daley—who thought it looked like the wings of Justice—and the city council paid tribute, posthumously, to the sculptor and his gift with a 1973 resolution: "Pablo Picasso became a permanent part of Chicago, forever tied to the city he admired but never saw, in a country he never visited, on August 15, 1967. It was on that day that the Picasso sculpture in the Civic Center Plaza was unveiled; it has become a part of Chicago, and so has its creator Picasso."

Chicago City Center and City Plaza were renamed Daley Center and Daley Plaza, respectively, in 1976 to honor the late mayor, but the odd sculpture is still known simply as "the Picasso."

- AUGUST 16 -

1980

EDWARDSVILLE ROCKS OUT TO THE FINAL
MISSISSIPPI RIVER FESTIVAL

The outdoor amphitheater in Madison County hosted the final Mississippi River Festival, which featured some of the biggest names in music since its 1969 inception, on this day in Illinois history.

The MRF was born on the campus of Southern Illinois University, Edwardsville in the summer of 1969, during the tumultuous days of "sex, drugs, and rock 'n' roll" in America. The festival began as a cooperative effort between SIUE and the St. Louis Symphony Society, and it featured a lineup ranging from classical music to show tunes to psychedelic rock. It soon came to be dominated by top performers of the era like The Beach Boys; Chicago; and Emerson, Lake and Palmer. It opened in 1969 with The Band and Bob Dylan being called out for an encore. The final show in 1980 included a memorable concert by The Grateful Dead. But due to lagging profits and the negative stigma of unruly rock 'n' roll concerts—often based on the reality of increased crime, drug abuse, and filth surrounding the venue—the festival itself was dead after a brilliant but short-lived run of twelve seasons.

The end was not abrupt. By 1980, state funding (through the university) had waned, original patrons at SIUE had either died or moved on, and the St. Louis Symphony Society had long since dropped out of the endeavor entirely. The crowds—who did come in large numbers from both sides of the river—were nevertheless not large enough to sustain the MRF any longer. The large open-air amphitheater erected upon sloping hills at the edge of campus began to deteriorate, and with no funds to support its renovation, the host site of the MRF seemed likely to go silent. The annual festival had few remaining advocates to respond to the continuing negative publicity.

The Mississippi River Festival rose up with the counterculture of the late-1960s and enjoyed a heyday that ended appropriately with the coming of a new generation.

- AUGUST 17 -

1803

FEDERAL TROOPS ARRIVE TO BUILD FORT DEARBORN

Captain John Whistler led a company of soldiers to the mouth of the Chicago River and ordered the construction of stockades and a shelter, on the future site of the great city of Chicago, on this day in Illinois history.

Completed over the next couple of years, the fort was named for Revolutionary War hero and Secretary of War Henry Dearborn, and served to protect the frontier and affirm America's authority in a region still inhabited by Native Americans. The complex was a basic quadrangle, 120 feet per side, surrounded by a double row of 12-foot high wooden palisades. A pair of blockhouses sat one each in the northwest and southwest corners, and an underground tunnel ran north to the riverbank as an escape route and for access to fresh water. Two-story barracks sat opposite the officers' quarters. A cluster of civilian homes sat outside the stockade, and the total population of the garrison and settlers was approximately 100.

Reconstructed Fort Dearborn at original site

Fort Dearborn was a peaceful trading post for several years. But with the outbreak of the War of 1812, most Indian tribes allied themselves with the British and set upon American frontier posts and settlements with a vengeance. On August 15, 1812, the fort was evacuated by then-commander Captain Nathan Heald, who negotiated safe passage in exchange for surrendering stores and provisions to the Native Americans assembling outside. Friendly Miami natives had tried to warn Heald against trusting the Potawatomi war chief Blackbird. Nevertheless, some 60–70 soldiers, 40 civilians, and 30 Miami warriors set off on a 150-mile trek to the protection of Fort Wayne, Indiana.

A 500-strong Potawatomi war party, some of whom started off escorting the departing columns as a ruse, descended on the evacuees within miles of their leaving the stockade. Nearly all the soldiers were killed, along with several Miami warriors and a number of civilians. Heald surrendered, was taken hostage along with his wife, and eventually ransomed to the British. Fort Dearborn was burned to the ground.

The fort was rebuilt in 1816 and used intermittently through the early 1830s, when it was permanently abandoned after Indian resistance in the region had ceased.

- AUGUST 18 -
1971
LINCOLN'S SPRINGFIELD HOME DEDICATED NATIONAL HISTORIC LANDMARK

On this day in Illinois history, Honest Abe's Sangamon County residence, the only home to ever be owned by Abraham Lincoln, became a National Historic Landmark.

The Lincolns moved into this house in 1844, and left in 1861 when the president-elect departed for Washington, D.C. It was originally built five years earlier for Reverend Charles Dresser, who in fact performed the marriage ceremony for Abraham

Passersby pose in front of Lincoln's home

Lincoln and Mary Todd on November 4, 1842. Assuming the $900 mortgage, Lincoln reportedly stated, "I reckon I can trust the preacher who married us." The Lincolns begot four sons here—Robert Todd, Edward Baker, William Wallace, and Thomas "Tad"—all of whom, except for the eldest, Robert, were born in the home. Robert Todd was tragically the only son to survive to adulthood. Lincoln hosted a grand reception at this house on February 9, 1861, to say goodbye to his neighborhood friends several days before his more famous farewell address at Springfield's Great Western Depot on February 11. He never returned to his beloved home or the city.

The two-floor hickory and oak frame house is now the centerpiece to the four-block Lincoln Home Historic District. Restored to its 1860s appearance, the interior is full of Lincoln memorabilia and period furniture. Abe's favorite rocking chair, Mary's sewing station, and an 1860 photograph taken for the presidential campaign are just three of the featured items. The Lincoln Home National Historic Site also sponsors the Annual Lincoln Colloquium, which is hosted on a revolving schedule by the Lincoln Studies Center in Galesburg, Illinois; the Lincoln Museum in Fort Wayne, Indiana; and the Chicago Historical Society. The colloquium was inaugurated at the Lincoln Home in 1986, and scholars—from college professors to amateur history buffs—gather every fall to share their ideas, discoveries, and judgments on Lincoln and his place in American history.

The other 11 original houses still standing in the district either have been or are in the process of being restored to appear exactly as they did in 1861, when Lincoln left Springfield.

- AUGUST 19 -
1889
LOUIS SULLIVAN MAKES HISTORIC LOAN
TO FRANK LLOYD WRIGHT

Frank Lloyd Wright's famous Oak Park home and studio, his first independent project, was the result of a $5,000 loan made by fellow architect and mentor, Louis Sullivan, on this day in Illinois history.

Interior of Frank Lloyd Wright's home

Wright had worked as the "pencil in Sullivan's hands," as he described himself, for years before asking for the loan. Serving as his family residence from 1889 to 1909 and work studio after 1898, this house was a continual work in progress for Wright as both his family and his architectural practice grew. It was here that Wright developed his distinct "Prairie Style" of architecture, experimenting with new ideas such as open space interiors and the use of natural lighting. Wright and his wife Catherine raised six children here. The most notable features of the building's design are the two-story polygonal Bay caps, added in 1895, and the studio annex, completed in 1898, which in itself—combining home and office—was a radical departure from the architectural norms of the day. From this Oak Park home Wright would revolutionize American architecture.

A Wright home, or one designed by his many imitators, is easily identified. His trademarks include an overall horizontality and low-pitched roofline that create the impression of a house growing right up from the prairie, blending with its natural surroundings. He designed hundreds of private residences and other structures in Chicago and its surrounding suburbs. Oak Park alone is home to numerous other Frank Lloyd Wright masterpieces, including Unity Temple, the congregation of which he was a member. "Not only do I fully intend to be the greatest architect who has yet lived," Wright once immodestly boasted, "but fully intend to be the greatest architect who will ever live. Yes, I intend to be the greatest architect of all time." In 1956, Wright—always the visionary—drew up and proposed plans for a mile-high skyscraper called The Illinois, which would have been approximately four times the height of the Sears Tower. It has not yet been built.

The Frank Lloyd Wright Home and Studio in Oak Park was designated a National Historic Landmark in 1976.

- AUGUST 20 -
1832
BLACK HAWK'S BAND BEGINS TO SURRENDER

Black Hawk's few remaining allies, devastated by military defeats and without provisions to carry on, finally started surrendering to the Sauk and Fox tribal councils and U.S. authorities, on this day in Illinois history.

Statue of Black Hawk at Rock Island

After three months of evading state militia and federal troops across northwestern Illinois, they had narrowly escaped the slaughter at the Battle of Bad Axe River on August 2. But even Black Hawk's last 30 followers were abandoning him, and the Winnebago who had given them refuge counseled Black Hawk and White Cloud, his prophet-ally, to surrender. Several leaders of Black Hawk's so-called British Band were captured and turned in by the peaceful chief, Keokuk, and the Sauk and Fox tribal councils that had opposed Black Hawk from the start. One of the saddest episodes in Illinois history had come to an end. Black Hawk, who had orchestrated much of the tragedy, was defeated, and would surrender himself a few days later.

The war had cost the lives of more than 600 Native Americans and 100 settlers. Scores of state militiamen and federal troops had also died—mostly from cholera. Among those whose political careers advanced through their service in the Black Hawk War of 1832 were four future governors of Illinois: Thomas Ford, John Wood, Joseph Duncan, and Thomas Carlin. Two future presidents also trailed Black Hawk that summer. A 23-year-old Abraham Lincoln was elected captain of a company of Illinois volunteers assembled in Beardstown, and Lieutenant Jefferson Davis, Lincoln's future adversary and president of the Confederacy, served with federal troops sent west under General Winfield Scott at the appeal of Illinois Governor John Reynolds. Neither saw combat.

Black Hawk spent several months in captivity before being sent by U.S. Secretary of War Lewis Cass on a tour of Eastern cities to impress upon him the vast power of the American people. It may not have been what he expected when he made his surrender speech: "Farewell, my nation. Black Hawk tried to save you and avenge your wrongs. He drank the blood of some of the whites. He has been taken prisoner, and his plans are stopped. He can do no more. He is near his end. His sun is setting, and he will rise no more. Farewell to Black Hawk."

The old Sauk warrior died in 1838, after living out his final years among his people on the Des Moines River in Iowa.

1867

CONSTRUCTION BEGINS ON EADS BRIDGE

Construction on Eads Bridge, which crosses the Mississippi River between East St. Louis and St. Louis, Missouri, began amid much doubt on this day in Illinois history.

It was an engineering feat dubbed "the finest example of a metal arch yet erected" by the *Encyclopedia Britannica* in 1875. The first bridge to be constructed of cast steel, it spans the river in three massive arches of 502, 520, and 502 feet, respectively. The supporting piers were sunk into solid bedrock more than 100 feet below the river's surface, through the loose sand and gravel at the river's bottom. The sunken remains of 20 steamboats needed to be cleared away first. This unprecedented feat was accomplished by the first-ever use of caissons. These submarine-like work stations—invented by the bridge's designer, James Buchanan Eads—were airtight chambers with open floors that allowed for underwater construction. (For nearly 100 years after its completion, no other underwater construction project had yet been attempted at such depths in America.) After seven years and $7 million, and the deaths of 14 workmen employed on the project, Eads Bridge was completed in the summer of 1873. It was called a "marvel of modern engineering."

Eads Bridge under construction

Eads's bold vision for the most ambitious bridge yet to cross the mighty Mississippi River did have its doubters and naysayers. The design was called "unsafe and impracticable." In 1867, a convention of engineers met in St. Louis to discuss the project and subsequently warned that Eads's idea of sinking piers into bedrock would be "perilous and futile." But it was crossed for the first time by horse-drawn carts and stagecoaches on June 4, 1873. In a mid-June publicity stunt, Eads led an elephant across the upper deck (for foot and wagon traffic), as it was believed that the large beasts had a natural instinct for unsafe structures. The elephant crossed without hesitation. To further silence his critics, a few weeks later, Eads proved the bridge's soundness by sending 14 locomotives back and forth across the lower deck (for rail traffic). At the time, lesser bridges would crumble under the weight of just one engine.

In 1992 Eads Bridge was closed for renovations. It reopened a decade later and remains among the greatest engineering marvels in the nation today.

- AUGUST 22 -
1814
MAJOR ZACHARY TAYLOR ASCENDS THE
MISSISSIPPI TO BATTLE THE SAUK

Major Zachary Taylor—future 12th president of the United States—led a small army upriver on this day in Illinois history, to secure the confluence of the Mississippi and Rock rivers during the War of 1812.

The United States declared war on Great Britain in June of 1812 over a litany of grievances, most notably the impressment of U.S. sailors into the British Navy and the continued incitement of Native American attacks on American frontier outposts. Illinois's Potawatomi, Sauk, and Fox allied themselves with the British in a last-ditch effort to stem the tide of American settlers coming to their traditional hunting grounds. The August 1812 massacre at Fort Dearborn in Chicago, which killed 67 soldiers and settlers, was the most well-known Native American victory in Illinois during that war; but there had been numerous other attacks on smaller isolated settlements. Territorial Governor Ninian Edwards called up hundreds of volunteer militiamen in response.

In August, Major Taylor, who had been assigned to St. Louis, Missouri, was ordered to sack the tribes' base near present day Rock Island, Illinois. It was then Saukenuk, capital of the Sauk and Fox nations and home to a still-young warrior named Black Hawk. Taylor commanded a small fleet of eight fortified keelboats carrying 40 U.S. Army regulars and more than 300 Illinois militiamen up river—against the current. In the meantime, Britain had sent Lieutenant Duncan Graham along with 30 Canadian troops to a strategic position on the Iowa side of the river. More than 1,000 Sauk warriors joined them to wait in ambush.

Taylor's flotilla reached their destination on September 4, set up camp on a wooded island, and were greeted the following morning by hostile fire from the opposite shore. Outnumbered and outgunned, Taylor ordered a defensive retreat downriver, the swivel guns on his keelboats holding off the pursuing Sauk warriors. Having suffered more than a dozen casualties, he decided that the three-to-one ratio was too great an advantage for the enemy. The militia fell back to the confluence of the Des Moines River near present day Warsaw, Illinois, and built a fortification on the high bluffs overlooking the waters below. It was abandoned a few weeks later.

This defeat at the hands of Black Hawk and his British allies was the only retreat in Taylor's illustrious military career.

- AUGUST 23 -
1911
OLYMPIC CHAMPION BETTY ROBINSON BORN IN RIVERDALE

On this day in Illinois history, Betty Robinson, who took home the gold in the 100-meter dash for women as a 16-year-old athlete at the 1928 Olympic Games in Amsterdam, was born in suburban Cook County.

Robinson was first woman to ever carry off an Olympic gold metal, as the 1928 Olympic Games were the first in which women—amid great controversy—were allowed to compete. She did so as a complete unknown, setting a course record of 12.2 seconds and earning the nickname, "Princess of the Olympics." Robinson added a silver medal with the women's 400-meter relay team. She accomplished this after only four months of part-time training and having entered but a few previous races. When Robinson, who was yet to graduate frm high school, returned home, she was greeted by ticker-tape parades. New York City held the first, and then Chicago, followed by a welcome-home parade and reception in Riverdale, Illinois, on August 28, 1928. The townspeople pooled their money to buy her a diamond watch in commemoration of her groundbreaking feat.

Robinson was nearly killed in a 1931 plane crash but miraculously survived and—perhaps even more miraculously—was able to push on and compete at the 1936 Olympics in Berlin. She survived the wreck—narrowly—with serious injuries to her head, arm, and hip, and fell into a seven-week coma. Even after she awoke, it was thought that Robinson would never walk again. But she would do more than walk. At just her second public appearance after the accident, Robinson set a world record of 12 seconds in the 100-meter dash at the Olympic tryouts in Chicago, earning herself a trip to Germany. There, the United States's women's 4-by-100-meter relay team, with Robinson running the third leg, snatched the Olympic gold from the favored German team before the eyes of Adolf Hitler.

Robinson returned, once again a hero, married and raised a family in the Chicago area, and died of cancer at the age of 87 on May 18, 1999.

Germanicus Kent, a land speculator, chose a beautiful ford on the Rock River's western bank in Winnebago County to plant a new settlement on this day in Illinois history.

The community was first known as the village of Midway because of its location between Galena and Chicago. Kent, taking advantage of the natural resources, built a

Photo courtesy of Eric A. Johnson

sawmill along the Rock River and used the plentiful lumber in the area to build homes for early settlers. In 1835, Daniel Haight built a small community on the river's opposite bank. The two settlements became rivals and were popularly called "Kentville" and "Haightville" until incorporated together as Rockford, seat of Winnebago County, in 1839. Rockford remained a small, agricultural village until the early 1850s. Citizens referred to their hometown as the "Forest City," for the elm- and oak-filled woods surrounding the Rock River.

Bird's-eye view of downtown Rockford

Rockford's transformation to one of Illinois's top industrial centers began in 1852, the year it was officially chartered as a city. The Galena & Chicago Union Railroad arrived that year, and with it came a new era of prosperity. Thousands of Swedish immigrants, who had left the east for "as far west as the train would take them," settled in Rockford, quickly earning reputations as skilled furniture makers. The Rockford Water Power Company—harnessing the power of the Rock River just as Kent's sawmill had done two decades earlier—was also established that year, further driving economic growth in the region. In 1853, John H. Manny arrived. His invention of a combination reaper-mower, and the Rockford plant he built to produce the machinery, became a constant thorn in the side of Chicago's McCormick Reaper Company. Cyrus McCormick tried to sue Manny in 1855 for patent infringement, but the Forest City industrialist's defense attorney was Abraham Lincoln, and the Chicago tycoon was defeated in court.

Nineteenth-century Rockford also hosted one of the nation's best baseball teams. The *Chicago Evening Post* commented in 1870: "If Chicago has no cause for local rejoicing over the achievements of her professional baseball representatives she can at least join heartily in the State pride resulting from the remarkable record made by the club of amateurs residing in the flourishing town of Rockford. . . . We consider the Forest City Nine the champion club of America." The Forest City Nine are long gone, but Rockford today is Illinois's second largest city.

- AUGUST 25 -

1819

ALLAN PINKERTON, ILLINOIS GREAT DETECTIVE, BORN IN SCOTLAND

Allan Pinkerton—America's premier 19th-century sleuth—was born in Glasgow, Scotland, on this day in Illinois history.

Photo courtesy of Library of Congress, LC-USZ62-117576

He would set sail for America as a young man while fleeing arrest by authorities in the United Kingdom. Son of a police sergeant, Pinkerton had a thirst for adventure and in his youth joined the "Chartists," a group of revolutionaries who agitated for governmental reform in the United Kingdom. On the day of his marriage, Pinkerton learned that a company of soldiers was en route to arrest him for these activities. The following day, with his wife Joan, Pinkerton fled to America. He settled in a community of Scottish immigrants about 40 miles west of Chicago, called Dundee, Illinois, in present-day Kane County. There, he set up shop as a cooper.

One day while gathering wood for his trade, Pinkerton discovered a secret hideout on an island in the Fox River. Together with Sheriff Bartholomew Yates, who had been searching for a gang of counterfeiters, Pinkerton staged a one-week stakeout of the island. The criminals were caught off guard, forged bills in tow, by the shotgun-wielding mayor and the newly deputized Pinkerton, and taken into custody. Thus the legendary career of America's greatest private detective was born.

Pinkerton moved his family to Chicago in the late 1840s, becoming the first detective on the city's police force, before resigning to set up the famous Pinkerton National Detective Agency in 1850. The trademark logo of an unblinking eye, hanging from his agency's entryway, inspired the slang term "private eye" used for detectives to this day. The agency broke a series of major train robberies; provided safe passage to Washington, D.C., for President-elect Lincoln, who was under threat of assassination; and later formed the U.S. Secret Service to spy for the Union during the Civil War. Pinkerton demanded a strict code of moral conduct from his agents: no bribes, no reward money, and no scandal. He played a prominent role in the Underground Railroad; hired the nation's first female detective, Kate Warne; and later earned the ire of organized labor when small armies of Pinkertons served as strikebreakers.

Allan Pinkerton died on July 1, 1884, and is buried at Chicago's Graceland Cemetery.

- AUGUST 26 -
1910
ELGIN HOSTS ITS FIRST NATIONAL ROAD RACE

The first Elgin National Road Race was held on this day in Illinois history, launching the city's brief reign as the automobile-racing capital of the world.

A local auto dealer, Frank Wood, petitioned the Chicago Motor Club in 1910 to host its annual road race in Elgin. The motor club had held its inaugural competition the previous year at Crown Point, Indiana, but poor track conditions and poorer accommodations for spectators had them looking for a new home. Wood argued that Elgin had a far superior track. The course featured a welcome scarcity of obstacles—no crossroads or railroad crossings, no residential areas to pass through, and no dangerous hills or curves—nothing but 8.5 miles of wide-open track. The Chicago Motor Club was convinced. On May 13, 1910, the Elgin Automobile Road Race Association was incorporated and plans set in motion for the inaugural races to be held that summer.

A boon to Elgin's economy and civic pride, the race became the focus of the entire community, and it attracted huge national interest in the early 20th century. The association had cut deals with local farmers, who allowed their land to be used for the races in exchange for licenses to build grandstands, run concessions, or open up makeshift motels to lodge the thousands of spectators expected. Townspeople were invited—and happily accepted—to drive their autos along the racecourse in order to compact the gravel, already covered with 50,000 gallons of oil to keep the dust down. The whole city, save for the service industry, closed down for the two-day event. Hotels were booked weeks in advance, and the nation's top drivers came to claim the coveted Elgin National Cup, a $5,000 trophy designed by Tiffany's of New York.

More than 125,000 spectators lined the track that opening weekend. Drivers, competing simultaneously in three separate races, left the starting line in 15-second intervals. Each was accompanied by a mechanic. Ralph Mulford won the trophy, averaging close to 62 miles per hour. But the race's heyday lasted from only 1910 to 1915, as the track was soon outclassed by oval raceways in Chicago and Indianapolis. Races resumed there in 1919 and 1920, but the obsolete roadway—once state-of-the-art—had lost its luster.

Danger was another factor in the Elgin National Road Race's losing its prominence, as five drivers had been killed there in as many years.

- AUGUST 27 -
1957
WORLD-CLASS HARNESS RACING COMES TO DU QUOIN

The most prestigious event in harness racing, the Hambletonian, debuted for its 24-year run at the Du Quoin State Fairgrounds, in downstate Perry County, on this day in Illinois history.

The Hambletonian is the jewel of harness racing's Triple Crown (Yonkers Trot and Kentucky Futurity being the other two), and it has been held every year since 1926 for the country's top three-year-old trotting Standardbreds. The race is named for Hamiltonian 10, a mid-19th-century trotter-turned-stud through whose lineage can be traced practically all Standardbred racehorses in America (quite literally, the "father" of modern-day harness racing.) The race was held in Goshen, New York, from 1930 through 1955, before being moved to southern Illinois as a result of a dispute between directors of the Hambletonian Society and their host site. It was initially a two-year contract but, finding the rural Illinois setting to be idyllic and the racing conditions superior, race officials stayed until 1981 before relocating again to the Meadowlands Racetrack in New Jersey.

The Du Quoin State fairgrounds had hosted harness racing for decades, but nothing this prestigious—nor with such a large purse—had been seen at the small Illinois coal-mining town. W. R. Hayes, a local Coca-Cola bottler who had done quite well, developed the racetrack in the 1920s and his two sons, Gene and Don Hayes, outbid competing racetracks across the United States to bring the illustrious event to Du Quoin. Gene's wife, Leah Hayes, wrote and performed the song, "Du Quoin's Hambletonian," which became an opening ceremony tradition. Hickory Smoke won the inaugural race at the new site and took $111,126 in prize money. Interestingly, the 21 entries that day necessitated two divisions each with two heats, with a run-off between the two division winners. Hickory Smoke and his driver, John Simpson Sr., thus became the only Hambletonian victors required to win three heats before taking home the trophy. And what was meant to be a temporary solution became a southern Illinois tradition—though wagering was not allowed until 1975.

Over the course of the next two and a half decades, the Du Quoin State Fairgrounds witnessed dozens of Hambletonian records set, millions awarded in prize money, and no less than five Triple Crown champions pass through its gates.

- AUGUST 28 -
1968
CHAOS REIGNS AT DEMOCRATIC NATIONAL
CONVENTION IN CHICAGO

Mayor Richard J. Daley is denounced on the convention floor while riots continue in the streets of Chicago, during the explosive 1968 Democratic National Convention, on this day in Illinois history.

A week of protests, counterprotests, and police violence at the 1968 DNC stands symbolic in the nation's memory of an America torn apart by war. The Democratic Party was itself split between its top two candidates: Vice President Hubert H. Humphrey, who wanted to carry on the policies of Lyndon B. Johnson and continue the Vietnam War effort, and antiwar candidate Eugene McCarthy, who campaigned for the immediate withdrawal of all U.S. troops. (President Johnson had withdrawn from the race in March, and front-runner Robert Kennedy had been assassinated in June.) The Tet Offensive in January and subsequent media coverage had galvanized the antiwar movement, and popular support for the war had been eroding as American casualties mounted. Passions about the war ran high.

Chicago found itself at the center of the maelstrom. The Yippies—leftist activists led by Abbie Hoffman, Tom Hayden, and Dave Dellinger—were intent on causing major disruptions. Other protest groups led by Mobilization to End the War in Vietnam and Students for a Democratic Society had been planning convention-week protests for months. They arrived in great numbers and were highly organized—and not all were peaceful. Mayor Daley would have none of it. He took draconian measures, refusing to issue many of the permits applied for by various protest groups, vowing to enforce an 11 p.m. curfew, and training special police units in riot control. Nearly 6,000 National Guardsmen were also mobilized.

Senator Abraham Ribicoff, while nominating George McGovern inside the Chicago Amphitheater, denounced "Gestapo tactics on the streets of Chicago," and thousands of protesters organized to march toward the convention site. Police lines clashed against groups of protesters, and the nation's television cameras famously caught the ensuing chaos. Clubs flew, tear gas sprayed, and squad cars were pelted with rocks and bottles. By week's end, 668 arrests were made, nearly 1,000 protesters and 200 police sustained injuries, and Chicago was so stigmatized that the DNC would not return to the city for 28 years.

Speaking at a press conference several days later, Daley made the famous gaffe, "The policeman isn't there to create disorder; the policeman is there to preserve disorder."

- AUGUST 29 -
1970
CITY OF RIVERSIDE NAMED NATIONAL HISTORIC LANDMARK

On this day in Illinois history the Cook County suburb—designed by landscape architect Frederick Law Olmsted and built beside the Des Plaines River—was designated a National Historic Landmark.

It was one of the first planned communities in the United States. Olmsted, along with his partner, Calvert Vaux, was commissioned by the Riverside Improvement Company in 1868 to plan a unique suburban community 9 miles west of Chicago. (Olmsted had already gained fame as the creator New York's Central Park, and he would be called on again by Chicago's Daniel Burnham to design gardens for the World's Columbian Exposition of 1893.) Riverside's winding roads, gas-lit streets, and landscaped parks appear to this day very much as planned more than 130 years ago. Olmsted and Vaux broke convention by dismissing the standard grid system for city streets and laid out Riverside's 1,600 acres to follow the natural bends of the Des Plaines River. The only straight roads in town are those that run parallel to the Chicago, Burlington & Quincy Railroad. Dozens of open parks, large and small, are scattered at intersections throughout the village.

Though initially hampered by the Great Chicago Fire of 1871, that disaster became a blessing in disguise for Riverside. At first, construction stopped and plans were put on hold. Available funds dried up, and it looked as if Olmsted and Vaux's dream might never come to fruition. But Riverside was the final stop on the commuter railroad line, and many Chicagoans who lost their homes ended up in Riverside building anew. Along with them came some of the eras most celebrated architects—Frank Lloyd Wright, Louis Sullivan, William Le Baron Jenney—who designed homes and building that still stand in the charming village of approximately 9,000. The village completed, Riverside was incorporated in 1875.

The original water tower and pump house, destroyed by fire in 1913, were fully restored and ceremoniously unveiled in September 2005 as a symbol of Riverside's unique history.

- AUGUST 30 -

1924

SOUTHERN ILLINOIS SHOOTOUT BETWEEN SHELTON GANG AND KKK

On this day in Illinois history, a shoot-out between Williamson County bootleggers and the Ku Klux Klan at Smith's Garage in Herrin left five Klansmen dead.

It happened amid the Prohibition-era gang wars. The Shelton brothers—"Handsome" Carl, Bernie, Earl, and Roy—were Herrin, Illinois, coal miners–turned–organized

criminals who sold illicit booze, operated gambling resorts, and ran a vast crime racket that thrived from East St. Louis to downstate Williamson, Saline, and Franklin counties. It was estimated that by the end of the decade the Sheltons were bringing in more than $6 million per year. The eldest brother, Carl, had reportedly worked out a deal with Al Capone: The Chicago syndicate would operate from Peoria, Illinois northward, while the Sheltons, for a monthly payoff, were allowed to maintain control over the southern half of the state. Their archnemesis in the early 1920s was S. Glenn Young, a former Prohibition agent and newly recruited leader of the local Ku Klux Klan who was determined to "clean up the area."

Forming an unholy (and temporary) alliance with rival southern Illinois mob boss Charlie Birger, the Sheltons started the infamous "Klan War" in May 1924. That month, they executed a drive-by ambush on Young, wounding the Klansman in the leg and leaving his wife blind. The KKK, which had considerable influence in the region, fought back. At Smith's Garage that late August, a furious gunfight left Carl and Earl Shelton injured and five Klansmen dead. The Sheltons were joined by Herrin's sheriff, George Gilligan, a staunch enemy of Young's who was eager to start trouble at the noted Klan hangout; he, too, was injured.

The war culminated in another shootout two years later, the famous "Election Day Riot" of April 13, 1926. Pro and anti-Klan forces, while vying for power at the polls, dragged the contest out into the streets of Herrin. Gunmen from both the Shelton and Birger gangs were involved; the battle ended the lives of six Klansmen and precipitated an end to their power in Williamson County. Three of Birger's men were also killed.

Thereafter, with the KKK out of the picture, a fierce rivalry between the Shelton brothers and Charlie Birger developed into an even bloodier gang war.

- AUGUST 31 -
1864
GEORGE B. MCCLELLAN NOMINATED AT DNC IN CHICAGO

On this day in Illinois history, the Democratic National Convention met at the Chicago Amphitheater to nominate General George B. McClellan amid rumors of conspiracy at the city's Confederate prison, Camp Douglas.

The convention had been postponed for several weeks as the Democratic Party awaited opportunistic headlines from the war front that would boost antiwar sentiments and solidify a national war policy among its members. The headlines never came. Their candidate, General McClellan, had been dismissed in 1862 as commander of all Union forces, and later as commander of the Army of the Potomac. President Abraham Lincoln accused him of being incompetent and overly cautious. McClellan, harboring a keen grudge against his former boss, was in turn highly critical of "Lincoln's War" and ran as a peace candidate. He was the near unanimous nominee, save for a congressman from Maryland who caused a riot at the amphitheater when he offered harsh words for the general. Nearly 30,000 out-of-towners flooded the city, despite the fact that Delaware, Kentucky, Maryland, and Missouri (slaveholding states remaining with the Union) were the only southern states to send delegates.

Meanwhile, concerns of a much more threatening situation swirled around Chicago's Camp Douglas. There, more than 8,000 Confederate prisoners wasted away under the watchful eyes of 736 Union soldiers. The conditions were miserable—"a tyranny and cruelty worse than the dark ages," as told by one survivor—and an estimated 4,000 to 6,000 prisoners died of disease, malnourishment, or frostbite during Chicago's harsh winters. Union spies from Chicago's Pinkerton Detective Agency foiled the plot that summer to free the prisoners, arm them, and form a "Northern Army of the South" to seize Chicago. Behind the plot was the Knights of the Golden Circle, a network of pro-Southern northerners who engaged in guerrilla warfare against the Union. One thousand reinforcements were sent down from Wisconsin to guard the camp. A large hoard of arms and ammunition, which had been smuggled in by the conspirators, was later found and confiscated from the basement of a known Knights member in Chicago. By the eve of the election, 100 conspirators had been arrested.

McClellan, who remained blunderingly silent in denouncing the failed coup of which he had no part, was defeated by Lincoln in an electoral landslide of 233 to 81.

This day in

September

- September 1 -
1928
Boy Scouts Place 175 Lincoln Highway Markers across Illinois

On this day in Illinois history, to preserve the namesake of America's most famous road, Boy Scouts placed commemorative markers at one-mile intervals, from Chicago Heights to Fulton, along Lincoln Highway.

Lincoln Highway was conceived in 1913, funded by automobile industry executives who formed the Lincoln Highway Association, and patched together by paving over a network of dirt and gravel roads running from coast to coast. It became the first successful cross-continental road system in America. Named for the 16th president, Lincoln Highway held special significance for Illinois, where it entered the state

at Chicago Heights and continued westward through Joliet, Aurora, DeKalb, Rochelle, Dixon, Sterling, and Morrison before crossing the Mississippi River at Fulton. By 1925, a number of copycat highway systems had popped up across the country, identified by a puzzling array of names and logos.

The American Association of State Highway Officials decided to establish a standard system for organizing this confusing web of roads—by number—which would obviate the use of all existing names. The great Lincoln Highway was to become US 1, US 30, US 530, US 40, or US 50, depending upon which stretch one drove. The Lincoln Highway Association, threatened by this loss of identity, decided to make sure that the nation's cross-country travelers never forgot the highway's original name.

Masters of promotion, the association placed memorial markers at every 3,000-plus mile of the historic road. Illinois landscape artist Jens Jensen designed the markers. Cast in concrete and a few feet tall, each marker was topped with a small bronze bust of President Lincoln and the words, "This Highway Dedicated to Abraham Lincoln." Of the approximately 175 markers erected in Illinois, only a handful remain—relics of an era nearly forgotten despite the association's best efforts.

The last remaining markers may still be found—along old Lincoln Highway—deteriorating gracefully on present-day US 30, IL 31, or IL 38, not far from the superhighways that replaced the original route in later decades.

- SEPTEMBER 2 -
1850
ALBERT GOODWILL SPALDING BORN NEAR BYRON

A. G. Spalding, inductee to the National Baseball Hall of Fame and cofounder of the sporting goods company that bore his name, was born in Ogle County on this day in Illinois history.

He moved to Rockford as a young boy. Spalding showed the character of a natural leader when he organized a group of 15- and 16-year-olds into a ball club that took on—and usually defeated—all comers. His ambitious team, the Pioneers, challenged the Mercantiles (an established amateur ball club composed of Rockford salesmen) to a ball game in the fall of 1865. The older club first dismissed the challenge as a joke; however, after much persistence by the youngsters (and some chaffing by the elder team's rivals) the Mercantiles agreed to take the field.

The game was not even close. Spalding pitched a gem, and the Pioneers won the game handily, 26–2, before a gathering crowd of spectators. Among the crowd were members of the Rockford Forest Citys Baseball Club, considered the city's "top nine," who rooted "good and hard" for the "kids." Spalding was promptly invited to join their team. With the young hurler on the mound, the Forest Citys became a powerhouse, winning 51 of 65 games through 1870. Spalding's 12–5 win over the champion Washington Nationals that season won him national renown.

His dominant pitching for Rockford launched a professional career that would land A. G. Spalding in Cooperstown. He led the Boston Red Stockings to four consecutive National Association pennants (1872–1875) and then returned to Illinois to win the inaugural National League pennant as player-manager for the 1876 Chicago White Stockings (now the Cubs). He retired from the field in 1877 and guided the White Stockings as team executive for much of the next 15 years. In the 1888–89 offseason, Spalding led an all-star club on baseball's first world tour, playing the national pastime in such faraway and exotic places as Hawaii, Australia, and before the pyramids of Egypt.

The far-reaching Spalding also pursued a successful Chicago sporting goods business with his brother, and for more than a century ambitious young hurlers have taken the mound clutching the baseball that bears his name.

- SEPTEMBER 3 -
1926
NOVELIST ALISON LURIE BORN IN CHICAGO

On this day in history, Alison Lurie, the writer and scholar who won the Pulitzer Prize for fiction in 1985, was born in Cook County.

A professor of literature and folklore at Cornell University since 1970, Lurie is best known as a novelist. Her *Foreign Affairs* won the Pulitzer 23 years after the publication of her first book, *Love and Friendship,* in 1962. Though a critic once called her writings "so simple a cat or dog can understand them," Lurie's use of clever yet non-obfuscating prose, lacking in any stylistic pretensions, has also been called addictive, haunting, and likened to the works of Jane Austen or Marcel Proust. Her social satire frequently mirrors her own life experiences, often taking place on fictional college campuses, in artists' colonies, or in eclectic small towns where the characters wrestle with modern-day mores and morality.

As a nonfiction writer, Lurie has also brought her pen of cultural commentary to the world of children's literature. (Her semiautobiographical heroine in *Foreign Affairs* is a plain-spoken Ivy League professor in the field.) She's pondered why, for example, Winnie the Pooh has become a 20th-century favorite and explored the subversive nature of Victorian-era classics in her 1990 collection of essays, *Don't Tell the Grown-Ups,* and she coedited the 73-volume *Garland Library of Children's Classics.*

Lurie has since explored a variety of themes and subjects. Her *Language of Clothes,* published in 1981, can best be described as a psychology of fashion. In 1994 Lurie published a collection of haunted tales, *Women and Ghosts,* followed four years later by a return to the subject of popular children's books with *Reading at Escape Velocity.* Her most recent work, the novel *Truth and Consequences,* was published in October 2005.

- SEPTEMBER 4 -

1890

WOODSTOCK OPERA HOUSE PREMIERE

On this day in Illinois history, the Woodstock Opera House—one of the oldest continuously operating theaters in the nation—hosted its premiere performance.

It was the musical *Margery Daw,* and critics raved that, "The scenic effects were excellent, and in every way the affair was a brilliant success." But the Woodstock Opera

House was built between 1889 and 1890 to be more than a mere auditorium. The building, a mixture of Victorian and Gothic with hint of Moorish style, also housed Woodstock's city hall, public library, and fire department. The auditorium was up on the second floor, and all was topped by an ornate five-story bell tower looming above the busy town square below. It was designed and constructed by architect Smith Hoag of Elgin, Illinois. The $25,000 building quickly became the center of McHenry County's political, economic, and communal activity. Traveling vaudeville acts played the auditorium after farmers had carried out their business at city hall, and local women socialized in the parlor or attended a public safety forum put on by volunteer firefighters. All would gather to see prominent speakers such as Jane Addams or Leo Tolstoy.

But it was the opera house that garnered national praise for being what actor, broadcaster, and director Orson Welles called the "grand capital of Victorianism in the Midwest." Welles was attending Woodstock's Todd School for Boys in 1934, when, as an aspiring 19-year-old actor, he led a Shakespearean summer troupe that performed at the auditorium. In addition, future stars Tom Bosley, Paul Newman, and Geraldine Page, members of a group called the Woodstock Players, formed in the late 1940s, all got their start on the opera house stage.

In dire need of repair, the building closed for renovations in 1975. Two years and $500,000 later, with a majority of the funds being raised by local businesses and area residents, it reopened as a completely modern yet historically authentic theater. Today, it hosts a variety of live acts, of both local and national renown, and is listed on the National Register of Historic Places.

One legendary patron, Elvira, is the ghost of a beautiful young actress who took her life by leaping from the bell tower after losing a leading role, forever haunting seat 113—or so some theatergoers believe.

- SEPTEMBER 5 -
1901
NATIONAL ASSOCIATION OF PROFESSIONAL BASEBALL LEAGUES BORN

Seven minor-league presidents met in a hotel room in Chicago, on this day in Illinois history, to form the National Association of Professional Baseball Leagues, the organization that to this day governs minor-league baseball.

Professional baseball was being torn apart by a "war" between the longstanding National League and an upstart American League that had just declared big league status. To protect their own leagues and teams from the "pirating" of players and the appropriation of cities, the presidents of several lesser leagues convened in Chicago to unite and form an umbrella organization to guide minor-league baseball into the 20th century. What emerged was an association that represented professional baseball from coast to coast, setting formal relations between the majors and the minors, and preserving the latter. The laws set down that day included territorial rights, a limited player draft, salary structure, and a classification system to rank leagues from lower to higher levels of competitive play. The national pastime was thus stabilized.

That first year there were 15 member leagues in the NAPBL, a number that jumped to 59 leagues, playing in more than 400 cities in the United States by the "Golden Age" of the late 1940s. Over the years, Illinois towns and cities have entered more than 100 teams into the NAPBL, from the Springfield Senators and Rock Island Islanders, who finished one-two atop the 1910 Three-Eye League standings, to the 2001 Midwest League Champion Kane County Cougars. Some of the more colorfully named ball clubs have been the Lincoln Abes (Class-D Illinois-Missouri League), the Peoria Tractors (Class B Three-I League), and the Quincy Gems (Class A Midwest League). One of the greatest major-leaguers to come through the "farm system" in Illinois was future Chicago Cub pitcher, Grover Cleveland Alexander. En route to a Hall of Fame career, Alexander—or Pete to his teammates—spent part of the 1909 season with the Galesburg Boosters, where a relay throw to the head knocked him unconscious for two days. He awoke to win 373 games, the third most in major-league history.

Minor-league baseball is played today in Peoria, Geneva, Cook County, Schaumburg, Rockford, Joliet, and Sauget—providing young players the dream of one day landing on the roster of the big league Chicago Cubs or White Sox.

- September 6 -
1860
Jane Addams Born in Cedarville, Illinois

Jane Addams, founder of the famous Hull-House settlement and recipient of the Nobel Peace Prize, was born in Stephenson County on this day in Illinois history.

Addams's mother died when she was only 2 years old, and she was raised by her father, for whom she had great admiration. He died in 1881, the same year Addams graduated from Rockford Female Seminary (later named Rockford College). She spent much of that decade traveling, including an 1888 trip to London, where she was inspired by a visit to Toynbee Settlement Hall to devote her life to social reform.

Addams, whose motto was "The excellent becomes the permanent," returned to Illinois in 1889 to excel as an educator and permanently influence for the better thousands of immigrants. Her Hull-House was established on Chicago's West Side to serve the various immigrant groups crowding into that neighborhood—Italians, Russian Jews, Poles, Irish, Germans, Greeks, and Bohemians. Addams and her fellow social workers forged a powerful reform movement. They provided work-training programs and classroom instruction for poor immigrants to facilitate their assimilation into American society, providing them greater opportunity to lift themselves up out of poverty. Hull-House offered day care, an employment bureau, and art and music classes; it also became a meeting place for labor unions and the site of the Juvenile Psychopathic Clinic.

Hull-House's success earned Addams national renown, and she used her celebrity to champion such causes as workers rights and women's suffrage. In 1910, she became president of the National Conference of Social Work. In 1915, she chaired the International Congress of Woman. She also helped found the American Civil Liberties Union in 1931. A committed pacifist, Jane Addams joined the Women's Peace Party during the First World War; in 1919, it became the Women's International League for Peace and Freedom, and she was elected its first president. She was awarded the Nobel Peace Prize for her life's achievements in 1931.

Jane Addams died May 21, 1935, in Chicago, and is buried near her Cedarville home.

- SEPTEMBER 7 -
1923
CHICAGO BEER WARS BEGIN

On this day in Illinois history, the O'Donnell Gang muscled in on the Prohibition-era business of the Torrio-Capone syndicate, launching the bloody Chicago Beer Wars of the Roaring Twenties.

Along with a federal ban on alcohol was born an illegal system of quenching the city's natural thirst. Its chief suppliers, or bootleggers, were led by Johnny "The Fox" Torrio, who had arrived from New York City in 1909 to build up the Chicago underworld. By the early 1920s, his top lieutenant was Al Capone, a recruit from Brooklyn's notorious Five Points Gang. Together they controlled and expanded the influence of the Chicago Outfit, running beer and liquor to speakeasies across the city (among other criminal dealings). But the South Side's O'Donnell Gang decided in the late summer of 1923 to move in on Torrio and Capone's territory. The O'Donnells were led by brothers Spike, Steven, Tommy, and Walter. Their thugs terrorized at least six saloon owners who were customers of the Outfit, beating one to within an inch of his life, and even shot up a Torrio-owned beer truck, shattering the relative peacefulness of the early years of Prohibition.

The Outfit's response was swift and brutal. Frank McErlane, an owner of one of the intimidated saloons, and others affiliated with Torrio and Capone sought revenge. McErlane, whom the Illinois Crime Survey would label "the most brutal gunman who ever pulled a trigger in Chicago," decapitated an O'Donnell hooligan who had participated in the raids with his sawed-off double-barrel shotgun. This "hit" sparked open warfare between rival gangs that would last for years. Mob bosses, bodyguards, informers—anybody who knew too much—became a target. The violence was enough to force one of the O'Donnell's drivers into retirement, declaring, "I'm through. I wouldn't peddle orange pop at a Sunday-school picnic."

By October 1926, when a truce was called, the spate of gangland shooting, bombing, kidnapping, and murder had killed scores and dominated the city's headlines for years in what was dubbed the Chicago Beer Wars.

- SEPTEMBER 8 -
1986
THE OPRAH WINFREY SHOW GOES INTO NATIONAL SYNDICATION

On this day in Illinois history, *The Oprah Winfrey Show*—already a hit in the Chicago market—first aired nationally.

The Mississippi-born entrepreneur came to Chicago in 1984 after working as a news anchor in several U.S. cities. "My first day in Chicago," she recalled. "I set foot in this city, and just walking down the street, it was like roots, like the motherland. I knew I belonged here." There, Winfrey got her big break when asked to host WLS-TV's *AM Chicago*, a struggling 30-minute morning talk show. It became an immediate hit, was renamed *The Oprah Winfrey Show*, and was extended to a full hour by the following television season. The show enjoyed tremendous success in Chicago, but before attaining national stardom, the host costarred in Steven Spielberg's *The Color Purple* and was nominated for an Academy Award for Best Supporting Actress in 1985. (She has also appeared in, among other productions, *Beloved, Native Son*, and *The Women of Brewster Place*.) The following year, *The Oprah Winfrey Show* went into syndication, and it hit number one in the ratings within months.

The Oprah Winfrey Show is produced by Winfrey at Harpo Studios in Chicago, built at the old Armory Building that served as a makeshift morgue during the horrid Eastland disaster of 1915. (Winfrey has reportedly claimed to feel at times the presence of spirits.) From there it has become the longest-running daytime talk show in the United States, with more than 20 million viewers in more than 100 countries across the globe.

Winfrey also supervises the Angel Network, which donates millions of dollars every year to various charities; publishes the popular *O, The Oprah Magazine;* and can create an instant best-seller overnight with a recommendation through Oprah's Book Club. She is also a founder of the cable-television network Oxygen.

Named by *Time* magazine as one of the 100 most influential people of the 20th century, Winfrey was revealed to be the first African American woman billionaire in America in 2003.

- SEPTEMBER 9 -
1836
ABE LINCOLN LICENSED TO PRACTICE LAW IN ILLINOIS

On this day in Illinois history, Abraham Lincoln, a self-educated jack-of-all-trades who lived for a time in the tiny town of Salem in Marion County, was declared competent to become an attorney.

Photo courtesy of Library of Congress, LC-USZ62-

Lincoln settled in Salem in 1831 and stayed through 1837, taking on a number of occupations to survive. He was a clerk at a general store, then a militiaman during the Black Hawk War of 1832, and a merchant, postmaster, and surveyor thereafter before being elected to represent Sangamon County in the state legislature in 1834. Meanwhile, Lincoln—whose childhood stints in formal schooling totaled less than 12 months—worked doggedly at sharpening his grammar, wit, and general knowledge through continuous self-education. Once in public office, Lincoln was motivated by fellow assemblyman John Todd Stuart to pursue law, and Stuart loaned him the necessary texts, which Lincoln studied while the legislature was out of session. After the Illinois Supreme Court examined Lincoln and issued his license to practice law, he moved from Salem to Springfield on April 15, 1837, to become Stuart's junior partner.

Lincoln practiced law in Springfield for 25 years before moving into the White House. In 1841, he formed a partnership with Stephen Logan, setting up shop at an ideally located third-floor office in downtown Springfield—above the federal courthouse, across the street from the America House Hotel (Springfield's premier destination for traveling lobbyists, lawyers, and politicians), and a mere block from the state capitol with its vast library and home to the Illinois Supreme Court. In 1844, the partnership with Logan dissolved and 26-year-old William Herndon became Lincoln's junior partner. They remained in practice together, at least in name, through President Lincoln's 1865 assassination. In total, Lincoln accepted more than 400 cases in Illinois, at all levels—city, county, circuit, appellate, and federal—earning a reputation most notably as the "Rail Splitter," arguing variously for or against the competing barges and railroads of the state's flourishing transportation industry.

In 1849, perhaps inspired by a legal case or two, the inventive Lincoln received a patent for a device designed to buoy rivergoing vessels over hard-to-pass shoals, an invention that was never manufactured but does qualify Abraham Lincoln as the only U.S. president to receive a U.S. patent.

The University of Chicago, by many standards the top-ranked institution of higher learning in the country, was founded on this day in Illinois history.

U of C was born from the millions ($35 million, to be exact) of oil magnate John D. Rockefeller and other wealthy patrons, built upon ten acres of land donated by Chicago

mercantile giant Marshall Field, and immediately established itself among the nation's elite colleges. William Rainey Harper, a noted Hebraic scholar, was the university's first president, and leading scholars from across the globe were attracted to instruct at the new campus by the promise of high salaries and unrivaled academic freedom. The philosophy department was home to such distinguished names as John Dewey and George Herbert Mead. Albion Small, father of modern sociology, was appointed head of that department. U of C physicists Albert A. Michelson, first chair of the physics department, became an early recipient of the Nobel Prize in science. Rockefeller and Harper's goal was to promote Christian morality while advancing scientific knowledge.

The university officially opened on October 1, 1892—young men and woman, books in arm, hopped from classroom to classroom in the as-yet unfinished Cobb Hall. The Gothic-style buildings and surrounding quadrangles exuded an aura of academia. But it was not all about the scholars in those early days. Amos Alonzo Stagg, the university's athletic director, built a legendary football team: The U of C Maroons were the original Monsters of the Midway, winners of seven Big Ten titles, and the only collegiate football squad that can boast of an undefeated lifetime record against Notre Dame. The second university president, Robert Maynard Hutchins, however, deemphasized athletics and dropped the football program in 1939; ten years later, when Northwestern University was in the midst of Rose Bowl celebrations, the U of C campus paper, *Chicago Maroon,* directed a caustic barb at their North Side academic rivals implying that the Wildcats were spending too much time studying the T formation while the Maroons were deciphering the mysteries of the atom.

The University of Chicago has had 78 recipients of the Nobel Prize affiliated with it—more than any other American university.

- September 11 -
1896
Chanute-Herring Biplane Flies 256 Feet at Lakefront

Chicagoan Octave Chanute successfully tested his newest flying machine, a biplane-glider, at the Indiana dunes on this day in Illinois history.

Chanute was a brilliant railroad engineer from Paris, whose accomplishments include designing and supervising the construction of Chicago's Union Stockyards in 1865. He had come to America as a teenager, inspired by the four-week steamship voyage to master the secrets of mechanical transportation. Retiring after a full career at age 57, in 1889, he turned to his true passion—aeronautical theory. He spent years studying the history of experimental aviation. This led to the publication of *Progress in Flying Machines* in 1894, the first-ever comprehensive work examining man's early attempts—and failures—at flight. In it, he wrote: "Let us hope that the advent of a successful flying machine, now only dimly foreseen and nevertheless thought to be possible, will bring nothing but good into the world; that it shall abridge distance, make all parts of the globe accessible, bring men into closer relation with each other, advance civilization, and hasten the promised era in which there shall be nothing but peace and goodwill among all men."

Having analyzed the problems of earlier innovators, Chanute set himself to the task of applying practical solutions to winged gliders of his own design. He conceived of and directed the International Conference of Aerial Navigation at the 1893 World's Columbian Exposition. There, he met many others of like mind and soon partnered with August Herring, a New Yorker who had likewise attempted to built his own gliders before relocating to Chicago. Their pilot was a local aviator named William Avery. The team had tested several designs—triplanes; six-winged gliders; and elastic-winged, batlike machines—before settling on the biplane glider. After numerous runs and modifications, the winged machine finally took flight, clinging to the wind for more than 250 feet. It was an unprecedented success that would become the model for all future biplanes and the inspiration for the Wright Brothers' historic first motored flight in 1903.

Chanute, whose vision set the foundation for modern aviation, died on November 23, 1910, in Chicago.

- SEPTEMBER 12 -
1680
IROQUOIS FORCE ATTACKS GREAT ILLINIWEK VILLAGE

Henri de Tonti narrowly escaped a fierce battle between his Illiniwek allies and an overwhelming Iroquois war party on this day in Illinois history.

Tonti, no stranger to battle, had been nicknamed "Iron Hand" by the Illiniwek for the iron hook attached to his arm where his right hand been lost in battle. He arrived in Illinois Country with La Salle earlier that year, befriended the Native Americans, and had been left behind to command the French outpost by the Illiniwek village near Starved Rock in La Salle's absence. The Illiniwek were at war with the mighty Iroquois. When a friendly scout reported the approaching band of 600 Iroquois warriors, including a chief wearing a French hat and vest, the village broke into panic, and suspicious eyes fell on the remaining Frenchmen.

They accused Tonti of treachery. Many Illiniwek believed that the uniformed chief indicated La Salle's collaboration with the hated Iroquois, and that Tonti had had knowledge of this all along. Tonti was bound and his life threatened, but he assured the warriors that no Frenchmen would be among the Iroquois war party. Winning their trust, he promised to fight at the side of the Illiniwek. With only 500 warriors—the rest off making war with the Sioux out west—his hosts conceded. Tonti's life, for the moment, was spared.

The Illiniwek warriors, now painted for battle, whooping and armed with war clubs and bows and arrows—but few guns—charged the invading Iroquois. Tonti and his handful of French troops followed. But seeing the greater numbers of better-armed Iroquois, he dropped his gun, raised a piece pipe, and, advancing slowly, signaled for peace. He soon found himself swarmed by enemy warriors. One stabbed him in the chest—the blade glancing off ribs—and Tonti was taken captive.

Then, diplomacy and Tonti's wits took over. He demanded to know why the Iroquois had harmed a Frenchman; the Illiniwek, like the Iroquois, were under the protection of the King of France. But when a warrior arrived to report that the Iroquois line had been broken, and that French soldiers had been seen among the Illiniwek force, Tonti improvised quickly. He told his interrogators that the assembled Illiniwek contingent consisted of 1,200 warriors, with 60 French gunmen approaching from the village to reinforce them—a gross exaggeration on both accounts.

The wounded Tonti was sent back to the Illiniwek with wampum, and an uneasy truce began, though the Iroquois would soon be back on the war path, spelling the beginning of the end for the Illiniwek Confederacy.

- SEPTEMBER 13 -

1918

ELGIN'S COMPANY E, THIRD REGIMENT MARCHES OFF TO WAR

On this day in Illinois history, the men of Company E from Elgin set off to fight in the Great War—a scene repeated in cities throughout the state.

Company E was organized in 1877. It had served most notably to settle a violent coal miners' strike in 1894 and a rail workers' strike a couple of years later. In 1898 the Elgin guardsmen served in Puerto Rico during the Spanish-American War, suffering far more from malaria and typhoid fever than from actual combat. In 1917 President Woodrow Wilson pledged all of America's "material resources" to support the Allies in the "War to End all Wars." Congress declared war on Germany, and with the recently enacted Selective Service Act bolstering U.S. forces via the draft, 18- to 30-year-old Elgin recruits were called up to serve in a mission unlike any Company E had ever seen.

The men crossed the Chicago Street Bridge toward Northwestern Station as crowds cheered and waved flags and a band played patriotic songs to see them off. Their first stop was Camp Logan in Texas for training. After that, it was off to the battlefields of Europe. Company E joined Illinois's 33d Infantry Division—the "Prairie Division"—just in time for the Meuse-Argonne offensive. This major battle began in September 1918 and employed more than 400,000 troops, 300 tanks, and 500 U.S. aircraft. One young Elgin recruit recalled advancing on German "pillboxes," concrete squares that sprayed forth devastating machine-gun fire from narrow windows: "[I]t kind of makes a fellow feel like ducking his head and staying close to the ground."

Photo courtesy of Jeff Ruetsche

Company E returned in July 1919. A grand parade and a welcome-home feast served outdoors by Elgin's prettiest young women awaited them. More than 7,000 residents of the city later contributed their dollars and dimes to erect a statue, *Over the Top*, as a memorial to local veterans of the Great War.

Thirty-eight men of Company E never made it back to their Kane County homes.

- SEPTEMBER 14 -
1886

GURDON S. HUBBARD—"THE SWIFT WALKER"— DIES IN CHICAGO

Gurdon Saltonstall Hubbard, whose life spanned Chicago's extraordinary rise from wilderness outpost to burgeoning metropolis, died on this day in Illinois history.

Hubbard first set foot in Chicago as a teenager employed by the American Fur Company. It was October 1818, and, according to his autobiography, the future city then consisted of "four and a half houses, a fort, and a Potawatomi town." The Native

Photo courtesy of John Freyer

Chicago as an early frontier town

Americans nicknamed Hubbard *Pa-pa-ma-ta-be,* or "he who walks swiftly." They had been skeptical of his boast of being able to walk 75 miles in a single day. He challenged their champion walker to set out beside him, and bets were placed to see who could go the greater distance in 24 hours. Hubbard prevailed, and the following day his competitor could barely move while the young trader strolled about seemingly unaffected.

Hubbard transported goods overland from Chicago to Danville, Illinois, and along the Wabash River, cutting a path that came to be known as Hubbard's Trail (later Illinois Route 1). As the settlement at the mouth of the Chicago River grew, all who resided there knew of the vigorous young man. Chief Waba of the nearby Kickapoo tribe even adopted him as a son. But Hubbard became much more than a local celebrity.

In the winter of 1828–29, he used the icy Chicago riverfront to store excess sides of pork, becoming the city's first meatpacker. A few years later, he built what was derisively called "Hubbard's Folly," an immense brick building used to store large quantities of produce—the city's first warehouse. In 1836, Hubbard used one corner of that building to open up a bank, making him Chicago's first banker. And he commissioned "Fire King Engine No. 1," establishing Chicago's first volunteer fire company in 1835. Hubbard was elected a representative to the Illinois General Assembly (1832–33), where he introduced a bill to construct the Illinois & Michigan Canal, and he wielded the ceremonial shovel at the canal's historic groundbreaking on July 4, 1836.

When Hubbard died, Chicago was a great city, and despite the significant role he played in its development, he is little remembered today.

- SEPTEMBER 15 -
1924
PIANIST-SINGER BOBBY SHORT BORN IN DANVILLE

On this day in Illinois history, cabaret great Bobby Short—champion of the "Great American Song"—was born in Vermilion County.

Robert Waltrip Short took to music as a very young child and began performing at Chicago nightclubs by the age of 11. Short was then nicknamed "the miniature King of Swing." He would eventually earn renown as the world's greatest cabaret performer, though he always referred to himself as a simple "saloon singer." He moved out East in the 1940s and became an institution at Cafe Carlyle in New York City by the late 1960s. His voice has been called an American treasure, compared to that of Frank Sinatra, and he sang with the same cheer and love-for-life that marked his personality. His rollicking piano playing, influenced by his classical training, distinguished Short from his peers. And his unique approach to standard hits from the likes of Cole Porter, George Gershwin, and Duke Ellington brought originality and freshness to the popular songs of the day.

Short, who played on more than 100 hit songs and was designated a living legend by the Library of Congress in 2000, never let go of his Illinois roots. He released more than two dozen live recordings, cameoed on television sitcoms and miniseries, and even appeared in four feature films—including Woody Allen's *Hannah and Her Sisters*—from the 1950s through the early 2000s. He returned to Danville regularly, often performing to raise money for various local charity drives. In 1988, for example, Short appeared on stage with fellow celebrities Gene Hackman, Donald O'Connor, and Dick Van Dyke to restore the city's historic Fischer Theater where he was inspired as a young boy to enter show business.

Bobby Short succumbed to leukemia just months after retiring and died on March 21, 2005, in New York City.

- SEPTEMBER 16 -
1966
UNSOLVED KENILWORTH MURDER OF
VALERIE PERCY TAKES PLACE

On this day in Illinois history, the daughter of a U.S. senator was brutally murdered in the family's North Shore suburban mansion, a crime that befuddled investigators and grabbed the attention of the national media.

Chuck Percy was a rising star in the Illinois Republican Party, a self-made millionaire on the campaign trail for U.S. Senate, when tragedy stuck. He had run against and narrowly lost to Otto Kerner in 1964, and now his opponent was Democratic incumbent Paul Douglas. His three-acre Kenilworth estate, overlooking Lake Michigan, was home to himself, his wife, and their five children. It was in Chicago's most exclusive suburban neighborhood, founded by retail mogul Joseph Sears, an area which had not seen a murder in 75 years. But before dawn on that Sunday morning, his eldest child, 21-year-old twin, Valerie Percy, would join the more than 11,000 victims of homicide in the United States that year.

Senator Paul Douglas

The murderer entered the house by cutting through a screen door, went directly to the young woman's upstairs room, and viciously bludgeoned and stabbed her to death in her bed. He escaped before Valerie's mother, awoken by the turmoil, could get a good look at his features. Nothing had been stolen from the home. Valuables, such as Valerie's purse and jewelry, sat untouched on the nearby dresser, so robbery was ruled an unlikely motive. Past boyfriends were questioned—perhaps it was a scorned lover—but those leads went nowhere. Family members and the family's two servants were questioned and dismissed as suspects. Campaign aids were subjected to lie-detector tests; leads again turning up empty as frustration mounted for the investigators. Local authorities and Federal Bureau of Investigation agents under the direction of J. Edgar Hoover pursued thousands of tips, and still had nothing to show for it—nobody was ever charged with the mysterious murder of Valerie Percy.

The funeral was a media circus attended by President Richard Nixon. Less than two months later, a grieving Chuck Percy was elected to the U.S. Senate.

- SEPTEMBER 17 -
1818
ILLINOIS'S FIRST PUBLIC ELECTIONS BEGIN

On this day in Illinois history, three days of polling, in which Shadrach Bond was elected the state's first governor, officially began.

At the same time Illinois's first constitution was being set in type, citizens of the soon-to-be 21st state of the Union hit the voting booths to elect their government officials. Illinois was poor and sparsely populated. "The first state government was as primitive and simple as frontier life itself," noted one historian, "Money was a chronic problem." Shadrach Bond, the nephew of a Kentucky man who had served under George Rogers Clark in capturing Illinois from the British in 1778, ran uncontested and was elected Illinois's first governor. Bond had settled in Illinois (then part of the Northwest Territory) in 1794, flourished as a farmer and politician in what is today Monroe County, and served as Illinois's territorial delegate to the U.S. Congress from 1812 to 1814. He never had much formal education, and desiring a man of letters by his side, designated Elias Kent Kane (the man who had researched, written, and revised the Illinois Constitution) as his secretary of state. The state's first General Assembly convened on October 5, 1818, and Bond was inaugurated the following day.

Limited in power by the new constitution, Bond nevertheless cooperated with the fledgling state's legislators to enact a number of internal improvements, most notably in transportation, during his single term (1818 to 1822). He proposed a canal be built to connect Chicago to the Illinois River, echoing the idea of a great waterway first envisioned by the French explorer Louis Jolliet one-and-a-half centuries earlier. During Bond's term, a road was built connecting Kaskaskia and Illinois's largest city, Shawneetown, though the capital would be moved to Vandalia in 1820. Bond also supported legislation creating toll bridges across Illinois's rivers and creeks to raise funds in support of these various projects, and he backed the expansion of slavery to provide the labor force—though these efforts were blocked by the antislavery camp in the Illinois General Assembly. He also wanted to begin a state lottery to raise money, a proposition that failed.

Shadrach Bond died on April 11, 1830, succumbing to pneumonia at the age of 60 on his Illinois farm.

- SEPTEMBER 18 -

1889

CHICAGO'S HULL-HOUSE FOUNDED

Jane Addams and Ellen Gates Starr moved into the Charles Hull mansion, on Chicago's West Side, and first opened their doors to neighborhood immigrants on this day in Illinois history.

Hull, who built the mansion in 1856, donated it to the two women of privilege for use as a settlement house to better the lives of underprivileged, newly arrived immi-

grants to the city. The neighborhood was once one of the more fashionable and affluent sections of Chicago. After the Great Fire of 1871, however, and the subsequent flight from the area by the upper classes, it had attracted wave after wave of southern and eastern Europeans who lived in wretched conditions in overcrowded tenement buildings. Few spoke English or had any ability beyond that of the unskilled laborer. They were perceived as ignorant, unwashed rabble who had little to contribute to the great city of Chicago. Both Addams and Starr, who had grown up in upper-middle-class families, gone off to college, and never had to hold a job to survive, felt differently and were committed to helping those without such advantages in life.

Their concern for social philanthropy was not new but their insistence on living among the poor was novel. They used Hull-House to teach English, train in job skills, and care for the children of men and woman who worked long hours at grueling jobs to support their families. Other volunteers joined the two women, and the project grew remarkably. What began on a single floor at the mansion had grown by the early 1900s to a fully staffed, two-block, 13-building complex where the city's poor could take literacy classes, join a sports club, or enter a theater and dance program, among dozens of other activities. Hull-House provided the opportunities—and the confidence—disadvantaged city-dwellers needed to lift themselves up from the slums. But by the 1950s and 1960s the city was changing, and Hull-House no longer played the critical role in social reform it had once enjoyed. It was sold to the city for $875,000 in 1963, and all but two of the buildings were demolished to clear ground for a new University of Illinois campus.

The original Hull mansion—today the Jane Addams Hull-House Museum—was designated a National Historic Landmark in 1967.

- SEPTEMBER 19 -

1932

COLUMNIST MIKE ROYKO BORN IN CHICAGO

Mike Royko, Pulitzer Prize–winning "voice of the city," was born in Chicago on this day in Illinois history.

Royko grew up in a working-class Northwest Side neighborhood, in an apartment above the bar his family owned. His writings reflect all the wit and wisdom of the proverbial everyman the young scribe must have encountered during his formative years in blue-collar Chicago. He worked as a bar-back at the family business and also labored setting bowling pins, pushing shopping carts, and as a cog at the local lamp-shade factory before turning to journalism, as he recalled, "because it was easier on my feet." Royko also served in the U.S. Air Force. His career as a columnist began with the newspaper for the Glenview Naval Airbase in suburban Glenview, and he started writing for the often-outspoken *Chicago Daily News* in 1956. A constant nuisance to the seemingly all-powerful Mayor Richard J. Daley, Royko's columns skewered the mayor's proclivity for abusing the English language and, more seriously, inquired doggedly into the corruption at city hall. In 1972 he published his first book, *Boss,* a biographical critique of Mayor Daley, and for it he won the Pulitzer Prize in commentary.

Mike Royko was not only talented but also amazingly prolific. He had a lot to say, on topics ranging from the Chicago Cubs to the mysteries of life itself. Over the course of four decades, Royko cranked out some 7,500 columns, at times paced at five or six per week, and was eventually syndicated in more than 600 papers throughout the United States. Though he gained national fame, the man of letters almost always declined invitations to appear on television, with the exception of filling in as color commentator for a Cubs game on WGN TV the day after broadcaster Harry Caray suffered a heart attack in 1980. When the *Daily News* called it quits in 1978, Royko moved his popular column over to the *Chicago Sun-Times*. When that paper was bought out in 1984 by media mogul Rupert Murdoch, Royko—always brutally candid—quit immediately, stating, "No self-respecting fish would be wrapped in a Murdoch paper." He then finished out his career at the *Chicago Tribune*.

Mike Royko died of a brain aneurysm at age 64 on April 29, 1997, working on fresh columns through his final days.

1972

CHICAGO'S *BOB NEWHART SHOW* DEBUTS ON TV

On this day in Illinois history, *The Bob Newhart Show,* featuring the Windy City and its foremost comedian, first aired on CBS.

George Robert Newhart was born on September 5, 1929, in Oak Park, and graduated from Loyola University Chicago to become an accountant. "The truth is, I look like an accountant, which was my trouble," Newhart recalls. "I'd always end up in the debits or credits by $3.76 or something, which I'd make up out of my pocket." Part-time work as a stand-up comedian and doing radio sketches supplemented his income, and in 1959 Bob Newhart was discovered by Warner Brothers and signed to a contract. *The Button-Down Mind of Bob Newhart,* a comedy album released the following year, went straight to the top of the Billboard 100 (beating out Elvis and the *Sound of Music* soundtrack). For it, Newhart was awarded the 1961 Grammy Award for Album of the Year. He was a Hollywood star in the 1960s, appearing as a regular on *The Dean Martin Show* and *The Ed Sullivan Show,* and later guest-hosting *The Tonight Show* for Johnny Carson more than 80 times.

Newhart returned to Chicago in the early 1970s to film his new television series. (Apparently he had little input editorially, at least regarding the show's intro. With the theme song playing in the background, Newhart is seen commuting from his Wilmette, Illinois, home to his office on North Lake Shore Drive, by way of the Loop—a circuitous route, to say the least.) The weekly sitcom was a huge hit. Bob delivered his stuttering, deadpan wit in the role of a Chicago psychiatrist, Dr. Robert Hartley, surrounded by a colorful supporting cast. The show was nominated for an Emmy as Outstanding Comedy Series. Newhart himself was nominated for a Golden Globe as Best Television Actor in a Comedy. After a break, he returned to television from 1982 to 1990. In *Newhart,* he played the owner of a quirky Vermont bed-and-breakfast. His character awoke—surreally—in the final episode back on the original 1970s Chicago set, having just experienced a very long dream.

Newhart received a star on the Hollywood Walk of Fame in 1999, won the Mark Twain Prize for American Humor in 2002, and, in the summer of 2004, a statue depicting him as Dr. Robert Hartley was unveiled in downtown Chicago.

- SEPTEMBER 21 -
1950
ACTOR BILL MURRAY BORN IN WILMETTE

Bill Murray—the actor and comedian of *Saturday Night Live* fame who is best known for films like *Caddyshack, Groundhog Day,* and *Lost in Translation*—was born in the Cook County suburbs on this day in Illinois history.

As a student at Loyola University in Chicago, Murray worked as a caddie (as did several of his eight siblings) to help pay his way through college. In 1973 he joined Second City, Chicago's famous live-theater improvisation group, and was an immediate—and unpredictable—hit on stage. "I was here for about 400 or 500 of those shows, and I only remember about six," Murray later recalled. He gained national fame as a writer and actor for NBC's *Saturday Night Live* from 1977 to 1980; an all-star cast that included Dan Aykroyd, John Belushi, and Gilda Radner. Murray, who filled the shoes of a departed Chevy Chase, was arguably the funniest of the bunch. His comedic approach, often described as "insincere," and his irreverent, dry wit broke out big-time on the big screen in the early 1980s. *Caddyshack* (1980) and *Ghostbusters* (1984) were two of the top-grossing comedies of all time, and so successful was Murray that his skills as both a comedic writer and actor seemed to peg him, exclusively, to that genre.

But Murray has also excelled in more serious roles. In *Rushmore,* (1998) he appeared to have finally broken the comedic mold, and the *SNL* alumnus was finally nominated for an Academy Award for his leading role in 2003's *Lost in Translation.* He did not win the Oscar but did bring home a Golden Globe for his performance. Murray has appeared in more than 30 major studio films, and was joined by brothers John, Joel, and Brian in 1988's holiday comedy *Scrooged.* (The Murray siblings have since opened a chain of golf-themed restaurants, called Caddy Shacks, where patrons receive the epicurean counsel to "eat, drink, and be merry.") A diehard Cubs fan, he also appeared in the 2004 documentary *This Old Cub,* about Chicago baseball great Ron Santo.

Bill Murray's movies have grossed billions worldwide, though whenever he sings "Take Me Out to the Ball Game" at Wrigley Field, he seems more like one of the crowd than a Hollywood megastar.

More than 80,000 people packed Champaign's outdoor Memorial Stadium, despite overcast skies, to attend the inaugural Farm Aid concert on this day in Illinois history.

It was hard times for America's family farmers. The agricultural boom of the 1970s had busted wide open, and land values, which had soared to record highs, came crashing to the ground. Farmers had overinvested in overhyped land speculations and now saw their land values plummet by as much as 60 percent. Overproduction and a 20 percent decrease in exports (the Carter Administration's grain embargo on the Soviet Union was carried on by President Ronald Reagan) spelled further financial ruin for thousands. Increasing numbers of farmers could not handle their debt and were forced to auction off their land. And there was no lack of buyers; the era of the corporate farm had arrived. Despite a record high $51-billion 1983 farm subsidy, which critics say was improperly distributed, too many could not escape the crisis and hundreds of the nation's small farms were sold every month.

To help out, more than 100 musical acts took the stage, including founders Willie Nelson, Neil Young, and John Mellencamp, in an unprecedented benefit concert to raise money and awareness for the plight of American family farmers. "Wouldn't it be great," Bob Dylan asked from the stage of a previous international aid concert, ". . . if we did something for our own farmers right here in America?" The idea for Farm Aid had been planted, and Nelson, Young, and Mellencamp cultivated it, organizing a concert to save America's small farms that has become an annual festival. Farm Aid featured a jumbled array of styles and artists: B. B. King and Roy Orbison, Loretta Lynn and Joni Mitchell, the Beach Boys and Johnny Cash. Arlo Guthrie shared a stage with Eddie Van Halen and Huey Lewis, and of course the program's founders headlined the show. They raised more than $7 million that day. The proceeds were channeled to various funds that primarily provided legal support to fight foreclosures.

Farm Aid returned to Illinois in 2005 for its 20th anniversary concert, playing Tinley Park's Tweeter Center amid criticism from the *Chicago Tribune* that over nearly 75 percent of past gross revenues had been eaten up by organizational expenses.

1987
Chicago's Award-winning Choreographer Bob Fosse Dies

On this day in Illinois history, Robert Louis Fosse—who won the Academy, Tony, and Emmy awards in 1973 (the only director to ever do so in a single year)—died at the age of 60.

Fosse was born in Chicago on June 23, 1927, the son of a vaudeville entertainer, and his parents steered him towards a life in show business. The industry would bring him great fame. He enrolled in dancing lessons as a young boy and performed in local nightclubs with his own dance group, the Riff Brothers, at 13. Two years later he choreographed his first routine, in which female dancers mimicked the risqué "fan dance" made famous by Sally Rand. The atmosphere of the theatrical world—the dark humor, the social satire, and the suggestive sexuality (he spent much time backstage with strippers)—emerged to define his later work. The chain-smoking Fosse became a brilliant director of musicals. He carried the title "Lord of the Dance." His trademarks included bowler hats, fishnet stockings, and props (chairs, canes) employed by dancers throughout his routines. (He often wore a hat himself as he began to bald as a teenager.) A Fosse number could always be identified by its intensely rapid gestures, a style he called "hand ballet" where parts of the body kick or jerk while others remain posed.

Bob Fosse—who said he "had fantasies of becoming the next Fred Astaire"—is one of the most decorated choreographers in the history of American theater. He was nominated for 15 Tony Awards and won 7 (6 as Best Choreographer and 1 as Best Director). He claimed the Academy, Tony, and Emmy awards in 1973 for *Cabaret*, *Pippin*, and *Liza with a Z*, respectively, all for Best Director, making him the only person in history to win all three in the same year. Fosse's semi-autobiographical *All That Jazz* won the Palme d'Or (Golden Palm Award) for Best Film at the 1979 Cannes Film Festival, the most prestigious such event in the world. After his death in 1999, a show about him, *Fosse*, won a Tony Award for Best Musical.

There was a resurgence of interest in Bob Fosse's life and work with the film revival of his 1975 hit musical, *Chicago*, which won the Oscar for Best Picture in 2002.

- SEPTEMBER 24 -
1963
ILLINOIS BOTANIST MARY AGNES CHASE DIES

On this day in Illinois history, Mary Agnes Chase, the Iroquois County–born botanist who became the leading grass specialist of her time, died at the age of 94.

Born Mary Agnes Meara on April 20, 1869, she moved to Chicago with her mother after her father's death two years later. She grew up in the city as it rebuilt and experienced a postfire renaissance, and in 1888 Meara married newspaper editor William Chase. He died within the year. To support herself, Mary Agnes Chase worked as a proofreader until her interest in plant life was born at a botany exhibit at the 1893 Chicago World's Fair. Chase, who had ended her formal education during grammar school, took to the study of grasses as a hobby, collecting and drawing plant specimens. She was hired as an illustrator for the Chicago Field Museum of Natural History in 1901. At the time, getting work as an illustrator was the lone avenue, for many woman, of entering the scientific community.

Leading botanists soon discovered her talent, and Chase began working alongside top specialists at the U.S. Department of Agriculture by 1903. By 1936, under the guidance of her mentor, Albert S. Hitchcock, Chase had become senior agrostologist (grass scientist) at the USDA. She traveled the world, from the Illinois prairies to the mountains of Brazil, gathering more than 12,000 specimens by the end of her career. She published 70 titles—page-turners all, for the lover of grass life—including *First Book of Grasses, Index to Grass Species,* and a revised edition of *Hitchcock's Manual of the Grasses of the United States.* (She had done most of the field work for the original.) Her work led to the development of nutritionally enhanced cereals and other crops.

Photo courtesy of Jeff Ruetsche

Agnes Chase's own Illinois—once home to vast seas of tall prairie grasses—has long since been transformed by the farmer's plow and paved over of by the steady march of industry, and only a handful of preserves remain.

- SEPTEMBER 25 -

1900

GOVERNOR JOHN PALMER DIES IN SPRINGFIELD

John McCauley Palmer— the state's 15th governor— died in his sleep at his Sangamon County home on this day in Illinois history.

Photo courtesy of Abraham Lincoln Presidential Library

Palmer, who changed party affiliation five times over his six-decade political career, came to Madison County, Illinois, from Kentucky as a 14-year-old boy with his family in 1831. At 17, after his mother's death, John was sent off by his father to make a life for himself in the Illinois prairie frontier. He taught school and sold clocks for years while studying law, was admitted to the bar in 1839, and then opened up a practice in Carlinville, Illinois, almost immediately. He made a name for himself in local politics, serving as a Macoupin County judge intermittently from 1843 to 1852. Palmer befriended Democratic powerhouse Stephen A. Douglas and, with his support, was elected to the Illinois Senate on that party's ticket in 1854. But he later split with Douglas over the controversial issue of the expansion of slavery—and stumped for Republican Abraham Lincoln during the 1860 presidential campaign.

Now a member of the Republican Party, Palmer was a delegate to a national peace conference in 1861, served as a major-general in the Union Army during the Civil War, and was appointed military governor of Kentucky by President Lincoln in 1864. After the war, Illinois Republicans persuaded him to run for state governor—an office he won easily in the 1868 elections. Governor Palmer was inaugurated on January 11, 1869. He blazed an independent trail, however, as Illinois's chief executive, taking a strong stand for state rights and vetoing many Republican-backed bills; and he became a sharp critic of Republican President Ulysses S. Grant. It was during Palmer's single term as governor that Chicago was engulfed in flames in 1871, and he became furious when federal troops were sent in to help restore order. Palmer chose not to run for reelection. He later joined the short-lived Liberal Republican Party, rejoined the Democrats to claim a U.S. Senate seat in 1890, and then formed the Gold Democrats in 1896 to run, unsuccessfully, for the U.S. presidency at the age of 79.

Palmer was interred at City Cemetery, near his family home, in Carlinville, Illinois.

- SEPTEMBER 26 -
1853
FIRST ANNUAL ILLINOIS STATE FAIR COMES TO A CLOSE

On this day in Illinois history, the first-ever state fair ended after a successful week of activities in Springfield.

The Illinois State Fair was conceived by the Illinois State Agricultural Society at a May 1853 meeting in the state capital. Its purpose was to encourage the "best in field and garden crops, cattle, and labor-saving implements," and "elevate the individual farmer's opinion of his own profession," which, in the view of the board members, was suffering at the time. In addition to displaying improved methods of farming, raising livestock, and promoting new ideas in agriculture, the Illinois State Fair also featured all the pageantry, art, and entertainment typical to major expositions of the day. Carnival rides, band concerts, and horse racing were all popular draws—perhaps even more so than the hog-judging contests.

Illinois State Fairgrounds, 1909

The event was an immediate success. The fair ran for six days, charged 25 cents for admission, and on the third day alone, which focused on family activities, it drew 20,000 attendees without, organizers bragged, "a single inebriated man seen among the crowd." The following year, Senator Stephen Douglas made a speech, as did Abraham Lincoln, anticipating their famous series of Illinois debates for the not-too-distant 1858 senatorial campaign. Over the next 40 years, the Illinois State Fair had many homes—Alton, Peoria, Freeport, Jacksonville, Decatur, Quincy, Ottawa, Du Quoin, Olney, and Centralia. Drama gripped the 1858 fair in Centralia when a hot-air balloon lost its mooring and sailed 18 miles with several children onboard, all landing unharmed in a farmer's field. After a lull during the Civil War, the fair returned permanently to Springfield. In 1895, the massive "Dome Building" was purchased from the Chicago World's Fair (1893) and reconstructed in Springfield. It became a permanent fixture on the Illinois State Fair grounds until it burned to the ground in 1917.

The original site in Springfield, which covers 366 acres, has now been home to the Illinois State Fair for more than 100 years, and it receives hundreds of thousands of visitors annually.

- SEPTEMBER 27 -
1817
FAMOUS DUEL GAVE BLOODY ISLAND ITS NAME

The famous Benton-Lucas duel resulted in bloodshed and death on the soon-to-be-named Bloody Island, located on the Mississippi River between St. Louis and East St. Louis, on this day in Illinois history.

Thomas Hart Benton, the future governor of Missouri, and Charles Lucas were two St. Louis lawyers who settled a war of words that began in the courtroom with pistols in the field. Benton accused Lucas of insulting him during a St. Louis Circuit Court trial, which Benton lost, and afterward challenged Lucas to a duel. He declined. A year later, during the 1817 elections, Lucas accused Benton of not paying taxes and therefore being ineligible to vote. Benton derisively refused to reply to charges made by "any puppy who may happen to run across my path." Lucas then challenged Benton to a duel, and Benton accepted. They first met on the island in late August 1817. (A no-man's land between Illinois and Missouri territory, and beyond any city jurisdiction, the sandstone bar began to rise up from the Mississippi River around 1800 and within years had grown into a mile-long island.) The initial meeting left both men wounded—Benton grazed in the leg and Lucas more seriously in the neck. Both survived. They met again the following month, and this time the distance was shortened from 30 feet to a mere 10 feet between the men. Lucas missed, took Benton's shot in the chest, and died 20 minutes later. It was this fatal exchange of lead that gave the island its name and its reputation.

Bloody Island became the preferred site for all manner of illegal activity. Subsequent duels—a socially acceptable way to end an argument at the time—left several men dead, including a U.S. district attorney and a member of Congress. Cock fights and bare-knuckle brawls, both outlawed in the mid-1800s, also became common activities on the island. But in the late 1830s Congress appropriated $65,000 for the construction of two dykes to redirect the flow of the river, which in effect washed away several hundred feet of sandbar and pushed Bloody Island closer to the Illinois shore. The construction was supervised by a young engineer from Washington, D.C., named Robert E. Lee. So successful was the project that Lee, future top general of the Confederacy, was promoted to captain of the U.S. Army Corps of Engineers.

Today the site is simply called the "Island" and is joined to the mainland at East St, Louis, Illinois.

- September 28 -

1920

Eight Chicago White Sox Indicted
for 1919 "Black Sox" Scandal

On this day in Illinois history, eight Chicago ballplayers—including one of baseball's greats, "Shoeless Joe" Jackson—were indicted for throwing the 1919 World Series.

The 1919 White Sox had won the American League pennant and were considered the cream of the crop in professional baseball. But they lost the best-of-nine World Series, three games to five, to the Cincinnati Reds that October. Illicit gambling in professional baseball was no novelty, and rumors soon spread of foul play at the Fall Classic. In December the *New York World* published an article implying the World Series had been fixed. Controversy rankled the baseball world into the 1920 season until finally, in mid-September, names were named and it was learned that gamblers had promised $80,000 to key Chicago players to lose the World Series.

Photo courtesy of Library of Congress, LOT 11147-1

Team owner Charles Comiskey immediately suspended all eight players for the rest of the 1920 season. He paid one of the lowest salaries in the major leagues; he was so parsimonious that he had refused to pay the team's laundry bill. The "Black Sox" nickname had actually been coined by the players themselves, in reference to their dirt-stained uniforms, long before the scandal ever broke. In suits and ties—cleaned and pressed—they went on trial in July 1921.

The players were cleared of conspiracy to defraud by a Chicago grand jury on August 2, in large part because the key confessions of hitter Jackson and pitcher Ed Cicotte mysteriously disappeared from the Cook County Courthouse files. Commissioner of Baseball Kenesaw Mountain Landis would have none of it, banning all eight players from the major leagues for life the following day despite the jury's acquittal. Joining Jackson and Cicotte were pitcher "Lefty" Williams, outfielder "Happy" Felsch, and infielders "Chick" Gandil, Fred McMullin, "Swede" Risberg, and "Buck" Weaver.

Shoeless Joe's .375 batting average, errorless play in the field, and lone home run (between both teams) of the series cast doubt on his complicity. He appealed for but was denied reinstatement to major-league baseball in later years.

- SEPTEMBER 29 -
1963

GEORGE HARRISON—THE "QUIET BEATLE"—ENDS AN IMPROMPTU TWO-DAY TOUR OF FRANKLIN COUNTY

Five months before the band's milestone appearance on *The Ed Sullivan Show*, Beatles guitarist George Harrison took the stage with local rock 'n' rollers The Four Vests at a Franklin County birthday bash, on this day in Illinois history.

It happened before he was "Fab." George Harrison's sister, Louise Caldwell, had moved to Benton, Illinois, with her husband, Gordon, from Canada earlier that year. Harrison arrived in mid-September for a two-week visit. There, he quickly hit it off with Louise's friend, Gabe McCarty. Gabe's band, The Four Vests, had a good local following and the two talked music constantly while shopping for records around town. In fact, Harrison purchased his famous Rickenbacker "cresting wave" guitar while visiting a Mount Vernon, Illinois, music store with McCarty.

The Beatles were just beginning to make it big in Britain, and George, noting Illinois's approximate size to England, thought it would therefore take some time for Beatlemania to sweep across all of America. But Louise was a huge fan and early promoter of her brother's band. A local teenage girl, Marcia Schafer Raubach, whose father owned the local radio station WFRX, had been happily playing Beatles songs like "From Me to You" and "Love Me Do" at the request of George's sister—making it one of the first American radio stations to spin Beatles records on the airwaves. Marcia also became the first American disc jockey to broadcast an on-air interview with a member of the Fab Four when Harrison spoke live in-studio with the girl one night during his visit.

The first impromptu gig occurred at a local VFW. Harrison was surprised to be invited on stage with his new friend's band, but they clicked. The next night, the budding superstar once again joined The Four Vests, this time at a birthday party at a neighborhood bocce ball club. The crowd at both shows was electrified. Harrison joined the local rock 'n' rollers in a rousing performance that included "Everybody's Trying to Be My Baby" and "Johnny B. Goode." They also played a number of popular Hank Williams country tunes.

The Caldwell home in Benton, Illinois, where Harrison stayed was saved from the wrecking ball in the 1990s and is now the aptly named Hard Day's Night Bed and Breakfast.

- SEPTEMBER 30 -

1917

FIRST RECRUITS FROM CAMP GRANT, ROCKFORD, LEAVE FOR WAR

On this day in Illinois history, the first units to arrive at Camp Grant in Winnebago County left for training in Texas, where they would help form the 33rd Division of the Illinois National Guard and be off to fight in Europe.

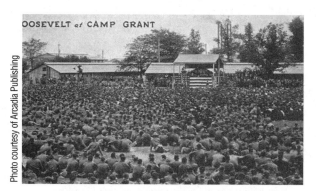

Photo courtesy of Arcadia Publishing

Camp Grant was organized after General Order 95 created a National Army Cantonment of Northern Illinois for training infantry and engineers to support the war effort. Construction began in July 1917 on Rockford's southern border, on 3,000 acres of farmland purchased by the U.S. government from area families for $835,000. By November, Camp Grant was virtually a self-contained city, with everything from soldiers' barracks to a YMCA. The complex comprised over 1,000 buildings, including stables for the cavalry with capacity for 500 horses.

Named after Civil War hero, former U.S. president, and Illinoisan Ulysses S. Grant, the camp was the starting point or demobilization center for roughly 1 million fighting men during the Great War. Among them was the celebrated Illinois 86th Infantry Division—nicknamed the Black Hawk Division for the Indian War of the previous century. In September 1917, former President Theodore Roosevelt delivered a 40-minute speech before 21,000 soldiers stationed at the camp, supporting U.S. intervention in the European war. One year later, Camp Grant was hit by the influenza epidemic which reaped a final death toll of 1,400 soldiers and 323 civilians.

Camp Grant was deactivated in 1921 and handed over to the state a few years later, when it became the peacetime training center for the Illinois National Guard. After use as a base for the Civilian Conservation Corps during much of the 1930s, it was reactivated to serve the draft for the U.S. Army as America edged ever closer to participation in World War II. More than `2,000 German prisoners of war called Camp Grant home from 1943 to 1946.

Deactivated once again in 1946, most of its facilities were auctioned off and the land where Camp Grant once stood is now, in part, Greater Rockford Airport.

This day in

October

- OCTOBER 1 -
1895

DeKalb Celebrates Awarding of New Teachers' College

A parade was held to the cheers of thousands on this day in Illinois history, when word reached DeKalb that it had been selected host city for the new Northern Illinois teachers' college.

In May 1893, a bill aimed at founding a new teachers' college in northern Illinois was passed into law by the Illinois legislature. Pressure applied to Governor John Altgeld and state representatives in Springfield by DeKalb newspaperman Clinton Rosette and businessman Colonel Isaac Elwood proved to be influential in passing the legislation. Several northern Illinois cities also coveted the promised school and the economic windfall it would produce and immediately offered incentives for the northern Illinois teachers' college to be brought to their respective communities. Rockford, Freeport, Oregon, Dixon, Fulton, and Polo all lobbied to be host city for the school; but DeKalb, with an all-out community effort, lobbied just a little bit harder.

Each of the other candidates boasted of a scenic location on the Rock River as an ideal campus setting, except for Fulton, which sat on the mighty Mississippi River. DeKalb, however, sits beside the modest Kishwaukee River—nice, but it simply did not compare. In July, a committee appointed to award the decision took a tour of all the sites, with DeKalb last on the schedule. The people of DeKalb built a damn outside of town, dredged up mud from the riverbed, and, reportedly, went without water for a whole weekend. When the inspectors arrived, and just before they crossed the "Kish" over what would become the Lincoln Highway Bridge, the townspeople opened the dam, and the river's water level rose to record heights. Fishermen nearby just happened to display strings of healthy fish in plain view, including one exceptionally large cod, which are not native to the river. The offer by local barbed wire entrepreneur, Joseph Glidden, to donate 67 wooded acres along the river for construction of the school and a promise to name its administrative center after the sitting governor, were too much for the committee to pass up.

The Northern Illinois Normal School opened in 1912 with 139 students. Today, as Northern Illinois University, its 23,000 annual enrollment makes it the second-largest state college in Illinois—quite a catch.

Photo courtesy of Library of Congress, PAN US GEOG Illinois

Unable to attend the opening day ceremonies, President Franklin Delano Roosevelt was nonetheless impressed by the achievements made at Chicago's Century of Progress World's Fair, which he visited on this day in Illinois history.

Opening on May 27, 1933, with the theme of "I Will" in defiance of the Great Depression, the fair deserved the president's praise. "I congratulate Chicago and its guests and wish the exposition unbounded success," the president declared, "success as a show, but more success in helping to bring about a binding friendship among the nations of the earth." Indeed, there was an international theme, with exhibits for Japan, Italy, Sweden, and many other nations around the globe. The futuristic and luminous

Photo courtesy of Library of Congress, LC-DIG-ggbain-05644

A young FDR

Art Deco buildings that dominated the fair's architecture—in striking contrast to Daniel Burnham's classically inspired white city of the 1893 Columbian Exposition—projected a sense of progress that offset, if only temporarily, the glumness of the day. In the fair's two years of operation, nearly 39 million people paid the 50-cent admission to escape the realities of the Great Depression.

Though it wasn't as expansive as Chicago's 1893 World's Fair, the 1933–1934 Century of Progress Fair was every bit as ambitious and just as full of pageantry. The exposition celebrated not only the city's centennial, but also all that had been achieved in science, industry, and transportation during the preceding century. The exhibit space was built on 437 acres of mostly landfill called Northerly Park (later to become Meigs Field). It featured a replica of the original Fort Dearborn; the spectacular Sky-Ride, which carried passengers between two towers 628 feet above the North Lagoon; and the marvelous Travel and Transport Building with its "breathing roof." Also to be found was the more customary stuff of carnivals, such as human "freaks of nature" and dancing fleas. But the biggest hits among fair goers were perhaps Free Beer Day and the expo's top attraction, fan dancer Sally Rand.

Most remarkable of all was that the Century of Progress, funded privately by a $10-million bond issued on October 28, 1929—the day before Black Tuesday sunk the nation into the Great Depression—actually turned a profit.

- OCTOBER 3 -
1907
PRESIDENT THEODORE ROOSEVELT VISITS, PRAISES CAIRO

Teddy Roosevelt made a visit to the state's southernmost city and seat of Alexander County to deliver a stirring speech extolling the virtues of the town and its people, on this day in Illinois history.

"Here is the breeding place not of disease," he said, "but of heroes, the best people that ever trod the face of the earth." This was in reference and stark contrast to the damning words penned by British author Charles Dickens, who, after visiting the city in 1842, wrote in *American Notes* that Cairo was a "detestable morass . . . a breeding place of fever, ague, and death." (Dickens used Cairo as the model "nightmare city" of Eden in his novel *Martin Chuzzlewit* the following year.) He spared no kind words for Cairo's neighbors either; Illinoistown (present-day East St. Louis), for example, was full of "muck and mire." But Dickens had invested unwisely in the Cairo City and Canal Company, losing money on the failed deal two years earlier, and it is suggested that these financial misfortunes may be the source of the scribe's bitterness toward southern Illinois.

Photo courtesy of Library of Congress, LC-H824- P01-

The 26th president of the United States had no such misgivings. "The American people abhor a vacuum," he famously told the assembled crowd at St. Mary's Park Pavilion. Cairo, Illinois— destination of Tom Sawyer in the fictional adventure by an American writer with a better opinion of the region—was anything but a vacuum. Resembling its Egyptian namesake as a river delta city, Cairo's location at the intersection of the muddy waters of the Mississippi and the yellow waters of the Ohio gave it prime importance in 19th-century America. It was connected to Chicago via the Illinois Central Railroad in 1856, played a central role in the Underground Railroad, and served as General Ulysses S. Grant's headquarters during the Civil War. By the 1880s, because of its centralized transportation links, the city had earned the highest per-capita commercial value in the entire United States. But gentle decay rather than economic boon has been the fate of the small city, which in the early 20th century became a largely abandoned, deteriorating shell of its former self.

Cairo was visited by two of Roosevelt's successors, President William H. Taft in 1909 and President William J. Clinton in 1996.

- OCTOBER 4 -

1931

DICK TRACY, CREATED BY WOODSTOCK'S CHESTER GOULD, HITS SYNDICATION

On this day in Illinois history, cartoonist Chester Gould saw his newest creation, *Dick Tracy,* one of the most popular comic strips of the 20th century, finally hit the nation's funny pages.

The fantastic plainclothes detective was born in the heyday of organized crime. "I decided that if the police couldn't catch the gangsters," Gould once commented, "I'd create a fellow who could." That fellow, Dick Tracy, was an otherwise normal 34-year-old family man when the murder of his father-in-law spurred him to devote his life to fighting crime. The dashing private eye squared off against some of the most colorful villains ever created in pulp fiction, most notably his arch-nemesis, Big Boy (his father-in-law's murderer who Tracy spent decades pursuing). There were also 88 Keys (a jazz pianist–turned–murderer who preyed on wealthy heiresses), Prune Face (a grotesquely distorted Nazi spy), and Breathless Mahoney (a blonde bombshell and master thief). Tracy's exploits often featured the aid of futuristic gadgetry—the two-way radio–wristwatch, for example—gifts from his friend, the blind inventor named Brilliant. To add realism to these otherwise outlandish stories, Gould enrolled in criminology classes at Northwestern University in Evanston, Illinois, and was a regular visitor at the Chicago Police crime lab on State Street.

Photo courtesy of Jeff Ruetsche

Gould came from Oklahoma to Chicago in 1921, an ambitious 21-year-old cartoonist with a lifelong dream of being publishing in the *Chicago Tribune.* It would be ten years before that dream came true. In the interim, he attended Northwestern University, married, and settled in Wilmette, Illinois, where he freelance-designed newspaper advertisements and wrote theater reviews for various local dailies. He kept submitting ideas to the *Chicago Tribune.* After nine years and more than 50 rejections, publisher J. M. Patterson saw something he liked—an action-packed detective thriller called *Plainclothes Tracy*—and Gould finally got his big break. Gould moved to Woodstock, Illinois, in 1935, and from his McHenry County home and studio he created the original *Dick Tracy* strip, which stayed in syndication until he retired in 1977.

Gould received a great deal of recognition during his illustrious career, including the 1980 Edgar Award (named for Edgar Allen Poe), the first time in the award's 34-year history that it went to the creator of a comic strip.

- OCTOBER 5 -

1979

POPE JOHN PAUL II CELEBRATES CHICAGO MASS

On this day in Illinois history, tens of thousands of Catholics packed Chicago's Grant Park to attend a Mass celebrated by Pope John Paul II.

In seeing the crowds gathered, one would have thought The Beatles had reunited for a tour of the Midwest. Not content to watch on television, the city's faithful—estimates say upward of 350,000—of the city's faithful flooded Grant Park to receive the historic blessing. The Pope's motorcade made its way up Michigan Avenue, lined by thousands of cheering citizens, before the Pope met the welcoming committee of 300 U.S. cardinals and bishops. A three-block-long greeting line of Illinois Knights of Columbus in full regalia formed a notable part of the parade route. The Mass celebrated that afternoon

Photo courtesy of Library of Congress, U.S. News & World Report Magazine Collection, LC-U9-38282-12

was the highlight of the Pope's 37-hour visit to Chicago, the type of international pilgrimage that earned him the nickname "The Pilgrim Pope," for having toured the world more extensively than all his predecessors combined. The Pope's two-hour Mass at Grant Park, for which thousands had camped out overnight to get prime seating, included a seven-page homily in praise of America.

The papal visit had a tremendous impact on Chicagoans, especially the city's large Polish community. Pope John Paul II was born in a small town outside of Krakow and became the first Polish-born pontiff. Except for Warsaw and perhaps the city of Lodz in central Poland, Chicago has the largest Polish population in the world. Earlier that day, the Pope had celebrated Mass at Five Holy Martyrs Church on the city's Northwest Side. Thousands of parishioners spilled out into the streets of the neighborhood, waving hundreds of red-and-white Polish flags. The Pope, speaking in his native language, commented on the cold and wet October morning, "This feels just like Poland." President Jimmy Carter, who met one-on-one with the pontiff at the White House a few days later, said Pope John Paul II was surprised by the massive outpouring of support in Chicago. "The pope represents truth, integrity, and humility," Carter added. "These are things we don't talk about much."

Mayor Jane Byrne renamed a stretch of road on the city's West Side Pope John Paul II Street to commemorate the historic visit.

- OCTOBER 6 -

1899

PEORIA'S SOLDIERS' AND SAILORS' MONUMENT DEDICATED

On this day in Illinois history, President William McKinley and 30,000 others attended the dedication of the Soldiers' and Sailors' Monument in Peoria's courthouse square.

Peoria's Soldiers' and Sailors' Civil War Memorial was the result of an all-out community effort. Funded by donations from city residents, it was erected by the Ladies' Memorial Day Association. It was designed by local artist Fritz Triebel, who created many of Peoria's most notable monuments, including "Love Knows No Caste" at city hall and the Robert Ingersoll statue at Glen Oak Park. Triebel originally called his work "In Defense of the Flag." At the base of a 30-foot column stands Lady Liberty, draped in robes and inscribing patriot verse onto a tablet. Triebel's Italian wife, Santina, served as his model. Small groups of heroic, battle-worn soldiers of the Union Army and sailors of the U.S. Navy flank her. The series of bronze sculptures, a combined 70,000 pounds, were cast in Italy, shipped to Illinois, and assembled by Triebel and his assistants where the monument stands today. Granite for its base had to be shipped in from the state of Maine twice—the original stone was so heavy that it sank the ship carrying it just a few hundred feet offshore.

Two time capsules were placed within the monument. A copper box located at the base contains the names of Peoria County schoolchildren, many of whom contributed their pennies to the memorial fund. A tin box within a globe, upon which the bronze eagle, "Old Abe," is perched, holds the names of local Civil War veterans. Stone benches for sightseers encircle the monument.

One Civil War veteran who attended the ceremony was not impressed with Triebel's work. He went home and wrote a critical letter to the artist: "I have never seen . . . a drummer boy with a pistol chasing one of the enemy; and never heard of a trumpeter mixing in with the infantry and tooting signals in the midst of battle." Triebel replied tersely, "To speak of art to you is the same as speaking to a jackass."

The monument has been the courtyard centerpiece of the Peoria County Courthouse—the current building and its predecessor were torn down in 1963—since its dedication.

- OCTOBER 7 -

1945

CURSE OF THE BILLY GOAT SETS IN

The Chicago Cubs lost game five of the 1945 World Series to the Detroit Tigers 2–1—succumbing to the Curse of the Billy Goat—on this day in Illinois history.

The Cubs had held a two-games-to-one lead and home field advantage for the remainder of the series going into game four. That day, Billy Goat Tavern owner William Sianis approached the gates with a pair of box-seat tickets and a guest—his pet goat, Murphy. Sianis and Murphy were reluctantly shown to their seats. They enjoyed at least a few innings of the game before Cubs owner, Philip K. Wrigley, having learned of the goat's disruptive presence and accompanying odor, ordered stadium ushers to evict the duo from the ballpark. Sianis—infuriated—placed a curse on the Cubs; they would lose this World Series and never again win the National League pennant, so long as they played at Wrigley Field. The Tigers won that day 4–1, eventually taking three of four games at Wrigley to steal the series from Chicago. The Cubs have not returned to the Fall Classic since.

The Curse of the Billy Goat rears its unwelcome head every time the Cubs come close to winning the pennant. Most devastating was the 1969 flop. After two decades of losing, the 1969 ball club headed toward September with a robust eight-and-a-half-game lead, only to be surpassed by the second-place New York Mets in a heartbreaking pennant race. In 1973, after leading their division in the first half of the season, the Cubs lost 49 of their 76 second-half games to finish near last place. They made the playoffs in 1984, 1989, and 1998 but fell frustratingly short of the National League pennant in each of those seasons. And in 2003—when the curse looked to be finally, mercifully broken—a now infamous botched play on a foul ball (and a subsequently unraveled team) once again ruined Cubs fans' dreams of a World Series at Wrigley.

Sianis died in 1970; his subterranean tavern in downtown Chicago was immortalized by a 1970s *Saturday Night Live* skit—"Cheezborger, cheezborger! No fries, cheeps! No Coke, Pepsi!"—and the fate of Murphy is unknown.

- OCTOBER 8 -

1871

CHICAGO ENGULFED IN FLAME

On this day in Illinois history, the Great Chicago Fire reduced 80 city blocks—nearly 3.5 square miles of prime Chicago real estate—to smoldering ruins.

Chicago was a virtual tinderbox, with block after block of wooden "shams and shingles" ready to ignite after several weeks of unremitting drought. On the dry October evening, a fire of unknown origins—widely attributed to Mrs. O'Leary's mythical cow—started at the corner of DeKoven and Jefferson streets, on the city's West Side. It was not an uncommon incident; in fact, the city's 185 firefighters were by that night exhausted after dousing 20 such blazes in the past week, including a substantial fire that destroyed four city blocks just the previous day.

A watchman sighted the fire from the courthouse tower downtown, but he telegraphed in the wrong location, sending fire crews astray. A shopkeeper across from the actual site at O'Leary's barn pulled the hook on a recently installed alarm box, but it failed to sound. Consequently, firemen did not arrive at the scene until 10 p.m., two hours after the conflagration began. By that time it was too late. Winds had lifted the columns of flame, which were so intense that heat blasts could be felt several miles away, northeastward across the Chicago River. The inferno advanced unmercifully, devouring practically everything in its path.

Twenty-seven hours later it was all over but the rebuilding. More than 17,000 buildings had been destroyed; only the limestone water tower and pumping station were left standing in the fire's wake. At least 250 people died, and one-third of Chicago's 300,000 residents were left homeless. Hundreds of stores and business were wiped out. The city's gasworks and waterworks sat among the ruins, leaving large sections of the city that had been spared by the flames without lights or clean drinking water. Residents had grabbed what belongings they could and fled north in droves to the safety of Lincoln Park.

"There was no sleep for us until we heard the welcome sound of rain," remembered Horace White of the *Chicago Tribune*. "How our hearts did rise in thankfulness to heaven for rain!"

- OCTOBER 9 -
1919
ILLINOIS WOMEN'S COMMITTEE (IWC) DISBANDS

The Illinois Women's Committee, after two years of coordinating the state's women in support of U.S. troops fighting in World War I, held its final executive meeting on this day in Illinois history.

The IWC—"First in Importance"—was created in May 1917 under the auspices of the Illinois State Council of Defense and the Council of National Defense Women's Committee. Leaders of the IWC cleverly utilized this joint state and federal status to play the two authorities off one another, thus acting with considerable independence from either. Chairman Louise deKoven Bowen, for example, was able to maintain control of IWC funds throughout the organization's existence. When the state defense council requested IWC funds be collected into its treasury, Bowen answered that the money had been raised on behalf of the national organization; when the federal defense council asked for the same funds, she gave the opposite answer. And the organization put that money to terrific use.

By the end of 1917 the IWC was the largest organization of its kind in the nation. Each of Illinois's 102 counties had appointed committee leaders, and more than 1,000 Illinois cities, towns, and townships were organized into local IWC chapters. (This number peeked at 2,136 by the time the Illinois Women's Committee disbanded.) Among other duties, the IWC posted patriotic literature—"educational propaganda"— at library, school, and church bulletin boards throughout the state. They organized meetings of church groups and attended county fairs to do the same. The women were also stalwart promoters of Victory Gardens, which encouraged people to grow their own produce, helping in the government effort to conserve and ration food for the troops. Ordered to mobilize Illinois woman to support the nation's war effort, which they accomplished to national praise, the IWC also used its semiautonomous status to broaden the definition of "war effort" and pursued their own agenda of social reform— women's suffrage, child welfare, and improved working conditions for Illinois's laborers.

Roughly one-third of the state's women and girls over the age of 16 joined their local IWC, supporting the war effort while establishing the most comprehensive organization of women Illinois has ever seen.

- OCTOBER 10 -
1765
BRITISH TROOPS ARRIVE TO TAKE COMMAND OF FORT DE CHARTRES

France's Illinois Country stronghold, Fort de Chartres, located "about a musket shot" from the Mississippi River near Prairie du Rocher, was surrendered to the British on this day in Illinois history.

The mammoth fortress was commissioned in 1718 by the Company of the Indies, under the auspices of King Louis XV. The company had been granted a trade monopoly in the region, and the fort was to protect their vast interests. It was completed in 1720 and served to consolidate French control and protect lucrative trade routes. It became

the administrative center of French colonial government in Illinois Country. After being rebuilt three times, from the mid-1750s through 1763, the final Fort de Chartres had walls 15 feet high and three feet thick, a full stockade, stables, barracks, bastions for cannons, and a powder magazine. It stood imposingly on four acres of ground amid the Illinois wilderness but was never manned by more than a small contingent of soldiers.

The French-Indian War, or Seven Years War, raged across the American colonies from 1756 to 1763, the last and greatest of four colonial conflicts pitting the French against the English. (Most Native Americans sided with the French, while American colonists, still loyal to the King, sided with the British.) The Treaty of Paris resulted in France relinquishing nearly all its North American possessions—including the Illinois stronghold—to the victorious British. In August 1765, two years later, Captain Thomas Stirling led a force of 100 men from Fort Pitt in Pennsylvania westward to secure Fort de Chartres. They arrived on October 9, and the following day, in a choreographed ceremony, the stone fortress officially passed into British hands. Louis de Bellerive, the French commander, wept at the site of the cross of St. George replacing the lilies of France. The British renamed it Fort Cavendish, but made little use of the site—finding it located too close to the unpredictable river—and finally abandoned it to corrosion in 1771.

The state of Illinois purchased the fort in 1913, after more than a century of neglect, and rebuilt much of it through the 1930s; it is today an Illinois State Historic Site.

- OCTOBER 11 -
1908
THE WORLD SERIES COMES TO WEST SIDE GROUNDS

The Chicago Cubs defeated the Detroit Tigers 6–0 in game two of the 1908 World Series—en route to back-to-back championships—on this day in Illinois history.

It was the first game of the series to be played in Chicago, and the Cubs had already taken game one in Detroit, 10–6. The Cubs's home ballpark, West Side Grounds, was packed with 17,770 screaming Chicago baseball fans who saw pitcher Orval Overall hold the American League champs to a lone, ninth-inning run. It was 0–0 going into the eighth, when Joe Tinker's home run led the Cubs to a six-run explosion. Three days later, Overall—who had a solid season with 15 wins, 4 saves, and an austere 1.92 ERA—shut down Ty Cobb and the Tigers to three hits before a World Series record-low crowd of 6,210 dispirited baseball fans at Detroit's Bennett Park. The Cubs had won the Fall Classic four games to one and returned to Chicago baseball heroes, the first team in major-league history to win back-to-back World Series. (They had dominated the American League Champion Tigers, four games to none with one tie, in the 1907 World Series, after having lost to the White Sox the previous year.)

Photo courtesy of Library of Congress, LC-DIG-ggbain-12246

At the core of both the 1907 and 1908 championships was the famous double-play combination of shortstop Joe Tinker, second-base man Johnny Evers, and first-base man–manager Frank Chance—the "peerless leader." So popular became the trio that they were immortalized in the poem "Baseball's Sad Lexicon," by New York sportswriter (and no Cubs fan) Franklin Pierce Adams: "These are the saddest of possible words: 'Tinker to Evers to Chance.' / Trio of bear cubs, and fleeter than birds, / Tinker and Evers and Chance. / Ruthlessly pricking our gonfalon bubble, / Making a Giant hit into a double— / Words that are heavy with nothing but trouble: / 'Tinker to Evers to Chance.'" Stellar pitching secured that season's 99-55 pennant-winning record. Starters Ed Reulbach (24-7, 2.03 ERA) and Mordecai Brown (29-9, 1.47 ERA) paced the staff.

The Cubs have not won the World Series—or inspired many poets—since, but as they say, "Any team can have a bad century."

- OCTOBER 12 -
1970
PAUL "SHOEBOX" POWELL'S HORDE OF CASH FOUND IN HOTEL ROOM

Illinois Secretary of State Paul Powell died on October 10 and left the famous cache of $800,000 in cash—stuffed in shoeboxes—in his St. Nicholas Hotel room in Springfield, which was found on this day in Illinois history.

Powell was born in the small town of Vienna, Illinois, in 1902 and spent his entire childhood and young adult life in Johnson County. From humble beginnings—member of the local school board to mayor of Vienna—the lifelong Democrat built a political career that landed him at the highest levels of state government over the course of four decades. He never lost an election. In 1935, he won a seat in the Illinois House of Representatives. Powell served as speaker of the house from 1959 to 1963, and became Illinois secretary of state in 1965, holding office until his death in 1970. He was an Illinois delegate to the Democratic National Conventions of 1944, 1948, 1952, 1956, and 1960. He was a shrewd politician who could secure southern Illinois votes, quid pro quo, for his Chicago friends.

Powell never earned an annual state salary of more than $30,000 in the political arena and did not lead an extravagant lifestyle. But the hometown hero amassed a personal fortune of world-class proportions during the era of the honor system— before politicians made public disclosures of campaign contributions. His estate, when finally settled in 1978, was valued at $4.6 million, including several hundred thousand dollars invested in horse racing. His office had been investigated for corruption in 1966, but Powell was then exonerated.

Two days after he died while visiting the Mayo Clinic in Rochester, Minnesota, Powell's staff discovered a treasure trove of cash and other goods in his Springfield hotel room. The $800,000 in large and small bills was horded not only in shoeboxes, but briefcases, envelopes, and metal security boxes as well. Also excavated from the site, according to some reports, were considerable stashes of whiskey, transistor radios, and canned cream corn. Exactly how and why Paul "Shoebox" Powell had collected such odd booty in his hotel room remains a mystery to this day.

He is buried, along with that secret, at Fraternal Cemetery in Vienna, Illinois.

- OCTOBER 13 -

1917

THE WORLD SERIES COMES TO COMISKEY PARK

The Chicago White Sox won game five 8–3, their last World Series victory at Comiskey Park, before 27,323 home fans on this day in Illinois history.

The Southsiders followed up by taking the sixth and deciding game 1–0 two days later at New York's Polo Grounds, defeating the National League champion Giants four games to two. The potent Sox offense was led by future Hall of Famer Eddie Collins. He batted .409 on the series and scored a key run, stealing the plate after an exciting run-down between third and home during the series-winning rally. The arms of Red Faber and Eddie Cicotte, who combined for all four wins, led Sox pitchers.

The series began well, with the White Sox winning the first two games at Comiskey Park before traveling to New York. The Giants responded in kind, shutting out the Sox in games three and four at the Polo Grounds. Back at Comiskey, Game Five looked shaky until seventh- and eighth-inning rallies delivered an 8–5 Sox victory to the thousands of South Side fans in attendance. Two days later, the White Sox broke the home-team winning trend to capture the series at the Polo Grounds.

Photo courtesy of Library of Congress, LC-US262-97873

The White Sox won 100 games in 1917 against 54 losses, the club's highest winning percentage (.649) ever. After several years of mediocrity, a frustrated team owner, Charles Comiskey, had begun assembling the team in 1914 with one goal—a World Series championship—in mind. Joe Jackson and Happy Felsch were the team's sluggers, with five home runs and six home runs, respectively, in 1917—a fair number during the so-called dead-ball era. They were also the only two Sox hitters to bat at a better-than-.300 clip. The pitching staff kept opposing batters in check with a team ERA of 2.16, led by Cicotte (28 wins), Lefty Williams (17 wins), and Faber (16 wins).

The White Sox have failed to the Fall Classic since—the second-longest championship drought in major-league history.

WHITE SOX DEFEAT CUBS IN SIXTH AND
DECIDING GAME OF WORLD SERIES

The Chicago White Sox shocked the baseball world, and their crosstown rivals, with a Game Six series-winning upset on this day in Illinois history.

It was the first and only all-Chicago World Series. The Chicago Cubs were three-to-one favorites going into the series, having won 116 regular season games to just 36 losses. Led by player and manager Frank Chance, the Cubs had run roughshod over the National League that year with 705 runs scored on 1,306 hits. White Sox hitters, by contrast, had combined for a league-low .228 team batting average.

The Sox's hopes looked even dimmer when their starting shortstop, George Davis, announced that he'd miss the opening game, and possibly the whole series, because of a sore back. The Cubs were "booming along at such a rate," wrote baseball historian Warren Brown, "practically no one in Chicago could see much sense in playing the World Series." But play they did. The Sox—living up to their nickname—battled the mighty Cubs to a two-games-to-two draw through game four, despite going an anemic 11 for 113 at the plate. George Davis then returned to the lineup and led the Sox

Photo courtesy of Library of Congress, LC-US262-53418

to an 8–6 victory in Game Five, driving in three runs off two doubles before 23,000 fans at the Cubs's West Side Grounds. The underdogs found themselves up three games to two and then headed for home, Southside Park.

But Game Six looked to be no easy task for the White Sox, aka "The Hitless Wonders." They would face ace Cubs pitcher Mordecai "Three Fingers" Brown, who as a boy had lost his right index finger to a corn shredder and had broken two others on that same hand while chasing pigs on his uncle's farm. Owing to his disfigurement, Three Fingers had developed a devastating curveball. Brown led the league in 1906 with a minuscule ERA of 1.04, but on this day he did not show his best stuff. The Sox delighted the 19,000 fans at Southside Park by knocking in seven runs off the feared curveballer in the first two innings. Hurler "Doc" White held the prolific Cubs offense to three runs on seven hits in nine innings.

The White Sox won the game 8–3, and with it the World Series—and Windy City bragging rights for a century.

ALTON, ILLINOIS, HOSTS FINAL LINCOLN-DOUGLAS DEBATE

The seventh and final Lincoln-Douglas Debate was held near the banks of the Mississippi River in Madison County, on this day in Illinois history.

In 1858, as the Union was dividing itself over slavery, the debate between "free soil" and "popular sovereignty" that hastened the coming of the Civil War became the central issue in the campaign for Illinois's seat in the U.S. Senate. Stephen A. Douglas, the incumbent Democrat, argued that settlers in each territory soon to become a state had the right to choose for or against slavery on a state-by-state basis. Abraham Lincoln, the Republican challenger, stated famously that such popular sovereignty would lead disastrously to a "house divided." Lincoln and Douglas took their opposing views on a seven-city tour of Illinois. The candidates contrasted as much in stature—Lincoln tall and lanky, Douglas short and stocky—as in their ideologies, but both men were skilled orators who expressed their views passionately.

They had already taken the controversy to the towns of Ottawa, Freeport, Jonesboro, Charleston, Galesburg, and Quincy, but it was at Alton where Abraham Lincoln summed up his free-soil argument with these memorable words: "That is the issue. . . . it is the eternal struggle between two principles—right and wrong—throughout the world. . . . The one is the common right of humanity, the other is the divine right of kings." He pointed to the lack of constitutional references to slavery to suggest that the framers had therefore anticipated it would eventually die out of its own inertia, and he asserted that the nation must be "all slave or all free." Douglas countered in part by warning the audience that Lincoln believed "a Negro was as good as a white."

The several thousand in attendance included prominent state and national figures and members of the New York, Boston, St. Louis, and Chicago press. Douglas won the election; nevertheless, the debates launched Lincoln onto the national scene and set the stage for a presidential nomination two years later.

Lincoln's free-soil reputation won the support of abolitionists nationwide as the Union approached the terrible divide of which he had warned.

Big-city commuters first rode Chicago's new subway—no small feat of engineering and one of the earliest federally funded projects of its kind—on this day in Illinois history.

Ground was broken for the new underground mass transit system by Mayor Edward J. Kelly and U.S. Secretary of the Interior Harold L. Ickes on December 17, 1938. The layers of wet clay that Chicago sat upon would make tunneling difficult—and costly. For that reason the long-planned-for subway did not become a reality until federal funds were loosened up by President Franklin D. Roosevelt in 1937. After nearly five full years of construction, further delayed by the onset of World War II, the state-of-the-art facility was ready for public use. Those without cars now had a convenient way to get across downtown. The subway provided a nice alternative to those who wanted to avoid the traffic-choked streets and avenues of the city above. Subway projects had in fact been proposed for the city since the turn of the century, but it was now made possible thanks to FDR's Public Works Administration. The project was, as Mayor Kelly put it, "absolutely necessary that Chicago have a truly great transportation system."

The modern amenities of the subway were the source of much publicity. Among its futuristic features were escalators ("moving stairways"), underground fluorescent lighting, and soundproof telephone booths. The full ventilation system was touted for providing safety and comfort, and the experience of riding the new subway was advertised as "carefree, convenient, and enjoyable." While most of the city's public transport rail remained in the above-ground "L," two tubes now ran beneath the city—one along State Street and one along Dearborn Street, though the latter was not officially opened until 1951. The original State Street platform, with several underground stations, extends 3,300 feet end-to-end, while Dearborn's is 2,500 feet.

Though more tunnels were planned, none (at least for the purpose of extending the subway system) were ever built.

- OCTOBER 17 -
1931
AL CAPONE CONVICTED

The 20th century's quintessential gangster—flamboyant, cocksure, and unabashedly brutal—32-year-old Alphonse Capone was convicted for tax evasion on this day in Illinois history.

Capone owned the city. His crime syndicate, having absorbed or otherwise eliminated virtually all competitors, was supplying beer and hard liquor to an estimated 10,000 speakeasies throughout Chicagoland. Capone amassed great wealth and power—his bribe money notoriously corrupted both city hall and the Chicago police force. Mayor "Big Bill" Thompson received generous campaign contributions from Capone, and many among the city's rank-and-file police would pose for the camera when busting open a barrel of beer, but secretly run a speakeasy on the side. Capone had also attracted notice from the White House, as President Herbert Hoover declared, "I want that Capone in jail."

The legal assault on Capone was twofold—violation of the Volstead Act and income-tax evasion. The latter charge was headed up by a group of federal agents dubbed the "Untouchables," so named because they were incorruptible—Capone's bribe money slipped right off them. Their leader, 26-year-old Eliot Ness—an Illinois native and graduate of the University of Chicago—recruited the nine top U.S. Treasury agents to assist him in bringing down Capone. He had scrutinized the records of dozens of candidates before selecting only the most reliable. Ness and his small team became an immediate thorn in Al Capone's side, infiltrating the underworld, raiding brewers, and seizing millions of dollars worth of the crime boss's assets.

But it was the tax-related evidence they uncovered that would ultimately bring down Capone. Various raids uncovered documents that suggested extravagant spending habits that just seemed impossible with Capone's declared income. His telephone bills were in excess of $3,000 per month, weekly butcher's bills were $250, and donations were made by the thousands of dollars to various local organizations, including, ironically, a Chicago Police widows' and orphans' fund. Al Capone was indicted on 22 counts of tax evasion and thousands of violations of the Volstead Act and eventually sentenced to eleven years in prison.

"I guess it's all over," gasped Capone after the sentencing.

- October 18 -

1924

University of Illinois Memorial Stadium Dedicated

The University of Illinois Fighting Illini defeated the mighty Michigan Wolverines, 39–14, before a Homecoming crowd of 67,000 cheering fans on this day in Illinois history.

The contest followed dedication ceremonies for a new world-class football stadium. Memorial Stadium—a "living war memorial" to Illinois youth recently lost in the battlefields of Europe—was the result of three years of determined fund-raising by University of Illinois students and faculty. In April 1921, mass meetings were held on campus where George A. Huff, the university's athletic director, rallied the assembled thousands of Illini: "I want to see a great stadium at the University of Illinois. . . . a memorial to Illinois men who have died in the war . . . an imposing place for our varsity games . . . an unprecedented expression of Illinois pride."

He certainly energized the crowd. More than $700,000 was pledged at student rallies that spring. A national Illinois Memorial Stadium Campaign was launched, symbolically, at an Illinois-Michigan football game that fall (the Wolverines had the type of winning program and national respect to which Illinois aspired). "Build That Stadium for the Fighting Illini" was a typical slogan from one of the many pamphlets mailed out to potential donors. Every county in Illinois was appointed a pledge captain, and local alumni were encouraged to pitch in a minimum donation of $100. Head football coach Robert C. Zuppke embarked on a barnstorming tour throughout the Midwest and East Coast to raise funds among out-of-state alumni. Nearly $3 million had been pledged by the end of the drive, a sufficient amount to build a premiere football arena.

Construction began in September of 1922. Memorial Stadium would help to establish U of I among the nation's college football elite. Two rows of Doric-style columns adorn the finished stadium. Each one commemorated one of the 187 University of Illinois students killed in the Great War; one for the Unknown Soldier; two more to signify "sportsmanship" and "fair play," and one additional column sponsored by Illinois rival, Michigan Coach Ned Yost, for a former Michigan player (and Illinois native) lost in the war.

A football legend was also born that day with Memorial Stadium: Red Grange thrilled Illinois football fans by rushing for 402 yards and scoring six touchdowns in the Illini rout.

310 | This Day in Illinois History

- OCTOBER 19 -
1897
GEORGE PULLMAN DIES IN CHICAGO

On this day in Illinois history, Chicago entrepreneur George Pullman, architect of the famous workers' district that bore his name, died in the wake of great controversy.

Pullman, a high school dropout at age 14, arrived in the city an ambitious 24-year-old engineer in 1855 and quickly made his mark as a leading citizen. He is widely credited for the success of the two-decade-long project that raised the city's buildings, streets, and plank sidewalks several feet up from the disease prone muck. But his most notable invention was of course the luxurious Pullman Sleeping Car, made famous when the body of President Abraham Lincoln made its slow return journey to Illinois in one in early May 1865. After that, orders came pouring in from railroads across the country. Pullman grew rich, and he built a novel workers' settlement and manufacturing plant south of Chicago.

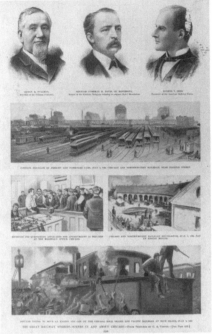

The town of Pullman gained worldwide praise as an example of the "broadest philanthropy to the working man." Pullman leased apartments to workers and offered markets, parks, and other neighborhood amenities under the auspices of the Pullman Palace Car Company. Living conditions were far healthier than those of the shoddy tenements many industrial workers and their families were crammed into during the era, but the experiment soured when Pullman lost revenues in the depression of the 1890s, cut workers' wages without cutting their rent, and refused to hear their grievances. The Pullman Strike of 1894 spread through several states and ended in violence when federal troops were called in to quash the strikers.

Virtually all of Pullman's workers were replaced by men who pledged to never join the union, but his model community was never again the same. When he died, the Illinois Supreme Court ordered the Pullman Company to auction off the town's houses and buildings, and the entire district was annexed by Chicago in 1889.

Buried beside George Pullman at Chicago's Graceland Cemetery are his daughter, Florence, and son-in-law–Illinois Governor (1917–1921) Frank Lowden.

- OCTOBER 20 -
1856
JAMES R. MANN BORN NEAR BLOOMINGTON

On this day in Illinois history, James R. Mann, author of the Mann Act prohibiting so-called white slavery, was born in McLean County.

Mann graduated from the University of Illinois in 1876 and Union College of Law in 1881 before being admitted to the bar and starting his own Chicago practice later that year. He later became involved in state politics, sitting on Chicago's city council (1892–96) and serving as chairman of the Illinois State Republican conventions in 1894, 1895, and 1902. He was elected to the first of 14 successive terms in the U.S. House of Representatives in 1896, serving through 1922. At various points during his time in Congress, Mann chaired many important committees, including the

Committee on Elections, the Committee on Interstate and Foreign Commerce, and the Committee on Women's Suffrage. He also served as House Minority Leader for the 62nd through 65th Congresses.

Representative Mann was a leading advocate of reform legislation. He introduced the Pure Food and Drug Act of 1906, which, in the wake of Upton Sinclair's *The Jungle,* provided for the inspection and setting of health standards for meat products. In 1910, he co-sponsored the Mann-Elkins Act, which likewise empowered the federal government, this time through the Interstate Commerce Commission, to regulate railroad rates. He also authored the Mann Act, which forbade the state-to-state transportation of women for "immoral purposes." (An endemic social problem at the time was white slavery, where European girls would be brought overseas to places like Chicago to work in bordellos. And it was under the authority of the Mann Act that the city's notorious Levee district was raided in 1907 and nearly 300 girls were freed from houses of ill-repute.) Through his final days in office, Mann also championed a Constitutional amendment to grant women's suffrage.

James R. Mann died in office on November 30, 1922, and was interred at Oakwood Cemetery in Chicago.

- OCTOBER 21 -
1984
WORLD RECORD SET AT THE CHICAGO MARATHON

On this day in Illinois history, a world record of two hours, eight minutes, five seconds was set at the Chicago Marathon as thousands of enthusiastic runners showed up to participate in what had become the world's largest long-distance foot race.

The idea for the big race in the City of the Big Shoulders was born at the LaSalle Street Young Men's Christian Association in downtown Chicago in November 1976. The race's founders met there and came up with a plan, taking their first steps with a successful ten-mile lakefront run the following May. Organizers expected no more than a few hundred participants to show up, but more than 1,000 runners came for what was then Chicago's first major long-distance race. It was an auspicious beginning. Others races followed that summer, as the city had "running fever"—some with up to 5,000 participants. Mayor Michael Bilandic, himself an enthusiastic runner, wanted his city to become the "running capital of the world" and funded the creation of five miles of track along the lakefront to accommodate the sport's explosive popularity. Chicago was now ready to host a world-class marathon.

The Inaugural Chicago Marathon was held on September 25, 1977, and it was an instant sensation. (It was originally called the Mayor Daley Marathon in honor of the late Richard J. Daley.) More than 4,000 men, woman, and even a few children paid the $5 entry fee and arrived stretched and read to go for the 8 a.m. start time. It was already the largest marathon in the world at its inception. More than 2,700 finished the race, including an 8-year-old boy who crossed the finish line at a little over three hours. Seven hundred volunteers helped make it all happen. Billed as the "people's race," the event drew large numbers of spectators as well, two of which were accidentally struck when the ceremonial cannon misfired (they were not hurt). Despite that one hitch, the day was a tremendous success, and the flat 26.2 mile course promised to be the site of many future world records. The 1984 record was set by Stephen Jones of the United Kingdom, a feat witnessed by the nearly 1 million spectators who lined the route.

With no required qualifying time to participate, the popular race accepts only the first 40,000 runners to register, and only those who finish within six hours are awarded an official running time.

Paul Johannes Tillich—"Apostle to the Intellectuals"—died while serving on the faculty of the University of Chicago on this day in Illinois history.

Tillich arrived in Illinois late in life, after having established himself as one of the great Protestant thinkers of the 20th century. Born on August 20, 1886, in Starzeddel, Prussia, he was ordained a Lutheran minister in 1912 and served as chaplain in the German army during World War I. He studied and then taught at a number of prestigious German universities through the early 1930s. Then, in 1933, his anti-Nazi views were cause for his replacement by a member of the National Socialist German Workers Party. The first non-Jew to be thus barred from teaching positions across the country, Tillich emigrated before things got worse and landed at the Union Theological Seminary in New York City. There, he would publish his first books integrating existentialism with Protestant theology and earn a reputation as a brilliant-yet-unorthodox Christian thinker. In 1952 he published *The Courage to Be*, which earned wide acclaim both within academia and beyond the confines of the ivory tower. Ten years later he became the chair of theology at the University of Chicago, where he also taught a course on divinity.

Tillich not only merged medieval theology with modern secular thought, but also infused a strong dose of Freudian psychology into his complex metaphysical system. The assertion that "faith need not be unacceptable to contemporary culture and contemporary culture need not be unacceptable to faith" was at the core of his writings. At the heart of being, for Tillich, was the fear of mortality, and it was this fear—the concept of "nothingness"—that defined finite existence. This realization both set mortal man apart from and necessitated the existence of an infinite God, since finitude could not be self-sustaining. And God, as the essence of being, remained beyond the capacity of finite human thought to comprehend; thus the necessity for Christian revelation.

Tillich, who was naturalized a U.S. citizen in 1940, is yet one more in a long list of revolutionary minds to be associated with the University of Chicago.

- OCTOBER 23 -
1975
AMERICAN BUFFALO DEBUTS AT
CHICAGO'S GOODMAN THEATER

On this day in Illinois history, Chicago playwright David Mamet's premiere of *American Buffalo* established the Second City as a national anchor for experimental live theater.

Mamet, born in suburban Flossmoor, Illinois, was 27 years old when he boldly promised management at the Goodman Theater that producing his drama would win them a Pulitzer Prize. The script was accepted. It was part of a trilogy of off-Broadway plays written by Mamet—*Sexual Perversity in Chicago, The Duck Variations,* and *American Buffalo.* The first takes a cynical and humorous look at modern relationships. The second involves the bizarre conversations of two old men with the recurrent imagery of water fowls. The third—scripted around an amateur heist attempt to reclaim a buffalo-head nickel—explores the themes of loyalty and betrayal in the ruthless world of American crime. His plays were unconventional, featuring rugged male leads and peppered with profane, blunt, and dynamic dialogue. The Pulitzer would have to wait until his 1984 prize-winning *Glengarry Glen Ross,* but *American Buffalo* grabbed the immediate attention of the city's critics nonetheless. Some, like the *Chicago Tribune,* scoffed at the "almost two hours of bleep-rated dialogue" surrounding the story of three small-time thieves and a botched robbery. Others, most notably the less conservative *Daily News,* applauded Mamet's work as "a triumph for Chicago theater." Two years later, *American Buffalo* had moved to Broadway and earned the New York Drama Critics' Circle Award as the best play in America.

Spurred by Mamet's success, the city's theater scene became ever-more audacious, energetic, and accomplished at thrusting the Chicago style of live drama onto the national stage. Experimental theater was not unknown to the city; *Grease,* for example, was first performed on a tiny Chicago stage before going on to become an international hit musical. With *American Buffalo* in 1975 came dozens of small independent theater groups with big-time aspirations. That same year, from a north suburban church basement, was born the Steppenwolf Theater Company, launching the careers of John Malkovich, Gary Sinise, and Laurie Metcalf, among others.

Mamet has since penned dozens of screenplays, some under the pseudonym of Richard Weiss, and even published two novels and a series of children's poetry.

- OCTOBER 24 -

1911

CHICAGO'S EVERLEIGH CLUB BORDELLO CLOSED DOWN

On this day in Illinois history, Chicago's most famed bordello, the Everleigh Club, was shut down by Mayor Carter Harrison, Jr.

In 1900, Ada and Minna Everleigh, recently arrived from operating a profitable brothel in Omaha, Nebraska, opened the opulent Everleigh Club in Chicago's First Ward red-light district called "The Levee." The strip was also home to such notorious houses of vice as the House of All Nations, Bed Bug Row, and Freidberg's Dance Hall. The "Everleigh" name derived from the sisters' grandmother's habit of signing her correspondence, "Everly Yours." (Their original surname was Lester.) The 50-room mansion quickly established a reputation for unrivaled luxury, extravagant furnishings (including gold-rimmed gold fish bowls, a library filled with hundreds of leather-bound volumes, and rich tapestries), and themed parlors. In a day when beer cost one nickel, the Everleighs charged $12 for a bottle of wine. Dinner started at $50. The menu featured caviar, roast duck, and fresh lobster. And, of course, private rooms were available. The Chicago Vice Commission called it, "the most famous and luxurious house of prostitution in the country." The Everleigh Sisters would tell their women that any client spending less than $50 was not to be invited back.

The club's demise was, ultimately, a result of its own success. It had been protected for years by bribe money paid out to neighborhood police and corrupt city alderman. But the sisters boldly issued a brochure targeting the city's elite and visiting dignitaries, which fell into the hands of the newly elected and straitlaced Mayor Carter Harrison Jr. Harrison immediately ordered the Everleigh House closed. It was the first of his sweeping reforms of the city's underworld. The sisters fled town with more than $1 million in cash and personal assets and eventually relocated to New York City. That was where Minna died in 1948 and Ada in 1960. They never returned to Chicago.

Having changed their names back to Lester, the once-notorious Everleigh sisters lived out their remaining days quietly, organizing a neighborhood pottery club, among other quaint pastimes.

- October 25 -
1917
Hansberry v. Lee Presented to the U.S. Supreme Court

A dispute in which a group of Chicago property owners barred "Negroes" from residential ownership was presented to the U.S. Supreme Court on this day in Illinois history.

The defendant, Carl Hansberry, a Chicago real estate broker who happened to be black, had bought a home for his family in the Hyde Park neighborhood on the city's South Side. Local property owners evoked a deed drawn up years earlier among themselves, which restricted the sale of residential property to blacks, and dragged Hansberry and his family to court. Accused of violating the local homeowners' agreement, Hansberry eventually lost the case in the Illinois Supreme Court. Refusing to give in, he appealed the much-publicized and bitterly fought dispute to the U.S. Supreme Court for final resolution.

Representing Hansberry was Earl B. Dickerson, a Chicago alderman (1939–1943) known as "the dean of Chicago's black lawyers." Dickerson presented a thoroughly researched and concisely argued case before Chief Justice Charles Evans Hughes and a full court, and he won a favorable decision ending the era of legalized residential segregation in the United States. "Jubilant over the handling of the case," wrote the *Chicago Defender* after the Supreme Court decision, "the Chicago lawyers feel that this cause . . . will bring about radical changes and more respect for the constitutional rights of Negroes to own and live in property which they are able to purchase."

Photo courtesy of Library of Congress, FSA-OWI Collection, LC-DIG-fsa-8e10738

The famous case of *Hansberry v. Lee* was the inspiration for Lorraine Hansberry's play *A Raisin in the Sun*, published in 1959. Lorraine was Carl Hansberry's daughter, and she was raised on the South Side of Chicago. The story, based on her father's famous court case, won wide critical acclaim when performed on Broadway. In 1961, the drama was made into a movie starring Sidney Poitier, but Lorraine Hansberry died young on her way to stardom, succumbing to cancer at age 34.

A 2004 revival of *A Raisin in the Sun* received two Tony Awards.

- OCTOBER 26 -
1837
ILLINOIS ANTISLAVERY CONVENTION MEETS IN ALTON

Amid rising tensions between slavery's critics and its defenders, a three-day meeting of the former convened in Madison County to boldly demand national abolition, on this day in Illinois history.

The convention—spearheaded by the Reverend Gideon Blackburn of Collinsville, Illinois—was not without precedent in the state. The St. Clair Society for the Prevention of Slavery in Illinois, founded by the Baptist Reverend John Mason Peck, was organized in March 1823. This was in response to proslavery forces, mostly residual French settlements along the Mississippi and Ohio rivers. Immigrants who had brought their "indentured servants" into Illinois just before statehood were agitating against the "hobbling" of slavery in the state constitution. The Morganian Society was likewise born in 1824, in downstate Morgan County, to confront the proslavery movement. "It is the declared design and intension of this society," articulated the Morganians, "to promote the public good . . . by using all honorable means to prevent the introduction of slavery into this state." While abhorring slavery, these earlier organizations did not challenge its existence beyond the state's borders, and were happy to accept the gradual demise of the existing system of indentured servitude—a form of quasi-slavery and a legal loophole—within state borders, in line with the status quo.

The 1837 meeting in Alton was much more radical, and it proved just how divided were the state's opponents of slavery. The three-day convention exposed a rift between those who would continue to work within the status quo to seek slavery's "quiet demise" and those demanding more immediate, far-reaching results. One of the most zealous proponents for full abolition was Alton's Reverend Elijah Lovejoy, whose newspaper, the *Alton Observer,* was indefatigable in its condemnation of the inhuman institution. Others, however, dissented and argued that Lovejoy's approach only served to anger slave owners and forced them to treat their slaves more harshly.

The convention minutes show that disorderliness reined, with much stomping and shouting in the hall; Lovejoy—likely one of the more vocal participants—would be murdered by a proslavery mob within a couple of weeks.

- OCTOBER 27 -

1946

ASTRONAUT STEVEN NAGEL BORN IN CANTON

Steven Nagel, highly decorated United States Air Force pilot and National Aeronautics and Space Administration astronaut, was born in Fulton County on this day in Illinois history.

Nagel, who graduated from high school in 1964, entered the University of Illinois at Urbana-Champaign the following year and signed up for the Air Force ROTC program. He graduated with honors with a degree in aeronautical and astronautical engineering in 1969. After serving several years in the Air Force—logging more than 9,400 hours of flight time, piloting F-100s and other jets, and doing a one-year tour of duty as flight instructor in southeast Asia in 1971 and 1972—Nagel returned to school to earn his master's degree in mechanical engineering from California State University, Fresno. Nagel became a NASA astronaut in the summer of 1979.

In four missions, he spent more than 700 total hours in outer space. Nagel first blasted off with the Space Shuttle Discovery on June 27, 1985, from Kennedy Space Center, Florida, making him the United States's 100th astronaut to reach the stars (metaphorically speaking). Subsequent missions came in October 1985 (Space Shuttle Challenger), April 1991 (Space Shuttle Atlantis), and April 1993 (Space Shuttle Columbia). In all, Nagel helped conduct hundreds of scientific experiments in everything from robotics to biology to extraterrestrial gamma rays; orbited the earth more than 100 times; and even participated in an unscheduled space walk to repair a broken communications satellite. He officially retired from the U.S. Air Force and as an astronaut in 1995, one year after being named Lincoln Laureate for the state of Illinois.

Photo courtesy of National Aeronautics and Space Adminis-

Honors Steve Nagel received over the years include the Air Force Distinguished Flying Cross; four NASA Space Flight Medals; and the Outstanding Alumni Award, University of Illinois.

Carter Henry Harrison Sr., the vice-friendly mayor of the Second City, was killed by an assassin's bullet after delivering the closing address for the World's Columbian Exposition, on this day in Illinois history.

The Kentucky-born politician came to Chicago as a young man, noting his two favorite pastimes in the city—making and spending money. He was elected to the first of an unprecedented four consecutive terms as the "common man's mayor" on April 1, 1879. Terms were then two years. Under Harrison's reign, vice thrived as crooked alderman such as "Bathhouse" John Coughlin and "Hinky Dink" Kenna protected local pimps, prostitutes, saloon-keepers, and gamblers. Mayor Harrison—no believer in legislating morality—was known to promenade through town on his white horse, boasting that his office was "always open." This accessibility would be his downfall. After several years out of office, Harrison was reelected in 1893, and inaugurated that April for what would prove an abbreviated fifth term as Chicago's mayor.

Photo courtesy of Library of Congress, LC-B2- 712-9

Relaxing at home—a lavish mansion on the city's south Side—at a dinner party celebrating the great success of the World Columbian Exposition of 1893, Mayor Carter Harrison Sr., met his fate. It was the week of the fair's official closing, and the mayor had delivered the ceremonial closing statements earlier that day. Patrick Eugene Prendergast, an unemployed Irish immigrant who was bitter over having been turned away by Harrison for the office of Chicago's chief attorney (for which he had no qualification), was the assassin. He arrived at the Harrison estate, unloaded three slugs from a .38-caliber pistol into the mayor, turned himself in, and pleaded insanity. Harrison died immediately. Chicago plunged into mourning. Even legendary defense attorney Clarence Darrow could not sell the jury on the insanity plea, and Prendergast hanged for his crime on July 13, 1894.

Carter Harrison Jr., son of the common man's mayor, was himself elected to four successive terms (1897–1905) and a later fifth (1911–1915) as mayor, but, unlike his father, lived to the old age of 93 after leaving office.

- OCTOBER 29 -

1955

CHICAGO'S O'HARE AIRPORT OPENS

O'Hare International Airport, among the largest and busiest airports in the world, opened for commercial flights on this day in Illinois history.

Midway Airport, on the city's South Side, once the world's busiest itself, had grown overwhelmed by commercial traffic as Chicago became the nation's hub for the passenger-airline industry. Expansion of O'Hare became the solution. It had been in use primarily as a manufacturing plant and U.S. Air Force base since the mid-1940s. Originally called Douglas Field and then Orchard Place Airport, it was renamed after World War II flying ace and Congressional Medal of Honor recipient Edward "Butch" O'Hare in 1949, and the first commercial flights began there six years later. By 1958, O'Hare Airport had built its first international terminal. By 1962, it had greatly expanded and was serving more than 10 million passengers annually. That number increased to 70 million per year by the end of the 20th century, making it the most congested airport in the world.

On the day of the airport's first commercial flight, Mayor Richard J. Daley prophesied: "I consider O'Hare's beginning as a long and firm step into the jet airline age now upon us. . . . We have the space for expansion for vast future developments that may now be entirely unguessed." And expand it did, much to the chagrin of many residential neighborhoods in suburban Cook County. On the one hand, O'Hare has created an unprecedented amount of noise pollution in the area; on the other, in the 1990s alone, it generated an estimated $12 billion in revenue per year and hundreds of thousands of jobs in the region.

It has also seen its share of tragedy. On May 25, 1979, American Airlines Flight 191 crashed upon takeoff from O'Hare, killing 275 people—the nation's deadliest airline disaster up to that time. American Eagle Flight 4184 crashed before landing on Halloween 1994, killing all 64 passengers and 64 crew onboard.

O'Hare International Airport is currently undergoing the $6.5 billion O'Hare Modernization Program to further expand its capacity while adding new terminals and runways to help offset congestion and delays.

- OCTOBER 30 -
1938

AN ILLINOIS ACTOR PULLS THE
GREATEST HALLOWEEN HOAX IN HISTORY

On this day in Illinois history, Orson Welles—who had honed his theatrical skills for three years at Woodstock's Todd School for Boys—sent an unintended wave of hysteria across the nation with his *War of the Worlds* broadcast.

An estimated 1.7 million listeners tuned in to scores of WABC-AM affiliates across the land to be stunned by the most famous 1 hour and 15 minutes in radio history. Welles, who had lost both parents as young child in Wisconsin, came to McHenry County as a precocious teenager. Without much formal education, he enrolled in the Todd School for Boys. There, in the early 1930s, headmaster Roger Hill took Welles under his wing. He introduced Orson to Shakespeare and encouraged his prodigy to be bold and experimental as he pursued a career in theater. And experimental he was during that Halloween-eve broadcast. Regularly scheduled music was interrupted by the special report about a fictional astronomer, a professor at Chicago's Mount Jennings Observatory, who had witnessed massive explosions on Mars. Despite an announcement during the show's introduction, thousands of listeners did not realize that this was indeed fiction. The "breaking news" continued, as the 23-year-old Welles conveyed to his listeners the growing pandemonium of a Martian invasion and their use of an awesome "heat ray" to lay waste to the East Coast.

Widespread panic ensued. People fled from their homes or barricaded themselves within as hundreds of phone calls flooded radio stations and newspaper offices in cities across America. The hysteria caused by Orson Welles's radio play of the then-little-known H. G. Wells's sci-fi thriller could have been far worse had it not aired opposite the nation's most popular radio program at the time, *The Chase and Sanborn Hour,* starring Illinois ventriloquist Edgar Bergen. But to some of those in Illinois who had the dial set for WABC's syndicated networks in Chicago, Rockford, or Peoria, the news of the unstoppable Martians caused wild speculation over how long it would be before the end of the world reached the Midwest.

Hours later, when the public realized that this product of a McHenry County theater school and former student of the Art Institute of Chicago had fooled them, some were outraged enough to threatened to sue the network.

- OCTOBER 31 -

1934

CHICAGO'S CENTURY OF PROGRESS CLOSES DOWN

On this day in Illinois history, Chicago's second World's Fair, the Century of Progress Exposition, closed down after its second season.

President Franklin Delano Roosevelt had delivered a "sound picture" address for the opening ceremonies of Chicago's "New" Century of Progress Exposition. The fair, which had been so successful in 1933 that it was held over for a second season, threw open its gates to admit 148,664 paying visitors on opening day. That was nearly 30,000 more than the opening-day number set the previous year. The city put on quite a gala for the grand opening, the highlights of which were the recorded messages of the president and first lady, Eleanor Roosevelt. The president's words were highly optimistic. "[T]he most critical days of national emergency have for the most part passed," FDR told the gathered celebrants by audio-visual recording. "Those who will come to the Exposition in 1934 . . . will see many signs pointing the way along that upward path on which we, as a nation, have set our feet." When he finished, he pressed a button, and a network of synchronized floodlights illuminated the fairgrounds for the first time.

For the next five months, fairgoers were treated to sites and sounds befitting the fair's motto: "Science Finds, Industry Applies, Man Conforms." The Century of Progress Fountain—at 650 feet long, the largest in the world—was just one of many marvels added to the 1934 World's Fair, which was touted as being "hugely augmented" from the previous summer. The expanded fairgrounds debuted 16 picturesque international villages, an expansive automotive industry exhibit, and free concerts performed by the Chicago Symphony. Total attendance was 16.3 million, down from 22.5 million just one year earlier. Henry Ford, who had refused to contribute to the 1933 fair, "switched gears" after rival General Motors's working assembly-line model had been such a big hit among fairgoers. Ford's dream cars competed with those of Cadillac, Lincoln, Nash, and Packard for the public's awe and attention.

The extended season of the Century of Progress was a welcome economic boon to a city in the midst of the Great Depression, employing more than 20,000 Chicagoans while being the first international exposition to actually pay for itself.

This day in

November

- NOVEMBER 1 -

1999

NFL GREAT AND BEAR LEGEND WALTER PAYTON DIES

Chicago Bears fans across the nation mourned on this day in Illinois history, when 45-year-old Walter "Sweetness" Payton succumbed to cancer.

Payton rose to stardom on the field and earned a special place in fans' hearts after being selected in the first round by the Chicago Bears (fourth overall) in the 1975 National Football League draft. A tough-as-nails running back from Jackson State University, he would eventually silence naysayers despite netting zero yards on eight carries in his first game as a Bear. And his in-your-face playing style was a big hit in the City of the Big Shoulders. In 1977, while suffering from the flu but refusing to sit on the bench, Payton pounded out an NFL record 275 yards in a single game against the Minnesota Vikings. He went on to win the NFL rushing title that year with 1,852 yards, followed by several seasons that established Sweetness—a nickname earned more by his personality than his punishing running style—as arguably the greatest football player ever to grace the nation's gridirons. On October 6, 1984, with a six-yard run against the Saints before his hometown fans at Soldier Field, Walter Payton surpassed Jim Brown as the NFL's all-time leading rusher. Payton's motto on the field: "Never Die Easy."

"He was the best football player I've ever seen," said his former coach, Mike Ditka, "and probably one of the best people I've ever met." Payton's career totals speak for themselves: 16,726 rushing yards; 125 touchdowns; 3,828 attempts—each is still on the NFL's all-time Top 5 list. Payton retired after the 1988 season and was inducted to the National Football League Hall of Fame in 1993.

After football, Payton continued to give to Chicago as an active philanthropist. The Walter and Connie Payton Foundation was founded to help many of the nation's neediest children. He always seemed available, happy to greet fans with that unrivaled sense of humor, at any number of local charity events. But in February 1999, the legendary No. 34 held a press conference to make public his tragic diagnosis of a rare form of liver cancer. Though visibly weakened, Walter Payton still seemed unstoppable. He died ten months later in his Barrington, Illinois home.

Today, the Walter Payton Cancer Fund sponsors research—"with the same grit and determination [he] showed on the football field"—seeking a cure for cancer.

- NOVEMBER 2 -
1948

"DEWEY DEFEATS TRUMAN" HEADLINE HITS THE PRESSES

Truman, of course, defeated Dewey in the 1948 U.S. presidential race, but the *Chicago Daily Tribune,* on this day in Illinois history, published the most famous faux pas in newspaper-headline history.

The paper was in a rush to scoop the competition on the big story and depended on erroneous exit polls, almost all of which indicated a win for Republican Thomas E. Dewey over Democrat Harry S. Truman. The *Chicago Daily Tribune*'s Washington, D.C., correspondent called in to the Chicago offices and echoed the predictions of Gallup, Roper, and Crossley pollsters, and the newspaper's early edition went to print on the evening of November 2. As late election returns were counted overnight, however, the pollsters—and the *Chicago Daily Tribune*—would be proven wrong. Truman had been the big favorite going in, but Truman would win by nearly four full percentage points. President-elect Truman posed with a copy of the front-page blunder the following day.

The *Chicago Daily Tribune,* like most major dailies back then, printed several city editions throughout the day. In an era not yet dominated by television news, this was how citizens kept up with major developments. The newspaper printed 11 editions for November 3, 1948, to update the election results. Later headlines told a different story: "DEWEY AHEAD! RACE CLOSE"; "DEWEY'S LEAD NARROWS"; and "IT'S TRUMAN BY 150,000." But the damage was done, and thousands of the "DEWEY DEFEATS TRUMAN" early editions had already hit Chicago newsstands and suburban homes. *Chicago Daily Tribune* staffers were sent out early in the morning with trucks to gather up the recalled papers, but it was too late, and the embarrassing headline was destined to become a part of Illinois history.

One columnist rightly commented that "the fatal flaw was the reliance on the public-opinion polls."

- NOVEMBER 3 -
1804

SAUK AND FOX INDIANS SIGN TREATY CEDING
ILLINOIS LANDS TO UNITED STATES

The allied Sauk and Fox Indians, on this day in Illinois history, signed a treaty with the U. S. government that would signify the beginning of the end of Native American sovereignty in Illinois.

Sauk and Fox chiefs circa 1855–1865

It was an unfortunate misunderstanding, a fraud, or a valid and binding contract—depending on whom one asked. In the fall of 1804 a young Sauk warrior had been imprisoned in St. Louis, Missouri, for his part in the murder of white settlers on the nearby Cuivre River. He was turned in by a Sauk delegation seeking to improve relations with the United States, fearful that the imprudent attacks of Sauk raiding parties might tip the balance of U.S. favor toward their traditional enemies, the Osage. Taking advantage of the delegation's conciliatory mood, Indiana Governor William Henry Harrison cajoled them—through wining and dining—to sign a treaty ceding all tribal lands east of the Mississippi River in exchange for an annual compensation of $1,000 in goods. The treaty also stated that the Sauk and Fox might continue to live and hunt in Illinois Country until the day said territory would be sold by the U.S. government for white settlement.

The treaty had been negotiated by the territorial governor, authorized by President Thomas Jefferson, and ratified by the U.S. Senate. (Illinois, until 1809, was part of the Indiana Territory.) But for the Sauk and Fox, the deal lacked validity; it had been signed, without consulting the tribal councils, by four lesser chiefs who represented only the Sauk and had no authority to bargain away the tribal land.

The area included the fertile lands of the Rock River Valley and the Native Americans' principal village of Saukenuk, at present-day Rock Island, Illinois. The village had been the political and spiritual capital of the Sauk and Fox nations since the early 18th century, when their war parties drove off the weakened Illiniwek Confederacy. Saukenuk was also the home of a young warrior, Black Hawk. Despite signing another treaty in May 1816, which reaffirmed the Treaty of 1904 and its huge cession of lands, Black Hawk obstinately viewed all such agreements as deceptive, illegal, and invalid.

He and his followers later formed a faction opposed to that of the more peaceful and subservient Chief Keokuk and they would not be easily removed from Illinois.

1960

MAYOR DALEY HOSTS PREELECTION PARADE FOR JFK

One million Chicagoans lined the parade route along Michigan and Madison avenues to greet the torchlight procession of Democrat presidential candidate John F. Kennedy, on this day in Illinois history.

The Chicago political machine was at the height of its power, and no other local politician in America exerted so much national influence as the city's machine boss, Mayor Richard J. Daley. At that summer's Democratic National Convention, Daley had thrown his weight behind Kennedy's nomination, rather than supporting his old political ally, fellow Illinoisan Adlai Stevenson. Luminaries such as Eleanor Roosevelt and Carl Sandburg, staunch Stevenson supporters both, were unable to convince Daley to reconsider. He was firmly in Kennedy's camp, and Illinois delegates obediently fell in line. Caucusing in secret, 59 of their 68 votes went to the young man from Massachusetts. Stevenson, crushed, dropped out of the running.

Daley's next move was to fine-tune the city's precincts for the general election. It promised to be a close contest against Republican nominee Vice President Richard M. Nixon, and huge voter turnout in Chicago would be vital to putting Kennedy in the White House. Machine workers went door-to-door—including more than a few barber shops, empty buildings, and vacant lots—to register a record number of voters. Nearly a quarter-million new Chicago voters added their names to the rolls. (One undercover reporter claimed to have moved into a "skid row" hotel room under the pseudonym "James Joyce" and later, when checking the registration rolls, saw his fake name signed up under that address.) Precinct captains were told that if they did not turn out the votes, they'd be removed from office. The Board of Election Commissioners filled 176 of its 180 positions with Democrats, and machine loyalists were assigned to accompany voters into booths—just to make sure.

The parade put a festive face on all these behind-the-scene machinations. It was an extraordinary event. Torchlight illuminated the floats and marching bands, and Daley, with Kennedy by his side, led the procession of party loyalists to the Chicago Stadium. There, before a rally of 28,000, the mayor promised the candidate that he'd win Chicago by half a million votes. He was off by 50,000. Kennedy took Illinois and its 27 electoral votes by a statewide margin of just 9,000, and with it he took the presidency of the United States.

Amid charges of election fraud, particularly from the *Chicago Daily News,* Daley fired back that his accusers were peddlers of conspiracy and slander, or worse—Republicans.

- November 5 -
1908

Fort Massac Officially Dedicated
Illinois's First State Park

The historic Fort Massac, located on a 50-foot rise above the Ohio River in present-day Metropolis, Massac County, became the state's first official state park on this day in Illinois history.

Massac was built by the French in 1757, as a bulwark against British encroachment into lucrative fur-trading territory. Originally named for Marquis de Massiac, a French naval minister, the fort played a critical role in frontier history for the next 50 years. It came under British control at the end of the French and Indian War in 1763. They found the site, abandoned by the French and the original fort burned to the ground, and built a new stronghold there. George Rogers Clark and his frontier soldiers, en route to capture Kaskaskia during the Revolutionary War, found the fort abandoned in 1778. It again fell into ruin.

Photo courtesy of Illinois Department of Natural Resources

President George Washington ordered the fort rebuilt and renamed Fort Massac in 1794. American troops garrisoned there were to protect the lower Ohio River valley. One decade later, in November 1803, Lewis and Clark and their Corps of Discovery obtained supplies and recruited volunteers at Fort Massac for their grand adventure into Louisiana Territory. In 1804, Massac was visited by Aaron Burr, former vice president of the United States, who during his visit failed to enlist General James Wilkinson into the so-called Burr Conspiracy—a plot to carve an independent nation from the American West.

Fort Massac was finally stripped of its garrison and abandoned, yet again, in 1814. Its wood and bricks were used by new Illinoisans to build nearby settlements. Vacant for decades, the site was used by the 3rd Illinois Cavalry and 131st Illinois Infantry as training grounds at the onset of the Civil War, but a measles epidemic in 1862 led to the final abandonment of Fort Massac as a U.S. military encampment. The 24 acres surrounding the original site were bought by the Daughters of the American Revolution in 1903 and later sold to the state.

In the 1970s a replica of Fort Massac was built near the original foundations. There, historical reenactments likely portray more action than was ever seen at the actual fort.

Novelist James Jones, who won the National Book Award for *From Here to Eternity* in 1952, was born in Robinson, Crawford County, on this day in Illinois history.

Jones joined the U.S. Army in 1939, a choice that would leave an indelible mark on his writing. He was present for the Japanese attack at Pearl Harbor on December 7, 1941, and subsequently was sent to fight Japanese forces in the South Pacific during World War II. Wounded at the battle of Guadalcanal, one of the bloodiest battles of the war, young Jones was sent to a military hospital in Memphis, Tennessee, went AWOL, and eventually returned to his quiet home town in southern Illinois. There, he began to write.

His first novel was published in 1951 and became an internationally acclaimed best seller. It was the first book in a trilogy—*From Here to Eternity, The Thin Red Line,* and *Whistle*—which address the psychological impact of war on the typical soldier, including accepting one's mortality as a warrior. "When all the . . . patriotic slogans are put aside," Jones would later explain, "the moment the individual soldier, sailor, or marine accepts this idea, he or she has reached the end of this evolutionary process and will be better able to function and survive in combat." Random House's Modern Library named *From Here to Eternity* one of the top 100 novels of the 20th century.

Jones believed that the brutality of battle was contradictory to American ideals. He was stunned by how the United States produced such an effective fighting force in so little time to defeat the totalitarian forces of Germany and Japan. Exploring Jones's own experiences, the trilogy of novels is an attempt to explain this, which he thought a miracle. While these nations were preparing their youth for war, he wrote, we "were teaching our young that war was immoral, and evil, and that, in fact, it was so costly in both treasure and spirit that mankind simply could no longer afford it. All conditions devoutly to be wished, but hardly a realistic description of the 1930s."

With his wealth James Jones helped establish a writer's colony in nearby Marshall, Illinois, and, following in the footsteps of Ernest Hemingway, later became a prominent expatriate in Paris.

- NOVEMBER 7 -
1837
ELIJAH P. LOVEJOY MURDERED BY PRO-SLAVERY MOB

Elijah Parish Lovejoy, the abolitionist editor of the *Alton Observer* newspaper, was gunned down on this day in Illinois History while defending his printing press from an Alton mob.

The Presbyterian minister had moved to free-state Illinois from slave-state Missouri in July 1836. He was forced across the Mississippi River after his first press was destroyed by a proslavery mob in St. Louis. Lovejoy's *St. Louis Observer*, a religious newspaper, had attracted the ire of Missouri slaveholders for its continued advocacy of the abolitionist movement. The editorials were penned by Lovejoy himself, and his opposition to slavery became increasingly strident after he witnessed a slave being burned at the stake.

Chased from Missouri, Lovejoy took his campaign of freedom from slavery—and freedom of the press—across the river to Alton, Illinois, where he was met, to his dismay, with the same outrage. He was hoping, at least, to now have the law on his side as the *Alton Observer* continued what its St. Louis precursor had started. Lovejoy supported the organization of the Anti-slavery Society of Illinois, which outraged many Alton citizens. Though living in a free state, many at this time in southern Illinois sympathized more with the South. Three times Lovejoy's press was wrecked and tossed into the Mississippi River by local proslavery mobs. Despite this intimidation, he persisted in writing and printing his controversial editorials—actions that would result in his eventual martyrdom.

On the night of November 7, Lovejoy and 20 supporters went to the Godfrey & Gilman warehouse on the riverfront to guard a newly arrived press. It was to be installed at the *Observer* the following day. As feared, the proslavery mob soon arrived, gathered in size, and became violent. Alton's mayor tried in vain to calm the agitators. They began throwing rocks at the warehouse windows. The defenders responded in kind, bombarding the assembled horde with bricks and pottery found within. Soon both sides opened fire, and Lovejoy was fatally wounded by a shotgun blast. The mob overran the warehouse and once again destroyed the press while Lovejoy's friends surrendered their arms and protected the body of their slain leader.

Elijah P. Lovejoy was buried two days later, on his 35th birthday, a fallen soldier in what some consider the opening battle of the Civil War.

- November 8 -
1838
State's First Railroad Locomotive Operates in Meredosia

On this day in Illinois history, the state's first-ever railroad locomotive traveled unceremoniously back and forth on a 12-mile track in Morgan County.

The idea of building a railroad through sparsely populated central Illinois was met with ridicule in the early 1830s. Illinois legislators, then meeting at Vandalia, repre-

sented mostly the larger cities and towns along the state's many rivers, and naturally they were strong advocates of the canal system. However, U.S. Congressman Joseph Duncan from Jacksonville, Illinois, championed the idea of a railroad, but he was literally shouted down by his peers while seeking a congressional appropriation to fund such a project. In 1834, Duncan was elected governor of Illinois, and one of his first major accomplishments was to win passage of the Illinois Internal Improvement Act. This landmark legislation authorized the use of state funds for the construction of a network of canals, roads, and—notably—railroads, to run across the state. Governor Duncan then laid out plans for the state's first railroad, which would run east to west between Quincy and Danville.

Meredosia was chosen for the groundbreaking. When construction finally began on the east bank of the Illinois River in November 1837, supporters of the state's canal system arrived to jeer their rivals. The first 8 miles of track, called the Northern Cross, were laid by the following April, then extended to 12 miles by the fall of 1838. In 1842, the line reached Springfield. In 1854, it reached Decatur. And then it crossed unsettled prairie to reach Danville in 1856 and completed the eastern branch of Governor Duncan's proposed line. By this time, the ridicule of Illinois railroad critics had fallen silent, but Duncan, who left office in 1838 and died in January 1844, missed this milestone.

The original Northern Cross in central Illinois formed the nucleus of a vast network of railroads—more than 700 miles of track—that span the American Midwest and continue to bring immeasurable prosperity to the Prairie State.

- NOVEMBER 9 -
1968
EARTHQUAKE SHAKES UP SOUTHEASTERN ILLINOIS

On this day in Illinois history, an earthquake registering 5.5 on the Richter scale with its epicenter at Hamilton County was felt as far north as Chicago.

Most Illinoisans do not associate their state with earthquakes. But southern Illinois sits atop the New Madrid fault line, which runs roughly from the confluence of the Mississippi and Ohio rivers at Cairo, Illinois, up to St. Louis and down to the banks of Missouri, Tennessee, and Kentucky rivers. The first recorded tremors in Illinois date to 1795, at Kaskaskia, when it was still a territorial outpost surrounded by sparsely populated frontier. The largest came in a series of cataclysmic earthquakes in 1811 and 1812, which are estimated to have been of far greater magnitude than the San Francisco earthquake of 1906. These quakes were felt as far north as Canada and as far south as New Orleans. More minor southern Illinois quakes occurred in 1857, 1903, and 1917, each marked by downed chimneys, falling plaster, and pedestrians tossed about on city streets and sidewalks. In 1909, a powerful earthquake in Menard County, northwest of Springfield, destroyed more than 100 buildings.

The 1968 quake was the most intense to hit Illinois in more than 100 years. "Earthquake Damage Probable at 90 Percent of County Buildings," read the headline of the *McLeansboro Times-Leader* in Hamilton County. Walls cracked and sections of brick and concrete fell from schools, churches, and the county courthouse in McLeansboro, and windows shattered as far away as Alton. Cemeteries near the epicenter had upturned headstones, and parked vehicles rocked violently. Grocery stores had major clean-up jobs on their hands.

"More frightening than destructive," reported the *St. Louis Post-Dispatch,* noting that the St. Louis area was shaken for about 20 seconds. The southern Illinois earthquake spawned tremors in 22 surrounding states.

Miraculously, there were no reports of serious injuries.

Vachel Lindsay, the vagabond poet who achieved great fame only to end his life in tragedy, was born in the state's capital city on this day in Illinois history.

Lindsay was born to deeply religious parents in Springfield's Campbellite Christian community. Educated at home by his mother on a steady diet of art, Sunday-school standards, and *Grimm's Fairy Tales,* he did not attend school until age 8. He attended Springfield High School, where he excelled at two subjects—long-distance walking and English composition. After high school he enrolled in a Campbellite college in Ohio to become a doctor like his father, but dropped out in his third year to pursue his love of art and poetry. He admitted to his sister that if he'd stuck out medical school, he would have made a lousy doctor and would likely have ended up killing somebody.

Photo courtesy of Sangamon Valley Collection, Lincoln Library

Lindsay enrolled at the New York School of Art in 1904 and, encouraged by his instructors, went from publishing house to publishing house seeking to be hired as an illustrator. Failing that, he took to the streets of New York selling his drawings and poems, as he said, "to the butcher, the baker, the candlestick maker." He returned to Springfield within a year. In 1906, he set off on a six-year journey traveling the country on foot, penniless, taking his poetry to the people. He walked more than 2,800 miles, avoiding larger cities, bartering a poem here and a song there for a meal and a bed in the small towns and farmhouses of America. After each excursion he would return to Springfield to recuperate.

After this amazing walking tour, Lindsay received his first major break when "General William Booth Enters Into Heaven" was published in *Poetry* magazine in 1913. His rhythmic, hopeful style was a big hit, and Lindsay enjoyed enormous success and accolades throughout the decade. He again toured the nation, but this time by train performing before large crowds. Perhaps his greatest moment was reciting "The Wedding of the Rose and the Lotus," which called for understanding between East and West, before President Woodrow Wilson in 1915.

The poet had become an entertainer, but, sadly, Lindsay's mental state deteriorated as his popularity declined in the postwar world of the 1920s, and he committed suicide in 1931. He left behind a wife and two children.

- November 11 -

1926

Route 66—"The Mother Road"—is Born

Route 66, the first fully paved highway to connect Chicago to St. Louis and eventually Los Angeles, was completed on this day in Illinois history.

No other stretch of highway so captures the American imagination. Cobbled together from a patchwork of gravel roads originally called "Pontiac's Trail," Route 66 linked the Windy City to Tinsel Town. It spanned more than 2,000 miles from start to finish. Its point of origin was the intersection of Jackson Boulevard and Michigan Avenue in downtown Chicago, and it wound gloriously through the cities of Cicero, Berwyn, and Joliet . . . Bloomington, Springfield, and Mount Olive . . . Collinsville, Granite City, and East St. Louis with innumerable small towns and roadside attractions along the way, before passing through St. Louis, the Gateway to the West.

Promoters of Route 66 put on an imaginative—if grueling—publicity stunt to promote the road in 1928. They sponsored a foot race from L.A. to Chicago and then on the New York City. The event's spokesperson was none other than legendary Illinois football player Red Grange, who fired the starting gun each morning to start that day's leg of the race. A circus arrived at towns along the way one day ahead of the runners with rides, games, and sideshows. Nearly 300 contestants signed up in hopes of winning the $25,000 first-place prize, but only 55 finished.

Recalling the era of great railroad construction, towns competed to have the route pass through their boundaries; those that were bypassed suffered. Tourists would bring an estimated $3.3 billion in annual revenues to soda shops and drive-ins, filling stations and motels, towns and one-of-a-kind landmarks along the open road. Nat King Cole crooned to a nation of road trippers, "Get your kicks on Route 66."

The "Main Street of America" was decommissioned as a national highway, replaced by the multilane Interstate 55, and the final black-and-white sign, emblazoned with the trademark double six, was removed from Chicago's Michigan Avenue in 1977.

Relics of the old road still exist, alongside the modern superhighways and in the collections of numerous Route 66 enthusiasts, as an indelible part of Americana.

- November 12 -
1926
First Aerial Bombing on U.S. Soil

On this day in Illinois history, amid the Prohibition gang wars of "bloody" Williamson County, the Shelton Gang dropped homemade bombs from an old "Jenny" biplane on the headquarters of local mob boss Charlie Birger.

It was the first known domestic air assault in American history. The southern Illinois turf wars between these rival gangs, beginning in 1926 and escalating in violence month after month, had gained as much notoriety in the nation's headlines as the bloody rift between Al Capone and his rivals in Chicago. Franklin, Saline, and Williamson counties had become a battleground over regional bootlegging rights. The sounds of machine-gun fire, sudden bombing raids, and even the sight of makeshift armored cars employed by both sides struck terror in the hearts of local residents.

The Birger Boys and the Shelton Gang had originally united to oppose the Ku Klux Klan—more for the latter's encroachment on local business than for any other reason—and succeeded in driving the Klan out of the region by 1925. With no one else to fight, they turned on each other. Assassinations provoked deadly reprisals, plunging southern Illinois's small towns and farming communities into what seemed an interminable state of chaos.

On the morning of November 12, 1926, the Shelton Gang coerced a barnstorming pilot (with the aid of $1,000 in cash) to take one of their men on a flyover of Birger's Harrisburg headquarters, called Shady Rest. Several bombs—jerry-rigged from sticks of dynamite bound to bottles of nitroglycerine—were dropped on the target-rich environment below. The first two hit dirt without exploding. By the third flyover, some of Birger's men began firing at the sputtering biplane. The third and last bomb landed and exploded—killing Charlie Birger's pet bulldog. There was otherwise no major damage.

The pilot—stunned by his role in the first air raid on U.S. territory—returned to the airfield, dropped off his passenger, and took to flight again in great haste.

- NOVEMBER 13 -
1909
CHERRY COAL MINE DISASTER KILLS 259 WORKMEN

A tragic fire took the lives of hundreds of workers at the Cherry Coal Mine, in Bureau County, on this day in Illinois history.

The St. Paul Coal Company, under the exclusive employ of the Chicago, Milwaukee & St. Paul Railroad, started mining the site in 1905. By 1909, it was producing more than 300,000 tons of coal annually. It was the first mine with an electrical grid, but it often failed. Kerosene lamps were used as a backup lighting system, which created an increased fire hazard, but Cherry Mine was still considered one of the safest in the United States. Young boys worked there along with their fathers.

Survivors mourn those lost at Cherry Mine

Hay was used as feed for mules that pulled the coal cars. Burning oil dripped from a lamp and ignited a small hay fire near the shaft of Mine No. 12. The fire, according to some versions of the tragedy, was initially ignored by workmen with more pressing concerns. When the workmen returned moments later to extinguish the fire, it had ignited nearby timbers and piles of coal. Flames and smoke were sucked through the mine's ventilation system, endangering the lives of nearly 300 coal miners trapped hundreds of feet below. A mere handful were able to escape. Only 20 men survived, pulled from the smoldering ruins after an heroic eight-day rescue effort that took the lives of another 12 men.

Conditions in the coal mines were notoriously dangerous—it was brutally hard work and accidents were common. Cherry Mine was not Illinois's first coal-mining tragedy, but it was the worst. The public responded by donating more than $400,000 in relief funds, which were organized by the Red Cross and distributed to survivors and victims' families by the Cherry Relief Commission. Another $400,000 was awarded in a settlement with the railroad company. This tragedy prompted the Illinois General Assembly to pass the Workmen's Compensation Act, which makes the employer liable for such disasters and forces greater responsibility on their part for the safety of employees. It was among the earliest legislation of the sort to be enacted in the United States.

In 1991, the United Mine Workers of America dedicated the Memorial to Victims of the Cherry Mine Disaster, which features the heartbreaking sculpture of a woman in mourning, at the site of the old mine.

M*A*S*H Actor McLean Stevenson
Born in Bloomington

On this day in Illinois history, McLean Stevenson—best known for his role as Lieutenant Colonel Henry Blake in the television series *M*A*S*H*—was born in McLean County.

The actor was born into an accomplished Illinois family. His paternal grandfather, Adlai E. Stevenson, was a two-time congressman in the U.S. House of Representatives (1875–1877, 1879–1881) and vice president of the United States under Grover Cleveland (1893–1897). McLean's first cousin, Adlai Stevenson Jr., was the former governor of Illinois (1949–1953), two-time presidential candidate (1952 and 1956), and the U.S. Ambassador to the United Nations who under the Kennedy administration famously presented evidence to the Security Council, which exposed the Cuban Missile Crisis of 1962. Another cousin, Adlai Stevenson III, became a two-time U.S. Senator from Illinois (1970–1981). Despite working for both of Adlai Jr.'s presidential campaigns and forming Young Democrats for Stevenson in 1952, McLean Stevenson chose a different course, drifting toward theater instead of politics. He debuted in a 1962 theatrical performance of *The Music Man* and became a comedy writer for the hit series *The Smothers Brothers Comedy Hour* later that decade.

Stevenson's happy-go-lucky Colonel Blake was one of the most memorable characters on one of the most successful sitcoms in TV history. At the end of season three, Blake—owing to Stevenson's desire to leave the show, reportedly not wanting to play second fiddle to Alan Alda's character Hawkeye Pierce—was written off the show (killed off, in fact, when the helicopter he boarded was shot down). This, one of the saddest moments in sitcom history, also turned out to be a disastrous career choice for Stevenson. *M*A*S*H* continued through 1983, enjoying enormous popularity and establishing itself as a timeless television classic; meanwhile, Stevenson's talent was wasted on long-forgotten shows, such as *In the Beginning, Hello Larry,* and *Condo,* that bombed season after season. McLean's career never again took off.

He died suddenly of a heart attack on February 15, 1996, in California and was recalled as a man with a "heart of gold" by fellow *M*A*S*H* star Gary Burghoff (Radar O'Reilly).

CHICAGO CARTOONIST BUD FISHER
INTRODUCES *MUTT AND JEFF*

On this day in Illinois history, a third-year University of Chicago dropout, Harry Conway "Bud" Fisher, debuted the nation's first wildly successful six-day-a-week comic strip, *A. Mutt.*

The title was soon changed to *Mutt and Jeff;* Fisher's characters presaged comedic duos like Laurel and Hardy. It went into newspaper syndication and brought great wealth and fame to its creator. Fisher's idea was not all that original, however, as the *Chicago American* published a similar strip in 1903 called *A. Piker Clerk.* Fisher, who was born in Chicago in 1884 and lived there through young adulthood, may have seen the earlier comic strip, but this cannot be proven. Regardless, Mutt (the lanky racetrack regular with woeful luck betting on the horses) and Jeff (his squat, affable sidekick) became a national phenomenon. The formulaic story line centered on Mutt's gambling, with daily antics that involved raising money for a bet, picking a horse's name through slapstick circumstances, and stumbling his way to the ticket booth. Readers would have to wait until the following day to see if he won or lost; sometimes he did win.

One first that definitely applies to *Mutt and Jeff:* It was the first such daily comic strip owned solely by its creator. Fisher wisely copyrighted his early cartoons, and when newspaper mogul William Randolph Hearst picked the strip up for syndication through his *San Francisco Chronicle,* the cartoonist commanded a lofty $1,000-per-week (for six strips) fee. By 1920, Fisher had gained celebrity status and, earning 60 percent of gross revenue from the wildly popular *Mutt and Jeff,* was well on his way to earning $5,000 per week. By the 1920s, the strip had inspired more than 300 Hollywood shorts. Fisher became a millionaire.

Bud Fisher turned over control of the comic strip to a number of other artists beginning in the early 1930s, though he kept on collecting profits from it until his death in 1954.

- November 16 -
1907
First Boat Travels the Hennepin Canal

The Hennepin Canal, sister waterway to the Illinois & Michigan Canal, opened its 33 locks to *The Marion* on this day in Illinois history.

The canal was first conceived as the Illinois & Mississippi Canal in the 1830s, but construction would not begin until 1892. Financial setbacks and political wrangling delayed its creation until well after the great canal-building era: the Erie Canal had opened in 1825 and the Illinois & Michigan Canal in 1848. (In 1885, a Cairo, Illinois, scientist published *Diluvium, or the End of the World* that argued canal building would alter the earth's climate, causing the polar ice caps to melt and ultimately destroying life on earth.) The Hennepin Canal officially opened six decades later. Though innovative in many ways, it would become obsolete as a commercial transportation route within only a few decades.

Built when railroads dominated commerce, the Hennepin Canal nevertheless shortened the route from Chicago to Rock Island by more than 400 miles. The 105-mile, man-made channel connected the Illinois River, just south of Hennepin in Putnam County, to Rock Island along the Mississippi River. Another 50-mile feeder route passed south from Rock Falls through Whiteside County to connect with the main channel. There were 33 locks—designed to narrow to accommodate the larger barges of the day—and nine aqueducts that allowed traffic on the canal to pass over intersecting streams.

The canal's 54- to 80-foot wide channel was planned to transport low-value, bulk commodities such as gravel, grain, and coal. By 1934, nearly 316,000 tons of commerce had been shipped via the canal. Tonnage, and federal funding, began to decline drastically in 1935 as the railroads and the widening of locks on the Illinois and Mississippi rivers obviated the canal's usefulness. Money was raised to maintain it by selling ice cut from the canal during the winters. Still, funding dried up, and the federal government officially closed the Hennepin Canal to commercial traffic in 1951.

The canal's entire parkway, totaling more than 5,000 acres, is listed on the National Register of Historic Places and is a popular recreation corridor for Illinoisans today.

On this day in Illinois history, master storyteller and Lake County native Ray Douglas Bradbury received the National Medal of Arts.

Bradbury was born in Waukegan on August 22, 1920, and the lakeside town of his childhood would make a deep impression on his later writings as an adult. He was one of the nation's most prolific 20th-century writers, publishing 30 novels—mostly in the sci-fi, fantasy, and horror genres—along with hundreds of short stories, poems, screenplays, radio scripts, and a few essays. Two of his earliest and most popular works—1957s *Dandelion Wine* and 1962s *Something Wicked This Way Comes* are set in the fictional "Green Town, U.S.A.," which is modeled after Bradbury's boyhood hometown. The nostalgia and imagery of 1920s and 1930s Waukegan, where he stayed until moving with his family to California at the age of 14, recur again and again in many of Bradbury's later works. And he returned to his hometown in 1984 for the dedication of Waukegan's Ray Bradbury Park.

Young Bradbury spent much of his youth at the public library (both in Waukegan and Los Angeles) and ended his formal education after high school. A self-described student of life, Bradbury supported himself by selling newspapers during the day while retiring at night to his typewriter, his imagination, and his perceptions of the human condition to produce story after story in his unique approach to the popular pulp fiction of the day. He was first commissioned to submit a story for the "fanzine," *Super Science Stories* in 1941 and had devoted himself to full-time writing by the following year. Soon his novels and collections of short stories were being published in rapid succession—*Dark Carnival* in 1947, *The Martian Chronicles* in 1950, *The Illustrated Man* in 1951. His literary masterpiece, the dystopian sci-fi classic *Fahrenheit 451,* published in 1953, cemented Ray Bradbury's place among the great writers of the 20th century.

In addition to the National Medal of Arts—awarded for "his incomparable contributions to American fiction"—Ray has won an Emmy Award, been nominated for the Oscar, and was honored by a star placed on the Hollywood Walk of Fame for the many studio adaptations of his work.

On this day in Illinois history, the largest convention center in the United States, named for one of the most prominent families in the city, opened for business in Cook County with the 1960 Home and Flower Show, the first of thousands of expositions and trade shows the enormous convention center has hosted.

Originally the idea of Robert R. McCormick, outspoken owner of the *Chicago Tribune,* the hall was conceived to anchor Chicago's place as the convention capital of the nation. McCormick did not survive to see its completion, but his newspaper called the $35-million McCormick Place greater than the Circus Maximus and "more durable than the [Roman] Colosseum." It burned down six years later. Rebuilt, McCormick Place reopened on January 3, 1971, on the same lakefront spot with a main exhibition hall of 300,000 square feet. Since then, it has brought in an average of $9 billion in convention-related revenue to Illinois annually.

Photo courtesy of Courtesy of Rotary Down Under, Australia

McCormick Place sprawls before the Chicago skyline

McCormick Place has continually expanded. In 1986, a North Building was added on the other side of an expressway and connected to the East Building (renamed Lake Side Center) by a pedestrian bridge. An additional 1 million square feet of exhibition space were added in 1997 with the completion of the South Building. A fourth venue, to be called the West Building, is scheduled to open in 2008.

Since 1960, the center has also been home to the Arie Crown Theatre, named for a Lithuanian immigrant who made it big as a businessman in the City of the Big Shoulders during the 1870s. The 5,000-seat theater was spared by the 1967 fire, but underwent a $6.5 million renovation as it entered the 21st century.

McCormick Place highlights over the years include the Chicago Auto Show, All Candy Expo, and World Wide Food Expo as well as stage acts ranging from Frank Sinatra to The Beach Boys to Jerry Seinfeld.

- NOVEMBER 19 -
1834
DR. SILAS HAMILTON DIES AT OTTERVILLE, ILLINOIS

Dr. Silas Hamilton, a former Mississippi slave owner, bequeathed in his will the funds to build Hamilton Primary School—the nation's first free integrated school—on this day in Illinois history.

The schoolhouse was built in 1835, and the site's present brick building replaced the original in 1873. The one-of-a-kind monument at the historic site reads, in part: "Erected by George Washington, born a slave, in memory of Silas Hamilton, his former master." Hamilton was a Mississippi plantation owner in the 1820s when, en route to visiting his mother in Vermont, he heard the cries of young George Washington, a slave child. Bound to a Virginia slave trader's wagon, the child was grieving the loss of his mother, who had just been sold. Overwhelmed with sympathy, Hamilton paid the peddler-in-human-flesh $100 for the boy, took George to his own mother's home, and raised him as an adopted son.

Finally abandoning the plantation he'd hoped would serve as an example of the operations of humane slave ownership—a seeming contradiction in terms—Hamilton and his conscience settled in Jersey County, Illinois, in 1830. On the way, he freed 28 slaves in Cincinnati, and in Illinois he immediately freed the last three—George Washington and an older couple—who stayed on to work legitimately for him. He was, at the time, the only physician in the county.

When he died four years later, Hamilton left $4,000 to pay for the construction of the integrated school and the salary of its teachers. "Believing in the very great importance of primary education," he wrote in his will, "and desiring that my friends and family have such." After Hamilton's death, George Washington moved in with another local family, and eventually became a successful farmer and community leader. When he died in 1864, Washington in turn bequeathed funds to build a monument honoring his former owner and bestowed "the rest of my estate to be used for the education of colored persons or Americans of African descent . . ." The George Washington Education Fund is still helping deserving students a century-and-a-half later.

Hamilton and Washington are buried together at the city cemetery at Otterville—the only known instance of a former slave and his former master interred side-by-side in America.

- NOVEMBER 20 -
1817
CAMPAIGN FOR ILLINOIS STATEHOOD BEGINS

Daniel Pope Cook published a persuasive editorial in the *Western Intelligencer* promoting statehood on this day in Illinois history.

Cook, a 23-year-old newspaperman, had just returned to Kaskaskia, Illinois, after serving as special envoy to Europe under President James Monroe. (He shared the

long sail back to the States with then-Secretary of State John Quincy Adams, forming a bond that would have tremendous influence on the young Cook's aspirations.) Upon his return, he immediately set upon his "pet project": advocating that Illinois Territory be admitted to the Union. Some historians suggest that he saw in it a lively challenge to beat neighboring Missouri Territory to statehood; others see an urgency born from his abolitionist convictions, as he advocated that Illinois enter the Union as a free state.

Cook launched his campaign for statehood from his home in the territorial seat of Kaskaskia, where he purchased the territory's only newspaper, the *Illinois Herald,* which he renamed the *Western Intelligencer.* (It was published weekly, and annual subscriptions cost $2.50 if paid in advance, $3 upon later collection.) His first editorial advocated statehood. The next issue appealed directly to the territorial legislators, who were scheduled to convene in Kaskaskia within two weeks, to bring the issue of statehood and slavery in Illinois before the U.S. Congress.

Daniel Pope Cook was then appointed clerk of the Illinois House of Representatives by the territorial governor, Ninian Edwards—who was to become Cook's father-in-law. In this official role, and having planted the argument for statehood in his recent editorials, the young Cook influenced the convention. The territorial legislators immediately introduced a resolution asking Congress to grant statehood for Illinois, in words strikingly similar to Cook's editorials. Some historians suggest that Cook composed the resolution himself. Eight days later—and just 22 days after Cook had returned from England—the territorial legislature adopted the resolution.

It was quickly presented to Congress by Daniel Cook's uncle Nathaniel Pope, a U.S. territorial delegate to the Congress, and Illinois's relentless march toward statehood was officially under way.

COACH ZUPPKE'S FIGHTING ILLINI
CLAIM NATIONAL CHAMPIONSHIP

The University of Illinois football team secured the Big Ten Conference championship, earning their first claim as National Champions, with a 24–9 rout over Wisconsin on this day in Illinois history.

Under the guidance of Robert C. Zuppke, in just his second year as head coach, the Fighting Illini went 7 and 0 while outscoring opponents 224–22—a ratio greater than 10–1—that season. They whitewashed division rivals Indiana, Ohio State, and Northwestern by a combined score of 121–0 during a three-week stretch in October. The nine points allowed to the Badgers this day was the largest single-game tally by an opposing team the entire season.

Coach Bob Zuppke, a German immigrant, was a Wisconsin graduate who had starred on that school's football team—before facing it from the opposing sideline. After college, he eschewed offers to coach high school football and instead moved to New York City, where he launched a brief and uneventful career as an artist and designer. In 1910 he returned to the gridiron, leading Oak Park High School, in suburban Chicago, to three straight undefeated seasons. The offers came pouring in—from Illinois, Purdue, Northwestern—and in 1913 Zuppke accepted the head coaching position with the Fighting Illini for a modest salary of $2,700 per year.

Innovative trick plays such as the screen pass, flea-flicker, and on-side kick were Zuppke's brainchilds—born from the creative mind of an artist—and contributed to the team's dominance of the Big Ten. His coaching tenure lasted 29 seasons, second only to Amos Alonzo Stagg's 41-year run at the University of Chicago. By the time he retired in 1941, Zuppke had established himself among the nation's most legendary coaches. His Illinois teams followed that astonishing 1914 season with six more Big Ten titles (1915, 1918, 1919, 1923, 1927, and 1928) and three more national Championships (1919, 1923, and 1927). The teams of the late 1920s featured Zuppke's crowning recruit, Red Grange—the "Galloping Ghost"—arguably the greatest college football star of all time.

Zuppke refused to award scholarships—ever—claiming that "the honor of playing for Illinois is payment enough."

The Northwestern University (NU) Wildcats were invited to their first Rose Bowl, and the Evanston campus exploded in celebration on this day in Illinois history.

It looked to be a special year when the Wildcats upset conference favorites Purdue, 21-0, in the Big Ten season opener. Northwestern's only losses came on the road to top-ranked Michigan (defending Rose Bowl champions) and undefeated Notre Dame. The Big Ten had a no-repeat rule in effect for Rose Bowl eligibility, and the Wolverines, despite winning the conference, could therefore not be invited back to Pasadena. The Wildcats headed into the final week of the season with a 7-2 record, in second place in the Big Ten, and in need of a victory against their traditional rivals, the Fighting Illini, to secure the Rose Bowl bid. At Dyche Stadium, the Wildcats trounced Illinois, 20-7, on November 20, to clinch their inauguration to the prestigious bowl.

What followed was one big party throughout campus. The football team carried Coach Bob Voigts off the field and NU Wildcat fans poured out of the stadium in a wild celebration that lasted through the weekend. At a "Rose Bowl Dance" held two days later, team captain Alex Sarkisian announced to thousands assembled that NU had, indeed, been officially invited to represent the Big Ten in the Rose Bowl. NU students, faculty, and fans were in college-football euphoria as classes were cancelled for the whole week in deference to pregame parties, dances, and pep rallies to cheer on the Wildcats.

The coming New Years Day saw one of the greatest games in Rose Bowl history. A sellout crowd of more than 92,000 fans—many clad in purple—packed Rose Bowl Stadium to see the Wildcats take on the Pacific Coast Conference champs, the undefeated University of California Golden Bears. After exchanging turnovers, Northwestern's Frank Aschenbrenner broke free for a 73-yard touchdown run, the longest in Rose Bowl history. Cal fought back and the Wildcats held to a 20-13 fourth-quarter lead with 43 seconds on the clock and the Bears driving toward the NU end zone. At that critical moment, Wildcat Pee Wee Day intercepted a Cal pass to the goal line, and the Wildcats won.

The Northwestern Wildcats were the Rose Bowl Champions; not bad for a team that had won only three games the previous season.

- November 23 -
1936
Robert Johnson Cuts First-ever Recording of "Sweet Home Chicago"

On this day in Illinois history, Delta blues singer and guitarist Robert Johnson recorded the song that would become a city anthem, "Sweet Home Chicago."

Johnson, who died at age 27 from bad whiskey, cut the recording in a Texas hotel room for the American Record Company. He was one of the most influential musicians of the 20th century, and the inspiration for an entire generation of great bluesmen who created the Chicago Blues style—Muddy Waters, Howlin' Wolf, and Sonny Boy Williamson among them. The music was old folk-blues driven by electric guitar and a rhythm section of bass, drums, and piano, with a saxophone often replacing the traditional harmonica. As poor blacks migrates from the South to Chicago, they brought the Delta blues with them, infused it with some big-city style, and made the Windy City the genre's new home. Johnson's song echoes the Delta blues's history: "Come on, baby don't you want to go / Come on, baby don't you want to go / Back to that same old place / Sweet Home Chicago . . ."

Nobody knows who originally wrote "Sweet Home Chicago," but one artist, Woody Payne, took credit. The song achieved immortality in the 1980 blockbuster hit movie, *The Blues Brothers*. Chicago-native comedians John Belushi and Dan Aykroyd, playing brothers Jake and Elwood Blues—in spin offs from their roles on television's "Saturday Night Live"—performed a memorable rendition of the old classic with living legend John Lee Hooker on guitar. A 1998 remake of the movie, with John Goodman replacing John Belushi, featured quintessential Chicago-style bluesman B. B. King on guitar.

The song has since become a blues-club staple throughout the city and can be heard everywhere from TV spots to sporting events where anything Chicago-related might be involved.

Joseph F. Glidden of DeKalb Receives
Patent for Barbed Wire

On this day in Illinois history, a DeKalb County farmer, Joseph Farwell Glidden, was granted U.S. Patent No. 157,124 for his invention of new-and-improved barbed wire fencing.

In 1843 Glidden, who had come westward from New York, purchased 600 acres outside the village of DeKalb, Illinois, and began to farm. He became a successful agriculturalist and community leader, expanding his acreage considerably and being elected sheriff of DeKalb County in 1852. Years later he attended a county fair where he observed the demonstration of crude wood and wire fencing with protruding nails. The locals, like farmers and ranchers throughout the country, needed such a contrivance to control their roaming livestock. It was then and there that Joseph Glidden had an idea that would forever transform the American heartland.

His design for a more perfect fencing, fashioned with the barbs of a coffee-bean grinder held at intervals by intertwining strands of wire—hence, "barbed wire"—was submitted to the U.S. patent office in the spring of 1874. After winning a multiyear legal battle that involved hundreds of copycat inventors, including fellow DeKalb entrepreneur Jacob Haish, who had patented a similar process, Glidden was declared the "Father of Barbed Wire." He would become fabulously wealthy off his invention. He formed a partnership with DeKalb merchant, Isaac Ellwood, and barbed wire frenzy swept across the land. Business for their Barb Fence Company of DeKalb, Illinois, boomed. Barbed wire, or the "Devil's Rope" as some called it, closed the open range and opened the vast plains to large-scale farming; the age of the western cowboy and his roundup had abruptly ended.

Known as the "Barbed Wire Capital of the World," the city of DeKalb benefited from Glidden's generosity. He donated 67 acres of land, a beauteous wooded area along the Kishwaukee River, to form the campus of the Northern Illinois Normal School—now Northern Illinois University. In 1876, he built Glidden House, a two-story combination hotel and market near downtown DeKalb. In 1879, Glidden cofounded the *DeKalb County Chronicle* with Clinton Rosette.

Glidden died in 1906, one of the wealthiest men in America.

- NOVEMBER 25 -
1932
HELEN SCOTT HAY, FAMOUS RED CROSS NURSE FROM ILLINOIS, DIES

Helen Scott Hay, who became director of the American Red Cross Nursing Personnel during World War I, died on this day in Illinois history.

"Nettie," as she was affectionately called by her parents and three siblings, was born in 1869 to a Carroll County farming family in northwestern Illinois. She graduated from Savanna High School along the Mississippi River in 1886 and later Northwestern University in Evanston before attending Illinois Training School for Nurses in Chicago. She was the "pride and despair" of the class of 1895, graduating with honors, and after various duties was appointed director of nursing at Cook County Hospital from 1905 to 1911. Hay next organized a nursing school in suburban Oak Park. At the outbreak of the Great War, she was central to launching the Mercy Mission—170 surgeons and nurses who set sail from the United States on the relief ship, USS *Red Cross*, in September 1914 for war-torn Europe. Their mission was to remain neutral and care for combat casualties from all nations.

In 1918, after the United States entered the war, Hay was appointed to the newly organized Red Cross operation in the Balkans. There, she worked as chief nurse for one year before being promoted to supervise all American Red Cross nursing commissions in Europe—administering from Paris nearly 20,000 nurses in the field and more than 50 hospitals. From 1914 to 1919, 296 American Red Cross nurses lost their lives. Hay stayed until 1922, training local nurses and directing a child-welfare program for the devastated continent's many orphans. She won numerous awards for her service along the way—including the Florence Nightingale Medal (the Red Cross's most distinguished award) and citations from a number of European heads of state.

Hay returned to Savanna, Illinois, to care for her ailing brother, and she remained active in local Red Cross activities until her death in 1932.

- NOVEMBER 26 -

1934

"BABY FACE NELSON" LAUNCHES LEADS THE FEDERAL BUREAU OF INVESTIGATION ON FATAL MANHUNT

Lester M. Gillis—aka Baby Face Nelson—on this day in Illinois history, stole a car while on the lam and launched the two-day manhunt in suburban Lake County that resulted in his own demise.

Gillis was born December 6, 1908, in Chicago. Described later in life as "something out of a bad dream," he as a youth embraced the criminal elements in the city's rough-and-tumble Back of the Yards neighborhood. There, stealing cars and running liquor for local speakeasies became his favorite pastimes. He graduated to armed robbery by the tender age of 14. Nicknamed "Baby Face Nelson" by his juvenile accomplices, Nelson stood just 5 feet 4 and weighed 130 pounds as an adult. Nelson's career as a hooligan reached levels of cruelty that belied his innocent appearance. He was among the most trigger-happy and heartless gangsters of the era. Among his victims—many gunned down while unarmed and defenseless—was a man caught in the middle of a carjacking, at least one witness scheduled to testify in a federal court case, and several police officers and FBI agents. It was said he murdered not for self-preservation, nor even to avoid arrest, but because he simply enjoyed it.

After escaping prison in 1932 and falling in with notorious bank robber John Dillinger, Baby Face Nelson, and his wife Helen spent life on the lam. They went from hideout to hideout, often narrowly escaping the grasp of local and federal authorities, bouncing mostly between Illinois, Wisconsin, Nevada, and California. In late November 1934, with Inspector Sam Cowley of the FBI hot on his trail, Nelson stole a car in Chicago and hoped once again to find sanctuary in Wisconsin. A bulletin went out and all eyes were looking for the wanted criminal. The following day, November 27, the stolen car was spotted in Barrington, Illinois, after Baby Face behind the wheel. A fierce multicar gun battle ensued, with Nelson fired the first shot. Two special agents (including Cowley) were mortally wounded, and Nelson's car was riddled with bullets.

Later that evening, the body of Baby Face Nelson was found miles away, dumped by the road in the town of Niles. He was buried at St. Joseph Cemetery in River Grove, Illinois.

- NOVEMBER 27 -
1926
CHICAGO'S SOLDIER FIELD FORMALLY DEDICATED

On this day in Illinois history, during a college football game between Army and Navy, Chicago officially dedicated Soldier Field.

A plan drawn by architects Holabird and Roche won a competition to design a great sports palace for the city, and construction began in 1922, funded by Chicago's South Park Commission. The stadium's design recalled the imposing Greek and Roman stadiums of antiquity, with Doric-style colonnades rising more than 100 feet on either side of the playing field. It was not designed to accommodate a single sport but as a "showcase for all events and a playground for all people." In October 1924—on the 53rd anniversary of the Great Chicago Fire—the facility officially opened as Municipal Grant Park Stadium.

Renamed Soldier Field on Armistice Day 1926, as a memorial to American soldiers lost in World War I, the 74,280-seat venue (with temporary bleachers for an additional 30,000) was formally dedicated at the Army-Navy game later that month. set some attendance records over the next several decades. The famous Dempsey-Tunney boxing match brought a crowd of 104,000 in 1927. A record-setting crowd for a high school football game, 115,000 fans, packed Soldier Field to watch Austin Public High School win over Leo Catholic in the 1937 Prep Bowl. And an astounding 123,000 spectators—

Photo courtesy of Library of Congress, pan 6a27179

a collegiate-football attendance record—saw Notre Dame defeat the University of Southern California at Soldier Field in 1927. Capacity was cut to 57,000 in 1971, when the Chicago Bears started using Soldier Field as their regular home in the National Football League.

Soldier Field underwent remodeling in 2002 and reopened for the 2003 football season, its original columns preserved beneath the shadow of a massive new seating bowl, which some critics likened to the belly of a giant UFO.

FRANK DURYEA WINS "RACE OF THE CENTURY"

The *Chicago Times-Herald* sponsored the first automobile race in America, a 53-mile ramble up Lake Michigan's coast from Chicago to Evanston and back, on this day in Illinois history.

Frank Duryea, who co-owned a Peoria bicycle shop with his brother, Charles, won the race at a bustling average 7.3 miles-per-hour. The Duryea brothers are generally credited with building the first gasoline-powered American automobile, the Duryea "Power Wagon," in 1893. It was an upgraded version of this model that Frank rode to victory in the Thanksgiving Day race—the "dash for the cash"—claiming the $2,000 prize put up by the *Chicago Times-Herald*.

Despite dozens of entries, only six horseless carriages made it to the starting line of the contest. Most others were German built machines, and only two, including the Duryea's, finished what was more a race of endurance than speed. Sent off at timed intervals, Duryea started first and won the race despite facing a number of emergency roadside repairs along the way. The following day, the sponsor editorialized: "Persons who are inclined to decry the development of the horseless carriage will be forced to recognize it as an admitted mechanical achievement, highly adapted to some of the most urgent needs of our civilization."

The Duryea brothers opened the Duryea Motor Wagon Company in 1896 in Springfield, Massachusetts. They sold a total of 13 models, but nevertheless qualify as America's first commercial automobile dealers. Charles moved the company back to Peoria, Illinois, two years later. There, he designed the "Peoria Motor Trap," a three-wheeled, two-passenger, double-speeder (forward and reverse) with an optional rear-facing trailer in the back, disliked by passengers who complained of dirt and exhaust. It had a three-cylinder, water-cooled engine; featured 30-inch (rear) and 36-inch (front) wheels; and weighed a total of 700 pounds. But because of poor sales—owing to the negative publicity of one of their models being in the first known auto accident—the Duryea brothers put a halt to manufacturing in 1914.

A restored original Peoria Motor Trap is displayed at the Peoria Public Library.

- NOVEMBER 29 -
1963
CHICAGO CITY COUNCIL VOTES TO RENAME
NORTHWEST EXPRESSWAY AFTER JFK

On this day in Illinois history, one week after the assassination of John F. Kennedy, the Chicago City Council voted unanimously to rename the Northwest Expressway after the late president.

The John Fitzgerald Kennedy Expressway runs for 26 miles from Chicago's Loop to O'Hare Airport. The Northwest Expressway was constructed in the late 1950s and officially completed on November 5, 1960, just three days before Kennedy's defeat of Richard M. Nixon in the general election. Kennedy, who called it "one of the greatest highways in the United States," had made a number of memorable visits to Illinois during his presidential campaign and abbreviated term in the White House. Most notable was the famous September 26, 1960, Kennedy-Nixon debate, which aired nationally on CBS, ushering in the age of televised debates and turning the underdog Massachusetts Senator into the front-runner for the White House. Kennedy, who appeared young and vigorous, had a much better "television face" than the more experienced but haggard-looking vice president. The landmark debate was viewed by some 70 million impressionable Americans. Kennedy returned to Chicago one week later to attend an ostentatious torchlight election parade orchestrated by Mayor Richard J. Daley. President Kennedy used the state-of-the-art highway that would soon bear his name when he attended the dedication of O'Hare International Airport March 23, 1963.

Construction costs of the state-of-the-art roadway totaled more than $237 million. The Kennedy Expressway was the first to feature a rail line along its median, an addition by the Chicago Transit Authority in 1970 that was intended to greatly relieve rush hour traffic. (It was opted for instead of adding a lane in each direction.) It also features reversible express lanes, which switch at 1 p.m. (outbound) and 1 a.m. (inbound) daily to accommodate the traffic flow as it peaks to and from the city. The Kennedy Expressway saves an estimated 60,000 traffic-hours per day among commuters, bringing downtown Chicago 20- to 40-minutes closer to the city's northern and northwest suburbs, respectively.

- NOVEMBER 30 -

1930

MOTHER JONES, MATRIARCH TO ILLINOIS COALMINERS, DIES

Mary Harris Jones died on this day in Illinois history at 100 years of age, after a lifetime devoted to the American labor movement.

The self-described hell-raiser developed her strong antiauthoritarian bent in her native County Cork, Ireland. As a small child in the 1830s, she witnessed the rough treatment of her countrymen at the hands of British soldiers. She immigrated to Chicago by way of Toronto, Canada, as a teenager and took on work as a seamstress. There, Mary met and married George Jones, an ironworker and staunch member of the Iron Molders Union. His influence and Mary's own observations of the gross inequities between the working classes and the affluent Chicago families that employed her planted the seeds for her support for the labor movement in later years. She understood these disparities needed social and economic remedies.

Jones's life was transformed by tragedy. In 1867, she lost her husband and four children to an epidemic of yellow fever, all of them dying within one week. Four years later she lost her home and all her possessions to the Chicago fire of 1871. Without a family, a home, or an income, Jones joined the newly formed Knights of Labor and adopted those who toiled in Illinois coal mines as her kith and kin. She advocated fiercely for improved wages and better conditions on behalf of the American miners, and labor organizations embraced her as their "Mother." "My home," Jones once pronounced, "is wherever there is a fight."

She fought hard to survive, traveling the country for years representing the United Mine Workers of America. She organized strikes, led marches, and commanded attention on the stage—her gentle, grandmotherly appearance disguised a "towering rage" that was revealed whenever she spoke. The U.S. Senate called her the "grandmother of agitators," a title she proudly owned, and industrialists tried vainly to stop her. Mother Jones was jailed on more than one occasion, and in 1925 the *Chicago Times* won a $350,000 lawsuit against the 95-year-old labor activist. But Jones continued to work up right until her 100th birthday.

She was buried at Union Miners Cemetery in Mount Olive, Illinois, where the Mother Jones Monument was dedicated near the graves of victims of the 1898 Virden Mine Riot.

This day in December

Inaugural Issue of *Playboy* Hits Newsstands

On this day in Illinois history, Chicagoan Hugh Hefner launched a racy new magazine for men originally called *Stag Party* but changed at the last moment to *Playboy*.

Hefner invested $600—including $200 for photo rights to the pinup of Hollywood starlet Marilyn Monroe—in the first issue of *Playboy*. Monroe also graced the cover, which listed a newsstand price of 50 cents but not the release date because Hefner was unsure if there would be any follow-up issues. It sold out its 50,000-plus print run within the month. Collectors will pay up to $5,000 for near–mint condition originals of that issue today. The famous logo, the profile of a bunny rabbit with a bow tie, debuted with the second issue and has since become one of the most identifiable brands in corporate America.

Circulation peaked in 1972, with the November edition alone selling more than 7.1 million copies. The issue featured Swedish model Lena Soderberg—and the famous "Lena" centerfold set an industry standard in digitally enhanced imaging. "First, the image contains a nice mixture of detail, flat regions, shading, and texture," noted one expert in the field, adding: "It is a good test image!"

In addition to the sexy, digitally (and otherwise) enhanced girls, *Playboy* is also well known, of course, for its in-depth and often brazen celebrity interviews. Many consumers buy it for the articles. Since its inception, Hefner's men's magazine has featured articles on such fellow Illinoisans as Miles Davis (September 1962), Orson Welles (December 1983), and David Mamet (September 1995). Some celebs have been flown in for interviews at the famed *Playboy* mansion in downtown Chicago. The 69-room mansion was acquired by Hefner in 1959 as his lavish base of operations. A brass sign above the front entrance reads, "Si Non Oscillas, Noli Tintinnare"—"If you don't swing, don't ring." Hefner relocated to a new mansion in Los Angeles, California, in the mid-1970s.

Hugh Hefner, born in Chicago in 1926, has bought a spot for himself beside the crypt of Marilyn Monroe in a California cemetery so he can be buried alongside the blonde bombshell whose glossy image helped birth a publishing empire.

- DECEMBER 2 -

1942

UNIVERSITY OF CHICAGO SCIENTISTS ACHIEVE FIRST CONTROLLED ATOMIC REACTION

On this day in Illinois history, at the squash courts–turned–nuclear laboratory beneath the unused University of Chicago football field, Enrico Fermi and his team of scientists unleashed the atomic age.

It was an unlikely setting. Stagg Field, once home to the mighty Maroons of Big Ten glory, had fallen silent since the university eliminated its football program to focus solely on academics in 1933. Enrico Fermi, an Italian-born physicist, had immigrated to the United States with his wife and children in 1938—after accepting the Nobel Prize for physics in Stockholm, Sweden—to escape Mussolini's fascist reign over his native county. (Fermi's wife was Jewish, and Mussolini had recently enacted anti-Semitic legislation to complement his Nazi allies'.) The world's foremost atomic theorist, Fermi was appointed by President Franklin Roosevelt to join the Manhattan Project, a secret experiment aimed at harnessing the power of the atom for military means, and he led a team of scientists at one of the nation's first nuclear reactors (Chicago Pile No.1), built beneath the vacant gridiron at the University of Chicago. There, Fermi and his team sustained the world's first controlled nuclear chain reaction.

At 3:25 p.m., an atom of uranium-235 was split and atomic power released, constrained, and stopped under Fermi's meticulous guidance. A coded telephone alerted leaders in Washington, D.C.: "Italian navigator has landed in the new world.... The natives were very friendly." Three years later, the first atomic bombs were dropped on Hiroshima and Nagasaki, and World War II was essentially won.

The scientist left quite a legacy. After the war, in September 1945, the Enrico Fermi Institute was established at the University of Chicago to pursue interdisciplinary research ranging from nuclear theory to astronomy to the concentration of solar energy. In May 1974, Fermilab (formerly the National Accelerator Laboratory) was dedicated in Weston, Illinois (30 miles west of Chicago). At 6,800 acres, it is the nation's largest laboratory, where researchers seek answers to the beguiling questions of the universe—studying the cosmic relationships between matter, space, and time.

Fermi died November 28, 1954, and is buried at Oak Woods Cemetery in Chicago.

- DECEMBER 3 -

1818

ILLINOIS ADMITTED TO THE UNION

President James Monroe signed the congressional resolution bringing the 21st state into the Union on this day in Illinois history.

Photo courtesy of Library of Congress, LC-USZ62-104958

James Monroe

With just over 34,600 residents in 1818, Illinois was the least populous state ever to enter the Union; today, with more than 12 million people, it is the fifth largest. Nicknamed the Prairie State, Illinois officially adopted "The Land of Lincoln" as the state slogan in 1955. The official state song, "Illinois," introduced in a bill brought before the General Assembly by Senator Florence Fifer Bohrer in 1925, is a tribute to the state's early history. With words written by C. H. Chamberlain and music composed by Archibald Johnston, the lyrics are as follows:

By thy rivers gently flowing, Illinois, Illinois,
O'er thy prairies verdant growing, Illinois, Illinois,
Comes an echo on the breeze.
Rustling through the leafy trees, and its mellow tones are these, Illinois, Illinois,
And its mellow tones are these, Illinois.

From a wilderness of prairies, Illinois, Illinois,
Straight thy way and never varies, Illinois, Illinois,
Till upon the inland sea,
Stands thy great commercial tree, turning all the world to thee, Illinois, Illinois,
Turning all the world to thee, Illinois.

When you heard your country calling, Illinois, Illinois,
Where the shot and shell were falling, Illinois, Illinois,
When the Southern host withdrew,
Pitting Gray against the Blue, There were none more brave than you, Illinois, Illinois,
There were none more brave than you, Illinois.

Not without thy wondrous story, Illinois, Illinois,
Can be writ the nation's glory, Illinois, Illinois,
On the record of thy years,
Abraham Lincoln's name appears, Grant and Logan, and our tears, Illinois, Illinois,
Grant and Logan, and our tears, Illinois.

- DECEMBER 4 -
1820
ILLINOIS LEGISLATURE FIRST CONVENES IN VANDALIA

The second General Assembly, having abandoned the flood-swept Kaskaskia, convened at the new state capital in Vandalia on this day in Illinois history.

Vandalia was founded in 1919 with the specific intent of locating Illinois's second state capitol building there. The state legislature had been meeting at Kaskaskia, for-

Old State Capitol in Vandalia

merly home to the territorial governor and Illinois's capital city since the state had been admitted to the Union the previous year. They agreed, however, that the current site, threatened as it was by Mississippi River flood waters, was too precarious to serve such a central role. Vandalia was established the new capital city on January 27, 1821, but the town had yet to be settled. The legislature had procured a federal land grant and chosen a site 60 miles up the Kaskaskia River, in the forested area known as Reeve's Bluff, for the new capitol building. There, Vandalia, the present-day seat of Fayette County, was hastily built. The legislators convened in a crowded boarding house to administer the affairs of state until construction was complete.

By 1836, what was intended to be a permanent capitol building—Vandalia's third statehouse—had finally been erected. The first, a shoddy two-story frame house, was destroyed by fire in December 1823. The second was poorly built by residents who suspected Vandalia's temporary status as state capital; they rightly feared that the Illinois General Assembly might be wooed to another city with more a extravagant building. Within a decade the floorboards sagged and the walls bulged outward, and some Vandalians refused to even enter its doors for fear of collapse. The third Vandalia statehouse, unlike its predecessors, was a solidly built structure with room enough to host all three branches of government. But a movement to relocate the state capital yet again had been afoot for years, and the new building in Vandalia was scarcely used before being abandoned. Illinois's capital was relocated to Springfield by 1840.

During its 20-year tenure, the Vandalia statehouse hosted such giants in Illinois politics as Stephen Douglas, Abe Lincoln, and John Reynolds. Today it is an Illinois State Historic Site.

- DECEMBER 5 -

1821

EDWARD COLES ELECTED ILLINOIS'S SECOND GOVERNOR

Edward Coles, a staunch abolitionist with Virginia roots, was elected the state's second governor on this day in Illinois history.

Coles's time in Illinois, including his four years in office (1822–1826), had a profound influence on the state's rejection of slavery before the Civil War. He first visited Illinois in 1815, between stints as private secretary and then diplomat for President James Madison, traveling to Shawneetown and Kaskakia. He fell in love on these trips with the frontier territory and returned in 1818 to attend the budding state's constitutional convention. There, he advocated that Illinois enter the Union as a free state.

Coles returned to his home in Virginia, where he had inherited a plantation along with his father's slaves, in 1819. He promptly sold the plantation and headed back to Illinois, bringing the slaves with him. Coles freed them all once he crossed the border of the new state, promising 160 acres of land to each family. This act shocked many slavery sympathizers in southern Illinois, and future political opponents.used it against him. He was appointed registrar to the land-grant office in Edwardsville, Illinois, by President James Monroe. But with the slavery issue still unsettled, he was ambitious to hold a more influential office. He aimed to be governor.

Coles ran for governor on an antislavery ticket, winning with one-third of the vote—a mere 50 ahead of the second-place tally—as the rest of the ballots were split between three other candidates. After he took office in 1822, Governor Coles's adversaries seized upon his recent act of manumission in a move to destroy him. Madison County filed a lawsuit against him for failing to post a $1,000 bond per freed slave, as required by law to insure against their becoming wards of the young, cash-strapped state. The case was eventually dismissed. Also, during his term, Coles scored a major constitutional victory against proslavery forces. A movement to introduce formal slavery in the state forced a statewide referendum before the 1824 constitutional convention. Coles organized an antislavery society, campaigning against proponents of slavery and stating that if they won, "we should write the epitaph of free government." It came down to a vote: 4,972 Illinoisans for slavery, 6,640 against.

Governor Coles, who is largely credited for the Prairie State becoming a free state, had a relatively brief stay in Illinois. In 1832, he left for Philadelphia, Pennsylvania, where he died in 1868.

- DECEMBER 6 -

1847

ABRAHAM LINCOLN TAKES HIS FIRST SEAT IN CONGRESS

Abe Lincoln, after years of personal struggle in the midst of political success, took his seat in the U.S. House of Representatives on this day in Illinois history.

For Lincoln, the road to Washington, D.C., was not an easy one. While rising to prominence in the Illinois Whig Party he had been suffering a private melancholy described by his first law partner, John T. Stuart, as "wrapped in abstraction and gloom." A defeat in the 1832 campaign for the Illinois General Assembly had been followed by four successive victories (1834, 1836, 1838, and 1840) and a nomination for the U.S. Congress in 1846. Despite this and a prospering law practice, Lincoln had wrestled with an intense sense of hopelessness throughout. In 1841, while paying daily visits to a personal doctor, Lincoln wrote his law partner to say that he was "the most miserable man living." He dealt with this odd melancholy by reading, reciting, and composing poetry—selecting works which tended to brood over the theme of death. Friends feared that Abe was suicidal and, according to some contemporaries, he admitted it. But a profound sense that he was here to accomplish something of greatness instilled in him the desire—the "irrepressible desire" in his own words—to live on.

Photo courtesy of Library of Congress, LC-USZC4-2439

His first chance at greatness came with the congressional seat in 1846. But his minority position of opposing the war with Mexico in 1848 led to a temporary political letdown. Lincoln failed to distinguish himself in the nation's capital as he'd hoped and did not seek a second term. President-elect Zachary Taylor offered Abe the governorship of Oregon Territory in 1848, but he turned it down. While in Washington, D.C., he had sent his wife Mary and their boys back to Springfield, because they had become a hindrance, and he said that "having nothing but business—no variety—[was making life] exceedingly tasteless." It looked like Abe's political aspirations may have ended. He returned to Springfield and refocused for several years on his law practice.

The passage of the antiabolition Kansas-Nebraska Act in 1854, championed by Lincoln's Illinois rival, Stephen A. Douglas, drew the somber attorney back into politics. He had found his great calling and threw all his energy into the fight against extending slavery.

Aaron Montgomery Ward—founder of the nation's first mail-order business—died on this day in Illinois history at his Highland Park home.

Ward began his retail career in 1859 as a salesman for a St. Joseph, Michigan, general store. He was hired at $6 per month, plus room and board, and three years later was a manager earning $100 a month. The ambitious and energetic clerk left for Chicago, capital of the nation's wholesale dry goods industry, in 1865. There, he became a traveling salesman for Marshall Field's, working on commission.

Photo courtesy of Library of Congress, LC-USZ62-117982

In the crossroads of rural America, he observed the frustration farmers, merchants, and their small-town customers had with being overcharged by the big city "middleman." Montgomery Ward conceived of a remedy—buying goods for cash at wholesale and delivering them directly to the rural market by mail, eliminating the traveling salesman and his commission, thereby lowering the mark-up price for consumers. His competitors thought Ward's plan was pure lunacy.

Despite his critics and early setbacks, including losing his entire initial inventory to the Chicago fire of 1871, Montgomery Ward mailed his first catalog in August 1872. It was a single-sheet price list featuring some 150 items and ordering instructions. By 1888, annual sales for Montgomery Ward & Co.'s popular "wish book" had reached $1 million. Ward's motto: "Satisfaction Guaranteed." By 1904, more than 3 million Montgomery Ward catalogs, each weighing in at a robust four pounds each, were circulating to households across the American landscape. Ward's one-time critics had turned into copycats, including retailers Richard W. Sears and Alvah C. Roebuck, whose own booming mail-order business would compete with Ward's for much of the 20th century.

Beginning in 1890, Ward battled tirelessly to preserve Chicago's lakefront park land, "which city officials would crowd with buildings, transforming the breathing spot for the poor into a show ground for the educated rich." When Ward died, he bequeathed a considerable part of his estate to Northwestern University in Evanston, Illinois, and to other educational facilites.

His greatest legacy, however, was in offering a "fair deal" to American consumers while revolutionizing the retail industry.

- DECEMBER 8 -
1969
ILLINOIS CONSTITUTIONAL CONVENTION MEETS IN SPRINGFIELD

On this day in Illinois history, 116 delegates convened at the old capitol building for the state's first constitutional convention in 100 years.

The movement for a renewed constitution was launched by Marjorie Pebworth, former president of the League of Women Voters and then member of the Illinois House of Representatives, in 1965. Illinois voters called for a new constitutional convention by a majority of two to one in the 1968 elections, and they would be represented by an equal number of Democrats and Republicans, a diverse group including lawyers, businessmen, educators, bankers, farmers, and union officials. Chicago attorney Samuel W. Witwer, who had been active in constitutional reform for 20 years, was chosen by the delegates to preside over the convention. Together, they decided to strip away the clutter of the 100-year-old constitution and focus its replacement on only the most fundamental concerns, such as taxation and the roles of the various branches of government.

The simplified Illinois Constitution featured a number of radical changes but maintained much that voters wished to retain from its unwieldy predecessor. The governor was given unprecedented powers, particularly in the use of a line-item veto and the freedom to create or reorganize state agencies without the approval of the General Assembly. To avoid the political quibbling that had obstructed the legislative process in the past, the new constitution mandated that the governor and the lieutenant governor be of the same political party. A home-rule article was introduced that gave larger municipalities (at least 25,000 in population) the ability to levy taxes and pass ordinances without approval of the state's General Assembly. Critics argued that created carte blanche for rampant taxation.

Illinois voters settled several important issues directly at the polls. The first was to retain three representatives from each of the 59 districts (one senator and two representatives in the house). Voters likewise chose to continue the direct election of judges (rather than having them appointed by a special committee). They rejected a motion to reduce the voting age to 18 from 21 (which was nevertheless imposed nationally by the U.S. Supreme Court soon after) and also, by a measure of two to one, rejected a motion to abolish the death penalty.

Voters ratified the new Illinois Constitution on December 15, 1970, and, evidently satisfied, voted down a ballot to call another convention for further revisions in 1990.

101 "WOBBLIES" GO ON TRIAL IN
CHICAGO UNDER ESPIONAGE ACT

On this day in Illinois history, 101 members of the Industrial Workers of the World (IWW)—nicknamed the "Wobblies"—stood before Judge Kenesaw Mountain Landis for "conspiracy to hinder the draft" in a Cook County courtroom.

The IWW was born in Chicago in 1905. Their motto was: "One Big Union." An amalgam of activists—socialists, anarchists, and radical trade unionists—their goal was to unite workers of the world against their employers. "The working class and employing class have nothing in common," reads the IWW Constitution, "There can be no peace. . . . . Between these two classes a struggle must go on until the workers of the world organize . . . take possession of the means of production, abolish the wage system, and live in harmony with the Earth." The group's more famous members included "Big Bill" Haywood, Eugene V. Debs, and Mary Harris ("Mother") Jones.

In Chicago the Wobblies received a death blow. Just before the United States entered World War I, an antiwar IWW newspaper, *The Industrial Worker*, declared: "Capitalists of America, we will fight against you, not for you! There is not a power in the world that can make the working class fight if they refuse." When the United States declared war on Germany, however, the IWW leadership ordered all antiwar propaganda to cease; if not in support of the war, they would not actively oppose it. Employers and those in the U.S. government, who saw the IWW as a threat, seized the climate of war hysteria to condemn the Wobblies as anti-American conspirators. (The fact that so many members were of German heritage did not help.) More than 100 leaders of the organization were arrested for violating the new Espionage Act—wartime legislation that made hindering the war effort punishable by both fines and prison time—and found guilty in a federal court in Chicago.

Judge Landis sentenced the Wobblies to up to 20 years in prison or hard labor, but suspecting a "stacked" jury, the U.S. Supreme Court overturned some of the convictions on a technicality in 1921.

- DECEMBER 10 -
1907
UNIVERSITY OF CHICAGO PHYSICIST BECOMES
FIRST AMERICAN TO WIN NOBEL PRIZE IN SCIENCE

On this day in Illinois history, the University of Chicago's Albert Abraham Michelson—a Prussian-born physicist most noted for measuring the speed of light—became the first American to be awarded the Nobel Prize for physics.

Michelson immigrated to the United States at age 2 in 1854, with his parents, who were lured by the California Gold Rush. He entered the U.S. Naval Academy in 1869, proved to be a fine scientist but poor sailor, and graduated with a degree in physics four years later. He taught science for a while in the Navy and resigned from the armed services in 1881 to pursue his life's passion: solving the problematic question of how best to quantify the speed of light. After professorships at universities in Cleveland, Ohio, and Worcester, Massachusetts, Michelson was appointed head of the physics department at the newly organized University of Chicago in 1892. There, he achieved national renown as a groundbreaking physicist.

Photo courtesy of Wikipedia

The annual Nobel Prize presentation speech in 1907 was canceled because of the death of King Oscar II of Sweden (home of the distinguished award) two days earlier. But the text of the speech notes Michelson's inestimable contributions to human knowledge in the fields of precision metrology and spectroscopy—the measure of light waves—and his work is considered by some to be as significant as that of Galileo. Just a few years before winning the Nobel Prize, Michelson—who never earned a PhD but held numerous honorary degrees—announced the results of one of the most significant studies in the history of physics: The Michelson-Morley Experiment. Along with American chemist Edward Williams Morley, Michelson set out to measure the speed of light based on the then-accepted notion of "luminiferous aether," a supposed cosmic substance that underlay all matter and acted as the transportive vehicle for water, sound, light, etc. Using the Michelson-built interferometer, an instrument designed to split in two a beam of light and measure the varying velocities against the ether, the pair discovered that, indeed, no such ether existed. This discovery led Michelson to conduct further experiments while at U of C that eventually determined the speed of light in 1933 (after he died) at 299,774 kilometers per second.

Michelson remained at the University of Chicago until he retired in 1929, after serving as president of the National Academy of Science from 1923 to 1927.

- DECEMBER 11 -

1949

JOHNNY LUJACK LEADS CHICAGO BEARS OVER CHICAGO CARDINALS IN SEASON FINALE

The Chicago Bears defeated in-town rivals the Chicago Cardinals 52–29, thanks to quarterback Johnny Lujack's record-setting 468 yards and six touchdown passes, on this day in Illinois history.

Both organizations were inaugural members of the National Football League. Their rivalry is the oldest in the league, despite the fact that the Bears and Green Bay Packers have played more games and the Cardinals left town in 1960 for St. Louis (later Arizona). (The Bears have a lifetime record of 56-26-6 against the Cardinals.) By 1949, the Bears had established themselves as one of the premier teams in the NFL, with five championship titles and consistent winning records. The Cardinals, meanwhile, were mired in mediocrity. After stumbling week after week and season after season with lackluster results, Chicago's South Side team (they played at Comiskey Park) had finally ended up on top, winning the 1947 NFL Championship. The 1949 Cardinals went into the final week of the season in the middle of the pack at 6–4–1 with a golden opportunity to spoil the 8–3 Bears's hopes of claiming first place in the NFL West.

Bears quarterback Johnny Lujack had different ideas. Drafted from the University of Notre Dame, where he had won the Heisman Trophy in 1949, Lujack was a master of the Bears' famous T formation. His 468 passing yards that day set an NFL single-game high mark (since broken) and his six airborne touchdowns are second in team history—Sid Luckman had tossed seven back on a Sunday afternoon in 1943. (Despite this great performance, and two subsequent Pro Bowl appearances, Lujack lasted only four seasons in the NFL, completing exactly half of his 808 career attempts and 54 interceptions.) The victory jettisoned the Bears to a 9–3 record to top the NFL West, while the Cardinals finished smack in the middle of the five-team pack at 6-5-1.

Lujack's Bears were denied a shot at the NFL Championship, as the 8-2-2 Los Angeles Rams instead represented the West against the East champion Philadelphia Eagles, and lost.

- DECEMBER 12 -
1803
LEWIS AND CLARK SET UP CAMP RIVER DUBOIS

Meriwether Lewis and William Clark, along with their Corps of Discovery, arrived at the site along the Wood River in present-day Madison County where they built Camp River Dubois on this day in Illinois history.

They spent the next several months in Illinois Country preparing for the historic exploration of Louisiana Territory. They first crossed into Illinois with 20 men on November 11, 1803, and stayed at Fort Massac for just two days to resupply and solicit

volunteers. Among their recruits was George Drouillard, a half–Shawnee Indian, half-French adventurer who became the group's top hunter and interpreter. On December 13, the party headed down the Ohio River.

The next day, according to Lewis's journal, the team "landed on the point at which the Ohio and Mississippi form their junction"—present-day Cairo. There the group practiced using the latest instruments for reading latitude and longitude. On December 28 they reached Kaskaskia, where they found 12 more volunteers. François Labiche, an Indian trader and expert boatman, became yet another valuable Illinoisan to the expedition. Sergeant John Ordway, who also signed up at Kaskaskia, became the Corps of Discovery's third in command. The only officer to come from the regular Army, he kept a detailed journal throughout the journey.

In early December, Lewis and Clark reached Cahokia—the oldest European settlement on the Mississippi—and used its post office to correspond with President Thomas Jefferson back in Washington, D.C. One week later, they set up their winter camp at Wood River, across from the mouth of the Missouri River a bit north of present-day Granite City. Barred from entering Louisiana Territory by Spanish authorities still in St. Louis—though Spain no longer held claim to those lands—they stayed until mid-May before launching the official mission. Lewis and Clark constructed Fort Dubois as their base, and, in the interim, focused their efforts on training their men, organizing their supplies, and gathering intelligence on what lay across the mighty river.

A replica of Camp Dubois was built near the original site in 2003 to commemorate the bicentennial of the Lewis and Clark exploration.

- DECEMBER 13 -

1900

THE "BIG FIX" SENDS CHICAGO BOXING TO THE CANVAS

The sport of boxing—the "manly art"—was banned from Chicago for 25 years after Joe Gans took a dive against "Terrible Terry" McGovern in an infamous championship bout on this day in Illinois history.

The Gans-McGovern fight was the most anticipated ring event of its day, and Chicago's Tattershall Arena was packed to the rafters with more than 17,000 boxing fans. Gans and McGovern—without question the top two prize fighters in the country—were a study in contrasts. Gans, considered by many the "uncrowned" lightweight champion, was America's first native-born black champ; he was a scientific boxer who studied an opponent's strengths and weaknesses and was known for his fancy ring maneuvers and landing punches with pinpoint accuracy. McGovern, current featherweight champion, was a white slugger from Brooklyn, New York; he was a ferocious, hard-hitting puncher who lacked strategy but whose raw power instilled fear in his opponents—most of whom he knocked out. They were to square off for six rounds, the regulation limit those days.

Uncrowned champ Joe Gans

The bout was filmed ringside, and on the primitive reel-to-reel footage Joe Gans can be seen hitting the canvas in round two after a ghost left hook by McGovern—and staying down for the count. Gans had come into the ring looking scared and was knocked down several times in the first two rounds before being counted out, which was highly uncharacteristic. Despite McGovern's knack for flooring opponents, eyebrows were immediately raised; Gans was no average opponent, and fans and authorities suspected foul play. Mayor Carter Henry Harrison Jr, was outraged, and the city council issued an order banning professional boxing that would be in effect through 1925. The much-hyped bout had generated plenty of betting. Gans, a gambler himself, later admitted to throwing the fight, to fixing the dive along with his manager and an unnamed crony. McGovern had no knowledge of the fix.

The Big Fix, as the infamous 1900 bout came to be known, threw Chicago boxing into a state of limbo for a full quarter century thereafter.

WINNETKA'S CROW ISLAND SCHOOL DESIGNATED
NATIONAL HISTORIC LANDMARK

On this day in Illinois history, a small, once-experimental grammar school in suburban Cook County was dedicated a National Historic Landmark.

Crow Island School, built upon a small "island" in former marshland where crows once gathered, opened in 1940 and has since revolutionized elementary-school archi-

Photo courtesy of Jeff Ruetsche

tecture in America. Its inside-out design put the needs of children first and features many characteristics that are now universal in school buildings across the nation, including self-contained classrooms with low windows, child-sized furnishings, and exit doors leading to an outdoor courtyard. Crow Island School originally had three wings for such classrooms, with a fourth added in 1954; each is connected to a common auditorium, a library, and administrative offices in the center. Its playground boasted the nation's first jungle gym with activity areas zoned by age to promote safety. As a whole, the basic concept of Crow Island School, the Winnetka Plan, has been replicated a thousand times over across the country.

The Winnetka Plan is based on the educational philosophy of Carleton Washburne, school superintendent for Winnetka from 1919 to 1943, and incorporates the progressive child-centered school concepts reflected so well in Crow Island's design. Each child, according to this plan, is to be treated as an individual, both socially and academically, and their education is to be fostered in an environment that meets the student's physical and developmental needs. This idea gained currency in the years following the school's opening and has been embraced as the core principal by many of the nation's educational systems ever since.

Crow Island School's chief architect, Lawrence B. Perkins, received the American Institute of Architects' 25 Year Award in 1971 for the school—the second building after Rockefeller Center in New York to be recognized with that honor.

- DECEMBER 15 -

1838

CHEROKEE ENTER ILLINOIS ON THE TRAIL OF TEARS

On this day in Illinois history, more than 8,000 Cherokee Indians began to cross the Ohio River at Pope County in one of the saddest episodes in 19th-century America.

Nearly 15,000 Cherokee—a Native American nation that fought beside the United States during the War of 1812—were forcibly removed from their Smoky Mountain homes by the U.S. government in the winter of 1838–39 and made to walk the 1,000 miles to lands in Oklahoma under the supervision of 7,000 federal troops. The trail was called *Nunna Daul Tsuny*—"The Trail of Tears"—by the weary exiles who survived.

Photo courtesy of Library of Congress, LC-USZC4-2954

As the May 1838 deadline for voluntary removal passed, General Winfield Scott, who had commanded U.S. troops in Illinois during the Black Hawk War of 1832, directed the removal of 15,000 Cherokee at gunpoint. Anywhere from 2,000 to 4,000 Cherokee died along the way, enduring harsh weather, malnourishment, and rampant disease. The larger group was divided into smaller ones of about 1,000, who traveled together. The largest contingent passed through southern Illinois following a path that is today traced by IL 146.

General Winfield Scott

It took them several weeks to traverse southern Illinois. They first crossed the Ohio River by ferry into Golconda, at an exorbitant fee of $1 per head, which the Cherokee had to pay from their own pockets. The brutal march took them on through Dixon Springs, Vienna, Pleasant Grove, and Jonesboro before they reached Dutch Creek and another ferry at the Mississippi River. There they had to wait for the ice to thaw before crossing, and many perished. A cluster of unmarked graves at a church near Anna, Illinois, is believed to be the final resting place for many of these Cherokee.

While camped at Dutch Creek, legend has it that a Cherokee chief sold his slave, Priscilla, to a Mulkeytown couple, who immediately set the 13-year-old girl free and adopted her into their family. The story goes that she brought with her from Tennessee a pocketful of hollyhock seeds that she scattered around her new home. The unusual red flowers that grew—known locally as Priscilla hollyhocks—still bloom today.

A small monument in Brownfield, alone along this stretch of the Trail of Tears, marks this tragic chapter in the state's history.

The Second City, a small comedy troupe that would change the face of live theater and late-night television in America, debuted at a former North Side Chicago laundromat on this day in Illinois history.

The Second City—named for Chicago's famous epithet—had its humble beginnings at the University of Chicago in the 1950s and by the end of the 1970s had transformed itself into a worldwide comedic tour de force. The Compass Players were a short-lived group of talented, young performers who got their start at the U of C campus in 1955. Their brisk skits, performed at a local cafe, featured political and social satire wrapped up in the techniques of improvisation, audience participation, and theatric games that would make The Second City famous in later years.

With some of the same actors, The Second City debuted a show called *Excelsior & Other Outcries* in 1959 to rave reviews and enthusiastic audiences By the mid-1960s, the cabaret had recorded its first comedy album (*Comedy from the Second City* on Mercury Records), performed on Broadway, in London, and in Toronto, and had been hosting workshops on improvisation for aspiring comedians in Chicago for years. In 1967, The Second City moved into its permanent home at the city's Piper's Alley Theater and produced some of the biggest names the world of comedy has ever known.

The Second City hit its stride in the 1970s. "Pioneers of Improv," an assemblage of Second City alumni including Dan Aykroyd, John Belushi, Bill Murray, and Gilda Radner, brought the trademark skills and stretches of the risk-taking Chicago cabaret into America's living rooms with the advent of *Saturday Night Live*. The Second City launched its own syndicated late-night television show in 1976 featuring the likes of John Candy, Harold Ramis, and George Wendt. Today, the satire and silliness continue at live theaters in Detroit, Las Vegas, Los Angeles, New York, and Toronto. The Chicago group, still the anchor of the Second City phenomenon, approaches its 50-year anniversary in 2009 with the same outlandish wit and irreverence from which it was born. Current television audiences enjoy yet another graduate of The Second City, the "Ivy League of Comedy": Dan Castellaneta, the voice of Homer Simpson.

FORMER GOVERNOR GEORGE H. RYAN
INDICTED FOR RACKETEERING

George Ryan—a hero to many for his opposition to the death penalty—was indicted on federal charges relating to the notorious "licenses for bribes" scandal on this day in Illinois history.

Ryan, a Kankakee pharmacist who rose through the ranks of the Illinois Republican Party to become governor from 1999 to 2003, was the 66th person to be charged in a bottom-to-top investigation of corruption in the secretary of state's office. He had served as Illinois secretary of state during the 1990s when the scandal broke. In 1994, six Chicago children—all siblings under 10 years of age—were killed in a fiery auto crash involving a truck driver who spoke no English and had zero qualifications for holding the trucking license issued him by Ryan's office. A terrible scam was exposed when local news reporters inquired how the driver acquired the license. Hundreds of thousand of dollars in bribe money had passed hands—swindling taxpayers and leading to the deaths of innocents—so drivers could buy licenses without first passing a driving test.

Whistleblowers reported that the practice had become endemic and that when they expressed concern they were told by higher-ups to keep silent—to "leave it alone." From instructors at truck-driving schools to managers at the Department of Motor Vehicles, indictments and convictions (more than 50) continued to work their way up the chain of command. Despite rumors that Ryan himself was receiving thousands of dollars in kickbacks, he was elected governor in 1998 with more than 51 percent of the vote.

The pressure, along with the evidence, continued to mount throughout his governorship. In August 2001, Ryan, adamantly maintaining his innocence, announced he would not be running for reelection. Meanwhile, he shocked the nation by issuing a moratorium on executions. Citing uncertainty of guilt and racial inequality in application of the death penalty, Ryan issued a blanket commutation of the sentences of the state's 167 death-row inmates. To some, this turned the scandal-ridden governor into an international hero, and he was in fact nominated for the Nobel Peace Prize for these actions; others, however—particularly the survivors of victims of heinous crimes where guilt was not in question—were outraged. "I don't think a blanket anything is a good idea," said incoming Governor Rod Blagojevich, a Democrat, as many (rightly) forecast that the scandal would deliver a near–death blow to the Illinois Republican Party.

Governor Ryan has not been proven to have had knowledge of the scam.

- DECEMBER 18 -
1913
LEGENDARY BASKETBALL COACH RAY MEYER BORN IN CHICAGO

On this day in Illinois history, the man who put DePaul University basketball on the map, Raymond J. Meyer, was born in Cook County.

The Vincentian Fathers built a church on the city's then–Far North Side in 1875 and established the adjoining St. Vincent's College—DePaul's predecessor—on the site in 1898. With seven faculty members, 70 students, and a $40 tuition fee, St. Vincent's began its first ten-month term that fall. Nicknamed at first the "D-Men," the school's athletic teams had by 1923 adopted the nickname of "Blue Demons," an ironic nickname for a Christian institution, and one which would stick. By then enrollment had reached 3,000. As the university continued to grow, the Blue Demons gained fame under head basketball coach Ray Meyer, who was appointed in 1942 and remained in charge through much of the 1980s.

Meyer had played basketball at St. Patrick's High School in Chicago, been named twice to All-Conference honors, and helped lead the team to the 1932 National Catholic High School Basketball Championship. In 1933 the 5-foot-11 forward went on to play for the University of Notre Dame, where he captained the Irish squad in 1937 and 1938. After a brief amateur career, Meyer was hired as the Blue Demons's assistant coach in 1941. He took the helm the following season.

In 1945, Meyer and superstar center George Mikan led DePaul to the National Invitational Tournament (NIT) Championship, the first and only postseason title in Blue Demon history. Coach Meyer had a career record of 723-354, chalked up 12 20-plus win seasons, and led the Blue Demons to the National Collegiate Athletic Association (NCAA) Final Four in 1943 and 1979. A fierce competitor and terrific motivator of ballplayers, Meyer never claimed that elusive NCAA tournament title, which would have been the crowning achievement in an otherwise remarkable tenure as head coach of one of the nation's most consistent college basketball teams. He retired in 1984.

Coach Ray Meyer was inducted into the basketball Hall of Fame on April 30, 1979, while he was still coaching.

- DECEMBER 19 -

1975

CHICAGOAN JOHN PAUL STEVENS IS SWORN IN AS U.S. SUPREME COURT JUSTICE

John Paul Stevens, born in Chicago in 1920, was sworn in to the U.S. Supreme Court on this day in Illinois history.

Son of a Chicago hotel mogul, Stevens graduated from the University of Chicago in 1941 before joining the U.S. Navy as an intelligence officer. He earned the Bronze Star for his efforts as a cryptographer during World War II. After the war, he attended Northwestern University's School of Law. Stevens became editor-in-chief of the law review, graduated at the top of his class in 1947, and earned the highest grade point average in the school's history. He was admitted to the Illinois bar in 1949 and two years later opened his own Chicago practice, specializing in antitrust law.

Photo courtesy of Wikipedia

His early successes forecast a meteoric rise through the nation's courts. A Republican, Stevens stayed clear of partisan politics and won universal respect as a moderate, honest, and highly capable attorney (and later, judge). He served as associate counsel to a U.S. House of Representatives subcommittee studying monopoly power in 1951 and was appointed to the attorney general's national committee to study antitrust law in 1953. In 1970, President Richard M. Nixon appointed Stevens to the Seventh Circuit Court of Appeals. Five years later, when Justice William O. Douglas retired from the U.S. Supreme Court, President Gerald Ford nominated Judge Stevens to assume that vacancy in the nation's highest legal body. He was confirmed by the Senate, 98–0, on December 17, 1975, and was sworn in two days later.

As a Supreme Court justice, John Paul Stevens continues to eschew ideology for pragmatism; with a voracious appetite for facts, Stevens decides cases one-by-one, not in obedience to a social agenda. *Federal Communications Commission v. Pacifica Foundation* (1978) is a case in point: Rather than fall back on abstract notions of free speech, Justice Stevens looked at the relevant facts of the case and determined that a radio program is distinct from a play or a movie, and therefore the First Amendment must be applied differently. The "Filthy Words" broadcast mistakenly tuned in by a child during the daytime (the basis for a father's complaint against a radio station), Stevens argued, infringed upon "the privacy of the home, where the individual's right to be left alone plainly outweighs the First Amendment rights of an intruder."

In recent years, Stevens has tended to side with the more liberal justices on the more contentious issues faced by the Supreme Court.

- DECEMBER 20 -

1918

AUDREY TOTTER, QUEEN OF FILM NOIR, BORN IN JOLIET

On this day in Illinois history, actress Audrey Totter, world-famous film noir star of the late 1940s, was born in Will County.

She grew up attending live theater with her father and all the popular big screen movies with her mother, and Totter knew from an early age that she wanted to be a star. As a child she performed in school plays and on stage at the local YMCA. After high school, Totter began acting professionally, reading show-scripts on Chicago and New York radio in the 1930s. She soon signed a seven-year contract with MGM Studios. Her debut film was *Main Street After Dark,* in 1945, which she describes as a "tongue-in-cheek story about a family of pickpockets." The following year she put in an unforgettable performance in *The Postman Always Rings Twice,* and—though versatile—Audrey Totter was thereafter pegged as the leading lady of film noir, the pulp-fiction-inspired genre of dark detective stories that dominated post–World War II box offices.

Her career thrived for several years. Totter won leading roles—playing the sweet-voiced, tough-talking damsel at the center of the action—in *Lady in the Lake* (1947), *The Saxon Charm* (1948), *The Set-Up* (1949), and *Any Number Can Play* (1950). Her personal life was far different from that of the adventurous, often bad-girl characters she portrayed on film, such as getting mixed up with the devil himself in the Faustian *Alias Nick Beal* (1949). Though she dated the likes of Cary Grant and Clark Gable, with whom she costarred, Totter married a doctor, Leo Fred, and they stayed together until his death 42 years later.

Audrey Totter—for whom "age is just a number, and mine is unlisted"— appeared in few films by the end of the 1950s. She settled down to do occasional television cameos, the last of which was an 1987 episode of the film noir–inspired *Murder She Wrote.*

- DECEMBER 21 -

1977

PATRICIA ROBERTS HARRIS OF MATTOON
SWORN IN AS FIRST BLACK FEMALE CABINET MEMBER

Patricia Roberts Harris, a native of Moultrie County, became the first African American woman in America to serve in a presidential cabinet, on this day in Illinois history.

Patricia Roberts was born in Mattoon on May 31, 1924; her life's work would take her far from her humble beginnings in central Illinois. She graduated with honors from Howard University in Washington, D.C., in 1954 and later returned (1969–1972) as dean of the law school. After attending graduate school at the University of Chicago in 1949, Roberts worked for the American Council on Human Rights through 1953. Married in 1955, Harris parlayed her political activism into a government career while many in Washington, D.C., took notice. In 1960 she graduated at the top of her class from George Washington University National Law Center. That year, she was appointed as an attorney for the Department of Justice—her first federal position—and by 1963 she was serving as cochair of President John F. Kennedy's National Women's Committee for Civil Rights. The following year she seconded the nomination of President Lyndon B. Johnson at the Democratic National Convention and thereafter served as Ambassador to Luxembourg from 1965 to 1967.

Photo courtesy of Abraham Lincoln Presidential Library

President Jimmy Carter, the next Democrat to claim the White House, appointed Harris to his cabinet. As the secretary of urban housing and development, and later the secretary of health, education, and welfare, Harris was 13th in line of succession to the presidency of the United States.

She never forgot her Illinois roots. During the confirmation hearings before the Senate committee, Harris declared, "I am one of them [the underclass] . . . the daughter of a dining-car worker. I am a black woman who could not buy a house eight years ago in parts of the District of Columbia!" Secretary Harris served through the end of Carter's presidency in January 1981.

After that, she was a professor at George Washington University National Law Center until her death on March 23, 1985.

Grote Reber, pioneer in radio astronomy, was born in DuPage County on this day in Illinois history.

Reber grew up in Chicago and graduated from the Illinois Institute of Technology in 1933. A ham radio operator, he was fascinated with the mystery of cosmic radio waves and the technology involved in their discovery. He applied for a position at Bell Labs, where scientists had discovered radio waves emitting from outer space, but he was turned down because of Depression-era budgeting. Undeterred, Reber decided to blaze his own trail. While employed manufacturing radios by day for various Chicago companies, he would spend his spare time at home taking his hobby a few steps further. He built an advanced radio telescope in his Wheaton, Illinois, backyard. Completed in 1937, it was nine meters in diameter with an eight-meter antenna, mounted on a titling stand, and more complex in design than those found at Bell or any of the other astronomical observatories across the land.

The neighborhood children thought it an odd sight, this enormous backyard dish. But Reber launched into his work of scanning the night skies for radio waves. Testing a number of different frequencies, he finally—at 160 Mhz—detected emissions bouncing off the Milky Way. The receiver within the telescope amplified the dim celestial signals millions of times over, and the width of the radio waves were recorded on a chart, represented by "peaks" and "spikes" and "fuzz." Reber confirmed and expanded on the earlier discoveries at Bell Labs. Among his many accomplishments are the first-ever radio-frequency maps of the sky. Grote Reber, after years of observation and study, published his findings in the *Astrophysical Journal* and, in the astronomical community, a new star was born.

After receiving numerous awards and being recognized by the Royal Astronomical Society for his life's work, Grote Reber died in Tasmania, Australia, in 2002.

- DECEMBER 23 -
1860
HARRIET MONROE, FOUNDER OF
POETRY MAGAZINE, BORN IN CHICAGO

On this day in Illinois history, Harriet Monroe, whose *Poetry* magazine featured poems by many of the greatest poets America ever produced, was born in Chicago.

Monroe was educated at Dearborn Seminary in Chicago, where she embraced art and theater as a student. She would decide to become a poet and dramatist well before her 20th birthday and went on to revolutionize how poetry was popularly viewed in America and around the world.

Photo courtesy of Courtesy of archives of Poetry magazine, circa 1910

Her first poem, "With Shelley's Poems," was published in *Century* magazine in 1888. Monroe was granted the honor of reciting another work, her "Columbian Ode," at the 1893 Columbian Exposition in Chicago. She quickly rose to become one of the city's more prominent poets, wrote book and theater reviews for local newspapers, and published a biography of noted Chicago architect, John Wellborn Root, in 1896. A few years later Monroe's "Cantata," an ode to Chicago's history, was chosen to be sung at the dedication ceremonies for the Auditorium Building, masterpiece of modern architect Louis. Sullivan. But it was as publisher, not composer, that Monroe would achieve her greatest fame. Her revolutionary publication, *Poetry* magazine, debuted in October 1912.

Readers of *Poetry* were happily exposed to some of the greatest poets of the early 20th century. Monroe, who championed modernism but did not eschew more traditional forms, conceived of a format that would bring about a renaissance in American prose. "We shall read with special interest poems of modern significance, but the most classic subject will not be declined if it reaches a high standard of quality," she advertised. Ezra Pound submitted two poems for the inaugural issue and then served to recruit local poets for Monroe from London. Others whose works graced the pages of *Poetry* included T. S. Eliot, Robert Frost, and Vachel Lindsay. In 1914, the magazine featured a group of poems by Carl Sandburg, then little known, and awarded him a prize for the wonderful "Chicago." This recognition was vital in boosting Sandburg's career.

Monroe died in 1936, but *Poetry* continued to break ground for decades thereafter, thanks to the open-door policy she established from the start—accepting submissions based on quality rather than the stylistic or political mores of the author.

- DECEMBER 24 -
1932
54 MINERS ENTOMBED AT MOWEAQUA COAL MINING DISASTER

On this day in Illinois history a tragic Christmas Eve coal-mining disaster took the lives of 54 workers in Shelby County.

Coal mining came to the Moweaqua area in the early 1890s. As with other miners at operations throughout the state, Moweaqua workers were at the mercy of harsh working conditions; the whim of their employers in providing for safety and other needs as they, often lived in company towns; and how much tonnage they could produce for pay. This was later summed up in the popular song of the 1950s by Tennessee Ernie Ford, "16 Tons": "You load 16 tons and what do you get? / Another day older and deeper in debt, / Saint Peter don't call me 'cause I can't go, / I owe my soul to the company store."

Illinois has certainly had more than its share of mining disasters, both before and after this fateful Christmas Eve in Moweaqua. In 1883, 63 miners drowned when the Diamond Mine in Wilmington flooded. In 1909, 259 perished at the Cherry Mine Disaster. Gas explosions took the lived of 52 Franklin County mine workers in 1914; another 111 at Centralia in 1947; and 119 at Chicago's Wilmington and Franklin Coal Co. on Christmas Day 1951. Despite the enactment of safety legislation and the establishment of the Office of Mines and Minerals by 1917, coal mining remained a hazardous industry.

Moweaqua Coal Mine, Shelby County's largest, took the lives of all 54 workers who entered the shaft that day. At 8:00 a.m. a rare drop in barometric pressure allowed large amounts of methane gas to enter the mine. Open lanterns ignited the gas and a terrific, terrible explosion occurred. Rescue workers scrambled to the scene, many from assorted holiday gatherings, and dug frantically and futilely in a desperate attempt to save lives. No survivors were found. The mine was permanently closed down.

This tragedy put a damper on the holiday spirits of the region—to say the least—but because it was Christmas Eve some workers had taken the day off and were spared.

- DECEMBER 25 -
1865
CHICAGO'S UNION STOCK YARD AND TRANSIT COMPANY OPENS

On this day in Illinois history, many of Chicago's smaller stockyards consolidated into the newly constructed Union Stock Yard on the city's Southwest Side, establishing the nation's central link for the transportation of livestock be-tween the East and West coasts.

In the city's early days, tavern owners usually offered ad hoc pasture for cattle before small herds were brought to market. With the arrival of the railroads, and the expansion of Chicago, more formal stockyards were set up along rail lines throughout the city. These yards proved insufficient when the city's meatpacking industry experienced explosive growth. In 1864, nine railroad companies came together to purchase 320 acres of Chicago swampland, at a price of $100,000, to build a vast centralized complex to serve as a hub for all this activity. It opened on Christmas Day 1865.

Octave Chanute, a civil engineer who was famous for his pioneering work in aviation, designed the Chicago Union Stock Yard, the largest and most modern in the world at that time. His plan featured 15 miles of track, connecting the stockyard to every major rail line running through the city. The compound covered one square mile bounded by 39th and 47th streets to the north and south, and Halsted and Ashland avenues to the east and west. Cattle, sheep, and hogs arrived from farms across the Midwest and were herded into pens that occupied roughly 40 acres of land. Half a million gallons of water, pumped daily from the Chicago River, drained waste into "Bubbly Creek," a contaminated stream branching off from the river.

Major meatpacking firms moved their plants to the vicinity of the stockyards, and by the turn of the century Chicago employed approximately 25,000 people in the meatpacking industry and provided more than 80 percent of the nation's pork and beef. Armour and Company offered daily tours to hundreds of visitors who tolerated the pungent odor in order to view what was considered a wonder of modern industry. "This was," recalls Les Orear, former stockyard employee and future president of the Illinois Labor History Society, "a fabulous way of taking a pig apart."

After peaking in 1924, the Chicago Union Stock Yard started its gradual decline, as the industry was decentralized into regional markets, and finally closed down on July 30, 1971.

JOHN A. LOGAN DIES

John Alexander Logan—Union General, U.S. Senator, and originator of Memorial Day—died on this day in Illinois history.

Logan is considered by many to be the greatest hero of southern Illinois. He was born on February 9, 1826, in Jackson County. A lawyer, he served as a Democrat from Illinois in the U.S. Congress from 1859 to 1861 before resigning to join the Union Army when the Civil War broke out. He fought at the Battle of Bull Run and returned home to give a lecture before a large crowd at Murphysboro, Illinois, arguing the case

for supporting the North. Logan, like many in the audience, was torn between sympathies for the South and loyalty to the state of Illinois. His speech that day is credited with rallying southern Illinois to the Union cause.

He was appointed colonel of the 31st Illinois Infantry, which he had organized from local volunteers, and fought alongside Ulysses S. Grant at many major battles. At Fort Donelson, in Tennessee, Logan suffered wounds from cannon fire as the 31st lost half its men, and he was promoted to Brigadier General by Grant on the battlefield after at first being thought dead. It was the Union's first major victory.

Further heroics at the battles of Vicksburg and Atlanta and his saving the city of Raleigh, North Carolina, from an angry mob of soldiers in the wake of Lincoln's assassination in 1865 earned Logan a national reputation rivaled by few on either side of the conflict. After the war, he returned to Congress and founded the popular veterans' organization, the Grand Army of the Republic (GAR).

As commander of the GAR in 1868, he issued General Order No. 11, establishing the first Memorial Day: "The 30th day of May, 1868, is designated for the purpose of strewing with flowers or otherwise decorating the graves of comrades who died in defense of their country during the late rebellion, and whose bodies now lie in almost every city, village, and hamlet churchyard in the land. In this observance no form or ceremony is prescribed, but posts and comrades will in their own way arrange such fitting services and testimonials of respect as circumstances may permit."

Logan was elected as a Republican to the U.S. Senate after the war and served until his death. He was buried at Soldier Home National Cemetery in Washington, D.C.

- December 27 -
1996
Rose Bowl–Bound Wildcats Tour the West Coast

En route to the 1995 Rose Bowl, on this day in Illinois history, the Northwestern University (NU) Wildcat football team—sole Big Ten champs for the first time since 1936—headed west for a pre–bowl game publicity tour.

It had been a miraculous year. The Wildcats won the Big Ten Conference with a record of 10-2, after a grand total of one victory in the previous three seasons. They had not won the Big Ten in 59 years nor been to the Rose Bowl (or any bowl game) since 1948. The Cats had suffered 24 successive losing seasons going in to the 1995 opener at Notre Dame. But when NU—28-point underdogs—shocked the Fighting Irish, 17–15, Wildcat fans everywhere had just witnessed the renaissance of Northwestern football. Wildcat head coach, Gary Barnett, had told his team at the start of the game, "Expect victory. . . . Don't carry me off the field after we win. Act like you've done this before."

His team would grow accustomed to winning by season's end. They were the "Mildcats" no longer. The former practice dummy of the Big Ten was now pummeling its Midwestern rivals. The Wildcats went 8-0 in conference play that season, and earned not only the respect but also fired the imagination of the entire nation. They were among the top teams in the country and scheduled to play the University of Southern California in the Rose Bowl.

Celebrating this remarkable turn of fate and their newfound fame, the Wildcats were invited to appear on *The Tonight Show*. Teammates crowded behind host Jay Leno wearing their jerseys while NU alumnus Charlton Heston raised a staff—conjuring his role of Moses in *The Ten Commandments*—triumphantly above his head. Heston introduced the upcoming game: "For all of us who ever walked the halls of Northwestern University as students, this New Year's Day is a heartlifting experience. . . Whatever happens, it will be a great day for the Purple and White."

Alas, after a valiant effort, the Northwestern Wildcats fell to the USC Trojans by a score of 41–32.

- DECEMBER 28 -
1993
GREAT CHICAGO-BORN HISTORIAN WILLIAM L. SHIRER DIES

On this day in Illinois history, William Shirer—a Cook County native who documented the crimes of Nazi Germany while finding himself blacklisted from American media—died in Massachusetts.

Shirer, whose 1,200-page *Rise and Fall of the Third Reich* is considered a historical masterpiece, was born on February 23, 1904, the son of a prominent Chicago attorney. After graduating from Coe College in Cedar Rapids, Iowa, Shirer began his career as a foreign correspondent in Paris for the *Chicago Tribune*. It was 1925, and the rise of Adolf Hitler was but a nascent and unseen phenomenon. Originally hoping to become a novelist, he noted that "[contemporary] history now seemed more interesting to me. . . . Vaguely the idea began to take root that there might be a great deal of history to write about from here for a daily newspaper back home." And it turned out to be true.

He spent the next 12 years covering events such as Charles Lindbergh's flight across the Atlantic, the League of Nations meetings in Geneva, and—venturing through India in 1931—met and befriended Mohandas K. Gandhi. And in 1937, Shirer began live radio broadcasts from Europe for Columbia Broadcasting System, announcing to the world, among other events, the fall of Paris to the Nazis. He caught the attention of the Gestapo and, under threat of arrest for espionage, narrowly escaped back to America in 1940.

As war ravaged Europe, William Shirer set out to publish from his experiences abroad. His first book, *Berlin Diary*, which he had smuggled out of Europe, was published in 1941. He continued to write throughout the war, but was labeled a Communist sympathizer in the postwar years and found great trouble finding work thereafter. It was during this time that he wrote his masterpiece, one of the most important works of the 20th century—*Rise and Fall of the Third Reich*—which both documented and denounced the brutality of modern-day totalitarianism, published in 1959.

After authoring more than a dozen titles that helped color America's perceptions of the tumultuous 20th century, William L. Shirer—who claimed, "I have never been bored for a minute in my life"—died at the age of 89.

- DECEMBER 29 -
1963
MONSTERS OF THE MIDWAY WIN THE NFL CHAMPIONSHIP

The Chicago Bears played host to the New York Giants in the National Football League Championship on this day in Illinois history. In nine-degree weather, the Bears won the title, 14–10.

Coach George Halas had felt a touch of destiny about the 1963 season, despite the previous two championships being won by the team's archrival the Green Bay Packers. The Bears were led by quarterback Billy Wade and Pro Bowl tight end Mike Ditka on offense, and a rugged line-backing core of Bill George, Joe Fortunato, and Larry Morris on the defensive side of the ball. Halas's team did not feature any superstars that year—aside from Ditka, whose 794 yards and eight touchdowns revolutionized the tight-end position—and its success was guided more by a solid roster and dependable teamwork than any individual acts of greatness. They went 11-1-2 on the season.

Halas, who said the Bears would need to defeat quarterback Bart Starr and the Green Bay Packers twice to win the NFL title, got half his wish delivered on opening day—a close 10–3 Bears victory at Green Bay. The winning continued all season. Despite a week-six road upset to San Francisco, the Monster of the Midway dominated opponents and completed the two-game sweep of the defending champions with a week-ten 26–7 whipping before a packed house at Wrigley Field.

The NFL championship game against the Giants was a close one. New York had lost four championship games over the past five years, and they were hungry for victory. But their explosive offense, which had set an NFL high-mark of 32 points per game that season, was virtually shut down by an opportunistic Bears defense. Halas's squad clinched it with a late third-quarter interception by Bears defender Ed O'Bradovich—one of five Bears picks on the afternoon—setting up a game-winning quarterback sneak from the one yard line.

The next Bears championship would come in New Orleans, Louisiana, more than 20 years later, under the leadership of the 1963 team's star tight end, Mike Ditka.

- December 30 -
1903
Iroquois Theater Fire Breaks Heart of City

More than 600 perished—mostly women and children—when the supposedly fire-proof Iroquois Theater burned to the ground on this day in Illinois history.

It had opened one month earlier. The Iroquois Theater was the city's newest and finest palace for the arts, and that Wednesday—a Christmas holiday from school—it was filled with 1,900 guests for a daytime performance of *Mr. Blue Beard,* a popular children's musical. It was standing room only. Stage decorations—large canvases painted with flammable oils—caught fire from nearby hot lights, about halfway through the performance.

The theater's fire-safety measures proved to be either insufficient or nonfunctional as the flames, and widespread panic, quickly engulfed the auditorium. The one fire-fighter on hand (larger theaters usually had at least three in those days) was immediately overwhelmed. There were no fire hoses. The asbestos fire curtain, which was designed to fall between the stage and the seated crowd in just such a circumstance, malfunctioned and snagged on joists and rafters when dropped by stagehands. The exits were either locked to keep out freeloaders or opened only inwards, remaining shut against the desperate onrush of victims trying to get outside. By the end of the horror, bodies were piled several feet high, crushed and charred, at these failed escape routes. The second- and third-floor fire escapes were unfinished. All but one (a tightrope walker) of the more than 400 actors, dancers, orchestra members, and assorted crew of the theater company managed to escape through the back door.

The city was outraged. Several individuals, ranging from the building's owner to the theater manager to Mayor Carter Harrison Jr., were indicted for negligence, but none were ever convicted. (The only conviction related to this tragedy was that of a local tavern owner who coldly picked the pockets of the remains of those who had perished.) Because of the Iroquois Theater fire, all manner of safety regulations became standard across the nation. All theater exits to this day, for example, must be clearly marked, unlocked, and open outward.

The Iroquois Theater reopened as the Colonial Theatre, which was torn down to become the Oriental Theater in 1926.

- DECEMBER 31 -

1855

PLAN ADOPTED TO RAISE STREETS OF CHICAGO

The Chicago Board of Sewage Commissioners conceived of a plan to raise the city up from the mud on this day in Illinois history.

Mid-19th-century Chicago was a city reeling from cholera and dysentery and desperately searching for a solution. (At the time, the fact that the diseases were waterborne was unknown, and some residents blamed frogs or Irish immigrants.) The city streets were sunk in mud, a breeding ground for disease, and thousands were dying every year—60 per day by the summer of 1854. That year, almost 6 percent of Chicago's population died of cholera, and the burgeoning boomtown was in a panic.

A three-man Chicago Board of Sewage Commissioners, headed by former mayor of Chicago William Ogden, was appointed by the Illinois General Assembly. Boston engineer E. S. Chesbrough was brought in to help solve the problem. He suggested a sewage system—the first comprehensive plan for an American city—to lift the city streets and sidewalks (wooden planks) up from the muck. The commission, facing an enormous crisis as thousands were fleeing the city, accepted that proposal on the last day of 1855.

It was an ambitious plan that called for extraordinary measures. In order to lay the sewage pipes, the entire city—homes, businesses, streets, and sidewalks—then only a few feet above Lake Michigan's water level, would need to be raised by six to ten feet. The gradation increased closer to the river. Over the next two decades, smaller structures were relocated and larger buildings were jacked up manually by teams of men operating jackscrews in unison. New foundations were laid, storm sewers inserted, and the streets filled in to be level with the first floors of homes and businesses up and down the block. A 26-year-old inventor named George Pullman, the future railroad sleeping car manufacturer, played a pivotal role in devising and coordinating these efforts. In 1858, Pullman directed the lifting of the posh six-story Tremont Hotel while guests remained in their rooms. Entire city blocks were sometimes completed in a single day.

The project was completed in 1878. For decades, one could spot parts of the city where residents or business owners had refused to participate because of incongruent first floor or basement steps leading up to the sidewalk.

ABOUT THE AUTHOR

Jeff Ruetsche is a lifelong resident of Illinois and a graduate of Northeastern Illinois University. A love for his native state has been cultivated by a lifetime of adventures, from the Cahokia Mounds to Lincoln's old stomping grounds to the neighborhoods of Chicago. He is a member of the Illinois State Historical Society, the Chicago Historical Society, and the Society for American Baseball Research, and has worked with historians and historical societies throughout the Midwest as an acquisitions editor for Arcadia Publishing since the summer of 2001. Jeff lives in Crystal Lake, Illinois, with his wife, Stacy, and his children, Sam, Marcus, and Zoe.

Index

d

Fuller, Melville Weston, 216

G

Gacy, John Wayne, Jr., 81
Gaines, Gen. Edmund, 172
Galena & Chicago Union
    Railroad, 22, 179
Galesburg, 12
Gallatin, Harry "the Horse," 126
Gallery, Daniel Vincent, 168
gambling, Riverboat Gambling
    Act, 45
Gans, Joe, 369
Giancana, Sam "Momo," 183
Giants baseball team, 51
Gibault, Father Pierre, 200
Gillis, Lester ("Baby Face
    Nelson"), 350
Giorgi, E. J. ("Zeke"), 45
Glenview Naval Air Base, 64
Glidden, Joseph F., 348
Goings, Melissa, 156
Goldberg, Arthur Joseph, 236
Goldman, George, 199
Gosden, Freeman, 18
Gould, Chester, 296
governors
    Altgeld, John Peter, 80, 293
    Bissell, William H., 166
    Blagojevich, Rod, 373
    Bond, Shadrach, 277
    Coles, Edward, 361
    Dunne, Edward, 175
    Edwards, Ninian, 41, 101,
        241, 250, 344
    Fifer, "Private Joe," 31, 80
    Ford, Thomas, 42, 191
    French, Augustus C., 74

    Green, Dwight, 111
    Harrison, William, 241
    Horner, Henry, 194, 198
    Kerner, Otto, Jr., 109
    Lowden, Frank Orren, 14, 160
    Oglesby, Richard James, 36, 66
    Palmer, John McCauley, 285
    Reynolds, John, 145, 150, 172
    Ryan, George H., 373
    St. Clair, Arthur, 127
    Thompson, "Big Bill," 53, 65,
        309
    Thompson, James R. ("Big
        Jim"), 140
    Walker, Dan, 45
    Yates, Richard, 121, 123, 189
Graham, Bruce, 223
Grand Army of the Republic
    (GAR), 106, 382
Grange, Harold Edward
    ("Red"), 177, 310, 335
Grant, Gen. Ulysses S., 89, 118,
    121, 123, 135, 142, 285,
    290, 295, 382
Graves, Henry T., 129
Great Fire of 1871. See
    Chicago Fire of 1871
Great Flood of 1937, 37
Great Lakes Naval Training
    Center, 197
Great Tri-State Tornado, 1925,
    86
Green, Gov. Dwight, 111
Grosse Point Lighthouse, 69

H

Hake, Terrence, 233

Halas, George S., 88, 220, 385
Hale, George E., 59
Hall, Glenn, 116
Hambletonian harness racing,
    255
Hamilton, Dr. Silas, 343
Hansberry v. Lee, 317
Harpe Brothers, 13
Harper, William Rainey, 59,
    270
Harpo Studios, 268
Harris, Patricia Roberts, 377
Harrison, George, 289
Harrison, Gov. William, 241
Harrison, Mayor Carter, Jr.,
    316, 369, 386
Harrison, Mayor Carter, Sr.,
    320
Harvey, Paul, 119
Hatch, Fred, 34
Hay, Helen Scott, 349
Haymarket anarchists, 80
Haymarket Square Riot, 136
Heald, Capt. Nathan, 245
Hebron H.S. Green Giants, 90
Hefner, Hugh, 357
Hemingway, Ernest, 217
Hennepin Canal, 340
Herndon, William H., 49, 180,
    269
Herrin coal-miner riot, 186
Heston, Charlton, 219, 383
Hickok, James Butler "Wild
    Bill," 87, 159
Hinckley, John, Jr., 98
hockey, Chicago Blackhawks,
    112, 116
Hood, Raymond, 174
Hoover, Herbert, 194, 309

BOOKS OF INTEREST

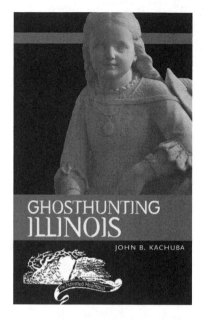

GHOSTHUNTING ILLINOIS
By John Kachuba

Ghosthunting Illinois is your ticket to thirty-two of Illinois's most legendary haunted places. Ghosthunter John Kachuba maintains an open mind, a healthy dose of skepticism, and a razor-sharp wit as he describes his encounters. John's accounts are sometimes humorous, sometimes hair-raising, and quite often simply unexplainable.

✍ Harpo Studios, Chicago—Home to the "The Oprah Winfrey Show," the building served as a temporary morgue when a steamer capsized in 1915. Oprah's employees have encountered the ghosts of the victims floating through the halls.

✍ Abraham Lincoln's Tomb, Springfield—Lincoln's coffin was moved seventeen times in Oak Ridge Cemetery due to fears of grave robbers. Could unrest be the source of the sobbing, whispering, and tapping noises visitors to his tomb report?

✍ Mineral Springs Hotel, Alton—Illinois's most haunted hotel is inhabited by at least four ghosts. One is the ghost of a child who drowned in the basement swimming pool; it seems she now enjoys drawing in coloring books a sympathetic employee leaves for her.

✍ And 29 other spooky spots in the Prairie State.

Since all these establishments are open to the public, you can seek out Illinois's supernatural presences for yourself—if you dare. Use the detailed map at the beginning of each section and start planning your fright inerary today!

Price $14.95 Paperback
ISBN: 1-57860-220-3

AVAILABLE AT LOCAL OR ONLINE BOOKSELLERS, OR AT WWW.EMMISBOOKS.COM
EMMIS BOOKS 1700 MADISON ROAD CINCINNATI, OHIO 45206